Core

Mathema IGCSE®

June Haighton
Andrew Manning
Gina McManus
Margaret Thornton
Keith White

Series Editor:
Paul Metcalf

Published in 2012 by:
Nelson Thornes Ltd
Delta Place
27 Bath Road
CHELTENHAM
GL53 7TH
United Kingdom

12 13 14 15 16 / 10 9 8 7 6 5 4 3 2 1

A catalogue record for this book is available from the British Library

ISBN 978 1 4085 1650 8

Cover photograph: Franck Boston/iStockphoto
Page make-up and illustrations by Tech-Set Ltd, Gateshead
Printed in China by 1010 Printing International Ltd

Contents

Introduction

This book has been written by teachers and examiners who not only want you to get the best grade you can in your IGCSE exam but also to enjoy your maths. The authors have worked together to ensure that the content is suitably planned and thoughtfully matched to the IGCSE syllabus. Examples and questions have been chosen to give you a flavour of the breadth and style of the examination papers, as well as make you think mathematically.

Each chapter has the following features to make learning as interesting and effective as possible:

Learning outcomes:

After this chapter you should be able to:

The **learning outcomes** at the start of the chapter give you an idea of what you will be covering. It also offers you a checklist of content so you can assess what you know and understand.

Learn 1.1

Learn: Each chapter is divided into a series of Learn sections to carefully take you through the required content. The Learn sections include key information and examples about each topic. Each Learn section should be followed in order to help you build up your knowledge.

Apply 1.1

Apply: Each Learn section is followed by an Apply section which includes questions that allow you to practise what you have just learned. The questions are carefully chosen to mirror the style of the exam papers. We have also included some questions that will develop your ability to think about mathematics.

Study tip

Study tip: Regular study tips are included to help you avoid common errors and mistakes. Make sure you read these tips very carefully as they will help you a lot in your exam.

Assess 1.1

Assess: An Assess section is included at the end of each chapter to check your understanding of the content. You can use these questions to identify any further work you have to do on the chapter.

Practice exam questions

Practice exam questions appear after every few chapters. These offer further practice for your exams. You should work through the exam questions when you have completed the chapters. You can also use these questions as part of your revision.

Key words: The first time they appear in this book key words are highlighted in **bold blue** text. A definition can be found in the glossary section so that you can check the meaning of words and practise your mathematics vocabulary.

1 Basic number

Learning outcomes:

After this chapter you should be able to:

- identify and use:
  - natural numbers
  - integers (positive, negative and zero)
  - prime numbers
  - square numbers
  - common factors and common multiples
  - rational and irrational numbers
  - real numbers
- put numbers in order of size
- use the symbols $=$, $\neq$, $<$, $>$, $\leqslant$, $\geqslant$

You probably first learned numbers by counting: 1, 2, 3, 4, 5, ...

Next you might have used 0.

Negative numbers, -1, -2, -3, -4, ..., might have come next.

Or you might have used fractions and decimals.

Historically, numbers were first used in this order:

- Numbers were used for counting as long ago as 3400 BCE.
- Fractions were first used around 300 BCE.
- Zero was first used in about 130 CE.
- Around 600 CE, negative numbers were being used in India.

Learn 1.1 The structure of numbers

The counting numbers, 1, 2, 3, 4, 5, ... are called **natural numbers**.

Natural numbers are given the symbol $\mathbb{N}$.

..., -5, -4, -3, -2, -1, 0, 1, 2, 3, 4, 5, ... are called **integers**.

Integers are given the symbol $\mathbb{Z}$. Z comes from the German word *Zahl*, meaning 'number'.

Integers are whole numbers.

So integers include the natural numbers, negative whole numbers, and 0.

0 is not a natural number but it is an integer.

Rational numbers are all the numbers that can be written in the form $\frac{p}{q}$, where p and q are integers.

Integers are rational numbers, as $3 = \frac{3}{1}$ and $-4 = \frac{-4}{1}$

Terminating decimals, like 0.71, are rational numbers, as $0.71 = \frac{71}{100}$

Recurring decimals, like $0.\dot{3}\dot{5}$, are rational numbers, as $0.\dot{3}\dot{5} = \frac{35}{99}$

Rational numbers are given the symbol $\mathbb{Q}$. Q comes from *Quotient*, the result of dividing.

Irrational numbers are all the numbers that *cannot* be written as a fraction.

Examples include the square root of 2, (or $\sqrt{2}$) and π.

$\sqrt{2}$ is the number which multiplies by itself to equal 2.

It is approximately 1.414213562…, but it carries on forever without recurring.

The **real numbers** are all the rational numbers and irrational numbers.

Real numbers are given the symbol $\mathbb{R}$.

All natural numbers are integers.

All integers are rational numbers.

All rational numbers are real numbers.

This can be shown in a diagram. This type of diagram is called a **Venn diagram**.

Each shape contains everything inside. Examples are given in red.

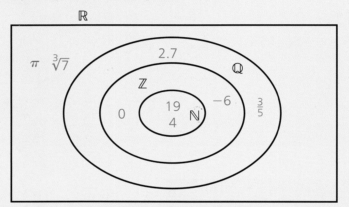

Ordering numbers

To order integers, draw or imagine a number line.

The numbers increase from left to right.

To order 4, −3, 1 and −5:

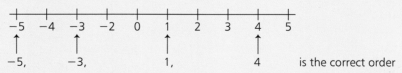

−5,   −3,   1,   4   is the correct order

To order decimals, write them in a table.

Put digits with the same place value in the same column.

Example
Four parcels weigh 2.4 kg, 1.69 kg, 1.8 kg and 1.64 kg.

List the weights in order, starting with the smallest.

Solution

To put the weights in order, write them with a column for units (U), a column for tenths (T) and a column for hundredths (H):

U	.	T	H
2	.	4	
1	.	6	9
1	.	8	
1	.	6	4

2.4 is the largest, as it has the most units.

1.8 is second largest, as the remaining three all have 1 unit, and 1.8 has the most tenths.

1.69 is larger than 1.64, as they have the same number of units and tenths, but 1.69 has more hundredths.

The weights of the parcels, from smallest to largest are: 1.64 kg, 1.69 kg, 1.8 kg, 2.4 kg.

Using the symbols $=$, $\neq$, $<$, $>$, $\leq$, $\geq$

When two quantities are equal, you can show it with the equals sign, $=$.

For example: $5 + 2 = 7$.

If quantities are not equal, you can use the 'is not equal to' sign, $\neq$.

For example: $5 - 2 \neq 4$

You could also write $5 - 2 < 4$, meaning $5 - 2$ is less than 4.

And $5 - 2 > 1$, meaning $5 - 2$ is greater than 1.

An aeroplane can seat 350 passengers.

The number of passengers must not be more than 350.

The number of passengers is less than or equal to 350.

This is written as: number of passengers ≤ 350.

$\leq$ means 'is less than or equal to'.

$\geq$ means 'is greater than or equal to'.

Example

n is an integer, and $n \geq 6$.

Which of these are possible values of n?

a 5   **b** -7 **c** 6   **d** 6.4   **e** 11

Solution

a 5 and **b** -7 are too small, as n must be greater than or equal to 6.

d 6.4 is not an integer.

c 6 and **e** 11 are possible values.

Apply 1.1

1 From the numbers 3, $\sqrt{5}$, −2, 4.5, −$1\frac{1}{2}$, write down all the numbers that are:

  a integers   **c** real

  b rational   **d** irrational.

2 For each set of numbers, write them in order starting with the smallest.

a	5	−4	−3	0	2
b	1.2	1.19	2.01	2	1.71
c	−2.4	2.5	−3.1	1.8	−2.45

3 For each of the following numbers, write down which of these words apply:

  natural   integer   irrational   real

  a 1   **b** $\sqrt{8}$ **c** 16   **d** 5   **e** −7   **f** $\frac{5}{11}$

4 Write down a number between 1 and 3 that is not an integer.

5 For each statement, say whether it is true or false.

  a All integers are rational numbers.

  b All integers are natural numbers.

  c All natural numbers are integers.

  d $-2 > -3$

  e $-5 \leqslant 1$

6 Arrange these five cards to make a true statement:

$$\boxed{5} \quad \boxed{9} \quad \boxed{+} \quad \boxed{3} \quad \boxed{<}$$

Learn 1.2 Types of number

Factors, multiples, primes and squares

Twelve bottles could fit into a rectangular box that is 2 bottles wide and 6 bottles long.

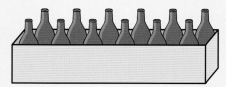

This is because 12 is a **multiple** of 2. This means 12 is in the 2 times table.

2 is a **factor** of 12, because 12 can be divided exactly by 2, with no remainder.

Nine bottles will not fit exactly into a rectangular box that is 2 bottles wide.

This is because 9 is *not* a multiple of 2.

Nine bottles will fit in a 3 by 3 box:

This is because 9 is a multiple of 3 ($9 = 3 \times 3$).

Numbers that fit into a square box, e.g. $16 = 4 \times 4$, $100 = 10 \times 10$, are called **square numbers**.

A square number is the result of multiplying an integer by itself.

Seven bottles will *only* fit in a 1 by 7 box:

This is because 7 is a multiple of 1 and 7.

7 has no other factors.

Numbers, like 7, that have exactly two factors are called **prime numbers**.

> **Study tip**
> - 1 is not a prime number as it has only one factor.
> - 2 is the only even prime number.

Common factors and common multiples

The factors of 28 are 1, 2, 4, 7, 14 and 28.

The factors of 42 are 1, 2, 3, 6, 7, 14, 21, and 42.

1, 2, 7 and 14 are factors of both 28 and 42.

1, 2, 7 and 14 are **common factors** of 28 and 42.

The **highest common factor (HCF)** of 28 and 42 is 14.

The multiples of 12 are 12, 24, 36, 48, 60, 72, 84, 96, 108, 120, …

The multiples of 16 are 16, 32, 48, 64, 80, 96, 112, 128, 144, 160, …

48 and 96 are **common multiples** of 12 and 16.

There are more common multiples of 12 and 16, for example, 144, 192, …

48 is the **least common multiple (LCM)** of 12 and 16.

Apply 1.2

1 From the numbers 16, 17, 18, 19, 20, write down:

   a a prime number   **c** a factor of 100

   b a square number   **d** a multiple of 3.

2 Explain why 15 is not a prime number.

3 For each statement, say whether it is true or false:

   a 5 is a factor of 20.

   b 3 is a factor of 20.

   c 20 is a factor of 4.

   d 36 is a square number.

   e The factors of 24 are 1, 2, 3, 4, 6, 8, 12, 16 and 24.

   f The highest common factor of 20 and 36 is 4.

   g The least common multiple of 8 and 10 is 80.

4 Find:

   a the highest common factor of 12 and 18

   b the least common multiple of 12 and 18.

5 Write down all the prime numbers between 10 and 20.

6 100 is a square number. It can be made by adding two prime numbers together in six different ways:

   $3 + 97 = 100$ $11 + 89 = 100$ $17 + 83 = 100$

   $29 + 71 = 100$ $41 + 59 = 100$ $47 + 53 = 100$

   a Find five ways of making 64 by adding two prime numbers.

   b Find four ways of making 36 by adding two prime numbers.

7 Find a way through this maze, only passing through squares containing a prime number or a square number.

7	**Start**	15	37	17	11
19	21	8	16	21	49
9	1	23	81	33	64
12	99	85	20	45	100
5	25	13	2	4	41
29	65	77	87	39	50
3	19	36	31	**Finish**	6

Assess 1.1–1.2

1 Which of the words: natural, prime, integer, square, irrational, apply to these numbers:

   a 1   **c** 16   **e** −7

   b $\sqrt{8}$ **d** 5   **f** $\frac{5}{11}$?

2 Write down all the factors of 40.

3 Write down the first five multiples of 7.

4 Find two prime numbers that are factors of 20.

5 Find the highest common factor of:

   a 60 and 84   **b** 56 and 42   **c** 60 and 42.

6 Find the least common multiple of:

   a 20 and 30   **b** 15 and 12   **c** 18 and 30.

7 Put these numbers in order of size, starting with the smallest:

   a 4.2, 4.08, 3.999, 4.19   **b** −4, 7, −2, −5, 8

8 Match the clues on the left with the numbers on the right.

A factor of 100	0
A square number	6
A prime number	13
Not a natural number	20
A multiple of 8	32
The HCF of 18 and 24	36

9 Which of these statements is true?

   a $4 \times 2 > 7$ **d** $5 \times 2 = 20 \div 2$

   b $3 + 5 \leqslant 4 + 4$ **e** $10 - 4 < 6$

   c $9 - 1 \geqslant 7 + 2$ **f** Highest common factor of 24 and 36
                                $\leqslant$ least common multiple of 6 and 4.

10 There are two numbers less than 10 with exactly three factors.
Find the two numbers.

11 Three cars are racing around a track. They all start together.
The green car completes a lap every 3 minutes.
The blue car completes a lap every 4 minutes.
The red car completes a lap every 5 minutes.

   a Which cars will be back at the start line after:

      i 6 minutes   **ii** 12 minutes   **iii** 15 minutes   **iv** 20 minutes?

   b How long will it be before they are all back at the start line together?

12 a How many square numbers are there between 1 and 50?

   b How many square numbers are there between 51 and 100?

   c How many square numbers are there between 101 and 150?

   d How many square numbers are there between 151 and 200?

2 Basic algebra

Algebraic representation and formulae

This chapter introduces you to the use of letters to represent numbers. The mathematical rules that work for arithmetic also work for algebra.

Learning outcomes:

After this chapter you should be able to:

- simplify an expression in one or more variables
- express basic arithmetic processes algebraically
- work out the value of an expression
- use a formula in words or letters.

Learn 2.1 Using letters for numbers

Addition of one variable

What do we mean by $3x + x + 2x$?

The letter symbol x stands for an unknown number.

It is a **variable** because it can take different values.

$3x$ means three lots of x. x means one lot of x. $2x$ means two lots of x.

| x | x | x | + | x | + | x | x |

> We usually write just 'x' rather than '$1x$' but the 1 is left in front of 'x' in the working below to help you to understand the process.

There are six xs altogether

So $3x + 1x + 2x = 6x$

'$3x + 1x + 2x$' is called an **expression** and $3x$, $+x$ and $+2x$ are the **terms** of the expression.

Working out the addition to get '$6x$' is called **simplifying** the expression.

Addition of two variables

This expression: $5a + 2b + a + 4b + 3b$ contains two variables, a and b.

In this expression there are **like terms** and **unlike terms**.

  $5a$ and $2b$ are unlike terms.

  $5a$ and $+a$ are like terms and can be simplified to $6a$.

  $+2b$ and $+4b$ and $+3b$ are like terms and can be simplified to $+9b$.

  $5a + 2b + a + 4b + 3b = 6a + 9b$

Addition and subtraction of variables

To simplify an expression that has some negative terms, use your knowledge of negative numbers.

The expression $4a + 5a - 7a$ can be simplified to $2a$. $4 + 5 - 7 = 2$

The expression $3y - 5y - 2y$ can be simplified to $-4y$. $3 - 5 - 2 = -4$

> Be very careful with the signs, especially when there are two variables.

To simplify $5a + b - 2a - a - 4b$ collect the like terms.

$$5a - 2a - a = 2a$$
$$+ b - 4b = -3b$$
$$5a + b - 2a - a - 4b = 2a - 3b$$

Study tip

The sign (+ or −) in front of each term in an expression stays with that term when you collect like terms.

Apply 2.1

1 Simplify these expressions.

   a $3a + 4a + 2a$

   b $3b + 5b - 2b$

   c $5x - 4x + 3x$

   d $3y + 2y + 4y - 7y$

   e $2p + 7p - 3p - 3p$

   f $q + q - q + q - q$

   g $4t - t + 3t - t$

   h $m + 7m + m - 7m$

   i $11c - 3c - 4c + 2c$

   j $8d - d - 3d - 4d$

2 Simplify these expressions by collecting like terms.

   a $a + 2b + 3a + 4b$

   b $2c + 5c + d + 8d + c$

   c $3p + 6q + 4p - 2q$

   d $2m + 4n - 3n - m$

   e $x + 6y - 2y + 4x$

   f $5t + 2k - t - 3k$

   g $5p + 2q - 3p + q$

   h $7x - 3y + 3y - x$

   i $4p - 5q - 2q - 3p$

   j $3m + 8 - m - 3$
      [Hint: + 8 and − 3 are like terms.]

3 Write an expression with four terms, which simplifies to $8a + 5b$.

4 Write an expression with four terms, which simplifies to $3x - 5y$.

5 Tania simplifies $5p - 2q - 2q - p$.

   Her answer is $5 - 4q$.

   Write down the correct answer and explain Tania's mistake.

6 Joe simplifies $2m + n - 3p - 2m + 4n - 5p$.

   His answer is $-3n + 8p$.

   Joe has made two mistakes.

   Write down the correct answer and explain his mistakes.

Learn 2.2 Expressing basic arithmetic processes algebraically

Addition and subtraction

$5 + 2$ is the same as $2 + 5$.

$5 - 2$ is *not* the same as $2 - 5$.

$a + b$ is the same as $b + a$.

$a - b$ is *not* the same as $b - a$.

Multiplication and division

3×4 is the same as 4×3.

$3 \div 4$ is *not* the same as $4 \div 3$.

$a \times b$ is the same as $b \times a$.

$a \div b$ is *not* the same as $b \div a$.

More about multiplication

$2a$ means 2 lots of a or $2 \times a$.

ab means a lots of b or $a \times b$.

$4ab$ means 4 lots of ab or $4 \times a \times b$.

$a \times a$ is written as a^2.

> We do not show the multiplication sign, but write $2a$.

> **Study tip**
>
> Do not confuse a^2 with $2a$.
> a^2 means $a \times a$ but $2a$ means $a + a$.

Example

Write $p \times q \times 3 \times p$ in the correct algebraic form.

Solution

We write the number first, then the letters, usually in alphabetical order.
The multiplication signs are taken out.
$3 \times p \times p \times q = 3p^2q$.

> $3 \times p \times p \times q$
> $p \times p$ is written as p^2.

Example

Simplify: $3ab - 2a - 5a + ba$.

Solution

ba is the same as ab so $3ab$ and $+ ba$ are like terms.
$3ab - 2a - 5a + ba = 4ab - 7a$

Example

Simplify: $5c^2 + 4c - c^2 - 2c$

Solution

$5c^2$ and $-c^2$ are like terms.
$5c^2 + 4c - c^2 - 2c = 4c^2 + 2c$

Apply 2.2

1 Write these expressions in the correct algebraic form.

  a $c \times b \times a$

  b $m \times m \times 4$

  c $t \times t \times 5 \times a$

  d $q \times p \times t \times 3$

  e $y \times z \times z \times 8 \times y$

2 Peter is asked to simplify $4ab - 3ba$. He thinks it is impossible.
Is he correct? Explain your answer.

3 Simplify these expressions by collecting like terms.

  a $3pq + 5pq$

  b $2cd + 5cd - 3cd$

  c $6mn - mn + 4mn$

  d $3xy + 2yx + xy$

  e $zt + 4tz - 3zt + tz$

  f $p^2 + p^2$

  g $q^2 + 2q^2 + 3q^2$

  h $5t^2 + 3t^2 - 2t^2$

  i $4a + a^2 + 2a + 3a^2$

  j $7gh + 2g - hg - 2g$

4 Write down an expression with four terms, which simplifies to $5xy + x^2$.

5 Write down an expression with four terms, which simplifies to $pq - 7yz$.

6 Elena simplifies $a^2 + a^2 + a^2$ and her answer is $6a$.
Explain why Elena's answer is wrong.

7 Simplify these three expressions and find the odd one out.

  $4c + 3d - 5d + c$ $3c + d - 8c + d$ $2c + 6d - 7c - 4d$

8 Find three pairs of like terms from the list below.

  $+4ab$ $-2a^2$ $+ba$ $-5a$ $+2b$ $+4b^2$ $+a^2$ $-2a$

Learn 2.3 Substitution

When each letter in an expression represents a given number, you can find the value of the expression.
This is called **substitution**.

Example

$a = 5$ and $b = 4$

Find the value of:

  a $4a - 3b$ **b** $2ab$ **c** a^2 **d** $\dfrac{b}{2a}$

Solution

a $4a - 3b = (4 \times 5) - (3 \times 4)$

$\qquad\quad = 20 - 12$

$\qquad\quad = 8$

b $2ab = 2 \times 5 \times 4$

$\qquad\quad = 40$

c $a^2 = 5 \times 5$

$\qquad = 25$

d $\dfrac{b}{2a} = \dfrac{4}{2 \times 5}$

$\qquad\; = \dfrac{4}{10}$

$\qquad\; = 0.4$

Example

$c = -3$ and $d = -2$

Find the value of:

a $2c + 4d$ **b** $2c - 4d$ **c** $3cd$ **d** $c^2 + d^2$

Solution

a $2c + 4d = (2 \times -3) + (4 \times -2)$

$\qquad\qquad = -6 + -8$

$\qquad\qquad = -14$

b $2c - 4d = (2 \times -3) - (4 \times -2)$

$\qquad\qquad = -6 - -8$

$\qquad\qquad = -6 + 8$

$\qquad\qquad = 2$

c $3cd = 3 \times -3 \times -2$

$\qquad\quad = -9 \times -2$

$\qquad\quad = 18$

d $c^2 + d^2 = (-3 \times -3) + (-2 \times -2)$

$\qquad\qquad = 9 + 4$

$\qquad\qquad = 13$

Study tip

Putting in brackets when you are substituting will help you to sort out positive and negative signs.

Apply 2.3

1 $p = 3$ and $q = 7$

Find the value of:

  a $2p + q$ **b** $5p + 2q$ **c** $3p - q$ **d** pq **e** $4pq$ **f** $p^2 + 2q$

2 $x = 9$ and $y = 2$

Find the value of:

  a $x + 6y$ **b** $2x + 3y$ **c** $3x - 4y$ **d** xy **e** $x^2 - y^2$ **f** $\dfrac{x}{y}$

3 $m = 5$ and $n = -2$

Find the value of:

a $m + n$ **b** $2m + 5n$ **c** $4m - 3n$ **d** mn **e** $n^2 + 3m$ **f** $\dfrac{5n}{m}$

4 $z = -1$ and $t = -4$

Find the value of:

a $z + 2t$ **b** $8z + t$ **c** $3z - 4t$ **d** $5zt$ **e** $z^2 + t^2$ **f** $\dfrac{3t}{4z}$

5 $a = 5$ and $b = 9$

  a Show that $2ab - 4b = 54$.

  b Write down another expression in a and b that has the value 54.

6 $c = 8$ and $d = -3$

  a Show that $3c + 2d = 18$.   **b** Katya says that $c^2 + d^2 = 55$.

                                                Can you explain Katya's mistake?

7 Pierre says that when x is an even number, $2x + 1$ is always a prime number.

  a Show that this is true when $x = 6$.

  b Give an example to show that it is not always true.

Learn 2.4 Using formulae

If a worker earns \$9 an hour, pay is worked out by multiplying \$9 by the number of hours worked. This can be written as a **formula** in words:

> pay equals \$9 multiplied by hours worked

Using p to represent pay in dollars and h to be the hours worked, this formula is written in symbols as:

> $p = 9h$

We can work out the pay by substituting a number for h in this formula.

For example, if he works 8 hours, $p = 9 \times 8 = 72$, so his pay is \$72.

Example

This is a rule for finding out how far away a thunderstorm is:

> 'Count the number of seconds between the lightning and the thunder.
> Divide your answer by 3. This gives you the distance in kilometres.'
> Asif counts 15 seconds between the lightning and the thunder.
> How far away is the thunderstorm?

Solution

$15 \div 3 = 5$

The thunderstorm is 5 km away.

Example

The time needed to cook a chicken is 45 minutes per kilogram plus an extra 20 minutes.

a Write this as a formula, using t for the time needed, in minutes, and n for the weight of the chicken, in kilograms.

b Work out the time needed to cook a chicken weighing 3 kg.

Solution

a $t = 45n + 20$

b $t = (45 \times 3) + 20$

$= 135 + 20$

$= 155$

It takes 155 minutes, or 2 hours and 35 minutes, to cook this chicken.

> **Study tip**
>
> Remember BIDMAS and do the multiplication or division before the addition or subtraction. The 'I' means Indices. Brackets first, then squares and cubes, which are types of indices.

Apply 2.4

1 'To change a nautical mile to kilometres, multiply it by 1.85'

Use this rule to change four nautical miles to kilometres.

2 The charges on a railway are worked out by this formula:

'$2.50 per kilometre plus $6'

What is the charge for a journey of 24 kilometres?

3 An approximate rule for converting temperatures in degrees Celsius (°C) to temperatures in degrees Fahrenheit (°F) is:

'multiply by 2, then add 30'

Use this rule to convert 26 °C to °F.

4 Roberto works in a bicycle shop.

His pay for a week's work is $42 plus $10 for every bicycle he sells.

Work out his pay for a week when he sells 11 bicycles.

5 The population density of an island is worked out by the formula:

$$\text{population density} = \frac{\text{population}}{\text{area}}$$

Find the population density of an island which has an area of 300 km² and a population of 96 000 people.

6 The cost, $C, of a take-away meal for n people is worked out from the formula: $C = 12n + 18$.

Work out the cost of a take-away meal for five people.

7 Tickets for a ferry cost \$16 for adults and \$10 for children.
   The total cost, \$$F$, for x adults and y children is given by the formula: $F = 16x + 10y$.
   Find the total cost for four adults and nine children.

8 The formula $V = IR$ gives the voltage in a circuit with resistance R and current I.
   Find the voltage when the resistance is 22 and the current is 11.

9 Juana uses this formula in her science lesson: $E = \frac{1}{2}mv^2$.
   Find the value of E when $m = 5$ and $v = 8$.

10 The rule for converting Celsius (°C) to Fahrenheit (°F) is:
$$F = \frac{9C}{5} + 32$$
   Use this rule to convert 35 °C to °F.

Assess 2.1–2.4

1 Simplify these expressions.

   a $5a + 2a + a$

   b $4b + 3b - 2b$

   c $7c - 4c - 2c$

   d $4d + 4d - 2d - 3d$

   e $3e - e + 2c - 4c$

   f $5f + 2g - 4f + 7g$

   g $9h + k - 4h - k$

   h $m + 8n - 3m - 2n$

   i $p + q + 5r - 2q - 3p$

   j $3x - 3y - 3z + x + 5y - 4z$

   k $9t + 5 - 3w - 4t - 4 + w$

2 Write down two expressions, each with four terms, which simplify to $3a + 8b$.

3 Write down two expressions, each with four terms, which simplify to $p - 4q$.

4 Simplify these three expressions and find the odd one out:
   $5x + 2y - 3x - 2y + z$
   $4y + 3z + 2x - 2z - 3y$
   $8z - 3x + y - 3z - 4z + 5x$

5 Sue tries to simplify: $5p + 2q - 3p + q$.
   She writes down:
$$5p + 3p = 8p$$
$$2q - q = 1q$$
   Answer: $8p + q$
   Describe Sue's mistakes and write down the correct answer.

6 Find three pairs of like terms from the list below.
   $3x^2$ -3 $+xy$ $-2yx$ $-y^2$ $+x^2$ $-2x$ -2

7 Simplify these expressions by collecting like terms.

a $2x^2 + 5x - 4x - x^2$

b $4y + 9 - 3y - 2y^2 + 8y^2$

c $mn - m^2 - 3mn + 5mn - m^2$

d $4pq + 8p + 5q - pq - 3p$

e $7 - 2k + 1 + 3k^2 - 2k$

8 Simplify these three expressions and find the odd one out.

$c^2 - 2c - 9 + 5c + 7$ $4c + 2 - c - 2c^2 + 3c^2$ $6 - c^2 + c + 2c^2 - 8 + 2c$

9 $a = 7$ and $b = 1$

Find the value of:

a $2a + 3b$ **b** $2a - 3b$ **c** ab **d** $4ba$ **e** $a^2 - b^2$

10 $p = 10$ and $q = -3$

Find the value of:

a $p + 2q$ **b** $p - 2q$ **c** $2pq$ **d** $p^2 + q^2$ **e** $\dfrac{3p}{2q}$

11 $x = 8$ and $y = -5$

a Show that $2x + 3y = 1$.

b Show that $x^2 - y^2$ has the same value as $3x - 3y$.

12 An approximate rule for converting gallons to litres is 'multiply by 9 and divide by 2'.

Use this rule to convert 10 gallons to litres.

13 To find the perimeter of a rectangle, double the length and double the width.

Then add them together.

Use this formula to find the perimeter of a rectangle whose length is 12 cm and width is 4 cm.

14 Paola uses the formula 'speed equals distance divided by time'.

The distance is 75 km.

The time is 3 h.

What is the speed in kilometres per hour?

15 The cost, in dollars, of hiring a machine for n days is given by the formula

$C = 16n + 20$

What is the cost of hiring this machine for 11 days?

16 The formula $K = \dfrac{8M}{5}$ can be used to change distances in miles to distances in kilometres.

Use this formula to change 35 miles to kilometres.

3 Mensuration: perimeter and area

Learning outcomes:

After this chapter you should be able to:

- work out perimeters
- find the area of a rectangle, parallelogram, triangle and trapezium
- calculate the circumference and area of a circle
- find the perimeters and areas of composite shapes.

Perimeter and area of 2-D shapes

Two-dimensional (2-D) shapes have length and width, but no depth.
Examples of 2-D shapes include triangles, squares, rectangles, parallelograms, trapezia and circles.

Learn 3.1 Perimeters and areas of basic 2-D shapes

Perimeter is the total distance around the sides of a shape. In the metric system, perimeters are measured in millimetres, centimetres, metres or kilometres.

Area is the amount of space inside a shape. In the metric system, areas are measured in square millimetres, square centimetres, square metres or square kilometres.
The diagram shows one square centimetre, written as 1 cm^2.

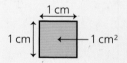

Perimeter and area of a rectangle

Perimeter of a rectangle = length + width + length + width

You can go around the shape adding the sides or add the length and width, then multiply by 2.

Area of a rectangle = length × width

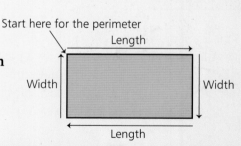

Area of a parallelogram

A parallelogram has two pairs of parallel sides.

> **Study tip**
>
> The height must be perpendicular to the base – this means at 90° to the base, shown as ⌐

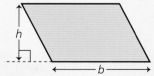

This parallelogram has base b and perpendicular height h.

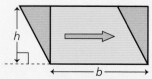

Moving a triangle from one side to the other gives a rectangle with the same area as the parallelogram.
Area of the rectangle = $b \times h$

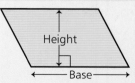

Area of a parallelogram = base × perpendicular height

Area of a triangle

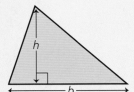 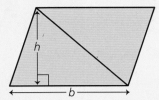 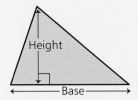

This triangle has base b and perpendicular height h.

Joining two identical triangles like this gives a parallelogram. The area of the triangle is half of the area of the parallelogram.
Area of the parallelogram $= b \times h$

Area of a triangle
$= \frac{1}{2} \times b \times h$
$= \frac{1}{2} \times$ base $\times$ perpendicular height

Area of a triangle $= \frac{1}{2} \times$ base $\times$ perpendicular height

Study tip

The height must be at 90° to the base.

Area of a trapezium

A trapezium has one pair of parallel sides.
The other two sides are not parallel.
The plural of 'trapezium' is 'trapezia'.

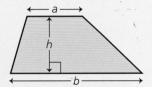 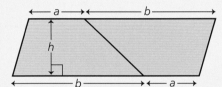 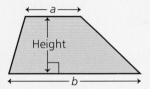

This trapezium has parallel sides a and b and perpendicular height h.

Joining two identical trapezia like this gives a parallelogram. The area of the trapezium is half of the area of the parallelogram.
Area of the parallelogram $= (a + b) \times h$

Area of a trapezium
$= \frac{1}{2} \times (a + b) \times h$
$= \frac{1}{2} \times$ sum of parallel sides $\times$ perpendicular height

Area of a trapezium $= \frac{1}{2} \times$ sum of parallel sides $\times$ perpendicular height

Study tip

The height must be at 90° to the parallel sides.

Example

Find the area and perimeter of these shapes.

a   **b**   **c**

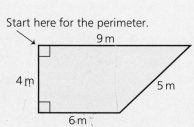 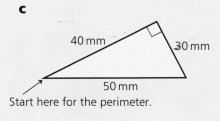

Solution

a Perimeter $= 6 + 5 + 6 + 5$

$= 22$ cm

Area $= 6 \times 4$

$= 24$ cm^2

b Perimeter $= 9 + 5 + 6 + 4$

$= 24$ m

Area $= \frac{1}{2} \times (6 + 9) \times 4$

$= \frac{1}{2} \times 15 \times 4 = \frac{1}{2} \times 60$

$= 30$ m^2

c Perimeter $= 40 + 30 + 50$

$= 120$ mm

Area $= \frac{1}{2} \times 40 \times 30 = 20 \times 30$

$= 600$ mm^2

or $\frac{1}{2} \times 40 \times 30 = \frac{1}{2} \times 1200 = 600$ mm^2

Study tip

Take care to use the correct dimensions.
Remember the base and height must be at 90°.

Apply 3.1

1 Find the perimeter and area of each shape on this centimetre grid.

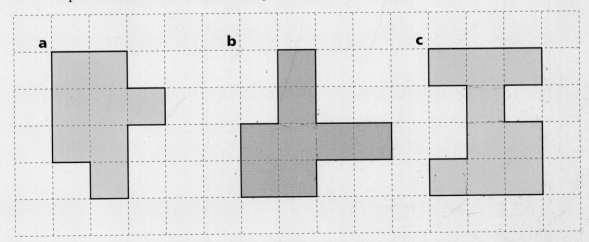

2 For each shape on this centimetre grid:

   i write down the mathematical name of the shape

   ii work out the area of the shape.

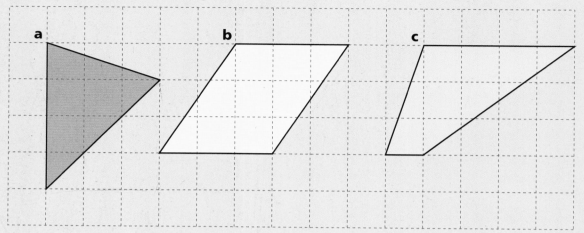

3 For each shape below, calculate: **i** the perimeter   **ii** the area.

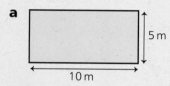

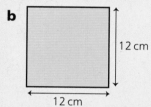

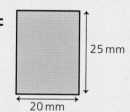

4 Work out the areas of these parallelograms.

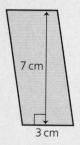

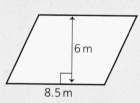

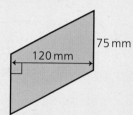

5 Calculate the areas of these triangles.

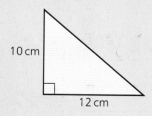

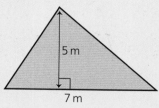

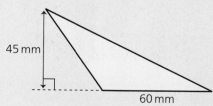

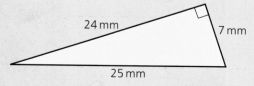

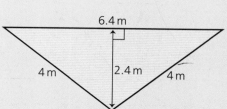

6 Work out the areas of these trapezia.

a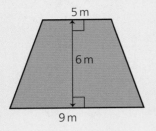

c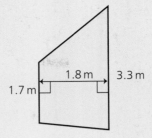

b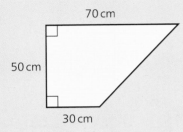

d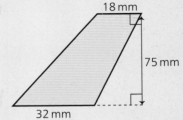

7 For each shape below, work out: **i** the perimeter   **ii** the area.

a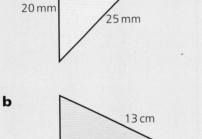

c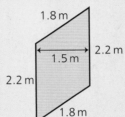

b

d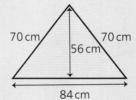

8 The shapes in the table below are all rectangles or squares.

Copy the table and fill in the gaps.

Shape	Length	Width	Perimeter	Area
Rectangle	9 cm	7 cm		
Square	8 cm			
	7 m		26 m	
Square				100 mm²
		6 cm		72 cm²
			34 m	30 m²

9 A teacher asks her class to write down the area of this rectangle.

Meera writes 24 m² and Jake writes 35 m. They are both wrong.

a Explain each error.

b Write down the correct answer.

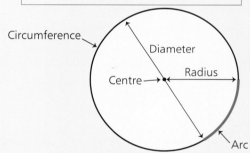

10 A rectangular lawn is 8 m long and 7 m wide.

a Sahid wants to put edging strip around the perimeter of the lawn.
What length of edging strip does he need?

b Sahid has a 2 kg bag of fertiliser to spread on the lawn.
The label on the bag says 'Use 35 g of fertiliser per square metre.'
Does Sahid have enough fertiliser for the lawn? Explain your answer.
[Hint: 1 kg = 1000 g]

Learn 3.2 Circles

Circumference of a circle

The **circumference** of any circle is always just over three times as long as its **diameter**.

> You can check this by measuring some objects with circular faces such as cans, coins or clocks.

A part of the circumference is an **arc**.

The accurate value for the circumference divided by the diameter of any circle is a number called 'pi'. This number, 3.14159 … , has an infinite number of decimal places and it is usually written as π.

> This means the figures after the decimal point.

You can find π on your calculator and use it to see more decimal places. Or you can add 3.142.

For any circle $C \div d$ is equal to π and so C is equal to $\pi \times d$.

Area of a circle

The diagram shows a circle, of **radius** r (plural **radii**), cut into 16 **sectors**.

> **Study tip**
>
> Answers should be given to three significant figures unless you are asked differently.

The length of the circumference $= \pi \times d = \pi \times 2r = 2\pi r$

The sectors are then rearranged as shown.

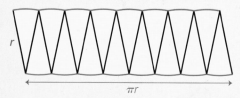

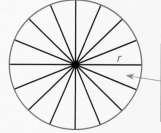

> A sector is part of a circle enclosed by two radii – like a slice of pie.

The shape they make is approximately rectangular.

The length is πr (half of $2\pi r$) and the width is r.

So, the area is approximately $\pi r \times r = \pi r^2$

This process can be repeated with more sectors.

The more sectors there are, the closer the shape becomes to an exact rectangle.

The area of a circle is exactly equal to πr^2.

Circumference of a circle = π × diameter

This is often written as $C = \pi d$

Area of a circle = π × radius × radius

This can be written as $A = \pi \times r \times r$ or πr^2.

> Diameter of a circle = 2 × radius.
> This can be written as $d = 2r$ where d is the diameter and r is the radius.

Example

The radius of a circular pond is 0.6 m.

Work out: **a** the circumference of the pond   **b** the area of the pond.

Solution

a circumference of a circle = π × diameter
diameter = 2 × radius = 2 × 0.6 = 1.2 m
circumference = π × 1.2
           = 3.77 m

> The answer is rounded off.

b area = $\pi \times r^2$
      = π × 0.6 × 0.6
      = 1.13 m²

> The answer is rounded off again.

Apply 3.2

1 Calculate the circumference of each of these circles.

a
6 cm

b
50 mm

c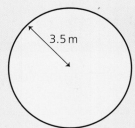
3.5 m

d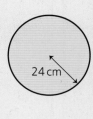
24 cm

2 Work out the area of each circle in question 1.

3 A circular clock has a diameter of 30 cm.
  a Calculate the circumference of the clock.
  b Calculate the area of the clock.

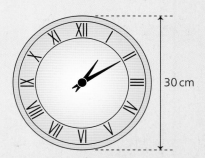
30 cm

4 The table gives the diameters of some American coins.

Copy and complete the table. Give circumference and area to the nearest whole number.

Coin	Diameter	Radius	Circumference	Area
Penny (1 cent)	19 mm			
Nickel (5 cents)	21.2 mm			
Dime (10 cents)	17.9 mm			
Quarter (25 cents)	24.3 mm			

5 A car wheel has a diameter of 0.4 m.

a Calculate the circumference of the wheel.

b Work out how far the car travels when the wheel turns 400 times.

0.4 m

6 Copy the table and fill the gaps.

Radius	Diameter	Circumference	Area
60 cm			
	2.6 m		
		470 mm	
		18π	

Learn 3.3 Composite shapes

A **composite shape** is made from simple shapes.
The shape in the example below is made from rectangles. You need to find the lengths of the unknown sides before you can work out the perimeter or area.

Example

Find the area and perimeter of this room.

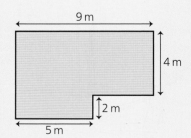

9 m

4 m

2 m

5 m

Solution

The perimeter of the room

$= 9\,m + 4\,m + 4\,m + 2\,m + 5\,m + 6\,m$

$= 30\,m$

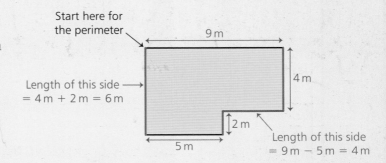

Start here for the perimeter

9 m

4 m

Length of this side $= 4\,m + 2\,m = 6\,m$

2 m

5 m

Length of this side $= 9\,m - 5\,m = 4\,m$

To find the area of the room, divide it into rectangles A and B.

The diagram shows one way of doing this.

Area of A $= 9 \times 4 = 36\,m^2$

Area of B $= 5 \times 2 = 10\,m^2$

The total area of the room $= 36 + 10 = 46\,m^2$

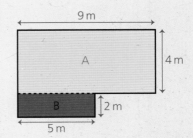

9 m

A

4 m

B

2 m

5 m

Study tip

Remember to include the units.

The units for area are usually m^2 (from m × m), mm^2, cm^2 or km^2.

There are other ways to find the area of the room. It could be split into different rectangles:

Area of A $= 6 \times 5 = 30\,m^2$

Area of B $= 4 \times 4 = 16\,m^2$

The total area of the room $= 30 + 16 = 46\,m^2$

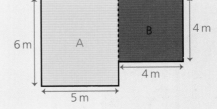

B

4 m

6 m

A

4 m

5 m

Alternatively, you can subtract the area of one rectangle from another as shown below.

Area of rectangle A (including B) $= 9 \times 6 = 54\,m^2$

Area of B $= 4 \times 2 = 8\,m^2$

Area of the room $= 54 - 8 = 46\,m^2$

Each way gives the same answer for the area.

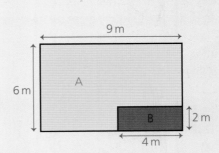

9 m

6 m

A

B

2 m

4 m

Example

This window consists of a square and a **semicircle**.

Work out: **a** the perimeter of the window

b the area of the window.

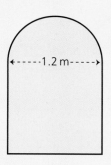

Solution

a The window has three straight sides, AD, BC and DC, all of length 1.2 m.

The length of the semicircular edge $AEB = \frac{1}{2} \times \pi \times$ diameter

$$= \frac{1}{2} \times \pi \times 1.2$$

$$= \pi \times 0.6 = 1.8849...$$

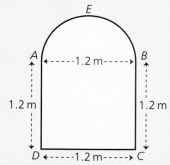

> The bottom of this window is a square, so all of its sides are equal to 1.2 m.

Total perimeter of the window $= 1.8849... + 1.2 + 1.2 + 1.2$

$$= 5.48 \text{ m}$$

Study tip

Continue this calculation on your calculator, rather than entering 1.8849... again.

b Area of the square $= 1.2 \times 1.2 = 1.44 \text{ m}^2$

Area of the semicircle $= \frac{1}{2} \times \pi \times$ radius $\times$ radius

$$= \frac{1}{2} \times \pi \times 0.6 \times 0.6$$

$$= 0.5654...$$

> Work out the area of the semicircle then add the area of the square without re-entering any of the numbers.

Total area of the window $= 0.5654... + 1.44$

$$= 2.01 \text{ m}^2$$

Apply 3.3

1 For each shape below, calculate: **i** the perimeter   **ii** the area.

a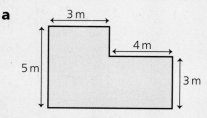

b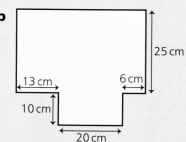

c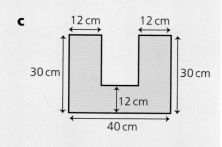

2 The diagram shows the dimensions of a picture frame.

  a Find the total length of

   i the outer perimeter

   ii the inner perimeter.

  b Work out the area of the front of the frame (the area shaded on the diagram).

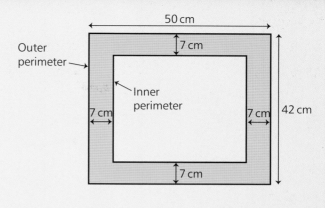

3 The diagram shows a farmer's field, *ABCD*. Work out the area of this field.

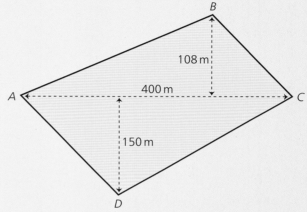

4 Six identical triangles are joined to form a hexagon as shown.

  Work out: **a** the area of one triangle

     b the total area of the hexagon.

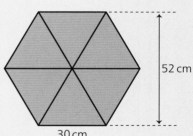

5 The diagram shows a circular mirror inside a frame. The diameter of the mirror is 24 cm. The width of the frame is 6 cm.

  Work out: **a** the area of the mirror

     b the area of the frame.

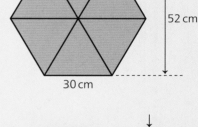

6 For each shape below find: **i** the perimeter   **ii** the area.

  a

  b

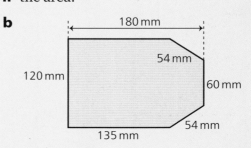

c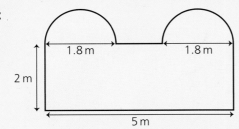

d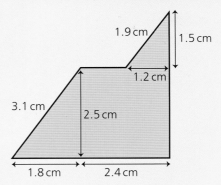

7 Work out the total area of this arrow.

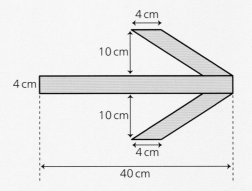

8 The diagram shows a circular hole of radius 5 cm cut
from a square piece of card.
The sides of the square are 12 cm long.
Work out the shaded area.

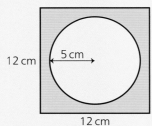

9 The diagram shows a garden in the shape of a trapezium.
It has a circular flowerbed of diameter 1.5 m.
The rest of the garden is lawn.

Work out: **a** the perimeter of the garden
 b the circumference of the flowerbed
 c the area of the lawn.

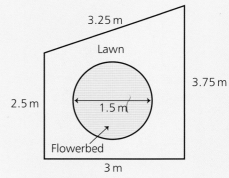

10 The diagram shows the dimensions of a window on a plane.
It has a rectangular section in the centre and semicircular ends.

Calculate: **a** the area of the window
 b the perimeter of the window.

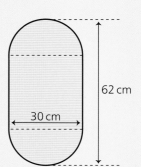

Assess 3.1–3.3

1 Find the area of each shape.

In part **a** give an estimate.   [Hint: Count those squares with half or more shaded. Omit those squares that are less than half shaded.]

In parts **b** and **c** give the exact value.

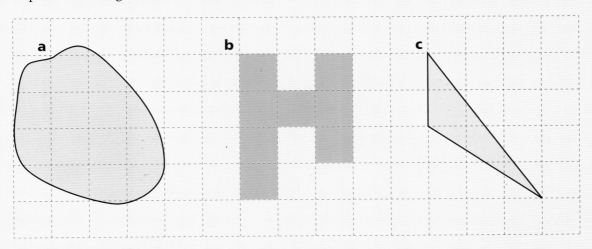

2 For each shape below, calculate: **i** the perimeter   **ii** the area.

a

5 cm

12 cm

d

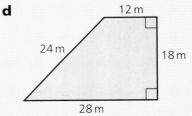

12 m

24 m

18 m

28 m

b

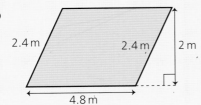

2.4 m

2.4 m

2 m

4.8 m

e

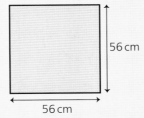

56 cm

56 cm

c

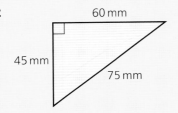

60 mm

45 mm

75 mm

f

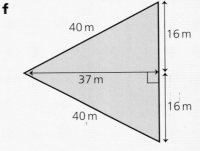

40 m

16 m

37 m

40 m

16 m

g

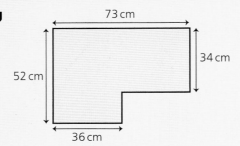

i

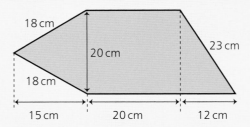

h

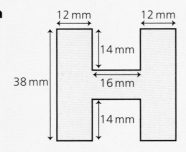

3   Find the area of each shape.

a

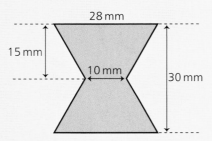

c

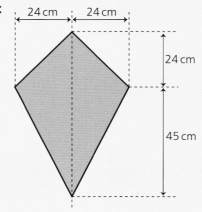

b

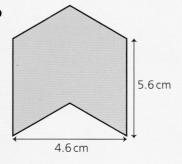

4   For a circle of radius 9 m, calculate: **a**   the circumference   **b**   the area.
Give each answer to the nearest whole number.

5   The circumference of a circular plate is 54 cm.
  a   Calculate the diameter of the plate.
  b   Calculate the area of the plate.

6 Calculate the area of this shape.

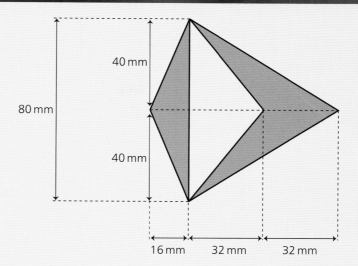

7 This shape consists of a semicircle and a trapezium.

   a Work out the perimeter of the shape.

   b Calculate the area of the shape.

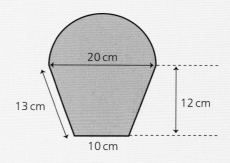

8 The diagram shows a brick wall with an opening.

   Calculate the area of the brick wall.

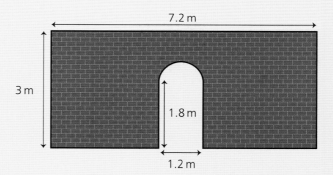

4 Mensuration: volume and surface area

Learning outcomes:

After this chapter you should be able to:

- calculate the volume of a cuboid, a prism and a cylinder
- calculate the surface area of a cuboid and a cylinder
- sketch the net of a cuboid and the net of a cylinder.

3-D shapes

Three-dimensional (3-D) shapes (or solids) have length, width and depth (or height). Examples include cubes, cuboids, prisms, and cylinders. This chapter is about the area of the surface of some of these 3-D shapes and the space inside them.

Learn 4.1 Volume of a cube or cuboid

Finding the volume of a cube or cuboid

Volume is the amount of space inside a 3-D shape. In the metric system, volume is measured in cubic millimetres, cubic centimetres, cubic metres or cubic kilometres.

The diagram shows 1 cubic centimetre, written as 1 cm^3.

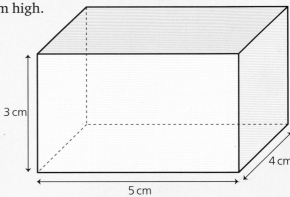

The **cuboid** opposite is 5 cm long, 4 cm wide and 3 cm high. Imagine that the cuboid is divided into cubic centimetres as shown.
There are 3 layers of cubes.

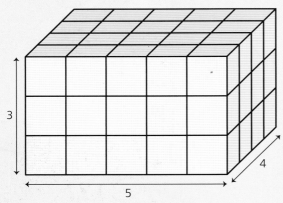

The number of **cubes** in each layer = 5×4
The total number of cubes = $5 \times 4 \times 3$

The volume of the cuboid = 60 cm^3

> The units for volume are cm^3 (from $\text{cm} \times \text{cm} \times \text{cm}$) or m^3 (from $\text{m} \times \text{m} \times \text{m}$), and so on.

You can find the volume of any cuboid quickly by using the following formula:

volume of a cuboid = length × width × height

Example

a A water tank has the dimensions shown in the diagram.
The amount the tank holds when it is full is called its **capacity**.
Find the amount of water the tank holds when it is full.
Give your answer in litres. [Hint: 1 litre = 1000 cm³]

b The water is used to fill bottles.
Each bottle holds 1.5 litres.
How many bottles can be filled from the water
in a full tank?

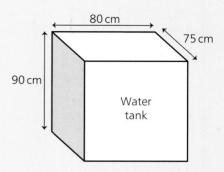

Solution

a Volume of water = length × width × height
$$= 80 \times 75 \times 90$$
$$= 540\,000 \text{ cm}^3$$

In litres, the capacity of the tank = 540 000 ÷ 1000 (since 1 litre = 1000 cm³)
$$= 540 \text{ litres.}$$

b Number of bottles = 540 ÷ 1.5 = 360 bottles

Apply 4.1

1 The following shapes are made from centimetre cubes.
Find the volume of each shape.

a

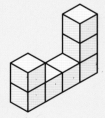

b

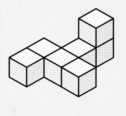

c

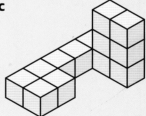

2 Calculate the volume of each cuboid below.

a

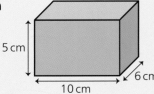

b

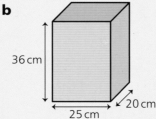

c

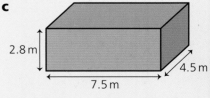

3 A box is in the shape of a cube with sides of length 80 centimetres.
Calculate the volume of the box.

4 The diagram shows the dimensions of a concrete base for a building. Calculate the volume of concrete in this base.

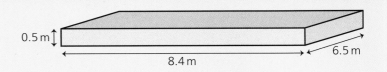

0.5 m

8.4 m

6.5 m

5 A water tank is in the shape of a cuboid.
It measures 2.5 metres by 1.2 metres by 0.6 metres.
Calculate the volume of the water in the tank when it is full.
Give your answer in litres. [$1 \text{ m}^3 = 1000$ litres]

6 a The diagram shows a seed tray.
It is 30 cm long and 20 cm wide.
The seed tray is filled with compost to a depth of 5 cm.
Work out the volume of compost in the seed tray.

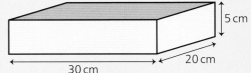

5 cm

30 cm

20 cm

b A farmer wants to fill 240 seed trays with compost.
How much compost does he need?
Give your answer in litres. [1 litre $= 1000 \text{ cm}^3$]

7 The diagram shows the dimensions of a fish tank.
The surface of the water in the tank is 5 centimetres below the top of the tank.
Find the volume of the water in the tank.
Give your answer in litres. [1 litre $= 1000 \text{ cm}^3$]

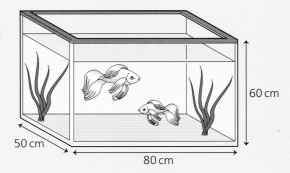

60 cm

50 cm

80 cm

8 A teacher asks his class to find the volume of a cuboid.
The cuboid measures 5 metres by 4 metres by 2 metres.
Ahmed says the answer is 11 m^3 and Sanjay says it is 40 m^2.
Is either of these answers correct? Explain your answer.

Learn 4.2 Volume of a prism

Finding the volume of a prism

A **prism** is a 3-D shape that has the same **cross-section** throughout its length (sometimes called a *uniform* cross-section).
The **solids** to the right are prisms.

This prism has a triangular cross-section.

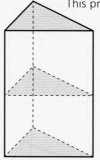

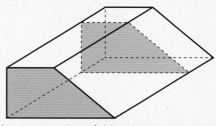

The cross-section of this prism is a trapezium.

The same formula can be used to find the volume of any prism. It is usually written as:

volume of a prism = area of cross-section × length

Example

The diagram shows the dimensions of a metal bar. Find the volume of this metal bar.

If you need a reminder of how to do this refer to Learn 3.3.

This shows how to find the area of composite shapes like this cross-section.

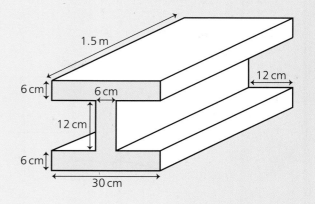

Solution

The cross-section is a composite shape. It can be divided into three rectangles.

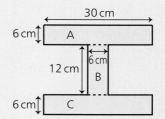

Area of rectangle A = 30×6
          $= 180 \text{ cm}^2$

Area of rectangle B = 12×6
          $= 72 \text{ cm}^2$

Area of rectangle C = Area of rectangle A
          $= 180 \text{ cm}^2$

Area of cross-section = $180 + 72 + 180$
          $= 432 \text{ cm}^2$

Volume of prism = area of cross-section $\times$ length
          $= 432 \times 150 = 64\,800 \text{ cm}^3$

← $1 \text{ m} = 100 \text{ cm}$, so $1.5 \text{ m} = 150 \text{ cm}$.

> **Study tip**
>
> Make sure all dimensions are in the *same units* before you use the volume formula.

Apply 4.2

1 The diagram shows a prism of length 12 cm.
The cross-section of the prism is a right-angled triangle *ABF*.
$AB = 8$ cm and $BF = 5$ cm

Calculate: **a** the area of triangle *ABF*
        b the volume of the prism.

2 A prism is 24 cm long.

The cross-section is a parallelogram with base 7.5 cm and height 6.4 cm.

Calculate: **a** the area of the cross-section
        b the volume of the prism.

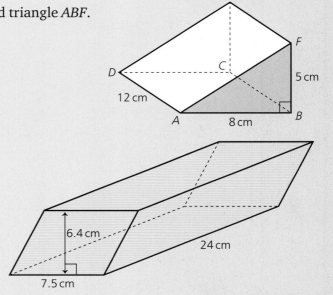

3

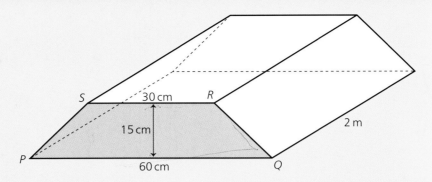

a In trapezium *PQRS*, *PQ* is parallel to *SR* and the perpendicular distance between them is 15 cm.
PQ = 60 cm and *SR* = 30 cm.
Work out the area of trapezium *PQRS*.

b *PQRS* is the cross-section of a prism. The length of the prism is 2 m.
Calculate the volume of the prism. Give your answer in cm³.

4 The diagram shows the dimensions of a waste skip.
The cross-section is trapezium *ABCD*.
AB = 1.6 m, *CD* = 2.4 m and *BC* = 1.2 m.
The width of the skip is 1.5 m.

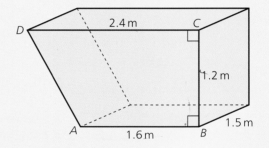

a Calculate the area of *ABCD*.

b Calculate the volume of the skip.

5 The diagram shows the dimensions of a feeding trough.
The cross-section is triangle *ABC* with *BC* = 60 cm.
The perpendicular distance from *A* to *BC* is 50 cm.
The trough is 140 cm long.

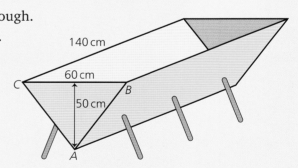

Work out: **a** the area of *ABC*

        b the capacity of the trough in litres.
[Hint: 1 litre = 1000 cm³]

6 a The diagram shows the dimensions of the cross-section
of a building.
Find the area of this cross-section.

b The building is 7 metres long.
Find the volume of the building.

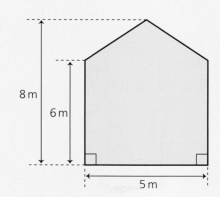

7 In the diagram, all the angles are 90° or 270°.

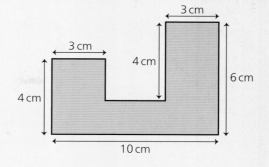

a Work out the area of the shape.

b The shape is the cross-section of a prism of length 15 centimetres.
Calculate the volume of the prism.

c A metal cuboid is melted down so that prisms as described in part **b** can be made.
The cuboid measures 120 cm by 60 cm by 30 cm.

i Calculate the volume of the cuboid.

ii Calculate the maximum number of prisms that can be made from this cuboid.

8 A chocolate manufacturer considers two possible shapes for a new chocolate bar.

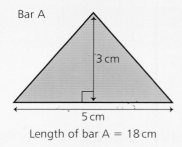

Bar A

Length of bar A = 18 cm

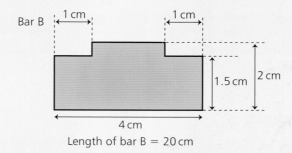

Bar B

Length of bar B = 20 cm

Each shape is a prism with cross-sections and dimensions as shown in the diagrams above.
Work out which bar takes less chocolate to make.

Learn 4.3 Volume of cylinder

Finding the volume of a cylinder

A **cylinder** is a prism with a circular cross-section.
The area of a circle of radius r is $\pi \times$ radius $\times$ radius $= \pi r^2$

If you need a reminder of how to do this refer to Learn 3.2.

This shows how to find the circumference and the area of a circle.

Using the volume formula for a prism gives:

    volume of cylinder $= \pi r^2 \times h = \pi r^2 h$

where r is the radius and h is the height of the cylinder.

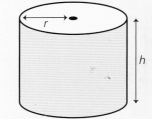

Example

A pipe is 36 metres long and has a diameter of 50 centimetres.
Work out how much water the pipe holds when full.
Give your answer to the nearest 10 litres. [Hint: 1 m^3 = 1000 litres]

Solution

50 cm

36 m

Diameter of pipe in metres = $50 \div 100 = 0.5$ m

Radius of pipe = $0.5 \div 2 = 0.25$ m

> All the dimensions must be in the same units.

Area of the cross-section of pipe = $\pi \times$ radius $\times$ radius

$\qquad = \pi \times 0.25 \times 0.25 = 0.196...$ m²

Volume of pipe = area of cross-section $\times$ length

$\qquad = 0.196... \times 36 = 7.0685...$ m³

Volume of water in litres = $7.0685... \times 1000$

$\qquad = 7068.5... = 7070$ litres (to nearest 10 litres)

Study tip

For an accurate answer carry on the calculation on your calculator. Do not round any values until the end of the calculation.

Apply 4.3

1 Find the volume of each cylinder below.

a 5 cm •

12 cm

b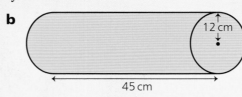

12 cm

45 cm

c 1.4 m

80 cm

Give your answer to part **c** in m³.

2 Find the volume of each cylinder.

a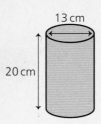

13 cm

20 cm

b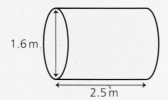

1.6 m

2.5 m

c 2.2 cm

4 mm

Give your answer to part **c** in mm³.

3 A litter bin has the dimensions shown in the sketch. Calculate the volume of the litter bin.

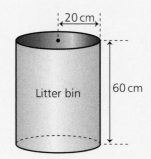

20 cm

Litter bin

60 cm

4 The container on a lorry is in the shape of a cylinder
with radius 125 cm and length 5.75 m.
Calculate the capacity of the container in litres.
Give your answer to the nearest 100 litres.
[1 m³ = 1000 litres]

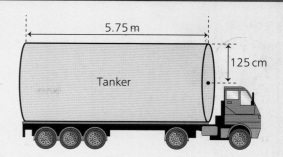

5 The diameter of a US dollar coin is 26.5 mm and it
is 2 mm thick.

Find the volume of metal needed to make
250 dollar coins.

6 A coffee mug is 10 cm tall and has a diameter of 7 cm.
Coffee is poured into the mug until it reaches 1 cm below the top.

a Calculate the volume of coffee in the mug.

b How many times could the mug be filled to this level with
2 litres of coffee? [1 litre = 1000 cm³]

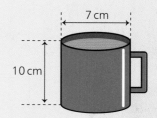

7 The diagram shows the dimensions of a can of soup and a saucepan.

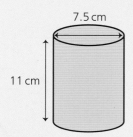
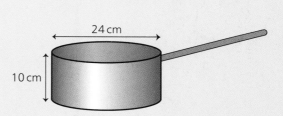

a Calculate the volume of soup in a full can.

b Calculate the capacity of the pan.

c How many whole cans of soup can be poured into the pan without it overflowing?

8

a An unsharpened pencil is in the shape of a cylinder of length 18 cm and radius 6 mm.
Calculate the volume of the pencil in cm³.

b The graphite inside the pencil is also cylindrical with length 18 cm.
The radius of the graphite is 1 mm. Calculate the volume of graphite in the pencil in cm³.

c The rest of the pencil is wood. Calculate the volume of wood in the pencil.

Learn 4.4 Surface area and nets

Finding the surface area of cubes and cuboids

The diagram shows some terms used when describing cuboids and other 3-D shapes (solids).

A **face** is the surface of a solid which is enclosed by edges.
A cuboid has 6 **faces**.

An **edge** is a line where two faces meet. A cuboid has 12 **edges**.

A **vertex** (plural **vertices**) is a point where three or more edges meet.
A cuboid has 8 **vertices**.

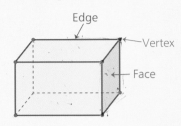

The **surface area** of a cube or a cuboid is the total area of its 6 faces.

Example

A cuboid is 10 cm long, 6 cm wide and 7 cm high.
Find the surface area of this cuboid.

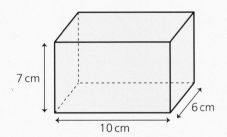

Solution

Area of front face = $10 \times 7 = 70 \text{ cm}^2$

Area of back face is also 70 cm^2

Area of face on right = $6 \times 7 = 42 \text{ cm}^2$

Area of face on left is also 42 cm^2

Area of top face = $10 \times 6 = 60 \text{ cm}^2$

Area of bottom face is also 60 cm^2

Total surface area of cuboid = $70 + 70 + 42 + 42 + 60 + 60 = 344 \text{ cm}^2$

Nets

Imagine you have a cuboid made out of card. Cutting along some edges and opening it out gives a 2-D shape called a **net** of the cuboid.

The diagram below shows a net of the cuboid in the last example.
The area of each face has been shown on the net.

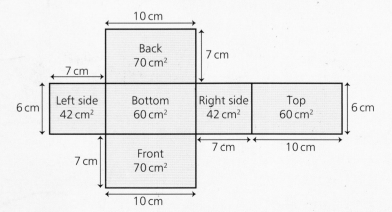

There are other ways of arranging the faces in this net.

Adding these areas together gives the total surface area of the cuboid.

Finding the surface area of a cylinder

The diagrams below show a cylinder and its net.

The ends of the cylinder are circles. Opening out the curved surface gives a rectangle. The area of the rectangle and circles are given on the second diagram.

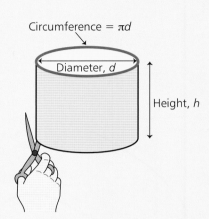
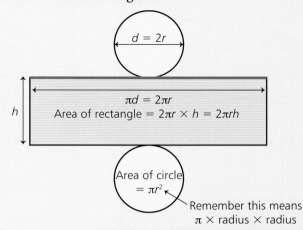

Total surface area of cylinder $= 2\pi r^2 + 2\pi rh$

> There are two circular faces: the top and the bottom.

> **Study tip**
>
> Do not try to remember this formula. When you need to work out the surface area of a cylinder, do it one part at a time.

Example

Find the total surface area of a cylinder of radius 6.5 cm and height 9.2 cm.

Solution

Area of each circular end $= \pi r^2 = \pi \times 6.5 \times 6.5 = 132.73\ldots$

> Put this value into a memory on your calculator to use later.

Opening out the curved surface of the cylinder gives the rectangle shown in the sketch.

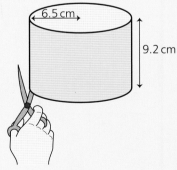
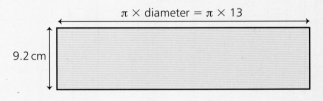

Diameter of cylinder $= 2 \times 6.5 = 13$ cm,

so length of rectangle $= \pi \times 13 = 40.84\ldots$

Area of rectangle $= 40.84\ldots \times 9.2 = 375.73\ldots$

Total surface area of cylinder $= 375.73\ldots + 2 \times 132.73\ldots$

$\qquad\qquad = 641$ cm^2 (to the nearest cm^2)

> **Study tip**
>
> Always work as accurately as you can. Only round your answer at the end of the calculation.

> Carry on the working on your calculator.

Apply 4.4

1 A room is 4.8 metres long, 3.5 metres wide and 2.4 metres high.

Find: **a** the area of the floor of the room

     b the area of the front wall

     c the area of the side wall

     d the total surface area of the room.

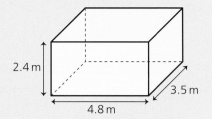

2 The diagram shows the dimensions of a can of cola.

Work out: **a** the area of the top of the can

        b the area of the curved surface of the can

        c the total surface area of the can.

3 Find the total surface area of each of the shapes below.

a 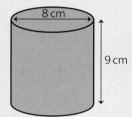   **b** 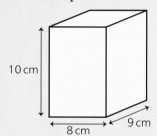   **c**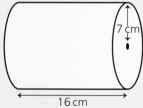

4 Which of these nets fold up to make a cube?

a   **b**   **c**   **d**   **e**

5 The cuboid in the diagram has $AB = 15$ mm, $BC = 11$ mm and $AE = 8$ mm.

a Draw a sketch of the net of this cuboid.

b Find the total surface area of the cuboid.

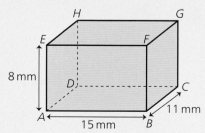

6 A cylinder is 2.5 metres long. The diameter of the cylinder is 1.2 metres.

a Sketch the net of the cylinder.

b Calculate the total surface area of the cylinder.

7 The diagram shows the net of an open-topped box and the length of three of its edges.

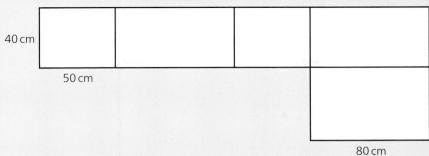

40 cm

50 cm

80 cm

a Copy the net and write the length on each of the other edges.
b Add another rectangle to give the net of a closed box.
c Find the total area of the closed box.

8 a Show that the volume of Tank A is slightly more than the volume of Tank B.
b Work out which tank has the smaller surface area.

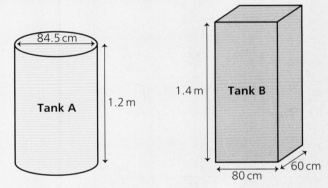

84.5 cm

Tank A

1.2 m

1.4 m

Tank B

80 cm

60 cm

Assess 4.1–4.4

1 Calculate the volume of each solid below.

a

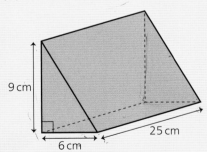

23 mm

12 mm

15 mm

c

9 cm

6 cm

25 cm

b

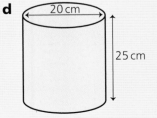

3 cm

4 cm

d

20 cm

25 cm

e

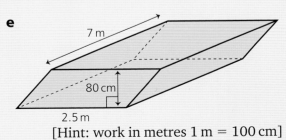

7 m

80 cm

2.5 m

[Hint: work in metres 1 m = 100 cm]

2 The diagram shows a block of stone in the shape of a prism of length 50 cm.

The cross-section is a trapezium *PQRS*.

PQ = 20 cm, *PS* = 25 cm, *SR* = 40 cm and angles *SPQ* and *PSR* are right angles.

Calculate: **a** the area of the cross-section *PQRS*

b the volume of the block of stone.

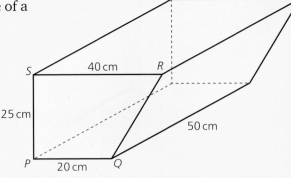

3 The cuboid shown in the diagram has *AB* = 10 cm, *AD* = 16 cm and *BF* = 7 cm.

Calculate: **a** the volume of the cuboid

b the surface area of the cuboid.

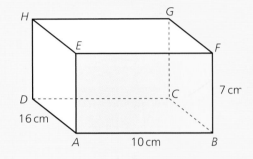

4 The diagram shows the net of a solid.

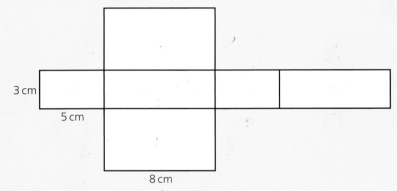

a Work out the perimeter of the net.

b Work out the area of the net.

c Write down the mathematical name of the solid.

d Work out the volume of the solid.

5 Find the volume of each prism.

a

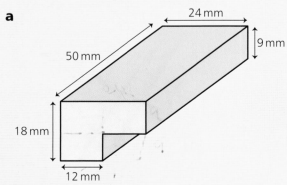

b

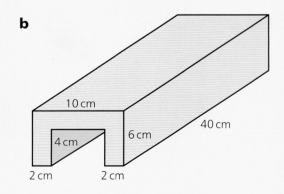

6 A cylinder has radius 12 cm and height 40 cm.

    a Draw a sketch of the net of this cylinder.

    b Work out the total surface area of the cylinder.

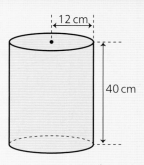

7 **a** A metal cuboid is 90 cm long, 50 cm wide and 40 cm high.
Calculate the volume of the cuboid.

    b The cuboid is melted down to make prisms.
The cross-section of each prism is a kite with the dimensions shown in the diagram.
Each prism is 30 cm long.

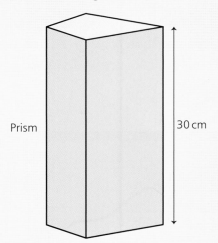

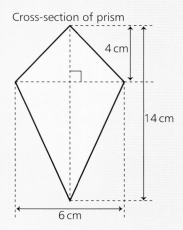

Cross-section of prism

      Calculate: **i** the area of the cross-section

              ii the volume of one prism

           iii the maximum number of prisms that can be made from the cuboid.

8 The diagram shows the dimensions of a padding pool.

    a Find the total area of the material used to make
the paddling pool.
Give your answer in m².

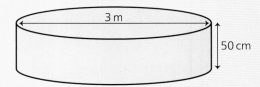

    b The pool is filled with water to a depth of 30 centimetres.
Work out the volume of water in the pool.
Give your answer to the nearest 10 litres. [1 m³ = 1000 litres]

5 Numbers and sequences

Learning outcomes:

After this chapter you should be able to:

- continue a given number sequence
- recognise patterns in sequences
- recognise relationships between different sequences
- find a term-to-term rule in a sequence
- write the terms of a sequence or a series of diagrams given the nth term
- write the nth term of a linear sequence or series of diagrams.

Sequences are shown as a list of numbers or as a pattern of connected diagrams.

You will extend sequences and describe them in words.

You will be asked to explain a sequence using the term-to-term rule or the position-to-term rule by finding the nth term.

Learn 5.1 The rules of a sequence

A **sequence** is a set of numbers or patterns with a given **rule** or pattern.

Each number in the sequence is called a **term**.

Examples of sequences include:

1, 3, 5, 7, 9, …	the odd numbers
2, 4, 6, 8, 10, …	the even numbers
1, 4, 9, 16, 25, …	the square numbers.

Sequences can also be patterns:

These are **infinite** sequences.

The dots '…' show that the sequence continues for ever.

In the following sequence, compare the terms.

1st 2nd 3rd 4th 5th 6th
term term term term term term

1,   2,   4,   8,   16, 32,   …
  ×2   ×2   ×2   ×2   ×2

Each term is twice the previous term.

To get from one term to the next you 'multiply by 2' or '× 2'.

This means that

　　1st term × 2 = 2nd term

　　2nd term × 2 = 3rd term

and so on …

This is called the **term-to-term rule**.

This rule can be used to continue the sequence. You can find the next terms using the rule '×2'.

1, 2, 4, 8, 16, 32, 64, 128, …

　　　　　　×2 ×2

Example

Write down the next two terms of the following sequence.

3, 9, 15, 21, 27, …

Solution

1st term	2nd term	3rd term	4th term	5th term
3,	9,	15,	21,	27, …

　　+6　+6　+6　+6　+6

These are called the **differences**

The rule is 'add 6' or '+6'.

The 6th term will be 27 + 6 = 33.

The 7th term will be 33 + 6 = 39.

3, 9, 15, 21, 27, 33, 39, …

　　　　　　+6 +6

Example

1st term　　　　　2nd term　　　　　3rd term

a Draw the next two patterns in the sequence.

b Copy and complete the following table.

Term	1	2	3	4	5	6
Number of dots	7	12	17			

c What is the rule for this sequence?

d By looking at the diagrams, explain why this is the rule.

Solution

a

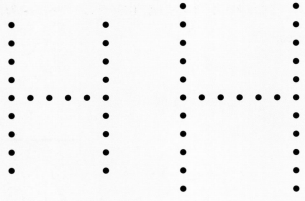

4th term   5th term

b

Term	1	2	3	4	5	6
Number of dots	7	12	17	22	27	32

c Finding the rule of a sequence is the same as finding the term-to-term rule.

This rule, for the number of dots, can be given in words or symbols.

'Add 5' or '+ 5'.

d When moving on from one term to the next, you are adding a total of 5 extra dots to the diagram; one at each corner and one in the middle.

1st term   2nd term

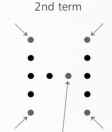

Example

Three terms are missing from this sequence.

5, __, __, −4, −7, __, …

a What is the rule?

b Find the missing terms.

Solution

a The rule is found by comparing two **consecutive** terms. Consecutive means 'next to each other'.

The 4th term is −4 and the 5th term is −7.

As you move from the 4th term to the 5th term, you are 'subtracting 3'.

The rule is 'subtract 3' or '−3'.

So every term in the sequence will be three less than the one before.

b 1st   2nd   3rd   4th   5th   6th
term term term term term term
5,   2,   −1,   −4,   −7, −10, …
  −3   −3   −3   −3   −3   −3

Apply 5.1

1 Draw the next diagram in the following sequences:

a

c

b

2 Write down the next two terms in the following sequences.

a 2, 6, 10, 14, …

b 20, 15, 10, 5, …

c 2, 8, 32, 128, …

d 1, 4, 9, 16, …

e $1\frac{1}{2}$, 1, $\frac{1}{2}$, 0, …

f 10, 100, 1000, 10 000, …

g −4, −2, 0, 2, …

h 1, $\frac{1}{2}$, $\frac{1}{3}$, $\frac{1}{4}$, …

3 Write down the rule for the following sequences.

a 8, 4, 2, 1, …

b 6, 11, 16, 21, …

c 1, 12, 23, 34, …

d 15, 8, 1, −6, …

e 1, 3, 9, 27, …

f 100, 10, 1, 0.1, …

g 1.5, 0.3, 0.06, 0.012, …

h $4\frac{1}{2}$, $4\frac{1}{4}$, 4, $3\frac{3}{4}$, …

4 Write down the first five terms of each of the sequences.

a 1st term = 1   Rule = add 9

b 1st term = 1   Rule = × 5

c 1st term = 13   Rule = − 3

d 1st term = 2   Rule = multiply by 2 and then add 1

e 1st term = 53   Rule = −3 then ÷ 2

5 The rule for a sequence is −2.
Write down three different sequences that fit this rule.

6 1, 1, 2, 3, 5, 8, 13, …
In this sequence each number is the sum of the two previous numbers
(this is called a Fibonacci sequence.)
For example 2 = 1 + 1 and 3 = 1 + 2

a What is the next term in the sequence?

Fibonacci sequences can start with different numbers.

b Find the next three terms of

   i 1, 2, …   **ii** 2, 4, …   **iii** 5, 10, …

7 Write down three different sequences that begin 1, 2, …
Show the first five terms of each sequence and explain how each is formed.

8

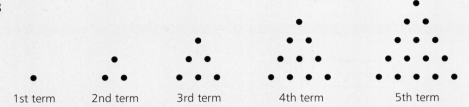

1st term   2nd term   3rd term   4th term   5th term

a   Count the number of dots in each diagram.

    Write down the sequence formed.

These are called the **triangular numbers**.

b   Copy and complete the following diagram for the sequence found in part **a**.

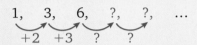

     1,   3,   6,   ?,   ?,   ...

     +2   +3   ?   ?

c   Find the 6th term of the sequence. Show your working.

d   Now look back at the diagrams. Explain your answer to part **c**.

9   1st pattern   2nd pattern   3rd pattern

These patterns are made from matchsticks.

a   Copy and complete the following table.

Pattern	1	2	3	4	5
Number of matches					

b   What is the rule for the sequence in the bottom row of the table?
     Explain your answer by looking at the patterns.

c   The patterns are changed by adding extra matches as shown.

     1st pattern   2nd pattern   3rd pattern

     Count the new total number of matches for each pattern.

     Write down the first five terms of the new sequence of numbers.

d   Find the rule for the new sequence.
     Explain your answer by looking at the new patterns.

10

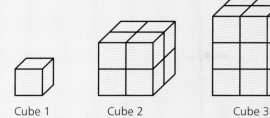

Cube 1   Cube 2   Cube 3

The diagram shows cubes of dimensions 1 cm by 1 cm by 1 cm, 2 cm by 2 cm by 2 cm, and 3 cm by 3 cm by 3 cm.

A 1 cm by 1 cm by 1 cm cube is referred to as a unit cube.

a How many unit cubes are there in each diagram?

Use these numbers to form a sequence.

b Add the next two terms of your sequence.

This is the sequence of cube numbers. You will meet these again in a later chapter.

c Now count the number of unit squares that can be seen on the outside surface of each cube. Copy and complete the following table. Try to do this without drawing any more diagrams.

Cube	1	2	3	4	5
Number of squares	6	24			

d Explain why there are 600 squares on the surface of cube 10 in the sequence.

Learn 5.2 The *n*th term of a sequence

You can work out terms in a sequence by identifying the rule.

The term-to-term rule compares one term to its previous term.

If you were asked to find the 100th term, you would have to know the 99th term.

To find these you would need the 98th, 97th, 96th, …

Instead of comparing a term to another term, you can compare the term to its position in the sequence.

Look at the sequence

6,   8,   10,   12,   …
+2   +2   +2

These differences are all +2.
+2 is the common difference

The common difference of +2 tells us that there is a 2*n* in the **nth term**.

Tables can be a useful way of showing your working.

n relates to the position of the number within the sequence.

That is *n* = 1 relates to the 1st term,

      n = 2 relates to the 2nd term,

and so on.

In the table below, the bottom row shows the values for $2n$.

Each value is 2 times the original number.

This gives the sequence 2, 4, 6, 8.

To return to the original sequence from this you add 4 to each of the numbers.

The nth term $= 2n + 4$

Check: 1st term $= (2 \times 1) + 4 = 6$

2nd term $= (2 \times 2) + 4 = 8$ and so on.

n	1st	2nd	3rd	4th
Sequence	6 +4	8 +4	10 +4	12 +4
$2n$	2	4	6	8

Example

The first four terms of a sequence are 1, 4, 7, 10, …

a Find the 5th term.

b Find the nth term.

c Find the 100th term.

Solution

a The 5th term can be found easily using the rule for the sequence.

1st   2nd   3rd   4th   5th
1,   4,   7,   10,   13,
+3   +3   +3   +3

$10 + 3 = 13$

b This term-to-term method cannot be used for finding the nth term.

The **position-to-term** method must be used.

This time, the number in the sequence is compared to its position 1st, 2nd, 3rd, …

You are comparing to the top line in the table, $n = 1, n = 2, …$

Comparing each term with the next, the common difference is 3.

There is a $3n$ in the nth term.

n	1st	2nd	3rd	4th
Sequence	1 −2	4 −2	7 −2	10 −2
$3n$	3	6	9	12

To return to the original sequence from the $3n$ row, you need to subtract 2 from each number.

The nth term $= 3n - 2$.

c To find the 100th term replace n by 100 in the formula for the nth term.

$$100\text{th term} = 3 \times 100 - 2$$
$$= 300 - 2$$
$$= 298$$

All sequences solved in this way are called **linear sequences**.

In linear sequences, the differences are the same for all terms in the sequence.

Example

The nth term of a sequence is $4n - 2$.

Find the first five terms of the sequence.

Solution

1st term $= 4 \times 1 - 2 = 2$

2nd term $= 4 \times 2 - 2 = 6$

3rd term $= 4 \times 3 - 2 = 10$

4th term $= 4 \times 4 - 2 = 14$

5th term $= 4 \times 5 - 2 = 18$

The sequence is

2, 6, 10, 14, 18, …

Example

A gardener needs some support for growing his plants.

He makes them out of straight pieces of wood joined together.

  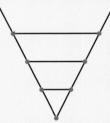

Diagram 1   Diagram 2   Diagram 3

a Draw the next diagram in the sequence.

b How many joins will there be in the 5th diagram?

c Copy and complete the table.

Diagram	1	2	3	4	5
Number of joins	3	5			

d How many joins would there be in the nth diagram?

e How many joins in the 25th diagram?

f The number of joins in diagram n is 81. Find n.

Solution

a

Diagram 4

b There will be 11. That is 2 more than in the previous diagram. The rule is + 2.

c

Diagram	1	2	3	4	5
Number of joins	3	5	7	9	11

d The top row is the diagram number.

Diagram (n)	1	2	3	4	5
Number of joins	3 ↑+1	5 ↑+1	7 ↑+1	9 ↑+1	11 ↑+1
$2n$	2	4	6	8	10

The bottom row shows the values for $2n$ because the common difference is + 2.

To return to the original sequence from the $2n$ row, you need to add one to each number.

The nth term is $2n + 1$. So there would be $2n + 1$ joins.

e Number of joins $= 2 \times 25 + 1 = 51$.

f The number of joins in the nth diagram $= 2n + 1$.
There are 81 joins.
So $2n + 1 = 81$

$$2n = 81 - 1 \quad \longleftarrow \boxed{\text{Subtract 1 from each side.}}$$
$$2n = 80$$
$$n = 40$$

Apply 5.2

1 Write down the first five terms of the linear sequence whose nth term is:

a $n + 1$ **c** $n + 7$ **e** $2n - 1$

b $5n$ **d** $2n - 3$ **f** $\frac{1}{2}n + 1$

2 Find the nth term of the following linear sequences.

a 6, 8, 10, 12, 14, ...

b 2, 5, 8, 11, 14, ...

c 0, 7, 14, 21, 35, ...

d 11, 10, 9, 8, 7, ...

e −1, 1, 3, 5, 7, ...

f $6\frac{1}{2}, 7, 7\frac{1}{2}, 8, 8\frac{1}{2}, ...$

g −5, −3, −1, 1, 3, ...

h 11, 22, 33, 44, 55, ...

3 Find the nth term for this non-linear sequence.

   a 1, 4, 9, 16, 25

   b Use the answer to part **a** to write down the nth term for:

      i 3, 6, 11, 18, 27   **ii** 0.5, 2, 4.5, 8, 12.5

4 The nth term of a sequence is $3n + 2$.

Maya says that if you add the 2nd and the 4th term together, it is the same as the 6th term.

Is Maya correct?

Give reasons for your answer.

5 Write down the nth term for the following non-linear sequences.

   a $1 \times 2, 2 \times 3, 3 \times 4, \ldots$

   b $1, \frac{1}{2}, \frac{1}{3}, \frac{1}{4}, \ldots$

   c 0.1, 0.2, 0.3, 0.4, ...

   d $2^1, 2^2, 2^3, 2^4, 2^5, \ldots$

   e $\frac{1}{2}, \frac{2}{3}, \frac{3}{4}, \frac{4}{5}, \ldots$

6 The diagram shows the first three patterns in a sequence.

Pattern 1   Pattern 2   Pattern 3

   a Copy and complete the following table showing the number of matches in each diagram.

n	1st	2nd	3rd	4th
Number of matches	5	8		
3n				

   b Use the table to find how many matches there are in the nth diagram.

   c How many matches are there in the 100th diagram?

7

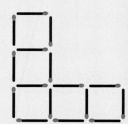

Pattern 1   Pattern 2   Pattern 3

   a Copy the table.

Complete the second row showing the total number of matches in each of the first five diagrams.

n	1st	2nd	3rd	4th	5th
Number of matches	4				
6n					

b Find the common difference and use this information to complete the third row of the table.

c Complete this formula for the number of matches in the *n*th diagram.

No. of matches = ___

d Use this formula to find the number of matches in the 60th diagram.

8

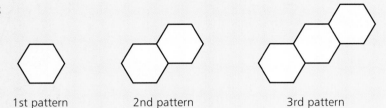

1st pattern   2nd pattern   3rd pattern

The hexagons in the diagrams are made from straight lines of equal length.

a Complete the table

Diagram (*n*)	1	2	3	4	5
Lines	6	11			

b How many lines in the 8th diagram?

c How many lines in the *n*th diagram?
(You might want to add another row to the bottom of your table to help you.)

d A diagram is made from 201 lines. How many hexagons are there in the diagram?

9

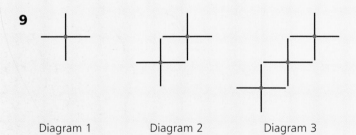

Diagram 1   Diagram 2   Diagram 3

a Draw the next diagram in the sequence.

b Copy and complete the table to show the number of lines and dots in each diagram.

Diagram (*n*)	1	2	3	4	5
Lines	4	8			
Dots	1				

c For the *n*th diagram, find an expression for:
   i the number of lines   **ii** the number of dots.

d How many dots are there in the 35th diagram?

e How many lines are there in the 50th diagram?

f Find the difference between the answers for **c i** and **ii**.
Simplify your answer.

10 These diagrams are made from lines and dots.

a Draw the next diagram in the sequence.

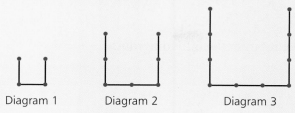

Diagram 1   Diagram 2   Diagram 3

b Copy and complete the table.

Diagram (*n*)	1	2	3	4
Lines	3	6		
Dots	4			

c Find the number of lines and dots in Diagram 6.

d For the *n*th diagram, find an expression for

    i the number of lines   **ii** the number of dots.

e How many lines and dots are there in the 100th diagram?

f Now look at the total number of lines and dots in each diagram.
Using your answers to part **c**, write down an expression for the total number in the *n*th
diagram. Simplify your answer.

Assess 5.1–5.2

1 Write down the next two terms in the following sequences.

    a 9, 12, 15, …   **d** 35, 24, 13, …

    b 20, 18, 16, …   **e** 2, 6, 18, …

    c 1, 8, 27, …

2 Write down the rule for the following sequences.

    a 27, 24, 21, 18, …   **d** 1, 4, 9, 16, …

    b 1000, 500, 250, 125, …   **e** 7, 14, 28, 56, …

    c 4, 13, 22, 31, …

3 Write down the first five terms of each of the sequences.

    a 1st term = 2   Rule = + 7

    b 1st term = 18   Rule = − 5

    c 1st term = 1   Rule = × 3, then − 1

4 Write down the first five terms of the linear sequence whose *n*th term is:

    a $n + 10$ **c** $5n - 3$

    b $3n + 1$ **d** $n^2 + 1$

5 **a** A sequence has the *n*th term of $2n + 1$.
Sahid says that the number 20 is in this sequence.
Is he correct? Explain your answer.

   b Roseanna's sequence has an *n*th term of $5n - 1$.
She says that the 5th term of the sequence is 6 times the 1st term of the sequence.
Is she correct? Explain your answer.

6 Find the *n*th term of the following sequences.

   a 9, 18, 27, 36, 45, …   **d** $1 \times 4, 2 \times 5, 3 \times 6, \ldots$

   b 13, 15, 17, 19, 21, …   **e** $10, \frac{10}{2}, \frac{10}{3}, \frac{10}{4}, \ldots$

   c 4, 3, 2, 1, 0, …

7 The *n*th term of a sequence $= \frac{1}{2}n(n + 1)$.

   a Find the first five terms of the sequence.

   b Use your answers from part **a** to find the *n*th term for the sequences

      i 2, 6, 12, 20, …   **ii** 3, 5, 8, 12, …

8 1st pattern   2nd pattern   3rd pattern

   a Copy and complete the table.

Pattern	1	2	3	4	5
Black dots	1	4			

   b Use the table to find the *n*th term of the sequence.

   c Write down the *n*th term of the sequence made from counting the total number of dots in each pattern.

   d If there is a total of 64 dots in a pattern, how many black dots are there?

   e If there are 79 black dots in a pattern number *n*. Find *n*.

9 1st   2nd   3rd

   a Draw the next diagram in the sequence.

   b Copy and complete the table.

Diagram (*n*)	1	2	3	4
Shaded squares	1	2		
Unshaded squares	3	4		

c Find the *n*th term for:

   i the number of shaded squares   **ii** the number of unshaded squares.

d Use your answers to **c** parts **i** and **ii**, to find the *n*th term for the **total** number of squares.

e Find the total number of squares in the 100th diagram.

f If there are 32 unshaded squares in a diagram, how many shaded squares are there?

10 These hexagon patterns are made from lines of an equal length.

         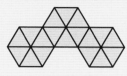

Pattern 1   Pattern 2   Pattern 3

a Copy and complete the following table showing the total number of lines used and the number of triangles enclosed in each pattern.

Pattern	1	2	3	4
Enclosed triangles	6	12		
Lines	12	23		

b Find the *n*th term for:

   i the number of enclosed triangles   **ii** the number of lines used.

c From your previous answers show that the *n*th term for the total number of triangles and lines is $17n + 1$

d Which pattern number has a total of 86 lines and triangles?

e How many triangles and how many lines are there in pattern number 7?

6 Directed numbers

Learning outcomes:

After this chapter you should be able to:
- understand what is meant by a directed number
- use directed numbers in practical situations
- add and subtract positive and negative integers
- multiply and divide positive and negative integers.

A directed number has a positive or negative sign.

The sign shows if it is less than or greater than zero.

A negative sign (−) shows that the number is less than zero.

A positive sign (+) shows that the number is greater than zero.

Directed numbers are often associated with temperatures and bank balances.

They are also used to describe height above/below sea level.

Learn 6.1 Using directed numbers

A **directed number** is any positive or negative number or zero.

An integer is any positive or negative whole number or zero.

Positive integers and **negative integers** can be shown on a number line.

The number line below shows the integers −9, −2, 0, +1 and +5.

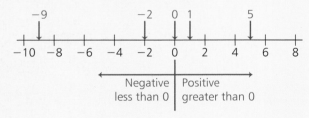

When writing positive integers, the + signs can be missed out.

Temperatures can be positive numbers or negative numbers.

When working with temperatures, it is useful to think of a thermometer. This is a vertical number line.
Temperatures are usually measured in degrees Celsius (°C).

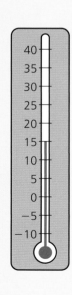

Example

The temperature is 5 °C.

The temperature falls by 7 °C.

What is the new temperature?

Solution

The new temperature is −2 °C.

You may have been asked for the 'drop in temperature'.

This is the same as the 'fall in temperature'.

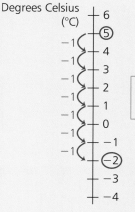

Temperature falls by 7 °C, moves 7 down.

Example

The minimum temperature in February in China was recorded as −7 °C.

The maximum temperature was 4 °C.

How many degrees Celsius had the temperature risen?

Solution

The temperature had risen 11 degrees.

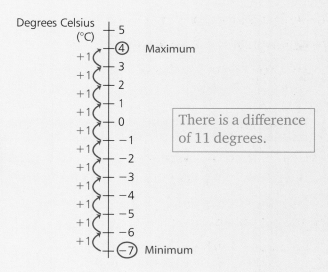

There is a difference of 11 degrees.

Study tip

When working with temperatures, think of a thermometer.

If you need to draw a diagram, use a simplified vertical number line.

Vertical number lines are helpful when working with temperatures.

Directed numbers can be used in other situations.

In these cases horizontal or vertical number lines may be used.

Example

Rashid has $70 in his savings account. He takes out $100.
How much does he have in his account now?

Solution

Rashid starts with $70.

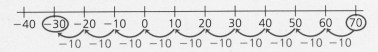

> This number line is labelled in 10's.

Rashid takes out $100, which is 10 lots of $10.

He finishes up with −$30.

This means that he has no money in his account.

He owes the bank $30. He is overdrawn by $30.

Apply 6.1

1 Place the following numbers on:

   a a horizontal number line

   b a vertical number line.

$$-4 \quad 3 \quad -1 \quad 5 \quad -3 \quad 0$$

2 **a** The temperature is 6 °C. It falls by 4 °C. What is the new temperature?

   b The temperature is −3 °C. It rises by 5 °C. What is the new temperature?

   c The temperature is 2 °C. It falls by 3 °C. What is the new temperature?

   d The temperature is −4 °C. It rises by 4 °C. What is the new temperature?

   e The temperature is −7 °C. It falls by 5 °C. What is the new temperature?

3

Monday	Tuesday	Wednesday	Thursday	Friday	Saturday	Sunday
4 °C	−2 °C	−4 °C	−3 °C	−1 °C	2 °C	5 °C

   a By how much did the temperature drop from Monday to Tuesday?

   b By how much did the temperature rise from Thursday to Friday?

   c What is the difference between the maximum and minimum temperatures for the week?

4 The table shows the average temperatures for the months of January and July in five different places. All temperatures were recorded at the same time on the same day.

Place	January temp (°C)	July temp (°C)
Male, Maldives	27	27
Resolute, Canada	−30	5
Jos, Nigeria	22	19
Bayandelger, Mongolia	−18	17
Mt John, New Zealand	13	−3

  a Write down the place with the warmest temperature in
   i January   **ii** July.

  b Write down the place with the coldest temperature in
   i January   **ii** July.

  c Find the difference between the January and July temperatures in
   i Mt John   **ii** Jos   **iii** Male.

5 The diagram shows a flood warning.

FLOOD WARNING

This path is likely to flood if
the water level rises to 2 metres
above sea level.

TAKE CARE!

The water level is presently at 3 m below sea level.

By how much would the level have to rise, for flooding to take place?

6 The table shows the maximum and minimum temperatures recorded for the city of Spurr
in Argentina.

	Jan	Feb	Mar	April	May	June	July	Aug	Sept	Oct	Nov	Dec
Maximum	41 °C	42 °C	37 °C	32 °C	29 °C	24 °C	26 °C	29 °C	32 °C	35 °C	38 °C	40 °C
Minimum	5 °C	2 °C	1 °C	−2 °C	−3 °C	−7 °C	−7 °C	−7 °C	−5 °C	−3 °C	−1 °C	−1 °C

Calculate the differences between the maximum and minimum temperatures for each of the
months.

7 Chembra Peak (2100 m above sea level) is the highest mountain in Kerala, India.
The lowest ground in Kerala is in Kuttanad which is 2 m below sea level.
What is the difference in height between these two places?

8 At the end of the month of May, Samirah's bank account is overdrawn by $70.
Overdrawn accounts can be shown using negative numbers (−$70).
The table shows the balances in her account for May and the following five months.

Month	May	June	July	August	Sept	Oct
Balance	−$70	−$40	$10	−$5	$35	$80

  a What was the most that she was overdrawn?

  b Between which two consecutive months was the difference the greatest?

  [Hint: consecutive months follow on from each other.]

  c Between which two consecutive months was the difference the smallest?

9 The highest mountain in Australia is Mawson Peak at 2745 m above sea level. The lowest place in Australia is at Lake Eyre which is 2760 m below this. How far below sea level is Lake Eyre?

10 All golf courses publish a par. The par is determined from the number of shots that are needed for a golfer to complete the course.

The par for the Doha Championship Course in Qatar is 76. So someone scoring 80 would be 4 over par $(+4)$ and someone scoring 73 would be 3 under par or (-3).

    a Habib scored -2. How many shots did he take?

    b Ibrahim scored $+3$. How many shots did he take?

Learn 6.2 Adding and subtracting positive and negative numbers

There are two uses for $+$ and $-$ signs:

- To show if a number is positive or negative. $+4$ or -4
- To show if you are adding or subtracting. $6 + 4$ or $6 - 4$

Questions can involve both uses of the signs. $4 - -3$ or $4 - (-3)$

For adding and subtracting numbers use the following rules:

Adding a positive number	$+\ +$	is the same as	$+$	adding
Adding a negative number	$+\ -$	is the same as	$-$	subtracting
Subtracting a positive number	$-\ +$	is the same as	$-$	subtracting
Subtracting a negative number	$-\ -$	is the same as	$+$	adding

When adding and subtracting positive and negative numbers you can use a vertical or horizontal number line.

Adding numbers

Example

Find the value of: **a** $5 + -2$ **b** $-5 + +3$ **c** $-3 + -4$

Solution

Always start by finding the first number on the number line.

a

Subtract 2 $+ - = -$

$5 + -2 = 5 - 2 = 3$

b

Add 3

$-5 + +3 = -5 + 3 = -2$

$+ + = +$

c

Subtract 4

$-3 + -4 = -3 - 4 = -7$

$- + = -$

Subtracting numbers

Example

Find the value of: **a** $2 - +4$ **b** $-2 - +3$ **c** $-2 - -3$

Solution

a

Subtract 4

$2 - +4 = 2 - 4 = -2$

$- + = -$

b

Subtract 3

$-2 - +3 = -2 - 3 = -5$

$- + = -$

c

Add 3

$-2 - -3 = -2 + 3 = 1$

$- - = +$

Study tip

Use either the $(-)$ key or the $+/-$ key for negative numbers on your calculator.

Check your own calculator to see if you need to press the key before or after you enter the number.

Apply 6.2

Work through the following questions. Use your calculator to answer check once they are complete.

1 Find the value of:

   a $3 + 5$ **b** $-3 + 5$ **c** $3 + -5$ **d** $-3 + -5$

2 Find the value of:

   a $-7 - -4$ **b** $7 - +4$ **c** $-7 - +4$ **d** $7 - -4$

3 Rewrite each of these in an alternative way and then calculate the answer.

   The first one has been started for you.

   a $5 - +7 = 5 - 7 = -2$ **e** $-2 - +6$

   b $7 - +3$ **f** $-5 - -1$

   c $8 + -9$ **g** $-2 + -3$

   d $7 + -7$ **h** $-4 - +3$

4 Calculate the following:

   a $-2 + 3$ **e** $-40 + 90$

   b $7 - 9$ **f** $-12 + 30$

   c $5 - -9$ **g** $55 - 25$

   d $-15 - 20$ **h** $16 - -16$

5 Write down two integers that add up to six where:

   a both integers are positive

   b one integer is positive and one is negative

   c both integers are negative.

6 **a** What must be added to -7 to give 12?

   b What must be added to -10 to give -3?

   c What must be subtracted from 11 to give -1?

   d What must be subtracted from -4 to give -9?

7 These are number pyramids.

   Two numbers are added together to give the number in the box above.

   Copy and complete the pyramids.

   a

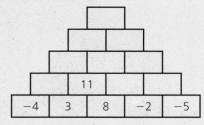

   b

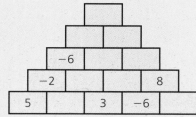

8 Julia chooses two numbers.

These numbers add up to six.

When you take one away from the other you get −2.

What are her numbers?

9 Ahmed is thinking of two numbers.

The difference between the numbers is five.

At least one of the numbers is negative.

Write down three possible pairs of Ahmed's numbers.

Learn 6.3 Multiplying and dividing positive and negative numbers

For multiplying and dividing numbers use the following rules:

For multiplication

$(+) \times (+) = (+)$

$(+) \times (-) = (-)$

$(-) \times (+) = (-)$

$(-) \times (-) = (+)$

For division

$(+) \div (+) = (+)$

$(+) \div (-) = (-)$

$(-) \div (+) = (-)$

$(-) \div (-) = (+)$

Study tip

When multiplying and dividing, remember the following:

Signs are the same, positive answer.

Signs are different, negative answer.

Example

Calculate:

a $-6 \div +3$

b $+8 \div -4$

c $-35 \div -5$

d $+4 \div +8$

Solution

a -2 $(-) \div (+) = (-)$

b -2 $(+) \div (-) = (-)$

c $+7$ $(-) \div (-) = (+)$

d $+\frac{4}{8} = +\frac{1}{2}$ $(+) \div (+) = (+)$

Apply 6.3

1 Find the value of:

a $+6 \times -3$

b -2×-8

c -5×0

d $+3 \times -2$

e -8×-1

f $+3 \times -10$

g $+8 \times +5$

h $-0.5 \times +9$

2 Find the value of:

a $+30 \div +3$

b $+21 \div -3$

c $-18 \div -9$

d $-40 \div +5$

e $+56 \div -8$

f $-81 \div +9$

g $-11 \div -2$

h $+7 \div 4$

3 Copy these and fill in the missing numbers.

a $-4 \times 6 = \ldots$

b $14 \div -2 = \ldots$

c $-24 \times \ldots = 48$

d $28 \div \ldots = 4$

e $9 \times -6 = \ldots$

f $\ldots \div 6 = -5$

g $\ldots \times -0.5 = 5$

h $13 \div -2 = \ldots$

4 Copy and complete these number pyramids.

Two numbers are multiplied together to give the number in the box above.

a

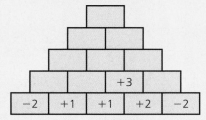

b

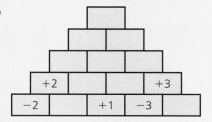

5 Two digits multiply together to give the answer -12.
Write down five different multiplication sums that would give this answer.

6 One digit divided by another gives the answer -9.
Write down five different divisions that would give this answer.

7 a Complete this sequence:

$$-1 \quad +2 \quad -4 \quad +8 \quad \ldots$$

b What is the rule for this sequence?

c Write down the first five terms of the sequence that has the rule 'Multiply by -3'.
The starting number is 1.

d Write down the first five terms of the sequence that has the rule 'Divide by -2'.
The starting number is 24.

8 a Find two integers whose sum is 6 and whose product is -16.

b Find two integers whose sum is -4 and whose product is -12.

c Find two integers whose sum is -7 and whose product is 10.

Assess 6.1–6.3

1 Calculate:

a $-5 + 3$

b $7 + -4$

c $5 - -6$

d $-2 - 9$

e 5×-3

f -4×-6

g $-12 \div 4$

h $-4 \div -8$

2 a Write down the number that is 5 less than -3.

b How many times does -2 go into -20?

c Explain why $-3 \times 6 - 2 = -20$.

3 On Monday the temperature at midday was 3° Celsius.
By noon the next day the temperature had dropped by 5 degrees.
What was the temperature at noon on Tuesday?

4 Lake Superior is the largest of the Great Lakes in Canada.

It contains approximately 10% of the Earth's fresh surface water.

The maximum depth of the lake is -406 metres.

The average depth of the water is -147 metres.

What is the difference between these water levels?

5 Calculate:

a $-5(4 - 9)$

b $(-3) - 3(-2)$

c $\dfrac{-8 - (-2)}{2}$

d $\dfrac{(-2 + 3 - 4) - 12}{-3}$

6 All freezers are given star ratings.
These depend on the temperature reached in the freezer and are shown below.

     * $-6\,°C$

    ** $-12\,°C$

  *** $-18°\,C$

****   below $-18°\,C$

A freezer is registering a temperature of $-14\,°C$.

By how many degrees does the temperature have to drop to be labelled a three star freezer?

7 Ulkar's bank account is overdrawn by $74.

She needs to save in order to buy a second-hand microwave from her neighbour.
This costs $250.

How much does she need to save in order to buy it?

8 a Write down three numbers whose sum is -8.

b Write down three numbers whose product is -8.

Practice exam questions

1   Write down the $\sqrt{16}$.   (*1 mark*)

2   Find the highest common factor of 24 and 40.   (*2 marks*)

3   A water container has a scale marked in cm as shown.

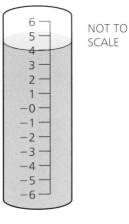

NOT TO SCALE

    a   7 cm of water are emptied from the container.
       What will the scale read now?   (*1 mark*)

    b   The container is then filled to the 6 cm mark.
       What depth of water has been added?   (*1 mark*)

4   For each of these statements, say whether it is true or false.

    a $5 + 2 < 8 - 1$

    b $8 - 5 \geqslant 2 + 1$

    c $8 \div 2 \neq 5 - 1$

    d $1 + 2 + 5 < 8$ (*2 marks*)

5   The lengths of five insects are:

    2.7 cm   3.02 cm   2.68 cm   2.4 cm   2.12 cm

    Write these lengths in order of size, starting with the smallest.   (*2 marks*)

6   From this list of numbers

    $\sqrt{10}$ $3\frac{1}{5}$ $4.\dot{6}$ -3 $\sqrt{4}$

    Write down:

    a   an integer

    b   a natural number

    c   an irrational number.   (*3 marks*)

7 $y = 5pq - 2q$

    Find the value of y when $p = -2$ and $q = 3$.   (*1 mark*)

8   Amalia earns a total of y dollars per week.
She works for x hours each week and is paid a fixed amount per hour.
She also receives a bonus of v dollars every week.
Her manager works out her pay using the formula $y = 9x + v$.

   a   Write down how much Amalia is paid per hour

   b   How much does Amalia earn in a week when she works 35 hours and her bonus is
30 dollars?   (*2 marks*)

9   The length, L, of an arc of a circle of radius r is given by the formula $L = \dfrac{2\pi r}{3}$.
Calculate the length when the radius is 8.5 cm.   (*1 mark*)

10   For this shape, work out:

   a   the perimeter   (*2 marks*)

   b   the area.   (*2 marks*)

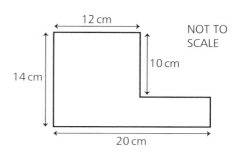

11   Find the circumference of a circle of radius 4.8 cm.
Write down your answer:

   a   exactly as it appears on your calculator   (*1 mark*)

   b   correct to the nearest centimetre.   (*1 mark*)

12   A model ship is flying two flags.
The first is a triangle with base 12 cm and height 20 cm.
The second is a rectangle of width 8 cm.
The flags are equal in area.
Find the length of the rectangular flag.   (*2 marks*)

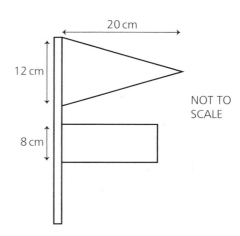

13   The diagram shows half of a circle.

   $AB = 18$ cm

   a   Calculate the perimeter of the shape   (*2 marks*)

   b   Calculate the area of the shape.   (*2 marks*)

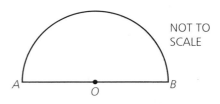

14 The diagram shows a prism of length 20 cm.
The cross-section of the prism is a trapezium
ABCD, with *AB* parallel to *CD*.
AB = 8 cm, *CD* = 16 cm and the
perpendicular distance between *AB* and
CD is 12 cm.

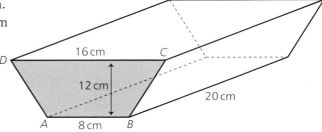

Calculate:

  a the area of the trapezium *ABCD*   (*2 marks*)

  b the volume of the prism.   (*1 mark*)

15 A cylindrical can of tomatoes has height 12 cm and radius 4 cm.
A label covers the curved surface of the can completely.
Calculate the area of the label.   (*3 marks*)

16 The diagram shows a swimming pool with cross-section *ABCDE*.
The pool is 12 m long and 8 m wide.
AB = 8 m, *AE* = 2 m and *CD* = 1.2 m.

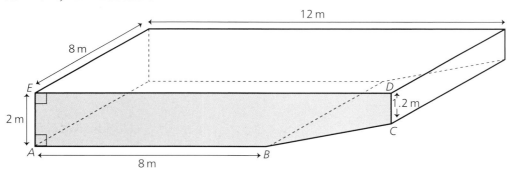

  a Calculate the area of the cross-section *ABCDE* and show your working.   (*4 marks*)

  b Calculate the volume of the water in the pool when it is full.
     Give your answer in litres. [1 m^3 = 1000 litres]   (*2 marks*)

  c One litre of water evaporates every hour from each square metre of the water surface.
     How many litres of water will evaporate in 6 hours?   (*2 marks*)

17 Find the next term and the *n*th term in the following sequences

  a 4, 6, 8, 10, …   **b** 1, 4, 9, 16, …   **c** $\frac{2}{3}, \frac{3}{4}, \frac{4}{5}, \frac{5}{6}$, …   (*3 marks*)

18 The *n*th term of a sequence is $\frac{n^2}{n+4}$.

  a Write down the first three terms of the sequence.   (*2 marks*)

  b Find the 10th term and the 50th term.   (*2 marks*)

  Leave your answers as fractions.

19 Each term in the Fibonacci sequence is the sum of the two previous terms.

> 1, 2, 3, 5, 8
> 4th term = 2nd term + 3rd term   5 = 2 + 3
> 5th term = 3rd term + 4th term   8 = 5 + 3

   a Find the 6th and the 7th terms. *(2 marks)*

   b Find the missing terms in the following sequences *(3 marks)*

      i 4, 5, 9, ..., ...   **ii** 2, ..., 7, ..., 19   **iii** ..., ..., 13, 20

20 The Kermadic Islands are home to some of New Zealand's most interesting volcanic features, both above and below sea level.

Volcanic feature	Height in metres
Raoul Island	516 m
MaCauley Island	238 m
Monowai Seamount	−100 m
Brothers Volcano	−1350 m

   a What is the difference in height between the highest feature and the lowest feature? *(2 marks)*

Submarine volcanoes are shown as negative numbers as they are below sea level.

   b Which feature is at the deepest point below sea level? *(2 marks)*

   c What is the difference in height between the two submarine volcanoes? *(2 marks)*

21 The table below shows the average maximum and minimum temperatures for January in three Chinese cities.

	Maximum	Minimum
Beijing	1 °C	−9 °C
Shanghai	7 °C	0 °C
Xi'an	4 °C	−4 °C

   a Which city has the coldest minimum temperature? *(2 marks)*

   b Calculate the difference between the maximum and minimum temperature for each city. *(2 marks)*

   c The temperature in Xi'an is 3 °C. How many more degrees would it have to fall to reach the average minimum temperature? *(2 marks)*

22 The water in a lake, during a drought, dropped to 1.8 m below its usual level.
After the rainy season, the level had risen to 0.6 m below its usual level.
How much did the level rise by? *(2 marks)*

Time and money

Learning outcomes:

After this chapter you should be able to:

- read clocks, dials and timetables
- calculate times using the 12-hour clock and the 24-hour clock
- calculate with money
- convert from one currency to another.

Time is universal. The same units, seconds, minutes and hours, are used everywhere in the world.

A currency is the unit of money that is used in a country. Different countries use different currencies.

Learn 7.1 Time

Dials and clocks

Some dials are **digital**. They show readings in a numerical display.

Here is an electricity meter:

0	5	7	2	3	8

It shows a reading of 57 238 units.

Cars have **odometers** that measure how far they have travelled.

These are usually digital.

Some scales are digital, but others are **analogue**.
This means they have a moving hand to show the reading.

These scales are marked in kilograms (kg).

The dial is marked in intervals of 0.1 kg.

The scales show a reading of 2.7 kg.

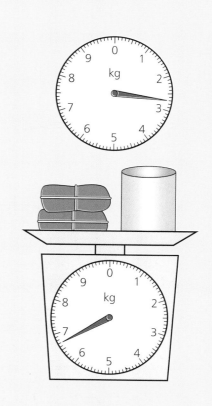

Example

Karl is weighing two identical parcels and a tin can.
The tin can weighs 3.9 kg.
Calculate the weight of each parcel.

Solution

The scales show a total weight of 6.7 kg.
The two parcels weigh 6.7 kg − 3.9 kg = 2.8 kg
Each parcel weighs 2.8 kg ÷ 2 = 1.4 kg

Many clocks have two hands, the hour hand and the minute hand.

The hour hand tells us the time in hours. Here the time is between 3 o'clock and four o'clock. In fact it is nearer 4 o'clock.

The minute hand tells us the time in minutes. Here the time is 20 minutes to the hour.

Calculating times

Times can be written in two ways: the 12-hour clock and the 24-hour clock.

The 12-hour clock
Times on a 12-hour clock use am to show morning and pm for an afternoon time.

So 3.45am is quarter-to-four in the morning, and 7.20pm is twenty-past-seven in the evening.

The time in between morning and afternoon is written as 12 noon, and in between night and morning as 12 midnight.

The 24-hour clock
When writing times in the 24-hour clock, hours and minutes are not separated by a full stop, and all times are written using four digits.

After 12 noon, the hours continue to be counted as 13, 14, 15, and so on to midnight.

Timetables are often written using the 24-hour clock.

To change from the 12-hour to 24-hour clock:
- For am times write using four digits.
- For pm times add 12 to the hours and write using four digits.

For example 3.45am is 0345 and 7.20pm is 1920.

Calculating
A maths exam contains five questions. Freda has 1 hour to answer them.

Freda divides 1 hour by 5 on her calculator and gets an answer of $1 \div 5 = 0.2$ hour.

She thinks she has 20 minutes for each question.
She is wrong.

There are 60 minutes in 1 hour.

She has $60 \div 5 = 12$ minutes for each question.

> Because time is not metric, it is difficult to calculate time on a calculator. It is often easier to work in hours and minutes separately.

Example

How long is it from 1150 to 1435?

Solution

From 1150 to 1200 =   10 minutes | This takes you to the next hour.

From 1200 to 1400 = 2 hours | These are the complete hours.

From 1400 to 1435 =   35 minutes | These are the remaining minutes.

Total = 2 hours   45 minutes

Example

a Write in 12-hour clock notation:

  i 1435   **ii** 0825

b Write in 24-hour clock notation:

  i 7.45am   **ii** 3.54pm

Solution

a **i** 24-hour clock times have 12 hours added to the hours, so 1435 is 2.35pm

   ii As 0825 is before 12 noon, it is 8.25am

b **i** 7.45am is 0745 using four digits

   ii 24-hour clocks have 12 hours added to the hours so 3.54pm is 1554.

Timetables

Timetables are often produced by airline companies to show departure times.

Here is an example:

from Jeddah (JED) to Colombo (CMB) via Dubai (DXB)

(+ indicates that the time is the day after the departure).

Depart		Arrive		Depart		Arrive	
JED	0100	DXB	0440	DXB	0745	CMB	1330
JED	2030	DXB	0010+	DXB	0245+	CMB	0845+

When flying from Jeddah to Colombo, you have to stop at Dubai and change planes.

You can either leave Jeddah at 0100 and arrive in Colombo at 1330, or leave at 2030 and arrive at 0845 the next day.

Example

a How long does the 0100 flight from Jeddah take to reach Colombo?

b How much shorter is the 2030 journey?

Solution

a The 0100 flight arrives at 1330. The journey time is 12 hours 30 minutes.

b The 2030 flight arrives at 0845 the next day.

From 2030 to 2100 =   30 minutes

From 2100 to 0800 = 11 hours

From 0800 to 0845 =   45 minutes

Total time = 11 hours 75 minutes = 12 hours 15 minutes

Difference in time = 12 hours 30 minutes − 12 hours 15 minutes = 15 minutes

Apply 7.1

1 Write these times using 12-hour clock notation, including am or pm where appropriate.

   a 1450   **c** 1715   **e** 2324

   b 0825   **d** 1200

2 Write these times using the 24-hour clock.

   a 7.25am   **c** 9.30pm   **e** 10.10pm

   b 3.25pm   **d** 11.15am

3 The measuring cylinder shows some oil floating on water.

   a What is the volume of water in the cylinder?

   b What is the volume of oil in the cylinder?

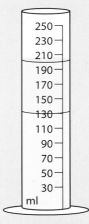

4 A television programme starts at 1450 and ends at 1620. How long is the programme?

5 A film lasts for 140 minutes. It starts at 1835. When will it finish? Give your answer using the 24-hour clock.

6 The odometer in my car shows how many kilometres the car has travelled.

   At the end of May, it looked like this:

0	4	5	8	3	6

   a I travelled 1276 m in May. What was the odometer reading at the start of May?

   b I travelled 1852 km in June. What was the odometer reading at the end of June?

Questions **7**−**10** are about the train timetable shown below:

Destination							
Paris	0601	0704	0801	0909	1201	1309	1601
Köln	0928		1148		1548		1948
Frankfurt		1113		1313		1713	
Berlin	1411	1523	1612	1725	2011	2125	0016+

7 How long does it take the 0601 train to travel from Paris to Köln?

8 Jean lives in Paris. He needs to be in Frankfurt for a meeting that starts at 2.00pm. Which train should he take from Paris?

9 How long does it take the 0601 train from Paris to get to Berlin?

10 One other train takes the same time as the 0601 train to travel from Paris to Berlin. Which train is it?

Learn 7.2 Money

Calculating with money

Your answers to calculations with money must have two decimal places.

As with other calculations, do not round off until the end.

Your calculator tells you that $12 \div 5 = 2.4$, but you must write your answer with units and two places of decimals, as $2.40.

Example

8 pens cost $5.30
Find the cost of 20 pens.

Solution

Each pen costs $5.30 \div 8 = \$0.6625$
20 pens cost $20 \times \$0.6625 = \$13.25$

Bills

A bill usually gives the unit price of an item.
The unit price is usually indicated by 'at'.
For example: '5 packs of screws at $2.10 per pack'.
The unit price for each pack of screws is $2.10 or each pack costs $2.10.
This unit price must be multiplied by the quantity being purchased to find the total bill.

Example

Find the total cost of these items:
5 packs of screws at $2.10 per pack
2.5 kg of nails at $3.50 per kg
1 hammer at $5.25
2 screwdrivers at $2.57 each.

Solution

5 packs of screws at $2.10 per pack	= 5 × $2.10	= $10.50
2.5 kg of nails at $3.50 per kg	= 2.5 × $3.50	= $ 8.75
1 hammer at $5.25	= 1 × $5.25	= $ 5.25
2 screwdrivers at $2.57 each	= 2 × $2.57	= $ 5.14
	Total	= $29.64

Currency conversion

Most countries have their own **currency**.

You need to **convert**, or change, from one currency to another to compare prices, or when you visit another country.

A conversion rate tells you how much of one currency you receive for 1 unit of the other currency.

For example, 1 Saudi riyal (SAR) = 0.3275 Singapore dollars (SGD) or 1 SAR = 0.3275 SGD

To change 250 SAR into SGD, multiply 250 by 0.3275

0.3275 Singapore dollars (SGD) = 1 Saudi riyal (SAR)

To change 350 SGD into SAR, divide 350 by 0.3275

Example

The exchange rate is $1 = €0.6765

a Change $250 into euros.

b Change €320 into dollars.

> When writing a sum of money, you must round answers off to two decimal places. This means writing the amount to the nearest cent.

c An item costs $350 in the USA and €220 in France. In which country is it cheaper?

Solution

a $1 = €0.6765

So $250 = 250 × €0.6765

$250 = €169.13

> 250 × €0.6765 = €169.125.
> This is exactly halfway between €169.12 and €169.13.
> When the answer is halfway you should round up.
> So the answer is €169.13.

b

$1 = €0.6765

€0.6765 = $1

$€1 = \$\dfrac{1}{0.6765}$

$€320 = 320 × \$\dfrac{1}{0.6765}$

$= \$473.02$

> $320 × \$\dfrac{1}{0.6765} = \$473.02291204...$
> This is between $473.02 and $473.03
> Halfway between these is 473.025, so the exact answer is less than this.
> So it is closer to $473.02.

c Either convert $350 into euros or €220 into dollars.

$350 = 350 × €0.6765 = €236.775 or €236.78 to the nearest cent.

Cost of item in the USA is €236.78. Cost of item in France is €220.

The item is cheaper in France.

Apply 7.2

1 Alicia can download an album for $9.50 or a track for $0.79.

She wants to download an album with 12 tracks. Is it cheaper to download the album or 12 separate tracks?

2 If 6 notepads cost $8.50, how much would 15 notepads cost?

3 I can buy 3 litres of oil for $4.25 or 2 litres for $2.90. Which is better value?

4 Find the total cost of this bill:

```
2 kg sugar @ $1.35 per kg
1.5 kg flour @ $0.90 per kg
2 lemons @ $0.40 each
6 eggs @ $1.70 per dozen
```

Use these conversion rates to answer questions **5−10**:

> 1 New Zealand dollar (NZD) = 6.2169 Hong Kong dollars (HKD)
>
> 1 Hong Kong dollar (HKD) = 0.8538 South African rand (ZAR)

5 Convert 350 New Zealand dollars into Hong Kong dollars.

6 Change 50 South African Rand into Hong Kong dollars.

7 Change 275 Hong Kong dollars into South African Rand.

8 Change 200 NZD into South African Rand.

9 A book costs 5.99 NZD, 37 HKD or 32.50 ZAR. Which is the cheapest price?

10 Complete these conversion rates, giving your answers to 2 decimal places.

    a 1 Hong Kong dollar = ... New Zealand dollars

    b 1 South African Rand = ... Hong Kong dollars

    c 1 South African Rand = ... New Zealand dollars

Assess 7.1–7.2

1 How many minutes is it from 12.36pm to 2.15pm?

2 a Write down the electricity meter reading shown below.

    b The meter reading for the previous quarter was 42 529.
Electricity costs $0.75 per unit. How much will the electricity company charge for the units used?

3 How much change do I receive from $20 if I buy seven items at $2.20 each?

4 How many minutes is it from 2314 on Thursday to 0115 on Friday?

5 Find the total cost of this garage bill:

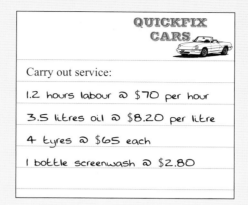

QUICKFIX CARS

Carry out service:

1.2 hours labour @ $70 per hour

3.5 litres oil @ $8.20 per litre

4 tyres @ $65 each

1 bottle screenwash @ $2.80

6 Before a journey, the odometer in Niranjan's car registered 027691 miles.

After the journey it looked like this:

| 0 | 2 | 7 | 8 | 2 | 4 |

How many miles was the journey?

7 The exchange rate between the Venezuelan Bolivar and the Tunisian Dinar is

1 Venezuelan Bolivar = 0.31294 Tunisian Dinar.

a How many Dinar would you receive for 375 Bolivar?

b How many Bolivar would you receive for 2000 Dinar?

8 Marsha is studying a plane timetable.

Hong Kong	0035	0455	1120
Dubai (arrive)	0430	0850	1515
Dubai (depart)	0855	1125	1715
Geneva	1410	1640	2230

a Which plane takes the shortest time to get from Hong Kong to Geneva?

b Each plane takes the same time to fly from Hong Kong to Dubai.
If the next plane arrives in Dubai at 1900, at what time does it leave Hong Kong?

9 Kris wants to change 2000 Egyptian pounds into Moroccan Dirham.

He is charged 30 Egyptian pounds commission, and the remainder is exchanged at 1 Egyptian pound to 1.28574 Moroccan Dirham.

How much will Kris receive?

Decimals, fractions and percentages

Numbers can be written in many forms. In this chapter you will be working with integers, fractions, decimals and percentages. You will also learn how to change a number from one form to another. Some questions involve many different operations and you will learn how to solve these.

Learn 8.1 Working with decimals

Addition and subtraction

Although you will be able to use your calculator in the examinations, it helps to know how to add, subtract, multiply and divide decimals without a calculator.

To add or subtract decimals you must make sure that you line up the decimal points.

Put 0s in any spaces to avoid making mistakes.

Example

Work out:

a $5.8 + 2.7$ **b** $7.2 - 1.8$ **c** $4.3 + 1.05$ **d** $9.1 - 7.25$

Solution

a
$$\begin{array}{r} 5.8 \\ +\ 2.7 \\ \hline 8.5 \\ \hline {\scriptstyle 1} \end{array}$$

b
$$\begin{array}{r} {}^6\!7^{\,1}2 \\ -\ 1.8 \\ \hline 5.4 \end{array}$$

c
$$\begin{array}{r} 4.30 \\ +\ 1.05 \\ \hline 5.35 \end{array}$$

d
$$\begin{array}{r} {}^8\!9^{\,10}\!\cdot\!^{1}\!1^{1}0 \\ -\ 7.25 \\ \hline 1.85 \end{array}$$

> **Study tip**
>
> If you are using a calculator to add or subtract decimals, you should always do a rough estimate in your head.

Multiplication and division

Example

Work out:

a 5.7×6.3 **b** $21.2 \div 0.4$

Solution

a There are various methods for multiplying decimals.

Two methods begin by taking out the decimal points to give 57×63.

Grid method:

×	50	7
60	3000	420
3	150	21

$3000 + 420 + 150 + 21 = 3591$

Column method:

$$
\begin{array}{r}
57 \\
\times\ \ 63 \\
\hline
171 \\
3420 \\
\hline
3591 \\
\hline
\end{array}
$$

Finally, put back the decimal point.

Estimate the answer by rounding each number to one significant figure.

5.7×6.3 is approximately 6×6. So the answer should be close to 36.

$5.7 \times 6.3 = 35.91$

Study tip

You should still do a rough estimate even if you are using a calculator and entering the exact decimal values.

b $21.2 \div 0.4$

To divide decimals without a calculator, you need to use numbers that are easy to work with.

To work out $21.2 \div 0.4$, first multiply both numbers by 10. This will mean you are now dividing by a whole number.

Dividing 21.2 by 0.4 is equivalent to dividing 212 by 4.

$$
\begin{array}{r}
53 \\
4\overline{)212}
\end{array}
$$

So $21.2 \div 0.4 = 53$

Check your answer by doing a rough estimate.

$200 \div 4 = 50$, so the answer should be near 50 ✓

Apply 8.1

1 Work these out without a calculator. Show all your working.

a $15.1 + 3.7$ **e** $0.07 + 1.7$ **i** $17.5 - 1.25$

b $8.7 + 2.9$ **f** $9.27 - 3.02$ **j** $6.05 - 0.605$

c $25.03 + 18.63$ **g** $6.18 - 3.05$

d $0.72 + 1.3$ **h** $7.87 - 3.2$

Use your calculator to check your answers.

2 Antoinette says that:

$5.7 + 0.5$ is 5.75

Pierre says that:

$5.7 + 0.5$ is 6.2

Who is correct? Explain what the other person did wrong.

3 Brad was ordering some food in Indonesia. He converted the menu to dollars.

Tom Yum Soup	$4.30
Chicken Sate	$3.84
Nasi Goreng	$3.26
Mie Goreng	$2.79

He decided to order the Tom Yum Soup, Chicken Sate and Mie Goreng.
He paid with a $20 note. How much change did he get?

4 Work these out without a calculator. Show all your working.

a 3.2×4 **e** 2.4×0.2 **i** 8.3×2.1
b 5×2.8 **f** 3.5×0.5 **j** 5.2×1.01
c 0.6×3 **g** 1.3×2.3
d 0.09×6 **h** 2.4×1.4

5 Use $21 \times 35 = 735$ to work out the answers to the following calculations:

a 2.1×35 **c** 0.21×0.35 **e** 0.021×0.035
b 21×0.35 **d** 0.021×3.5

6 Work these out without a calculator. Show all your working.

a $6.6 \div 11$ **e** $9.99 \div 0.9$ **i** $2.52 \div 2.1$
b $3.2 \div 0.2$ **f** $0.49 \div 0.7$ **j** $0.396 \div 0.04$
c $12 \div 0.4$ **g** $5.6 \div 0.8$
d $0.06 \div 0.03$ **h** $12.8 \div 0.004$

7 Cinema tickets cost $18.50 for an adult and $10.75 for a child. How much would it cost for a family of two adults and three children to go to the cinema?

8 Justice was cutting a rectangular piece of metal. It measured 4.3 metres by 3.6 metres and cost $6 per square metre. How much did he pay for the metal?

9 Catia moved into a new apartment. It cost her $25 for the meter to be reconnected and $0.021 per unit of electricity used. Her first bill was for $88.
How many units of electricity had she used?

Learn 8.2 Fractions

Fractions are used when you need to define a number that lies between two integers (whole numbers).

All fractions can be written in the form $\frac{a}{b}$.

The **numerator** is the number on the top of a fraction and the **denominator** is the number on the bottom.

$$\frac{2 \leftarrow \text{numerator}}{3 \leftarrow \text{denominator}}$$

Equivalent fractions are fractions that are equal in value.

For example: $\frac{1}{2}$ is the same as $\frac{5}{10}$.

$$\frac{1}{2} \overset{\times 5}{\underset{\times 5}{=}} \frac{5}{10}$$

Example

Which of these two fractions is the larger:

$\frac{5}{8}$ or $\frac{2}{3}$?

Solution

Change the fractions into twenty-fourths because 24 is the smallest number that both 8 and 3 divide into exactly.

$$\frac{5}{8} \overset{\times 3}{\underset{\times 3}{=}} \frac{15}{24} \qquad \frac{2}{3} \overset{\times 8}{\underset{\times 8}{=}} \frac{16}{24}$$

$\frac{16}{24}$ is larger than $\frac{15}{24}$.

So $\frac{2}{3}$ is larger than $\frac{5}{8}$.

Example

Simplify these fractions:

a $\frac{5}{35}$ **b** $\frac{88}{120}$ **c** $2\frac{4}{16}$

Solution

Simplify means to rewrite the fraction in its **simplest form**.

A fraction is in its simplest form when it is written as an equivalent fraction that has the smallest possible numbers in the numerator and the denominator.

a $\frac{5}{35} \overset{\div 5}{\underset{\div 5}{=}} \frac{1}{7}$

b $\frac{88}{120} \overset{\div 4}{\underset{\div 4}{=}} \frac{22}{30}$ and $\frac{22}{30} \overset{\div 2}{\underset{\div 2}{=}} \frac{11}{15}$ | Sometimes the fraction has to be simplified in stages. |

c $\frac{4}{16} \overset{\div 4}{\underset{\div 4}{=}} \frac{1}{4}$ so $2\frac{4}{16} = 2\frac{1}{4}$ | Simplify the fraction part first. |

You can simplify fractions using a calculator. The way to do this is not the same for all calculators, so make sure that you know how to do it using your own calculator.

Apply 8.2

1 Write each fraction in its simplest form.

  a $\frac{8}{16}$ **c** $\frac{7}{35}$ **e** $\frac{66}{120}$ **g** $\frac{76}{84}$ **i** $\frac{110}{154}$ **k** $\frac{315}{360}$

  b $\frac{9}{12}$ **d** $\frac{20}{64}$ **f** $\frac{18}{63}$ **h** $\frac{32}{48}$ **j** $\frac{126}{162}$

2 Copy and complete each pair of equivalent fractions.

a $\frac{5}{6} = \frac{15}{\square}$ **c** $\frac{6}{7} = \frac{\square}{14}$ **e** $\frac{2}{3} = \frac{14}{\square}$ **g** $\frac{\square}{11} = \frac{42}{66}$ **i** $\frac{3}{4} = \frac{\square}{60}$

b $\frac{3}{4} = \frac{\square}{44}$ **d** $\frac{5}{\square} = \frac{25}{35}$ **f** $\frac{4}{\square} = \frac{32}{40}$ **h** $\frac{45}{\square} = \frac{5}{8}$ **j** $\frac{\square}{12} = \frac{120}{144}$

3 Write down three fractions equivalent to:

a $\frac{2}{3}$ **b** $\frac{4}{5}$ **c** $\frac{3}{8}$

4 Arrange these fractions in order, smallest first:

a $\frac{3}{5}$ $\frac{7}{15}$ $\frac{7}{10}$ **b** $\frac{4}{7}$ $\frac{9}{14}$ $\frac{2}{3}$

5 Arrange these fractions in order, largest first:

a $\frac{1}{2}$ $\frac{5}{6}$ $\frac{11}{18}$ $\frac{5}{9}$ **b** $\frac{17}{24}$ $\frac{2}{3}$ $\frac{7}{12}$ $\frac{3}{4}$

6 Copy these pairs of fractions and write 'is less than' or 'is greater than' signs between each pair to make a correct statement.

a $\frac{4}{5} \ldots \frac{6}{10}$ **b** $\frac{1}{3} \ldots \frac{1}{6}$ **c** $\frac{2}{3} \ldots \frac{3}{5}$ **d** $\frac{7}{12} \ldots \frac{1}{2}$ **e** $\frac{1}{7} \ldots \frac{2}{9}$

7 Here are Keon's examination results:

Mathematics $\frac{52}{70}$

English $\frac{13}{20}$

Geography $\frac{24}{35}$

Chemistry $\frac{9}{14}$

a In which subject did he do best?

b In which subject did he do worst?

8 Emiko said that $\frac{1}{5}$ is smaller than $\frac{1}{6}$ because 5 is smaller than 6. Is he correct? Explain your answer.

Learn 8.3 Fractions, decimals and percentages

Changing fractions to decimals

To change a fraction to a decimal, divide the numerator by the denominator.

$\frac{5}{8}$ means '5 divided by 8', so $\frac{5}{8}$ is equivalent to 0.625

Example

Write the following fractions as decimals:

a $\frac{1}{8}$ **b** $4\frac{5}{6}$

Solution

a $\frac{1}{8}$ means 1 divided by 8.

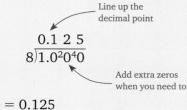

Line up the
decimal point

$$0.1\ 2\ 5$$
$$8\overline{)1.0^2 0^4 0}$$

Add extra zeros
when you need to

$\frac{1}{8} = 0.125$

b $4\frac{5}{6}$ Work out $\frac{5}{6}$ first

$\frac{5}{6}$ means '5 divided by 6'.

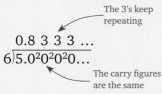

The 3's keep
repeating

$$0.8\ 3\ 3\ 3\ ...$$
$$6\overline{)5.0^2 0^2 0^2 0...}$$

The carry figures
are the same

This is a non-terminating decimal. It does not end.

The 3 keeps repeating. It is a **recurring decimal** and is written as $\dot{3}$.

So $4\frac{5}{6} = 4.8\dot{3}$

You can also use your calculator to divide.

Some calculators have a separate key that changes a fraction to a decimal, e.g.

Changing decimals to fractions

To change a decimal to a fraction, consider the place value of each digit.

Example

Change the following decimals to fractions in their lowest terms:

a 0.13   **b** 0.08   **c** 7.075

Solution

a

Units	·	Tenths	Hundredths
0	·	1	3

The 3 has the smallest value (3 hundredths), so change the decimal to hundredths:

$$0.13 = \frac{1}{10} + \frac{3}{100} = \frac{10}{100} + \frac{3}{100} = \frac{13}{100}$$

So $0.13 = \frac{13}{100}$

b

Units	·	Tenths	Hundredths
0	·	0	8

The 8 has the smallest value (8 hundredths), so change the decimal to hundredths:

$$0.08 = \frac{8}{100} = \frac{2}{25}$$ Cancel down where possible.

÷4

÷4

c

Units	·	Tenths	Hundredths	Thousandths
7	·	0	7	5

The 5 has the smallest value (5 thousandths), so change the decimal to thousandths:

$0.075 = \frac{7}{100} + \frac{5}{1000} = \frac{75}{1000} = \frac{15}{200} = \frac{3}{40}$

> Divide numerator and denominator by 5.

So $7.075 = 7\frac{3}{40}$

> **Study tip**
>
> Always read the question carefully. Sometimes you will *not* be asked to write your fractions in their lowest terms.

Changing percentages to fractions and decimals

One per cent (1%) means '1 out of every 100'.

A percentage is a number of hundredths.

To change a percentage to a fraction (or decimal), divide by 100.

$1\% = \frac{1}{100}$ or 0.01

So 47% would be written as $\frac{47}{100}$ or 0.47

This is because $0.47 = \frac{4}{10} + \frac{7}{100} = \frac{40}{100} + \frac{7}{100}$

Example

Rewrite 12% as:

a a fraction   **b** a decimal.

Solution

a To change a percentage to a fraction, divide by 100.

$$12\% = \frac{12}{100} \overset{\div 4}{\underset{\div 4}{=}} \frac{3}{25}$$

This fraction has been simplified.

b To change a percentage to a decimal, divide by 100.

$12\% = \frac{12}{100} = \frac{1}{10} + \frac{2}{100} = 0.12$

> **Study tip**
>
> Always read the question carefully to see if you need to simplify your answer.

Example

Work out each of the following as a percentage:

a 0.054   **b** $\frac{3}{20}$

Solution

To change a fraction (or decimal) to a percentage, multiply by 100.

a $0.054 \times 100 = 5.4\%$

Units	·	Tenths	Hundredths	Thousandths
0	·	0	5	4
5	·	4		

> × 100
> The number moves two places to the left.

b $\frac{3}{20}$ can be changed to a percentage as below.

Find $\frac{3}{20}$ of 100 by multiplying the fraction by 100.

Start by cancelling, i.e. dividing a number on the top and a number on the bottom by the same amount.

$$\frac{3}{{}_1\cancel{20}} \times \cancel{100}\%{}^{\,5} = 15\%$$

Divide 20 and 100 by 5, then divide the results, 4 and 20, by 4.

Example

Write these values in order of size starting with the smallest:

9% $\frac{9}{50}$ 0.1

Solution

It is easiest to write all the values as percentages.

9%

$\frac{9}{50} = \frac{18}{100} = 18\%$ This is more than 10%.

$0.1 \times 100 = 10\%$ This is more than 9%.

In order of size, smallest first, the values are: 9%, 0.1, $\frac{9}{50}$

Study tip

Read the question carefully. Make sure that your answer gives the numbers in the order that is asked for, that is smallest first (ascending) or largest first (descending).

Apply 8.3

1 Copy and complete this table showing equivalent fractions, decimals and percentages:

Fraction	Decimal	Percentage
		1%
$\frac{1}{10}$		
		20%
	0.25	
		50%
$\frac{3}{4}$		
	1.0	

2 Write each of the following percentages as:

a a fraction in its lowest terms   **b** a decimal.

  i 30%   **iii** 7%   **v** 44%   **vii** 36%   **ix** $12\frac{1}{2}\%$

  ii 23%   **iv** 80%   **vi** 2%   **viii** 1.5%   **x** $33\frac{1}{3}\%$

3 Write each of the following decimals as:

a a percentage   **b** a fraction in its lowest terms.

  i 0.7   **iii** 0.13   **v** 0.001   **vii** 0.12   **ix** 1.5

  ii 0.4   **iv** 0.05   **vi** 0.85   **viii** 0.025   **x** 1.6

4 Write each of the following fractions as:

    a a decimal   **b** a percentage.

      i $\frac{1}{4}$ **iii** $\frac{3}{5}$ **v** $\frac{7}{100}$ **vii** $\frac{3}{8}$ **ix** $\frac{1}{200}$

      ii $\frac{1}{10}$ **iv** $\frac{3}{20}$ **vi** $\frac{17}{50}$ **viii** $\frac{2}{3}$ **x** $1\frac{1}{2}$

5 Copy and complete each of these statements by inserting one of the following signs: >, < or =

    a $7\% \dots \frac{1}{7}$ **d** $20\% \dots \frac{1}{5}$ **g** $\frac{16}{50} \dots 30\%$

    b $0.5 \dots 50\%$ **e** $0.4 \dots 4\%$ **h** $12\frac{1}{2}\% \dots \frac{1}{8}$

    c $\frac{1}{25} \dots 0.25$ **f** $0.6 \dots \frac{13}{20}$

6 Write these numbers in order of size, smallest first:

    a 0.57 $\frac{26}{50}$ 56% **b** 33% $\frac{4}{11}$ 0.3

7 Write these numbers in order of size, largest first:

    a $\frac{2}{5}$ 41% 0.405 **b** 5% 0.5 $\frac{1}{5}$

8 Mei-Yin says that 30% is the same as $\frac{1}{3}$. Is she correct?

9 Find a percentage halfway between $\frac{4}{5}$ and $\frac{5}{6}$.

10 Find a fraction halfway between 24% and 25%.

Learn 8.4 Working with fractions: addition and subtraction

You can add and subtract fractions only when their denominators are the same.

If the denominators are different, you need to write equivalent fractions with the same denominator.

For example, if you need to add $\frac{3}{5}$ and $\frac{3}{4}$, you change the first of these to $\frac{12}{20}$ and the second to $\frac{15}{20}$. The number 20 is the smallest number that can be divided into whole numbers by both 5 and 4. It is called the **lowest common denominator**.

Study tip

You can always use the number you get from multiplying the two denominators together (here it is 5 × 4). This will be a common denominator but it will not always be the lowest one.

Mixed numbers are fractions that consist of two parts: a whole number part and a fractional part.

Whole number

$2\frac{1}{3}$ ← Fraction

When you add or subtract mixed numbers, you deal with the whole numbers and the fractions separately.

Example

Work out:

a $\frac{3}{11} + \frac{5}{11}$ **b** $\frac{1}{6} + \frac{3}{8}$ **c** $3\frac{5}{9} - 1\frac{1}{5}$

Solution

a $\frac{3}{11} + \frac{5}{11} = \frac{8}{11}$
> The denominators are the same, so the numerators can be added.

b $\frac{1}{6} + \frac{3}{8}$

$\frac{4}{24} + \frac{9}{24} = \frac{13}{24}$
> The lowest common denominator is 24. $\overset{\times 4}{\frac{1}{6} \underset{\times 4}{=} \frac{4}{24}} \qquad \overset{\times 3}{\frac{3}{8} \underset{\times 3}{=} \frac{9}{24}}$

c $3\frac{5}{9} - 1\frac{1}{5}$
> Subtract the whole numbers first $(3 - 1 = 2)$.

$= 2\frac{5}{9} - \frac{1}{5}$
> The lowest common denominator is 45. $\overset{\times 5}{\frac{5}{9} \underset{\times 5}{=} \frac{25}{45}} \qquad \overset{\times 9}{\frac{1}{5} \underset{\times 9}{=} \frac{9}{45}}$

Therefore: $\frac{5}{9} - \frac{1}{5} = \frac{25}{45} - \frac{9}{45} = \frac{16}{45}$

So $3\frac{5}{9} - 1\frac{1}{5} = 2\frac{16}{45}$

Example

Work out: $4\frac{1}{3} - 2\frac{3}{4}$

Solution

In this example the second fractional part is larger than the first fractional part.

You will need to change one of the whole numbers into an equivalent fraction.

$4\frac{1}{3} - 2\frac{3}{4}$
> Subtract the whole numbers first.

$= 2\frac{1}{3} - \frac{3}{4}$
> The lowest common denominator is 12. $\overset{\times 4}{\frac{1}{3} \underset{\times 4}{=} \frac{4}{12}} \qquad \overset{\times 3}{\frac{3}{4} \underset{\times 3}{=} \frac{9}{12}}$

$= 2\frac{4}{12} - \frac{9}{12}$

$= 1 + \frac{12}{12} + \frac{4}{12} - \frac{9}{12}$
> Change 2 into $1 + \frac{12}{12}$.

$= 1 + \frac{7}{12} = 1\frac{7}{12}$

Example

1 litre of lemonade is divided among three people.

Gjergi gets $\frac{2}{5}$ of a litre, Erikas gets $\frac{1}{3}$ of a litre and Saskia gets the rest.

What fraction does Saskia get?

Solution

$\frac{2}{5} + \frac{1}{3} = \frac{6}{15} + \frac{5}{15} = \frac{11}{15}$
> This is the total of Gjergi's and Erikas' fractions.

$1 - \frac{11}{15} = \frac{4}{15}$
> Subtract the total from 1.

Saskia gets $\frac{4}{15}$ of the lemonade.

Sometimes the numerator is larger than the denominator. This is called an **improper fraction** or top-heavy fraction. You should change this to a mixed number.

For example: $\quad \frac{9}{4} = \frac{8}{4} + \frac{1}{4} = 2 + \frac{1}{4}$
> There are 8 quarters in 2 whole ones.

$= 2\frac{1}{4}$

Apply 8.4

1 Work out:

a $\frac{3}{7} + \frac{2}{7}$ **c** $\frac{1}{10} + \frac{1}{5}$ **e** $\frac{1}{6} + \frac{1}{4}$ **g** $\frac{1}{7} + \frac{2}{3}$ **i** $\frac{1}{2} + \frac{1}{3} + \frac{1}{4}$

b $\frac{1}{4} + \frac{1}{2}$ **d** $\frac{8}{15} + \frac{1}{3}$ **f** $\frac{1}{3} + \frac{3}{4}$ **h** $\frac{7}{9} + \frac{1}{2}$ **j** $\frac{3}{4} + \frac{2}{9} + \frac{5}{18}$

2 Work out:

a $1\frac{1}{4} + 2\frac{1}{5}$ **c** $2\frac{1}{7} + 2\frac{1}{9}$ **e** $\frac{5}{7} + 1\frac{2}{21}$ **g** $3\frac{3}{4} + \frac{5}{8}$ **i** $4\frac{4}{5} + 1\frac{3}{7}$

b $3\frac{5}{11} + 1\frac{1}{2}$ **d** $2\frac{5}{6} + \frac{1}{12}$ **f** $2\frac{1}{3} + 1\frac{5}{6}$ **h** $3\frac{1}{6} + 1\frac{8}{9}$ **j** $1\frac{1}{2} + 2\frac{2}{3} + 3\frac{1}{4}$

3 Work out:

a $\frac{1}{2} - \frac{2}{5}$ **c** $\frac{4}{5} - \frac{1}{6}$ **e** $\frac{5}{7} - \frac{1}{6}$ **g** $\frac{6}{7} - \frac{1}{2}$ **i** $\frac{7}{8} - \frac{5}{6}$

b $\frac{3}{4} - \frac{3}{8}$ **d** $\frac{4}{9} - \frac{1}{6}$ **f** $\frac{5}{7} - \frac{1}{3}$ **h** $\frac{3}{4} - \frac{3}{5}$ **j** $\frac{1}{2} - \frac{1}{4} - \frac{1}{8}$

4 Work out:

a $3\frac{1}{2} - 1\frac{1}{4}$ **c** $3\frac{4}{7} - 1\frac{1}{3}$ **e** $7\frac{13}{15} - 4\frac{7}{10}$ **g** $3\frac{1}{3} - \frac{4}{5}$ **i** $2\frac{1}{4} - 1\frac{3}{7}$

b $2\frac{1}{2} - 1\frac{1}{5}$ **d** $5\frac{11}{12} - 2\frac{2}{3}$ **f** $2\frac{1}{2} - \frac{3}{4}$ **h** $4\frac{2}{5} - 1\frac{1}{2}$ **j** $6\frac{5}{6} - 1\frac{1}{3} - \frac{5}{12}$

5 By writing down all of your working, show that this calculation is correct:

$$\frac{5}{6} - \frac{5}{8} = \frac{5}{24}$$

6 By writing down all of your working, show that this calculation is correct:

$$2\frac{5}{6} + 1\frac{3}{7} = 4\frac{11}{42}$$

7 A pack of biscuits contains three types of chocolate biscuits. $\frac{1}{3}$ of them are plain chocolate, and $\frac{2}{5}$ of them are milk chocolate. The rest are white chocolate.

What fraction of them are white chocolate?

8 Maria was making tacos for a family celebration. $\frac{5}{7}$ of her family wanted chicken with cheese and $\frac{3}{14}$ wanted beef. The rest were vegetarian.

What fraction were vegetarian?

9 Rahni made $4\frac{1}{2}$ cups of lassi for her children. Subhan had $2\frac{1}{4}$ cups and Viraj had $1\frac{3}{4}$ cups. The remaining fraction was given to the baby.

What fraction did the baby get?

10 In Hawaii, distances are measured in miles. Keanu travelled from Waikoloa Market to Waimea, a distance of $17\frac{4}{5}$ miles. He had to stop to pick someone up from the airport, which was $15\frac{7}{8}$ miles from the market. How far did he have to travel to get from the airport to Waimea?

Learn 8.5 Working with fractions: multiplication and division

The methods used for multiplying and dividing fractions are completely different from those used for addition and subtraction.

Multiplying two fractions together

Example

Work out:

$\frac{4}{5} \times \frac{3}{4}$

Solution

You begin by 'cancelling'.

Then multiply the numerators and multiply the denominators.

$\frac{\overset{1}{\cancel{4}}}{5} \times \frac{3}{\cancel{4}_1} = \frac{3}{5}$

To multiply mixed numbers, first change them to improper (top-heavy) fractions.

Example

Change $2\frac{3}{4}$ to an improper fraction.

Solution

$2\frac{3}{4} = 2 + \frac{3}{4}$

$\qquad = \frac{8}{4} + \frac{3}{4}$

$\qquad = \frac{11}{4}$

Example

Show that

$2\frac{4}{7} \times 3\frac{1}{2} = 9$

You must show all your working.

Solution

$2\frac{4}{7} \times 3\frac{1}{2}$ First change the mixed numbers to improper fractions.

$= \frac{18}{7} \times \frac{7}{2}$ $2\frac{4}{7} = 2 + \frac{4}{7} = \frac{14}{7} + \frac{4}{7} = \frac{18}{7}$ $3\frac{1}{2} = 3 + \frac{1}{2} = \frac{6}{2} + \frac{1}{2} = \frac{7}{2}$

$\frac{\overset{9}{\cancel{18}}}{\underset{1}{\cancel{7}}} \times \frac{\overset{1}{\cancel{7}}}{\underset{1}{\cancel{2}}}$ Cancel by 2 and cancel by 7.

$= \frac{9 \times 1}{1 \times 1}$ Multiply the numerators, multiply the denominators.

$= 9$

Example

Find:

$\frac{4}{9}$ of $180

Solution

You could find the answer by dividing $180 by 9 to give $\frac{1}{9}$ and then multiplying this answer by 4 to give $\frac{4}{9}$.

$$\frac{1}{9} \times \$180 = \$20$$

So $\quad \frac{4}{9} \times \$180 = 4 \times \$20 = \$80$

Or you could work it out all in one step using the cancelling method:

$\frac{4}{9} \times \$180$

$= \$\frac{4}{{}_1\cancel{9}} \times \frac{\cancel{180}^{20}}{1}$ $\qquad$ | Divide top and bottom by 9. |

$= \$\frac{4 \times 20}{1 \times 1}$

$= \$80$

Dividing fractions

To divide by a fraction you must *multiply* by the **reciprocal**.

You find a reciprocal of a fraction by turning it upside down.

So $\frac{5}{4}$ is the reciprocal of $\frac{4}{5}$, and $\frac{4}{5}$ is the reciprocal of $\frac{5}{4}$

Also $\frac{4}{5} \times \frac{5}{4} = 1$.

Example

Work out:

$6\frac{1}{4} \div \frac{1}{2}$

Show all your working.

Solution

$6\frac{1}{4} \div \frac{1}{2}$ $\qquad$ | Change any mixed numbers to improper fractions. |

$= \frac{25}{4} \div \frac{1}{2}$ $\qquad$ | $6\frac{1}{4} = 6 + \frac{1}{4} = \frac{24}{4} + \frac{1}{4} = \frac{25}{4}$. |

$= \frac{25}{4} \times \frac{2}{1}$ $\qquad$ | Multiply by the reciprocal of $\frac{1}{2}$. |

$= \frac{25}{{}_2\cancel{4}} \times \frac{\cancel{2}^1}{1}$ $\qquad$ | Cancel by 2. Multiply the numerators, multiply the denominators. |

$= \frac{25}{2}$ $\qquad$ | Change the improper fraction to a mixed number. |

$= 12\frac{1}{2}$ $\qquad$ | $\frac{24}{2} + \frac{1}{2} = 12\frac{1}{2}$. |

Example

Work out:

$5\frac{1}{3} \div 3\frac{3}{5}$

Solution

$= 5\frac{1}{3} \div 3\frac{3}{5}$

$= \frac{16}{3} \div \frac{18}{5}$ Change any mixed numbers to improper fractions.

$= \frac{16}{3} \times \frac{5}{18}$ Multiply by the reciprocal of $\frac{18}{5}$.

$= \frac{{}^{8}\cancel{16}}{3} \times \frac{5}{\cancel{18}_{9}}$ Cancel by 2. Multiply the numerators, multiply the denominators.

$= \frac{40}{27}$ Change the improper fraction to a mixed number.

$= 1\frac{13}{27}$ $\frac{27}{27} + \frac{13}{27} = 1 + \frac{13}{27}.$

Study tip

Use your calculator to check conversions, such as mixed numbers to improper fractions, or to check your final answer.

Apply 8.5

1 Change the following improper fractions to mixed numbers:

   a $\frac{16}{3}$ **b** $\frac{13}{12}$ **c** $\frac{27}{20}$ **d** $\frac{8}{5}$ **e** $\frac{9}{4}$

2 Change the following mixed numbers to improper fractions:

   a $2\frac{1}{2}$ **b** $1\frac{2}{5}$ **c** $3\frac{1}{3}$ **d** $2\frac{7}{9}$ **e** 6

3 Work out:

   a $\frac{1}{2} \times \frac{3}{4}$ **c** $\frac{3}{4} \times \frac{3}{5}$ **e** $\left(\frac{3}{4}\right)^2$ **g** $\frac{3}{4} \times \frac{5}{9}$ **i** $\frac{7}{16} \times \frac{4}{5}$

   b $\frac{1}{5} \times \frac{5}{7}$ **d** $\frac{2}{3} \times \frac{1}{3}$ **f** $\frac{5}{6} \times \frac{3}{20}$ **h** $\frac{4}{9} \times \frac{3}{8}$ **j** $\frac{9}{5} \times \frac{20}{27}$

4 Work out:

   a $\frac{2}{3} \times 12$ **c** $15 \times \frac{2}{5}$ **e** $\frac{9}{11} \times 121$ **g** $\frac{1}{4}$ of $480   **i** $\frac{7}{8}$ of 2048 km

   b $\frac{1}{7} \times 70$ **d** $48 \times \frac{5}{8}$ **f** $\frac{1}{3}$ of 360 g   **h** $\frac{5}{6}$ of 396 miles   **j** $\frac{5}{7}$ of 357 ml

5 Work out:

   a $3\frac{1}{2} \times 4$ **c** $7 \times 2\frac{1}{3}$ **e** $3 \times 2\frac{5}{6}$ **g** $5\frac{5}{6} \times \frac{1}{7}$ **i** $3\frac{3}{4} \times 4\frac{4}{5}$

   b $2\frac{1}{4} \times 6$ **d** $5 \times 1\frac{3}{4}$ **f** $1\frac{1}{2} \times \frac{2}{11}$ **h** $2\frac{1}{3} \times 2\frac{3}{4}$ **j** $1\frac{5}{12} \times 1\frac{1}{3}$

6 Work out:

   a $\frac{3}{4} \div 8$ **c** $\frac{6}{7} \div 2$ **e** $2\frac{5}{6} \div 5$ **g** $8 \div \frac{2}{5}$ **i** $6 \div \frac{1}{4}$

   b $\frac{2}{5} \div 4$ **d** $1\frac{2}{3} \div 7$ **f** $10 \div \frac{1}{3}$ **h** $1 \div \frac{3}{7}$ **j** $5 \div 1\frac{3}{5}$

7 Work out:

   a $\frac{1}{2} \div \frac{2}{5}$ **c** $\frac{5}{8} \div \frac{1}{4}$ **e** $\frac{7}{9} \div \frac{1}{3}$ **g** $1\frac{7}{10} \div 2\frac{4}{5}$ **i** $2\frac{7}{9} \div 2\frac{2}{5}$

   b $\frac{1}{4} \div \frac{1}{5}$ **d** $\frac{4}{5} \div \frac{2}{3}$ **f** $2\frac{1}{2} \div 1\frac{1}{4}$ **h** $3\frac{2}{3} \div 1\frac{1}{4}$ **j** $3\frac{1}{6} \div 1\frac{1}{2}$

8 A piece of wood 60 cm long is cut into smaller pieces, each $3\frac{3}{4}$ cm long. How many smaller pieces are there?

9 Joshi is cutting lengths of material to use as a border for some tablecloths.
She has been given $4\frac{3}{4}$ yards. She has to cut it into strips each $\frac{1}{8}$ yard in width.
How many strips can she cut out?

10 In Brazil, the basic tax rate is $\frac{3}{20}$ of your income. Diego earns \$380 a week.
How much of this does he have to pay in tax?

11 Marlon lives in Manila, in the Philippines. He pays \$180 per month for his rent. Of this, $\frac{1}{5}$ is for the upkeep of the garden and area surrounding his apartment. How much does he pay for the actual apartment itself?

12 Faith works in a factory packing cocoa powder for export.
She has to take 25 kg bags of cocoa powder and pack them into small plastic bags.
Each small bag holds $\frac{1}{20}$ of a kilogram. How many small bags will she need for each 25 kg?

Learn 8.6 Ordering operations

Some calculations involve more than one operation.

The word **BIDMAS** helps you to remember the order in which you should perform them.

B Brackets

I Indices (powers: squares, cubes, …)

D Division
M Multiplication } Do these together and work from left to right.

A Addition
S Subtraction } Do these together and work from left to right.

Example
Work out:

a $6 + 10 \div 2$

b $80 \div (-16 - 4)$

c $2 + 5 \div 2 - 3^2$

d $\dfrac{12 \times 0.5 - 1}{2}$

Solution

a $6 + 10 \div 2$

$= 6 + 5$ Divide before adding.

$= 11$

b $80 \div (-16 - 4)$

$= 80 \div (-20)$ Brackets first

$= -4$

c $2 + 5 \div 2 - 3^2$

$= 2 + 5 \div 2 - 9$ | Indices first

$= 2 + 2.5 - 9$ | Divide before adding or subtracting.

$= -4.5$

d $\dfrac{12 \times 0.5 - 1}{2}$

$= \dfrac{6 - 1}{2}$ | Imagine the top part to have brackets around it.

$= \dfrac{5}{2}$ | Complete the top part before dividing.

$= 2.5$

Scientific calculators use the rules of BIDMAS.

Sometimes you will still have to put extra brackets in for yourself.

Example

Calculate:

$$\frac{9 - 4}{2 \times 6 - 2}$$

Solution

The calculator does not recognise that the whole of $9 - 4$ is divided by the whole of $2 \times 6 - 2$.

To get the right answer you need to insert brackets as shown:

$$\frac{9 - 4}{2 \times 6 - 2} = \frac{(9 - 4)}{(2 \times 6 - 2)} = \frac{5}{10} = \frac{1}{2}$$

The buttons would have to be pressed in this order:

$\boxed{(}\ \boxed{9}\ \boxed{-}\ \boxed{4}\ \boxed{)}\ \boxed{\div}\ \boxed{(}\ \boxed{2}\ \boxed{\times}\ \boxed{6}\ \boxed{-}\ \boxed{2}\ \boxed{)}\ \boxed{=}$

Another way to calculate this is to use the calculator's memory. Look at the instruction booklet to see how to do this.

Keys used include: , $\boxed{\text{RCL}}$

Apply 8.6

Use your calculator for questions **7** and **8** only.

1 Work out:

a $4 + 7 \times 2$

b $25 \div 5 - 2$

c $2 \times 9 - 3 \times 5$

d $20 \div 4 + 3 + 5$

e $\dfrac{7 + 4}{6 - 4}$

f $(4 + 7) \times 2$

g $36 - 24 \div 2$

h $(36 - 24) \div 2$

i $\dfrac{12 \times 3 \times 5}{6}$

j $\dfrac{(12 + (3 \times 5))}{6}$

2 Insert brackets in each of these to make them correct:

a $19 - 9 - 2 = 12$

b $10 - 3 \times 4 = 28$

c $36 + 4 \div 8 = 5$

d $21 \div 5 + 2 + 4 = 7$

e $45 \div 2 + 3 = 8$

f $20 \div 2 \times 3 + 2 = 50$

g $5 \times 5 - 3 - 1 = 23$

h $5 \times 5 - 3 - 1 = 9$

i $\dfrac{2 \times 3 + 5}{5 - 1} = 4$

j $\dfrac{3 - 4 \div 2}{4 \div 2 - 1} = 1$

3 Julie says that $5 - 3 - (3 + 1)$ is the same as $5 - 3 - 3 + 1$.
Is she correct? Explain your answer.

4 Sukina says that $12 \times 3 - 5 \times 2 = 62$.
Is she correct? Explain your answer.

5 Find the value of the letter in each of these calculations:

a $(2 + a) \times 3 = 15$

b $28 \div 7 + b \times 3 = 22$

c $2 \times (1 + c)^2 = 18$

6 Work out:

a $25 \times (30 - 15)$

b $120 \div 30 + 5$

c $\dfrac{(9 + 15) \times 3}{9}$

d $2 \times (-2) + 1$

e $6 \div (-2) - 1$

f $\dfrac{-3 \times -2 + 4}{(8 \div 2 + 1)}$

g $0.3 + 2.03 \times 2$

h $7.2 \div 0.9 + 0.5$

i $\dfrac{0.4 \times (0.2 + 0.3)}{5 \div 0.5}$

j $(7 \times (2 + 5)) \div 4$

7 Use your calculator to work these out:

a $192 \div 12 \div 8$

b $75 + 25 \div 5$

c $2 \times 40 \times 300 + 29$

d $3 \times 150 - 4 \times 86$

e $13^2 - 12^2$

f $693 \div 11 \div 3$

g $31 + 20 \times 42$

h $15 \div 5 \times 21^2$

i $25^2 \times 23 - 16^2$

j $2 + 5^2 + 200 \times 2^2$

8 Use your calculator to work these out. Put in your own brackets where you need to.

a $(2 + 23) \times (50 - 12)$

b $(10^2 - 24) \times 7$

c $10^2 - 24 \times 7$

d $(80 + 0.56) \times 4 + 15$

e $80 + 0.56 \times 4 + 15$

f $\dfrac{63 - 8}{7 + 4}$

g $\dfrac{6.4 + 3.6}{1.5^2 + 2.75}$

h $\dfrac{14^2}{13 - 5}$

i $\dfrac{9^2 - 6^2}{3^2 + 4^2}$

j $\dfrac{35^3 + 13^3}{2^3 + 1}$

Assess 8.1–8.6

1 Which is the larger fraction?

$\dfrac{7}{20}$ or $\dfrac{7}{15}$

2 a Work out each of the following as a decimal:

i $\dfrac{365}{1000}$ **ii** 36% **iii** $\dfrac{3}{8}$

b Write these in order of size, smallest first.

3 Show that:

a $\frac{3}{4} + \frac{2}{3} = 1\frac{5}{12}$ **b** $3\frac{1}{6} - 1\frac{4}{5} = 1\frac{11}{30}$

Show all your working.

4 A litre of juice is poured into three glasses. The first glass contains $\frac{3}{20}$ of a litre. The second glass contains $\frac{3}{5}$ of a litre. What fraction does the third glass contain?

5 Work out:

a $2\frac{1}{5} \times 1\frac{7}{8}$ **b** $3\frac{1}{8} \div \frac{1}{4}$

6 A tennis racket costs $75 but in a sale it is reduced by $\frac{2}{5}$ of the price.

How much does it cost now?

7 Work out:

a $45.5 + 94.9$ **b** $14.2 - 11.38$ **c** 0.21×5.6 **d** $28 \div 0.8$

Write down all of your working.

8 Josh says that:

$$6 + 4 \times 3 - 1 = 29$$

Is he correct? Explain your answer.

9 Algebra

Learning outcomes:

After this chapter you should be able to:

- expand and simplify expressions containing brackets
- extract common factors from an expression
- construct simple expressions
- set up and solve simple equations.

Using brackets, constructing expressions and solving simple equations

BIDMAS applies to algebra as well as to arithmetic. Use brackets to group terms together and to show which operation has to be done first.

Learn 9.1 Expanding brackets

When you **expand** a bracket, all the terms inside the bracket must be multiplied by the term outside the bracket. You will be given the instruction 'Expand' or 'Multiply out'.

Example

Expand $5(2x - 1)$.

Solution

You may find it helpful to work with a grid, as shown below.

$\times$	$2x$	-1
5	$10x$	-5

$5 \times 2x = 10x$

$5 \times -1 = -5$

The shaded squares contain the answer:

$5(2x - 1) = 10x - 5$

Example

Multiply out $2p(3p + 4)$.

Solution

$\times$	$3p$	$+4$
$2p$	$6p^2$	$+8p$

$2p \times 3p = 6p^2$

$2p \times +4 = +8p$

$2p(3p + 4) = 6p^2 + 8p$

If an expression contains more than one bracket, it may contain like terms.

'Expand and simplify' tells you to multiply out each bracket and then collect like terms.

Example

Expand and simplify $3(3y - 2) - 2(4y - 5)$.

Solution

Step 1 Expand: $3(3y - 2)$ to $9y - 6$

Step 2 Expand: $-2(4y - 5)$ to $-8y + 10$ ←───── $-2 \times -5 = +10$

Step 3 Merge these two answers by collecting like terms:

$9y$ and $-8y$ are like terms and simplify to y

-6 and $+10$ are like terms and simplify to $+4$

$9y - 6 - 8y + 10 = y + 4$

so $\quad 3(3y - 2) - 2(4y - 5) = y + 4$

Study tip

When you have a negative term in front of a bracket, make sure you multiply the signs with care.

Apply 9.1

1 Multiply out:

a $3(x - 2)$

b $2(2 + 4y)$

c $5(p - q)$

d $2(3t + 1)$

e $7(2a + 3)$

f $4(2b - c)$

g $-3(d + 2)$

h $-2(3 - 4k)$

i $-5(a + b)$

j $\frac{1}{2}(6x - 4)$

k $\frac{1}{3}(9 - 3y)$

l $-\frac{1}{2}(4v - 2)$

2 Gavin multiplies out $3(5x - 1)$ and writes down $15x - 1$ as his answer. Why is this wrong?

3 Expand:

a $x(x + 2)$

b $y(5 - y)$

c $z(3z + 1)$

d $2t(t + 3)$

e $4p(p - 1)$

f $3q(2 - 3q)$

g $a(7 + 3a)$

h $5b(2b + 1)$

i $c(c^2 - 4)$

j $2d(3d - 4)$

k $m^2(8 + m)$

l $xy(5 - z)$

4 Expand and simplify:

Think of this as $6(2 - n) - 1(5 - n)$

a $4(p + 2) + 3(p + 1)$

b $2(q - 4) + 5(q + 2)$

c $3(2t - 5) + 4(4 - t)$

d $6k + 3(3 - 2k)$

e $4(2p + 5) - 3(p + 2)$

f $5(q - 4) - 2(2q - 7)$

g $3(2t - 1) - 5(t - 2)$

h $3(2m - 1) + 2(5 - 3m)$

i $6(2 - n) - (5 - n)$

j $x(2x - 3) + 3x(x + 2)$

k $2y(4z + 1) - y(5z - 3)$

l $3a(4a - b) - 2a(6a - b)$

5 Each of the four cards P, Q, R and S has an algebraic expression on it.

P	**Q**	**R**	**S**
$2a - 7$	$3 + a$	$5a + 1$	$4 - 3a$

a Expand and simplify:

   i $P + 2Q$ **ii** $R - P$ **iii** $2S - 3P$

b Show that $P + Q + S = 0$

c Find a combination of three of these cards that simplifies to 12.

Learn 9.2 Factorising expressions

A bracket is multiplied out and the answer is $3x - 6$.

What was in the bracket and what was in front of the bracket?

Changing $3x - 6$ back to $3(x - 2)$ is called **factorising**.

It is the opposite of expanding.

To find the number in front of the bracket, look for a **common factor**.

The common factor could be a number, a letter or both.

You will usually be given the instruction 'Factorise'.

Example

Factorise: **a** $4x - 8$ **b** $y^2 + 3y$ **c** $5ab - 10a$

Solution

a $4x - 8 = 4(x - 2)$ $4x = 4 \times x$ and $8 = 4 \times 2$
Both terms have 4 as a common factor, so take this outside the bracket.

b $y^2 + 3y = y(y + 3)$ $y^2 = y \times y$ and $3y = 3 \times y$
Both terms have y as a common factor.

c $5ab - 10a = 5a(b - 2)$ $5ab = 5a \times b$ and $10a = 5a \times 2$
Both terms have $5a$ as a common factor.

Study tip

Always check that you have factorised correctly.
Multiply out the bracket to make sure you get back
to the original.

Apply 9.2

1 Factorise:

a $2p + 6$ **e** $6y + 9$ **i** $3a^2 + 5a$

b $3q - 9$ **f** $10 + 2k$ **j** $4c^2 - 6c$

c $7t - 28$ **g** $m^2 - 3m$ **k** $4de + 6e$

d $12 - 4x$ **h** $n + n^2$ **l** $9z^2 - 12az$

2 Explain why the expression $4x + 7y$ cannot be factorised.

3 Factorise each set of expressions to find the 'odd one out'.

a $4p + 12$ $3p - 9$ $p^2 + 3p$

b $2 - 4y^2$ $3y - 6y^2$ $5 - 10y$

c $6p^2 + 8q^2$ $6p + 8q$ $3p^2 + 4pq$

4 Match each expression with the correct factors:

Expression	Factors
$6x - 8y$	$2(4x - 3y)$
$6x + 8y$	$2(3x - 4y)$
$8x + 6y$	$2(3y - 4x)$
$8x - 6y$	$2(3x + 4y)$
$6y - 8x$	$2(4x + 3y)$

5 n is an integer.

Decide whether each of the following statements is true or false.

a $2n + 6$ is always even.

b $3n - 1$ is never a multiple of 3.

c $5n - 1$ is never prime.

Learn 9.3 Constructing simple expressions

We can use algebra to write an expression to describe a general statement.

For example: 'Anna is x years old.' This is a general statement as x could take any value.

If we know that Anna's sister, Julia, is 3 years older than her, we can write her age as $(x + 3)$ years.

This is an expression for Julia's age.

If we have a value for x, say $x = 11$, then we can work out Julia's age by adding 3 to 11.

> Put brackets around $x + 3$ to show that both x and 3 are numbers of years.

Example

Adam has y books.

Ben has 5 more books than Adam.

Daniel has one book less than Adam.

Jacob has twice as many books as Adam.

Rafael has three times as many books as Ben.

Write down expressions for the number of books each student has.

Solution

Adam has y books.

'5 more than y' is written in algebra as $y + 5$. Ben has $(y + 5)$ books.

'One less than y' is written in algebra as $y - 1$. Daniel has $(y - 1)$ books.

'Twice as many as y' is written in algebra as $2y$. Jacob has $2y$ books.

'Three times as many as $(y + 5)$' is written as $3(y + 5)$. Rafael has $3(y + 5)$ books.

Apply 9.3

1 Tania has x pencils.

    a Valentina has twice as many pencils as Tania.
Write down an expression for the number of pencils Valentina has.

    b Marco has five more pencils than Tania.
Write down an expression for the number of pencils Marco has.

2 Matt earns $\$a$ per week.

    a Chris earns $12 less than Matt.
Write down an expression for the amount Chris earns.

    b Bella earns three times as much as Matt.
Write down an expression for the amount Bella earns.

    c Jon earns twice as much as Chris.
Write down an expression for the amount Jon earns.

3 Elena buys six oranges.

The price of an orange is $\$m$.

Write down an expression for the total cost of the oranges.

4 Tareq buys 5 pencils and 2 pens.

The cost of a pencil is x cents.

The cost of a pen is y cents.

Write down an expression for the total cost of the pencils and pens.

5 Kim sells homemade cakes at $5 each.

She has to pay $12 to set up her stall.

She sells p cakes.

Write down an expression in p for the profit she makes.

6 Write an expression for each of these statements.

Use x for the unknown number.

  a Think of a number and add 4.

  b Think of a number and multiply it by 5.

  c Think of a number, double it and subtract 1.

  d Think of a number and add 2. Multiply the result by 3.

  e Think of a number. Square it and subtract 7.

Learn 9.4 Solving linear equations

Equations are used when you are trying to find an **unknown** value.

You will be asked to **solve** the equation.

- Think about the **operations** $(+, -, \times, \div)$ that have been applied to the unknown (x).
- Reverse these operations, *making sure you do the same to both sides of the equation.*

Example
Solve the equation: $5x = 40$

Remember that $5x$ means $5 \times x$.

Solution
$$\frac{5x}{5} = \frac{40}{5}$$
$$x = 8$$

Divide both sides by 5.

Example
Solve the equation: $x + 7 = 2$

Solution
$$x + 7 - 7 = 2 - 7$$
$$x = -5$$

Subtract 7 from both sides.

Example
Solve the equation: $\frac{x}{3} = 8$

Solution
$$\frac{x}{3} \times 3 = 8 \times 3$$
$$x = 24$$

Multiply both sides by 3.

Example

Solve the equation: $4x - 9 = 21$

Solution

The flow diagram shows the two operations: 'multiply by 4 and then subtract 9'.

$$x \longrightarrow \boxed{\times 4} \longrightarrow \boxed{-9} \longrightarrow 21$$

First, reverse the 'subtract 9' operation:

$4x - 9 + 9 = 21 + 9$ Add 9 to both sides.

$\qquad 4x = 30$

Then reverse the 'multiply by 4' operation:

$\dfrac{4x}{4} = \dfrac{30}{4}$ Divide both sides by 4.

$\quad x = 7\frac{1}{2}$

The flow diagram shows how the equation was solved.

$$7\tfrac{1}{2} \longleftarrow \boxed{\div 4} \longleftarrow \boxed{+9} \longleftarrow 21$$

Study tip

You can check your answer by substituting it back into the original equation.

Apply 9.4

1 Solve these equations:

  a $4x = 12$ **c** $9z = -9$ **e** $5 = 2q$

  b $7y = 14$ **d** $3p = -33$ **f** $4t = 18$

2 Solve these equations:

  a $x + 8 = 8$ **c** $14 = z - 3$ **e** $q + 2.5 = 5.8$

  b $y + 8 = 5$ **d** $p - 1 = -7$ **f** $4.4 + t = 3.2$

3 Solve these equations:

  a $\dfrac{x}{2} = 15$ **c** $\dfrac{z}{9} = 5$ **e** $\dfrac{q}{10} = -1$

  b $\dfrac{y}{3} = -11$ **d** $\dfrac{p}{5} = 0.6$ **f** $\dfrac{2t}{5} = 8$

4 Solve these equations:

  a $3m - 1 = 14$ **e** $4x - 7 = 7$ **i** $9c - 8 = 40$

  b $5n + 3 = 38$ **f** $5 = 14 - 6y$ **j** $8 - 5d = 6$

  c $2p + 7 = 1$ **g** $0 = 36 - 12a$

  d $3q + 16 = 4$ **h** $5 + 3b = 2$

5 Solve the equation: $\frac{x}{5} + 3 = 11$

Use these flowcharts to help you:

$x \longrightarrow \boxed{\div 5} \longrightarrow \boxed{+3} \longrightarrow 11$

$x \longleftarrow \boxed{\times 5} \longleftarrow \boxed{-3} \longleftarrow 11$

6 Solve the equations:

a $\frac{x}{2} - 3 = 4$ **c** $4 + \frac{p}{3} = 2$ **e** $2 = 5 + \frac{3t}{4}$

b $\frac{y}{5} + 2 = 9$ **d** $8 = 1 + \frac{2q}{3}$

7 Maria thinks of a number, doubles it and adds 5. Her answer is 21.
Write this as an equation in x and solve it to find Maria's number.

8 Angelo thinks of a number, multiplies it by 5 and subtracts 8. His answer is 47.
Write this as an equation in y and solve it to find Angelo's number.

Assess 9.1–9.4

1 Multiply out:

a $9(x + 2)$ **b** $7(2y + 1)$ **c** $-2(3 - 2p)$ **d** $\frac{1}{4}(8 - 4q)$

2 Multiply out:

a $k(3 + k)$ **b** $m(4m - 1)$ **c** $2n(n - 5)$ **d** $3t(2t + 3)$

3 Expand and simplify:

a $3(f + 2) + 4(f - 3)$ **c** $7(x + 3) - 2(2x + 5)$

b $2(3g - 7) + 5(4 - g)$ **d** $6(2 - y) - 5(3 - 2y)$

4

A	B	C	D
$3n + 2$	$5n - 1$	$n + 2$	$2n - 3$

a Expand and simplify

   i $A + 2D$ **ii** $B - 3C$

b Show that $3C + D - B = 4$

5 Factorise:

a $7p - 14$ **c** $8 - 2t$ **e** $a^2 + 3a$

b $5q + 5$ **d** $11v + 55$ **f** $2b^2 - 10b$

6 Tomas got n marks in his maths test.

   a Pierre got 9 more marks than Tomas.
      Write down an expression for the number of marks that Pierre got.

   b Damon got twice as many marks as Tomas.
      Write down an expression for the number of marks that Damon got.

7 Tina has a party.
She buys x balloons and y ribbons.
A balloon costs 8 cents and a ribbon costs 5 cents.
Write down an expression for the total cost of the balloons and ribbons.

8 Solve these equations:

   a $3x = 18$ **e** $a - 7 = 11$ **i** $\dfrac{m}{4} = 3$

   b $8y = -64$ **f** $4 = c + 9$ **j** $\dfrac{n}{2} = 3.6$

   c $60 = 5z$ **g** $d + 4.4 = 5.2$ **k** $\dfrac{p}{10} = -5$

   d $2w = 17$ **h** $e + 1 = 0$ **l** $\dfrac{3q}{2} = 12$

9 Solve these equations:

   a $4k - 3 = 17$ **c** $11 - 2x = 5$ **e** $23 = 5 + 12w$

   b $9 + 4y = 1$ **d** $14 = 2 - 3z$

10 Juana thinks of a number, multiplies it by 3 and subtracts 7. Her answer is 38.
Write this as an equation in x and solve it to find Juana's number.

Transformations 1

Reflections and rotations

A transformation changes the position or the size of a shape. The original shape is called the object and the new shape is called the image. Sometimes the transformation is said to map the object onto the image.

This chapter is about two types of transformation: reflection and rotation.

Learning outcomes:

After this chapter you should be able to:

- reflect simple plane figures in horizontal or vertical lines
- rotate simple plane figures about the origin, vertices or midpoints of edges of the figures, through multiples of 90°.

Learn 10.1 Reflection

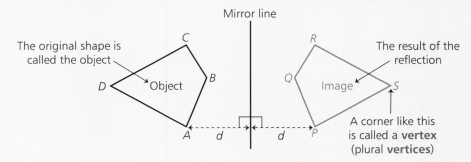

A **reflection** gives an **image** that looks like the reflection of the **object** in a mirror.

PQRS is the image of quadrilateral *ABCD* after reflection in the **mirror line**.
The reflection **maps** *A* onto *P*, *B* onto *Q*, *C* onto *R* and *D* onto *S*. The distance from each vertex of *ABCD* to the mirror line is equal to the distance from the mirror line to its image.

To use tracing paper to draw an image:

1. Carefully trace the object and mirror line.
2. Turn over the tracing paper.
3. Put the traced mirror line exactly over the actual mirror line (take care to match the ends).
4. Press a sharp pencil point on each vertex (corner) of the shape – this will give the vertices of the image.
5. Take away the tracing paper and join the vertices to give the image.

If the object is drawn on a grid, you can count squares to find the vertices of the image.

Example

a Plot the points *A*(3, 0), *B*(4, 6) and *C*(−3, 1) and draw triangle *ABC*.

b A reflection in the *x*-axis maps triangle *ABC* onto *PQR*. Draw triangle *PQR*.

Solution

a Triangle *ABC* is shown on the grid.

b *A* is on the *x*-axis (the mirror line), so its image, *P*, is also on the *x*-axis.

B is 6 squares above the *x*-axis, so its image, *Q*, is 6 squares below the *x*-axis.

C is 1 square above the *x*-axis, so its image, *R*, is 1 square below the *x*-axis.

Joining *P*, *Q* and *R* gives triangle *PQR*, the image of triangle *ABC*.

The order of the letters indicates that *P* is the image of *A*, *Q* is the image of *B* and *R* is the image of *C*.

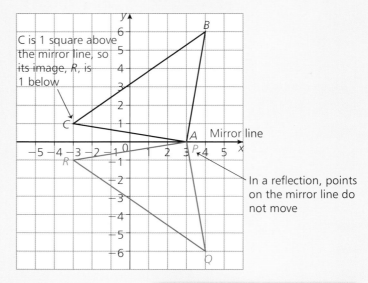

C is 1 square above the mirror line, so its image, R, is 1 below

In a reflection, points on the mirror line do not move

You can use tracing paper to check an image as follows:

1. Carefully trace the object, image and mirror line.
2. Fold the tracing paper along the mirror line. The image should lie exactly on the object.

When an object crosses the mirror line, each part is reflected to the other side.

Example

Draw the reflection of quadrilateral *ABCD* in the line *x* = 3.

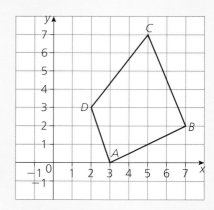

Solution

Joining points like (3, 1), (3, 2), (3, 3) and (3, 4) gives the mirror line *x* = 3.

Lines like *x* = 3 are parallel to the *y*-axis.
Lines like *y* = 3 are parallel to the *x*-axis.

Reflecting each vertex in this mirror line gives the vertices of the image.

Points of the object that are on the mirror line stay on the mirror line in the reflection.

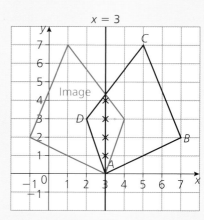

Sometimes questions like the next example ask you to find a mirror line. You must give the equation of the mirror line or describe exactly where it is.

Example

The points $A(-2, 3)$, $B(5, 3)$, $C(4, 1)$ and $D(1, 1)$ are the vertices of a trapezium.
A reflection maps $ABCD$ onto $PQRS$ with vertices $P(-2, -7)$, $Q(5, -7)$, $R(4, -5)$ and $S(1, -5)$.
Find the equation of the mirror line.

Solution

The distance from each point on $ABCD$ to the mirror line is equal to the distance from the mirror line to the image point. The mirror line passes through the midpoint of the line joining each vertex and its image.

$(-2, -2)$ is the midpoint of AP.
$(5, -2)$ is the midpoint of BQ.
$(4, -2)$ is the midpoint of midpoint of CR.
$(1, -2)$ is the midpoint of DS.

All points have a y-coordinate of -2.

So the equation of the mirror line is $y = -2$

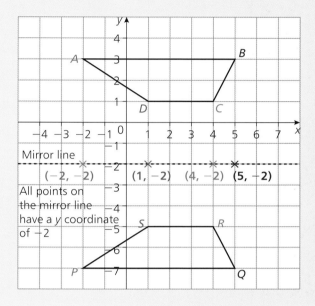

Apply 10.1

1 a Copy the diagram onto squared paper.

  b Draw the reflection of each shape in the mirror line.

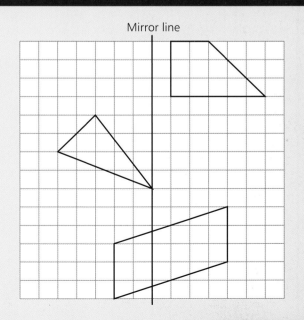

2 a Copy the diagram onto squared paper.

b Draw the reflection of each shape in the mirror line.

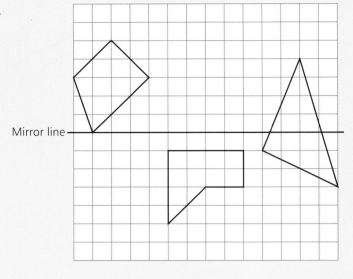

Mirror line

3 Copy the axes and triangle *PQR* onto squared paper.

a Reflect triangle *PQR* in the *x*-axis. Label the image *A*.

b Reflect triangle *PQR* in the *y*-axis. Label the image *B*.

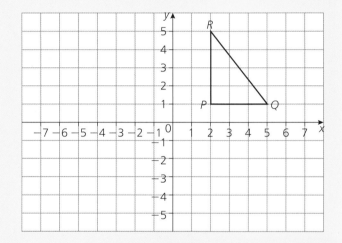

4 Copy the axes and trapezium *T* onto squared paper.

a Draw the image of *T* after reflection in the line $x = 1$. Label it *A*.

b Draw the image of *T* after reflection in the line $y = 1$. Label it *B*.

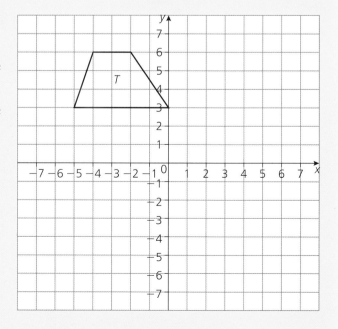

5 Copy the axes and rhombus *PQRS* onto squared paper.

Reflect *PQRS* in the line $y = 3$.

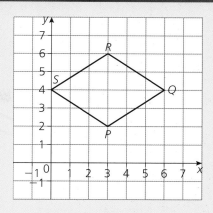

6 Copy the axes and quadrilateral *ABCD* onto squared paper.

A reflection in the line $x = 4$ maps *ABCD* onto *WXYZ*.
Draw *WXYZ*.

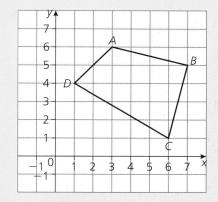

7 **a** On axes for *x* and *y* from −5 to 5, draw triangle *PQR* with $P(2, 4)$, $Q(-3, 1)$ and $R(3, -4)$.

b Draw the reflection of triangle *PQR* in the line $x = -1$.

8 **a** Draw axes for *x* and *y* from −8 to 8.

b Plot the points $A(-4, 2)$, $B(1, 4)$, $C(5, 0)$ and $D(-2, -5)$.

c Draw the reflection of quadrilateral *ABCD* in the line $y = -2$.

9 **a** Draw axes for *x* and *y* from −8 to 8.

b Plot the points $A(-3, 3)$, $B(4, 3)$, $C(4, 6)$ and join them to give triangle *ABC*.

c A reflection maps *ABC* onto *PQR* with vertices $P(-3, 1)$, $Q(4, 1)$ and $R(4, -2)$.
Find the equation of the mirror line.

10 The points $A(-5, 6)$, $B(-3, 2)$, $C(-4, -2)$ and $D(-8, 0)$ are the vertices of a quadrilateral.
A reflection maps *ABCD* onto *PQRS* with vertices $P(1, 6)$, $Q(-1, 2)$, $R(0, -2)$ and $S(4, 0)$.
Find the equation of the mirror line.

Learn 10.2 Rotation

A **rotation** turns an object through a given angle about a fixed point.

This fixed point is called the **centre of rotation**. It can be a point on the object itself or a point outside the object.

The angle of rotation is often 90° ($\frac{1}{4}$ turn), 180° ($\frac{1}{2}$ turn) or 270° ($\frac{3}{4}$ turn). The turn could be in a clockwise direction or an anticlockwise direction.

Use tracing paper to draw an image:

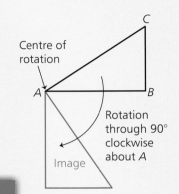

Centre of rotation

Rotation through 90° clockwise about A

Image

1. Carefully trace the object.
2. Use a sharp pencil or compass point to keep the centre in place as you turn the tracing paper through the angle.
3. Press a pencil point on each vertex of the object to give the vertices of the image.
4. Take away the tracing paper and join up the vertices to give the image.

Study tip

Remember you can use tracing paper in the exam to draw or check an image.

A rotation of 180° anticlockwise about M gives the same image.

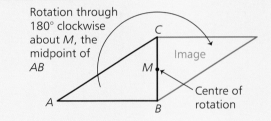

Rotation through 180° clockwise about M, the midpoint of AB

Image

Centre of rotation

Sometimes the object is drawn on a graph and the centre of rotation is the origin $(0, 0)$ or another point.

Example

Points $P(-1, 2)$, $Q(4, 2)$, $R(2, 5)$ and $S(-1, 5)$ are the vertices of a trapezium.
Draw $PQRS$ and its image after rotation through 90° anticlockwise about the origin, $(0, 0)$.

Solution

Tracing $PQRS$, then rotating the tracing paper anticlockwise through a quarter turn about the point $(0, 0)$ gives the position of the image.

Sometimes questions may ask you to describe a rotation. To do this, you must:

- give the angle of rotation

- say whether it is clockwise or anticlockwise

- give the position of the centre of rotation.

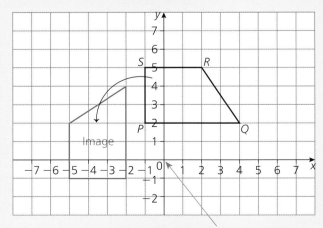

Example

Describe fully the rotation that maps the rectangle *ABCD* onto the rectangle *PQRS*.

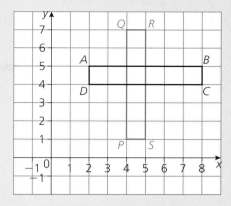

Solution

The order of the letters is very important.
In the rotation, *A* must be mapped onto *P*, *B* onto *Q*, *C* onto *R* and *D* onto *S*.
The rotation that does this is a rotation of 90° anticlockwise about the point (5, 4).

> Remember you must say *rotation*, then give three pieces of information: *angle*, *direction* and *centre*.

An alternative answer is a rotation of 270° clockwise about the point (5, 4).

> Sometimes there is another rotation that gives an image that looks the same, but maps the vertices to the wrong places. Use tracing paper to check that your rotation moves the vertices to the correct positions.

Apply 10.2

1 a Copy the diagram onto squared paper.

b Draw the image of rhombus *ABCD* after rotation through 180° clockwise about *A*.

c Draw the image of triangle *PQR* after rotation through 90° clockwise about *P*.

d Draw the image of flag *F* after rotation through 90° anticlockwise about *C*.

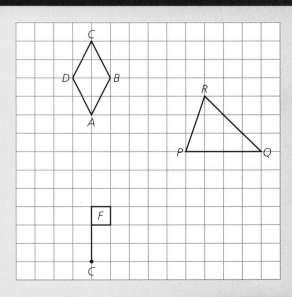

2 a Copy the diagram onto squared paper.

  b Draw the image of each letter after rotation through 180° clockwise about *O*.

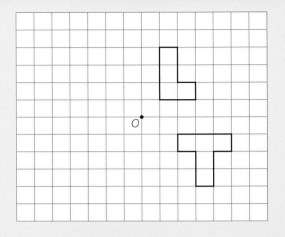

3 Copy the axes and parallelogram *PQRS* onto squared paper.

  a Draw the image of *PQRS* after a rotation of 90° clockwise about *P*. Label the image *A*.

  b Draw the image of *PQRS* after a rotation of 180° anticlockwise about *S*. Label the image *B*.

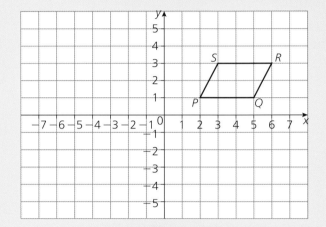

4 Copy the diagram onto squared paper.

  a Draw the image of *T* after a rotation of 180° clockwise about *M*. Label the image *A*.

  b Draw the image of *T* after a rotation of 180° clockwise about *N*. Label the image *B*.

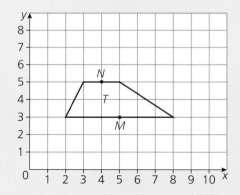

5 Copy the axes and the flag *F* onto squared paper.

  a Draw the image of *F* after rotation through 90° clockwise about the point (3, 2). Label the image *A*.

  b Draw the image of *F* after rotation through 90° clockwise about the point (3, 6). Label the image *B*.

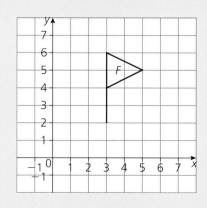

6 a On axes for x and y from -5 to 5, plot the points $P(0, 1)$, $Q(4, 2)$ and $R(1, 4)$.

b Draw the image of triangle PQR after rotation through 90° anticlockwise about P.

7 a Draw axes for x and y from -8 to 8.

b Plot the points $A(-4, 3)$, $B(2, 1)$, $C(5, 3)$ and $D(1, 7)$.

c Draw the image of quadrilateral $ABCD$ after rotation through 90° clockwise about the midpoint of AB.

8 Describe fully the rotation that maps:

a kite A onto kite B

b kite B onto kite A

c kite A onto kite C

d kite A onto kite D

e kite A onto kite E

f kite A onto kite F

g kite F onto kite A

h kite B onto kite G

i kite C onto kite H

j kite D onto kite A

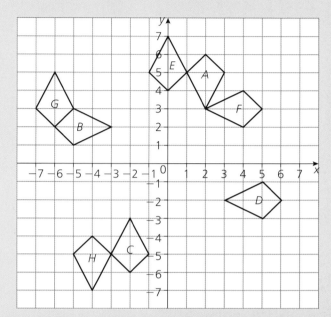

9 Describe fully the rotation that maps:

a square $ABCD$ onto square $QRSP$

b square $ABCD$ onto square $RSPQ$

c square $ABCD$ onto square $SPQR$

d square $PQRS$ onto square $DABC$

e square $PQRS$ onto square $BCDA$

f square $PQRS$ onto square $CDAB$

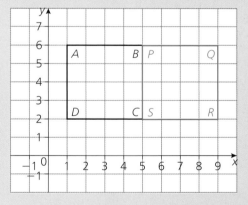

Assess 10.1–10.2

1 **a** Copy the diagram onto squared paper.

  b Draw the reflection of the object in the mirror line.

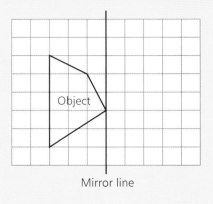

2 **a** Copy the diagram onto squared paper.

  b Draw the reflection of quadrilateral *ABCD* in the mirror line.

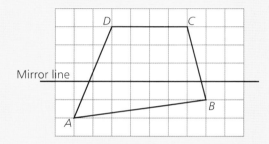

3 Copy the axes and triangle *T* onto squared paper.

  a Draw the image of *T* after reflection in the *x*-axis. Label the image *A*.

  b Draw the image of *T* after reflection in the *y*-axis. Label the image *B*.

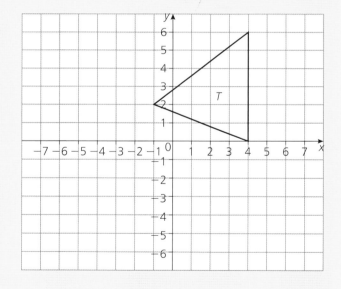

4 **a** Copy the axes and parallelogram *PQRS* onto squared paper.

  b Reflect *PQRS* in the *x*-axis. Label the image *A*.

  c Reflect *PQRS* in the line $x = 2$. Label the image *B*.

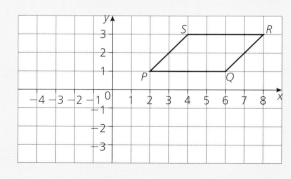

5 a Copy the diagram onto squared paper.

b Draw the image of the letter *H* after rotation through 90° clockwise about the centre, *C*.

c Draw the image of the letter *F* after rotation through 90° anticlockwise about the centre, *C*.

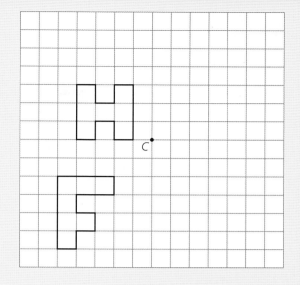

6 Copy the axes and pentagon *ABCDE* onto squared paper.

a Draw the image of *ABCDE* after a rotation of 90° clockwise about the origin. Label the image *P*.

b Draw the image of *ABCDE* after a rotation of 180° clockwise about the origin. Label the image *Q*.

c Draw the image of *ABCDE* after a rotation of 90° anticlockwise about the origin. Label the image *R*.

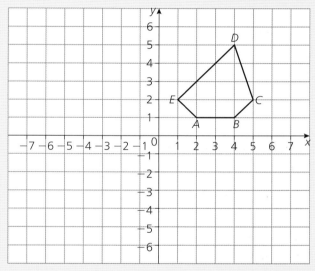

7 Copy the axes and the flag *F* onto squared paper.

a Draw the image of *F* after rotation through 90° anticlockwise about the origin. Label the image *A*.

b Draw the image of *F* after rotation through 90° anticlockwise about the point $(-3, 2)$. Label the image *B*.

c Draw the image of *F* after rotation through 90° anticlockwise about the point $(-3, 4)$. Label the image *C*.

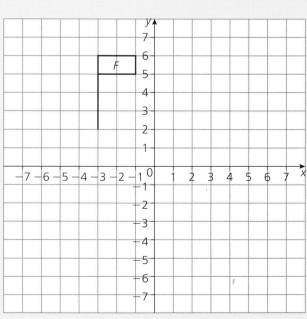

8 Copy the axes and the trapezium *ABCD* onto squared paper.

 a Draw the image of *ABCD* after rotation through 90° clockwise about *A*. Label the image *R*.

 b Draw the image of *ABCD* after rotation through 90° clockwise about *B*. Label the image *S*.

 c Draw the image of *ABCD* after rotation through 180° clockwise about the point $(-1, 3)$. Label the image *T*.

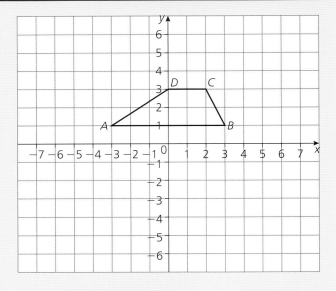

9 Describe fully the transformation that maps the triangle *T* onto:

 a *A*   **c** *C*   **e** *E*   **g** *G*

 b *B*   **d** *D*   **f** *F*   **h** *H*

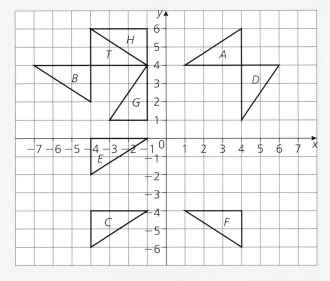

10 For this question use axes of *x* and *y* from 0 to 9:

 a Join points $A(7, 7)$, $B(9, 4)$, $C(7, 1)$ and $D(5, 4)$ to give rhombus *ABCD*.

 b Join points $P(3, 7)$, $Q(5, 4)$, $R(3, 1)$ and $S(1, 4)$ to give rhombus *PQRS*.

 c Describe fully the transformation that maps *ABCD* onto **i** *PSRQ* **ii** *RSPQ*.

11 Indices and standard form

Learning outcomes:

After this chapter you should be able to:

- calculate squares, square roots, cubes and cube roots of numbers
- use and interpret positive, negative and zero indices
- use the rules of indices
- use standard form.

In this chapter you will begin by learning about squares and cubes and continue by looking at other numbers written using powers.

You will then learn how to calculate with such numbers.

The chapter ends by looking at standard form, which is a very useful way to write down and calculate with very small and very large numbers.

Learn 11.1 Squares and cubes

Squares and square roots

A **square number** is the number you get when you multiply a number by itself.

The number 16 is a square number because $4 \times 4 = 16$ or $4^2 = 16$.

This way of writing a number is called **index notation**.

You say this as 4 squared or 4 to the **power** of 2.

The number 16 is also the square of -4 because -4×-4 gives 16 or $(-4)^2 = 16$.

The opposite or **inverse** of squaring is finding the **square root**.

When finding the square root of the number 16 you are looking for a number that when multiplied by itself gives 16.

So 4 and -4 are both the square root of 16.

This is written as $\sqrt{16} = 4$ (or -4).

All scientific calculators have a separate key for finding the square root.

This is usually $\boxed{\sqrt{\ }}$ or $\boxed{\sqrt{\square}}$. If you cannot find the correct key, check with your teacher.

So to find the square root of 64, enter the following on your calculator:

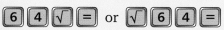 or

The square root of 64 is 8.

The $\sqrt{\ }$ sign usually means 'find the positive square root'.

Cubes and cube roots

A **cube number** is the number you get when you multiply three lots of the number together.

You say this as 2 cubed or 2 to the power of 3.

The number 8 is a cube number because $2 \times 2 \times 2 = 8$ or $2^3 = 8$.

Notice here that $-2 \times -2 \times -2 = -8$ so the cube of -2 is -8 and *not* 8.

The opposite or inverse of cubing is finding the **cube root**.

This means that:

the cube root of 8 is 2 $\qquad \sqrt[3]{8} = 2$

and the cube root of -8 is -2 $\qquad \sqrt[3]{-8} = -2$

You can find cube roots using either the $\boxed{\sqrt[3]{}}$ or $\boxed{\sqrt[3]{\square}}$ function key on a calculator.

So to find the cube root of 125, enter the following on your calculator:

$\boxed{1}\,\boxed{2}\,\boxed{5}\,\boxed{\sqrt[3]{}}\,\boxed{=}$ or $\boxed{\sqrt[3]{}}\,\boxed{1}\,\boxed{2}\,\boxed{5}\,\boxed{=}$

The cube root of 125 is 5.

Some calculators will have a separate key for finding the cube root, but most calculators show this function written above another key, such as above the x^3 key.

You may need to use the shift or the function key to select $\sqrt[3]{}$

You may need to use the following keys for:

finding any power or index $\qquad \boxed{y^x}$ or $\boxed{x^{\blacksquare}}$

finding any root $\qquad \boxed{\sqrt[y]{}}$ or $\boxed{\sqrt[x]{}}$ or $\boxed{\sqrt[\blacksquare]{x}}$

In either of these cases, if you cannot find the key you need, ask your teacher.

Example

Using your calculator, work out:

a $\sqrt{81} - 2^2$

b $\dfrac{25^3 + 15^2}{25 - 15}$

> **Study tip**
>
> When using a calculator, it is advisable to work in stages and write down each stage.

Solution

a $\sqrt{81} - 2^2 = 9 - 4 = 5$

b $\dfrac{25^3 + 15^2}{25 - 15} = \dfrac{15\,625 + 225}{10} = \dfrac{15\,850}{10} = 1585$

> **Study tip**
>
> Remember the rules for BIDMAS.
>
> The 'I' means Indices.
>
> Brackets first, then squares and cubes, which are types of indices.

To enter this calculation in one step on a calculator, you will need to insert brackets.

$\boxed{(}\,\boxed{2}\,\boxed{5}\,\boxed{x^3}\,\boxed{+}\,\boxed{1}\,\boxed{5}\,\boxed{x^2}\,\boxed{)}\,\boxed{\div}\,\boxed{(}\,\boxed{2}\,\boxed{5}\,\boxed{-}\,\boxed{1}\,\boxed{5}\,\boxed{)}\,\boxed{=}$

Working with algebra

$x \times x = x^2$ x times x equals x squared.

$x \times x \times x = x^3$ x times x times x equals x cubed.

$\sqrt{x^2} = x$ The square root of x^2 is x.

$\sqrt[3]{x^3} = x$ The cube root of x^3 is x.

$2x^2 = 2 \times x \times x$ 2 times x squared

$(2 \times x)^2 = (2 \times x) \times (2 \times x)$ 2 times x, all squared

Apply 11.1

1 Work out:

   a 3 squared   **c** 6^2 **e** the positive square root of 100   **g** $\sqrt{81}$

   b 5 cubed   **d** 3^3 **f** the cube root of 8   **h** $\sqrt[3]{64}$

2 Copy and complete the following tables:

   a The square of the numbers from 1 to 15:

Number	1	2		4		6			9	10	11			14	15
Square	1	4	9	16	25		49	64				144	169		

   b The cube of the numbers from 1 to 5 and the cube of 10:

Number	1	2		4	5	10
cube		8	27		125	

3 Write down all the cube numbers between 30 and 90.

4 Write down all the odd square numbers between 1 and 50.

5 n is an integer and n^3 is between 50 and 100. Find the value of n.

6 Work out:

   a $4^3 - 3^2$

   b $5^2 \times 2^3$

   c $7^2 + \sqrt{9}$

   d $\dfrac{6^2}{\sqrt{81}}$

   e $\sqrt{10^2 - 8^2}$

   f $\sqrt[3]{64} - \sqrt{64}$

   g $\dfrac{11^2 - 9^2}{10^2}$

   h $\sqrt[3]{512} \times \dfrac{3^2}{4^2}$

   i $\sqrt[3]{1000} - \dfrac{1}{\sqrt{100}}$

   j $(\sqrt{20})^2 + 3^2$

7 If you square a number ending in 2, the answer will end in 4.

If you square a number ending in 1, what will the answer end in?

Write similar sentences for the numbers 3 to 9.

There are some numbers that can never be at the end of a square number. What are they?

8 Julie says that $4x^2$ is equal to $(4x)^2$.

Substitute $x = 3$ into each of these expressions.

What do you notice? Can you explain why?

9 Sahid is estimating answers.

He says that $\sqrt{45}$ must lie between 6 and 7.

This is because 45 lies between 36 ($= 6^2$) and 49 ($= 7^2$).

Which two numbers do the following roots lie between?

a $\sqrt{32}$ **c** $\sqrt{420}$ **e** $\sqrt[3]{100}$

b $\sqrt{102}$ **d** $\sqrt[3]{12}$ **f** $\sqrt[3]{2000}$

Learn 11.2 Indices and powers

The **index** or *power* tells you how many times the **base number** has to be multiplied by itself.

Index (or power)

$$3^4$$

Base number

You say this as 3 to the power of 4.

So 3^4 means $3 \times 3 \times 3 \times 3 = 81$.

3^4 is in **index form** or index notation.

The $\boxed{x^{\blacksquare}}$ or the $\boxed{y^x}$ key on your calculator is used for finding powers other than 2 or 3.

Example

Write down the value of:

a 2^4 **b** $(-3)^5$

Solution

a $2^4 = 2 \times 2 \times 2 \times 2 = 16$

Or enter the following on your calculator:

b $(-3)^5 = (-3) \times (-3) \times (-3) \times (-3) \times (-3) = -243$

An odd number of negative signs multiplied together give a negative sign in the final answer.

Or enter the following on your calculator:

$$\boxed{(-)}\ \boxed{3}\ \boxed{x^\blacksquare}\ \boxed{5}\ \boxed{=}$$

Some calculators use the $\boxed{+/-}$ key instead of $\boxed{(-)}$ to input a negative number.

When finding roots of numbers use one of the following keys:

$$\boxed{\sqrt[x]{\ }},\ \boxed{\sqrt[x]{\ }}\ \text{or}\ \boxed{\sqrt[x]{x}}$$

These keys find roots of numbers other than 2 or 3.

Example

Write down the value of:

a $\sqrt[5]{32}$ **b** $\sqrt[4]{81}$

Solution

a When finding the 5th root of 32, you are trying to find a number (?) such that:

$$? \times ? \times ? \times ? \times ? = 32$$

Use the appropriate key on your calculator to find the 5th root:

$$\sqrt[5]{32} = 2$$

Check: $2 \times 2 \times 2 \times 2 \times 2 = 32$

b When finding the 4th root of 81, you are trying to find a number (?) such that:

$$? \times ? \times ? \times ? = 81$$

Use the appropriate key on your calculator to find the 4th root:

$$\sqrt[4]{81} = 3$$

Check: $3 \times 3 \times 3 \times 3 = 81$

The rules of indices

1 When *multiplying* powers of the same number, *add* the indices.

$3^2 \times 3^3 = 3^{2+3} = 3^5$ $\boxed{(3 \times 3) \times (3 \times 3 \times 3) = 3 \times 3 \times 3 \times 3 \times 3 = 3^5}$

2 When *dividing* powers of the same number, *subtract* the indices.

$3^6 \div 3^2 = 3^{6-2} = 3^4$ $\boxed{\dfrac{{}^1\cancel{3} \times {}^1\cancel{3} \times 3 \times 3 \times 3 \times 3}{{}_1\cancel{3} \times \cancel{3}_1} = 3 \times 3 \times 3 \times 3 = 3^4}$

3 To *raise a power* of a number to another power, *multiply* the indices.

$(3^4)^2 = 3^{4 \times 2} = 3^8$ $\boxed{(3 \times 3 \times 3 \times 3) \times (3 \times 3 \times 3 \times 3) = 3 \times 3 \times 3 \times 3 \times 3 \times 3 \times 3 \times 3 = 3^8}$

These rules can also be used for algebraic terms.

In general,

$$a^m \times a^n = a^{m+n}$$

$$a^m \div a^n = a^{m-n}$$

$$(a^m)^n = a^{m \times n}$$

Example

Simplify the following, leaving your answers in index form:

a $7^2 \times 7^6$ **b** $13^7 \div 13^3$ **c** $(5^7)^3$

Solution

a $7^2 \times 7^6 = 7^{2+6} = 7^8$ Add the powers.

Using a calculator:

$$\boxed{7}\ \boxed{x^2}\ \boxed{\times}\ \boxed{7}\ \boxed{x^\blacksquare}\ \boxed{6}\ \boxed{=}$$

This will give the answer 5 764 801, which is equivalent to 7^8.

The answer should be in index form so you can only use your calculator as a check.

b $13^7 \div 13^3 = 13^{7-3} = 13^4$ Subtract the powers.

c $(5^7)^3 = 5^{7 \times 3} = 5^{21}$ Multiply the powers.

> **Study tip**
>
> Whenever you are asked to give an answer in index form, always *check* your answer with a calculator.

Example

Simplify the following:

a $x^4 \times x$ **b** $\dfrac{a^{10}}{a^4}$ **c** $(2b^2)^3$

Solution

a $x^4 \times x = x^4 \times x^1 = x^{4+1} = x^5$ Add the powers. Remember x is the same as x^1.

b $\dfrac{a^{10}}{a^4} = a^{10-4} = a^6$ Subtract the powers.

c $(2b^2)^3 = 2^3 \times b^{2 \times 3} = 8b^6$ Multiply the powers. The 2 must be cubed and the power of b.

Negative indices

Indices can be negative or positive.

Using the second rule of indices may result in a negative index.

For example:

$$2^5 \div 2^8 = 2^{-3}$$

But what does 2^{-3} mean?

$$2^5 \div 2^8 = 2^{-3}$$

$$\frac{{}^1\cancel{2} \times {}^1\cancel{2} \times {}^1\cancel{2} \times {}^1\cancel{2} \times {}^1\cancel{2}}{{}_1\cancel{2} \times {}_1\cancel{2} \times {}_1\cancel{2} \times {}_1\cancel{2} \times {}_1\cancel{2} \times 2 \times 2 \times 2} = \frac{1}{2 \times 2 \times 2} = \frac{1}{2^3} = \frac{1}{8}$$

So $2^{-3} = \dfrac{1}{2^3}$

In general, $a^{-n} = \dfrac{1}{a^n}$

Zero indices

Indices can also be zero.

Again using the second rule of indices:

$$3^4 \div 3^4 = 3^{4-4} = 3^0$$

$$\frac{{}^1\cancel{3} \times {}^1\cancel{3} \times {}^1\cancel{3} \times {}^1\cancel{3}}{\cancel{3}_1 \times \cancel{3}_1 \times \cancel{3}_1 \times \cancel{3}_1} = \frac{1}{1} = 1$$

So $\qquad\qquad 3^0 = 1$

In general, $\qquad a^0 = 1$

Example

Work out

a 4^{-2} **b** 12^0 **c** $3^4 \div 3^7$

Solution

a $4^{-2} = \dfrac{1}{4^2} = \dfrac{1}{16}$ | Find the reciprocal. |

b $12^0 = 1$ | Anything raised to the power of 0 has a value of 1. |

c $3^4 \div 3^7 = 3^{4-7} = 3^{-3} = \dfrac{1}{3^3} = \dfrac{1}{27}$ | Subtract the powers. |

If you are not asked for your answers in index form, you may be able to use your calculator.

Do not give answers as rounded decimals. Fractions are more accurate.

Example

Simplify:

a $7p^{-4} \times 4p^2$ **b** $35q^2 \div 5q^3$ **c** $\left(\dfrac{3}{q^2}\right)^{-3}$

Solution

Always deal with the whole numbers separately from the indices.

a $7p^{-4} \times 4p^2 = (7 \times 4)p^{-4+2} = 28p^{-2} = \dfrac{28}{p^2}$

b $35q^2 \div 5q^3 = (35 \div 5)q^{2-3} = 7q^{-1} = \dfrac{7}{q}$

c $\left(\dfrac{3}{q^2}\right)^{-3} = (3q^{-2})^{-3} = 3^{-3} \times q^{-2 \times -3} = \dfrac{1}{3^3} \times q^6 = \dfrac{1}{27}q^6$

Notice that both the 3 and the q^2 must be raised to the power of -3.

Apply 11.2

1 Write the following in index notation:

   a $6 \times 6 \times 6 \times 6$ **c** $t \times t \times t \times t \times t$ **e** $d \times e \times e \times d \times d \times e$

   b $1 \times 1 \times 1 \times 1 \times 1 \times 1 \times 1$ **d** $a \times a \times b$

2 Work out each of the following. You may use a calculator.
Give all your answers as integers or fractions. Do not convert to decimals.

a 7^2 **c** 4^3 **e** 10^3 **g** 3^{-2} **i** 8^{-1}
b 2^7 **d** $(-4)^3$ **f** 5^0 **h** $\sqrt[4]{81}$ **j** $10^4 - 10^2$

3 Simplify the following. You may use a calculator.
Give all answers as integers or fractions. Do not convert to decimals.

a $2^5 \times 2^4$ **c** $6^4 \div 6^7$ **e** $10^{-4} \times 10^3$ **g** $5^6 \div (5^2 \times 5^3)$ **i** $\dfrac{3^5 \times 3^2}{3^9}$
b $(8^2)^3$ **d** 7×7^{-1} **f** $21^2 \times 21^0$ **h** $(10^4)^2$ **j** $4^3 \times 4^4 \div 4^9$

4 Simplify the following:

a $(c^2)^3$ **c** $5p^4 \times 3p^7$ **e** $(3y^2)^4$ **g** $\left(\dfrac{6}{t}\right)^{-2}$ **i** $32y^6 \div 4y^{-3}$
b y^0 **d** $(r^3)^{-2}$ **f** $q^7 \div q^2$ **h** $15x^8 \times 3x^2$ **j** $\dfrac{10^6 \times 10^4}{10 \times 10^2}$

5 Simplify the following:

a $x^2 \times x^3 \times y^2$ **c** $10x^4 \div 5y^2$ **e** $\dfrac{3x^2y \times 4x^2y^5}{2xy}$
b $3x^3y^2 \times 4x^2y^4$ **d** $(4x^2y^5)^0$

6 Write down the value of x when:
a $x^3 = 27$ **b** $2^x = 32$ **c** $x^{-1} = \frac{1}{10}$ **d** $\frac{1}{81} = 3^x$ **e** $6^x \div 6^2 = 6^9$

7 Write down the value of p when:
a $p^3 = -125$ **b** $\left(\frac{1}{2}\right)^p = \frac{1}{8}$ **c** $13^p = 1$ **d** $3^4 \div 3^p = 3^{-2}$ **e** $\dfrac{10^2 \times 10^5}{10^p} = 10^3$

8 $x^m \times x^n = x^9$ and $(x^m)^n = x^{20}$
Work out the values of m and n.

9 $p^a \div p^b = p$ and $p^a \times p^b = p^7$
Work out the values of a and b.

10 Write down five calculations that will give the answer x^{30}.
Try to use all the rules for indices and also include at least one calculation involving a negative power.

Learn 11.3 Standard form

A number can be written in many ways using powers of 10.

For example:

$3241 = 3241 \times 1$ 3241×10^0

$\quad\quad = 324.1 \times 10$ 324.1×10^1

$\quad\quad = 32.41 \times 100$ 32.41×10^2

$\quad\quad = 3.241 \times 1000$ 3.241×10^3

The same number can also be written using negative powers of 10:

$3241 = 3241 \times 1$ 3241×10^0

$ = 32\,410 \times 0.1$ $32\,410 \times 10^{-1}$

$ = 324\,100 \times 0.01$ $324\,100 \times 10^{-2}$

$ = 3\,241\,000 \times 0.001$ $3\,241\,000 \times 10^{-3}$

Standard form is used to write down very large and very small numbers.

Standard form is always written as:

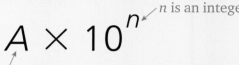

n is an integer.

$$A \times 10^{n}$$

A is a number between 1 and 10.

From the above lists, 3241, when written in standard form, is equal to 3.241×10^3.

You will need to investigate how to input numbers in standard form into your own calculator.

If you cannot work out how to do this, ask your teacher.

The following example has been solved without a calculator.

Example

Write these as ordinary numbers:

a 3×10^4 **b** 6.52×10^6 **c** 7×10^{-2} **d** 8.434×10^{-3}

Solution

a $3 \times 10^4 = 3 \times 10\,000$ | Move the number 4 places to make it larger. ←
$ = 30\,000$

b $6.52 \times 10^6 = 6.52 \times 1\,000\,000$ | Move the number 6 places to make it larger. ←
$ = 6\,520\,000$

c $7 \times 10^{-2} = 7 \times 0.01$ | Move the number 2 places to make it smaller. →
$\phantom{7 \times 10^{-2}} = 0.07$

d $8.434 \times 10^{-3} = 8.434 \times 0.001$ | Move the number 3 places to make it smaller. →
$\phantom{8.434 \times 10^{-3}} = 0.008434$

Now use your calculator to check these answers.

Study tip

Always check that you have moved the number the right way by asking yourself if you are expecting a smaller or bigger number.

Converting to standard form

Any number can be written in standard form.

You may be able to use a calculator to perform this conversion.

Example

Convert these ordinary numbers into numbers in standard form:

a 723   **b** 1827.45   **c** 0.0006   **d** 0.000000127

Solution

a 723

$= 7.23 \times 100$ | 7.23 is between 1 and 10. |

$= 7.23 \times 10^2$ | To get from 723 to 7.23, the number has moved 2 places. |

b 1827.45

$= 1.82745 \times 1000$ | 1.82745 is between 1 and 10. |

$= 1.82745 \times 10^3$ | To get from 1827.45 to 1.82745, the number has moved 3 places. |

c 0.0006

$= 6 \times 0.0001$ | 6 is between 1 and 10. |

$= 6 \times 10^{-4}$ | To get from 0.0006 to 6, the number has moved 4 places. |

d 0.000000127

$= 1.27 \times 0.0000001$ | 1.27 is between 1 and 10. |

$= 1.27 \times 10^{-7}$ | To get from 0.000000127 to 1.27, the number has moved 7 places. |

Now check the answers with your calculator.

> **Study tip**
>
> Large numbers have *positive* powers of 10 in standard form.
> Small numbers have *negative* powers of 10 in standard form.

Adding, subtracting, multiplying and dividing numbers in standard form

Use the rules of indices, but look out for shortcuts.

Example

Work out the following, leaving your answers in standard form:

a $(3 \times 10^3) \times (5 \times 10^{-5})$

b $(5.2 \times 10^2) \div (2 \times 10^4)$

c $(9.3 \times 10^2) + (2.1 \times 10^{-1})$

d $(4.5 \times 10^{-6}) - (4 \times 10^{-6})$

Solution

The solutions are given without using a calculator. You may use a calculator for all calculations in standard form.

Check that you get the same answer with your calculator.

a $(3 \times 10^3) \times (5 \times 10^{-5})$

$= 15 \times 10^3 \times 10^{-5}$ | Multiply the first part of each number together.

$= 15 \times 10^{3+ -5}$ | Use the 1st rule of indices.

$= 15 \times 10^{-2}$

$= 1.5 \times 10^1 \times 10^{-2}$ | Write 15 in standard form.

$= 1.5 \times 10^{-1}$ | Use the 1st rule of indices again.

b $(5.2 \times 10^2) \div (2 \times 10^4)$

$= 2.6 \times 10^2 \div 10^4$ | Divide 5.2 by 2.

$= 2.6 \times 10^{2-4}$ | Use the 2nd rule of indices.

$= 2.6 \times 10^{-2}$

c $(9.3 \times 10^2) + (2.1 \times 10^{-1})$

$= 930 + 0.21$ | Write each number in ordinary form.

$= 930.21$ | Add.

$= 9.3021 \times 10^2$ | Convert to standard form.

d $(4.5 \times 10^{-6}) - (4 \times 10^{-6})$

$= (4.5 - 4) \times 10^{-6}$ | You can only do this because the powers of 10 are the same.

$= 0.5 \times 10^{-6}$

$= 5 \times 10^{-1} \times 10^{-6}$ | Write 0.5 in standard form.

$= 5 \times 10^{-1-6}$ | Use the 1st rule of indices.

$= 5 \times 10^{-7}$

Answers may be given as whole numbers or in standard form.

Study tip

When calculating with numbers in standard form it is useful to put brackets around the number. This makes it easier to see what you are doing, e.g. $(5 \times 10^3) \times (3 \times 10^4)$.

Apply 11.3

1 Write the following numbers in standard form:

a 70 000	**c** 17 200 000	**e** 181 856	**g** 0.0007	**i** 0.000000057
b 650	**d** 2372.4	**f** 0.6	**h** 0.010101	**j** 0.000000202

2 Write the following numbers in ordinary form:

a 5×10^1	**c** 1.5×10^6	**e** 9.1909×10^8	**g** 8×10^{-1}	**i** 7.213×10^{-3}
b 9×10^4	**d** 3.142×10^3	**f** 7×10^{-2}	**h** 1.27×10^{-4}	**j** 2.111×10^{-7}

3 The population of Ghana after the census in 2010 was approximately 24 223 400.
What is this population written in standard form?

4 The speed of light is approximately 3.0×10^8 m/s.
a Write this as an ordinary number.
b What is this speed in km/s? Write your answer in standard form.

5 Qatar will host the football world cup in 2022. The cost of building the stadiums will be approximately 4 billion dollars.

1 billion is written as 1×10^9 in standard form.
a What is 4 billion as an ordinary number?
b Other work will cost 42.9 billion dollars.
What is this number in standard form?

6 Calculate the following, giving your answers as ordinary numbers. Show all your working.
a $(4 \times 10^3) \times (2 \times 10^2)$ **c** $(4 \times 10^3) + (2 \times 10^2)$
b $(4 \times 10^3) \div (2 \times 10^2)$ **d** $(4 \times 10^3) - (2 \times 10^2)$

7 Use your calculator to work out the following. Give your answers in standard form.
a $(7.2 \times 10^3) \times (1.5 \times 10^4)$ **c** $(3.4 \times 10^{-2})^2$
b $(7.2 \times 10^3) \div (1.5 \times 10^4)$ **d** $(6.3 \times 10^{-5}) + (3.7 \times 10^{-5})$

8 A factory is making a component for a computer.
The component is rectangular and measures 0.6×10^{-3} m by 7.2×10^{-3} m.
a Find the area of the component in square metres. Give your answer in standard form.
b Find the perimeter of the component. Give your answer in standard form.

9 The mass of the Earth is 5.97×10^{24} kg.
The average density of the Earth is 5515 kg/m^3.

    Volume = mass ÷ density

Find the volume of the Earth in m^3. Give your answer in standard form correct to 2 decimal places.

10 Senita says that $(7 \times 10^5) - (5 \times 10^5) = (2 \times 10^0)$.

Diana says that $(7 \times 10^5) - (5 \times 10^5) = (2 \times 10^5)$.

Who is correct? Give a reason for your answer.

11 The following table lists the population in 2010 of the five largest urban regions in New Zealand, together with the area of the region in km^2.

The population density is the number of people per km^2 or the average number of people per square kilometre.

a List the regions by population. Largest first.

Urban area	Population	Area in km²	Population density in people/km²
Auckland	1.35×10^6	1.09×10^3	
Christchurch	3.90×10^5	6.08×10^2	
Hamilton	2.03×10^5	8.77×10^2	
Napier-Hastings	1.24×10^5	3.75×10^2	
Wellington	3.90×10^5	4.44×10^2	

b List the regions by area. Largest first.

c Work out the population density for each of the areas.

d List the regions by population density. Largest first.

Assess 11.1–11.3

1 x is an integer between 40 and 80.

Find the value of x when:

a x is an odd square number
b x is a cube number.

2 Find all the square numbers that are also factors of 144.

3 Work out the following:

a $\sqrt[3]{125} + 2(5)^2$

c $\sqrt{(\sqrt{81} + 5^2 + 2)}$

b $\left(\frac{1}{4}\right)^3 \times 12^2$

d $\dfrac{6^3 + 2^3}{6^2 + 2^2}$

4 Simplify the following:

a 2^{-4}
b 7^0
c $\left(1\frac{1}{2}\right)^2$
d $\sqrt[5]{243}$
e $\left(\frac{1}{5^2}\right)^{-1}$

5 Simplify the following:

a $(3^2)^3$
b $4^6 \div 4^4$
c $5^{-1} \times 5^4$
d $(2^{-3} \times 2^5) \div 2^2$
e $(10^{19} \times 10^7)^0$

6 Find the value of p when:

a $p^3 = -1000$
c $2^3 \div 2^p = 2^5$
e $6^3 \times 6^p \times 6^5 = 6^{12}$

b $3^p = \frac{1}{9}$
d $(5^2)^p = 5^8$

7 a Write the following ordinary numbers in standard form:

　i 75

　ii 750 000

　iii 0.00000075

b Write the following as ordinary numbers:

　i 9.12×10^4

　ii 9.12×10^0

　iii 9.12×10^{-3}

8 Calculate the following giving your answers in standard form:

a $(2.9 \times 10^3) + (6.1 \times 10^4)$ 　　　　　**b** $(2.9 \times 10^3) \times (6.1 \times 10^4)$

9 A plane flew from Thimphu in Bhutan to Sydney in Australia.
The two places are 9.39×10^3 km apart. The flight took 7.26×10^2 minutes.

　　Average speed = total distance ÷ total time taken

What was the average speed of the plane in kilometres per minute?

10 Saturn does not have a circular orbit around the Sun, so it has a maximum and a minimum distance away from the Sun.
It has a minimum distance of 4.6×10^7 km and a maximum distance of 6.98×10^7 km.

What is the difference in kilometres between these two distances? Give your answer as an ordinary number.

Practice exam questions

1   Leo has $10 to spend.

He buys 2 kilograms of peaches at 85 cents per kilogram, 3 peppers at 35 cents each and 2 litres of juice at 95 cents per litre.

How much money does he have left?   (*3 marks*)

2   Tonia is travelling by plane.

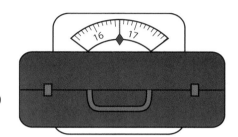

   a   She weighs her luggage.

   The maximum weight allowed is 22 kilograms.
   By how much is the weight of her case below the
   maximum allowed?   (*1 mark*)

   b   She changes 150 dollars into dinar.
   The exchange rate is 1 dollar = 72.47 dinar.
   Calculate how much she receives.   (*1 mark*)

   c   She checks in at the airport at 1345.
   She has to wait until 1610 to get on her plane.
   Work out how long she has to wait.   (*1 mark*)

   d   The plane takes off at 1645.
   The flight takes 4 hours and 20 minutes.
   What is the time when the plane lands?   (*1 mark*)

3   Complete this bill:

Item		Total cost of item
2 posters at	$6.25 each	$
3 magazines at	$2.75 each	$
5 newspapers at	$1.20 each	$
60 pencils at	$1.35 for 10	$
Total		$

(*3 marks*)

4   a   Show that: $3\frac{3}{8} \times 2\frac{2}{5} = 8\frac{1}{10}$.
   Do not use a calculator and show all your working.   (*3 marks*)

   b   A piece of wood 3 metres in length is cut into equal lengths. Each length is $8\frac{1}{3}$ cm long.
   How many lengths of wood are there?   (*2 marks*)

5   **a** Work out as a decimal:

        i $\frac{27}{50}$ *(1 mark)*

        ii 56%   *(1 mark)*

        iii $\frac{5}{9}$ *(1 mark)*

    b Write down the numbers in part **a** in order, starting with the smallest.   *(2 marks)*

6   Amita, Bella, Cosmas and Dimitri shared a large fruit pie between them.

    Amita ate $\frac{1}{6}$ and Bella ate $\frac{2}{9}$ of the pie.

    Cosmas ate $\frac{3}{4}$ of what was left.

    What fraction of the pie was Dimitri left with?   *(4 marks)*

7   Use your calculator to work out the following:

    a $13^2 - 24 \times 2$ *(1 mark)*

    b $(13 - 24)^2 - 2 \times 4^2$ *(1 mark)*

    c $15 \div 2 + 3 \times 2$ *(1 mark)*

    d $2 \times 7^2 - 3 \times 4$ *(1 mark)*

    e $\dfrac{13^2 - 12^2}{2^3 \div 4 + 3}$ *(2 marks)*

8   Factorise completely:

    a $4pq + 8qr$ *(2 marks)*

    b $3y^2 - 6y$ *(2 marks)*

9   Expand and simplify: $5(2x - 3y) - 2(4x + y)$.   *(3 marks)*

10   Solve the equations:

    a $7k - 11 = 24$ *(2 marks)*

    b $\frac{v}{5} = 12$ *(1 mark)*

11   A parallelogram has sides of length m cm and n cm.

    a Write down an expression for the perimeter of the parallelogram.   *(1 mark)*

    b The perimeter of the parallelogram is 88 cm. Write down an equation in m and n.   *(1 mark)*

    c If $m = 3n$, find the lengths of the sides.   *(2 marks)*

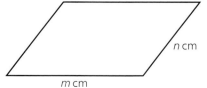

12 Juana has *x* dollars and Klaus has 3*x* dollars.

   a Juana is given another 5 dollars.
     Write down an expression for the number of dollars she has now.   *(1 mark)*

   b Klaus spends 25 dollars.
     Write down an expression for the number of dollars he has now.   *(1 mark)*

   c Klaus now has twice as much money as Juana.
     Write down an equation in *x* to show this.   *(1 mark)*

   d Solve your equation to find the value of *x*.   *(2 marks)*

13 Copy the diagram onto squared paper.

Then draw the reflection of the parallelogram
in the line *x* = 4.

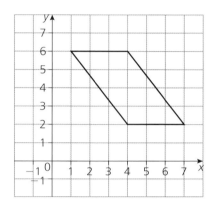

(2 marks)

14 Copy the diagram onto squared paper.

   a Draw the image of kite K after rotation through 90° clockwise about the origin.
     Label this image L.   *(2 marks)*

   b Draw the image of kite K after rotation through 180° clockwise about the origin.
     Label this image M.   *(2 marks)*

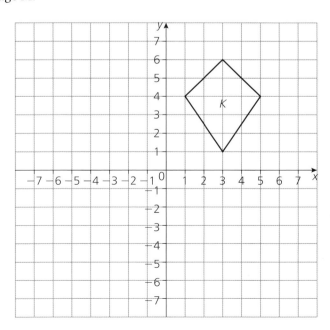

15 Copy the diagram onto squared paper.

a Draw the image of trapezium T after reflection in the *y*-axis. Label it A.

(*2 marks*)

b Draw the image of trapezium T after reflection in the line $y = -1$. Label it B.

(*2 marks*)

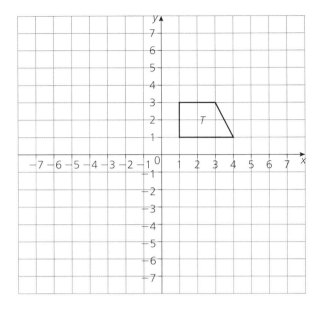

16 *x* is an integer between 30 and 40.

Write down:

a A multiple of 7. (*1 mark*)

b A square number. (*1 mark*)

c Two prime numbers. (*1 mark*)

d A factor of 408. (*1 mark*)

e The square root of 1444. (*1 mark*)

f Two numbers whose product is 1023. (*1 mark*)

17 Find the value of *n* in each of the following statements:

a $32\,000 = 3.2 \times 10^n$ (*1 mark*)

b $32^n = 1$ (*1 mark*)

c $0.000032 = 3.2 \times 10^n$ (*1 mark*)

d $32^4 \div 32^{10} = 32^n$ (*1 mark*)

e $\frac{1}{32} = 2^n$ (*1 mark*)

18 $x = 0.0471$ and $y = 29\,300$.

a Write the numbers *x* and *y* in standard form. (*2 marks*)

b Calculate, giving your answers in standard form.

   i $x + y$ (*2 marks*)

   ii $1000x - \dfrac{y}{1000}$ (*2 marks*)

   iii xy (*2 marks*)

   iv $\dfrac{5x}{y}$ (*2 marks*)

Give the answers to parts **i**–**iv** in standard form, correct to 2 decimal places.

Statistical diagrams

Learning outcomes:

After this chapter you should be able to:

- collect and tabulate data
- read and interpret information in tables and statistical diagrams
- construct and use bar charts
- construct and use pictograms
- construct and use histograms
- construct and use pie charts
- construct and use scatter diagrams
- draw a line of best fit
- understand correlation.

Tables, charts and graphs

Charts and graphs can be used to summarise statistical information.

You should choose the best diagram for the purpose carefully, draw it accurately and interpret it correctly.

Learn 12.1 Collecting and interpreting data

Common methods of putting data into tables are **tally charts** and **2-way tables**.

Tally charts

A tally chart is a method of showing a set of data.

Tallies are recorded in blocks of five, making it easy to find the total, or **frequency** for each category.

The tally chart shows how four friends recorded the number of text messages they sent in one day.

Every time they sent a text, they made a mark in the table. At the end of the day they counted up the number of texts sent, or the frequency.

Student	Number of text messages sent	Frequency
Denis	卌 卌 |||	13
Carla	卌 |||	8
Phil	卌 卌 ||	12
Lily	卌 ||||	9

Tally charts are also used for **grouping** data.

The **range** of a set of data is the difference between the largest item and the smallest item.

When data has a large range, it is useful to put the data into groups.

Example

Below are the ages of 30 people on a bus one morning:

| 11 | 54 | 35 | 45 | 21 | 17 | 16 | 56 | 45 | 33 | 29 | 31 | 14 | 15 | 13 |
| 39 | 57 | 62 | 29 | 44 | 28 | 12 | 73 | 56 | 36 | 41 | 74 | 26 | 18 | 29 |

Show this information in a tally chart.

Solution

The ages range from 11 to 74.

Grouping into tens (11 to 20, 21 to 30, etc.) will require seven groups.

Age (years)	Tally	Frequency
11–20	⦀⦀ |||	8
21–30	⦀⦀		6
31–40	⦀⦀	5
41–50	||||	4
51–60	||||	4
61–70			1
71–80	||	2
TOTAL		30

Aim to have between four and 10 groups. If possible, group into 5s or 10s.

Study tip

Always add up the frequency column and check that the total is equal to the number of elements of data.

Two-way tables

A two-way table is used when you need to show two different pieces of information. If you know the ages and gender of people on a bus, a two-way table would be used. The ages could be recorded in columns, and the gender in rows:

Age (years)	11–20	21–30	31–40	41–50	51–60	61–70	71–80
Male	5	2	4	2	0	0	1
Female	3	4	1	2	4	1	1

Example

a A store takes stock of the number of T-shirts for sale.

	White	Grey	Red	Blue	Black
Long sleeved	12	10	11	12	10
Short sleeved	23	22	23	21	26

a How many long sleeved T-shirts are there?

b How many red T-shirts are there?

c A customer wants a short sleeved T-shirt, but not a red one. How many can he choose from?

Solution

a There are 12 + 10 + 11 + 12 + 10 = 55 long sleeved T-shirts.

b There are 11 + 23 = 34 red T-shirts.

c He has 23 + 22 + 21 + 26 = 92 to choose from.

Apply 12.1

1 A manufacturer makes flowerpots.

The numbers made in one day are shown below.

	Large	Medium	Small
Brown	65	54	34
Green	24	18	12

a How many flowerpots do they make altogether?

b How many green flowerpots do they make?

c What fraction of all the flowerpots are medium?

2 The table below shows information about the gender and age of the teachers in a school.

	Male	Female
22–35	2	4
36–45	3	7
Over 45	9	17

a How many teachers are there in the school?

b What fraction are males under 45?

3 A class of 32 children has 17 girls. Twelve of the children wear glasses, of which seven are boys. Show this information in a two-way table.

Learn 12.2 Bar charts, histograms and pictograms

Bar charts

A **bar chart** has parallel bars or columns of the same width, usually with a space between them. Each bar shows the quantity of a different category of data.

Bar charts can be used for numeric (or **quantitative**) data or descriptive (or **qualitative**) data.

For example, quantitative data might be the ages of people at a concert; qualitative data might be the colour of shirt each person is wearing.

A company records the number of each model of photocopier sold during the year. The table gives the data for the last year:

Model	Photocopiers sold
Mono1	270
Mono2	330
Colour1	190
Colour2	450

> **Study tip**
>
> Remember that the vertical scale for a bar chart must start at zero.

The biggest number is 450, so we need a vertical scale that starts at zero and shows at least 450.

A scale of one square to 50 will take nine squares.

Then we can draw the bar chart:

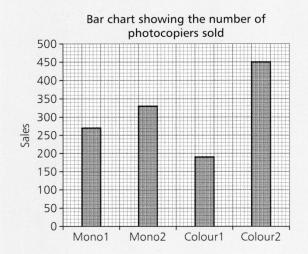

Histograms

A histogram is similar to a bar chart, but is used for **continuous data**.

Continuous data is data that can take on any value. As it is continuous, there are no gaps between the bars.

The histogram on the right shows the ages of people in a store at a particular moment.

The number of people (or **frequency**) aged 15 to 25 is 6.

There are 11 people aged between 25 and 35, seven aged between 35 and 45, and three aged 45 to 55.

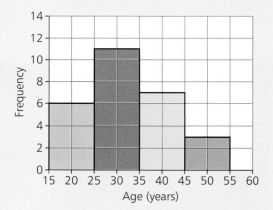

Example

Draw a histogram to show this data showing the mass of parcels being delivered.

Mass, m, kg	Frequency
$0 < x \leqslant 5$	3
$5 < x \leqslant 10$	7
$10 < x \leqslant 15$	11
$15 < x \leqslant 20$	9
$20 < x \leqslant 25$	7

Solution

$5 < x \leqslant 10$ This means the mass is greater than 5 kg but no greater than 10 kg.

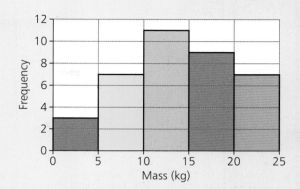

Pictograms

A **pictogram** is a way of displaying qualitative data.

The data is displayed by using pictures and a key shows the quantity that each picture represents.

For example, here is a pictogram showing how students in a class travel to school.

The key shows you that a complete drawing represents 4 students.

So $3\frac{1}{2} \times 4 = 14$ students walk, $1\frac{1}{4} \times 4 = 5$ travel by car, $3 \times 4 = 12$ go by bus and $1\frac{3}{4} \times 4 = 7$ cycle.

Walk	
Car	
Bus	
Cycle	

Key: represents 4 students.

Example

The bar chart shows the number of ice creams sold on a Saturday.

a How many people were in the survey?

b Draw a pictogram using the key to represent 4 ice creams.

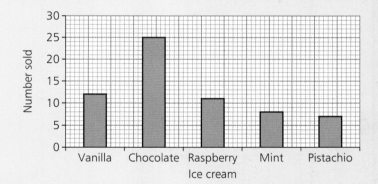

Solution

a The total number sold $= 12 + 25 + 11 + 8 + 7 = 63$.

b Vanilla: $12 \div 4 = 3$ pictures.

Chocolate: $25 \div 4 = 6\frac{1}{4}$ pictures.

Raspberry: $11 \div 4 = 2\frac{3}{4}$ pictures.

Mint: $8 \div 4 = 2$ pictures.

Pistachio: $7 \div 4 = 1\frac{3}{4}$ pictures.

Key: represents 4 ice creams.

> ### Study tip
>
> A pictogram uses the same picture for each category and the key shows what the picture represents.

Apply 12.2

1 The pictogram below shows the number of emails received by five friends one day.

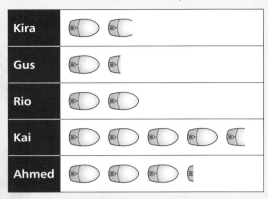

Key: represents 5 emails.

a How many emails did Kai receive?

b How many more emails did Ahmed receive than Rio?

c Show the information on a bar chart.

2 A library conducted a survey of the type of fiction books borrowed on one day. Here are the results:

Type	Frequency
Thriller	34
Romance	71
Science fiction	56
Detective	29

Show this information in a bar chart.

3 Below is a histogram showing the number of hours per week 30 athletes trained.

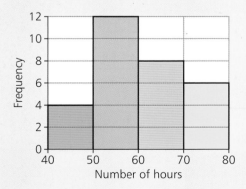

a How many athletes trained for more than 50 hours per week?

b Show the information in a pictogram, using to represent 4 athletes.

Learn 12.3 Pie charts and scatter diagrams

Pie charts

A **pie chart** is circular in shape. Pie charts show frequencies as proportions.

They are useful when representing a sample, where proportions are more important than the actual frequencies.

To construct a pie chart, the angle at the centre, 360°, must be divided into equal parts for each entry in the survey.

A survey of the colour of cars going past a school gave these results:

Car colour	Frequency
Red	3
White	7
Silver	9
Black	5

To put this information into a pie chart, we find the total size of the sample:

$3 + 7 + 9 + 5 = 24$

A full turn is 360°, so each car occupies $360 \div 24 = 15°$.

So the angles are:

Car colour	Frequency	Angle
Red	3	$3 \times 15 = 45°$
White	7	$7 \times 15 = 105°$
Silver	9	$9 \times 15 = 135°$
Black	5	$5 \times 15 = 75°$

And the pie chart looks like this:

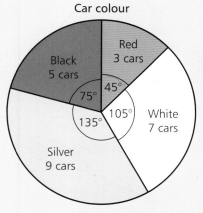

Car colour

Study tip

Before drawing the pie chart, make sure the angles add up to 360°.

Example

In a survey of 200 people, 45 chose 'orange' as their favourite fruit.

Calculate the size of angle for the orange sector.

Solution

Each person occupies $360 \div 200 = 1.8°$.

45 people will occupy $45 \times 1.8 = 81°$.

Scatter diagrams

Scatter diagrams are used to see if there is a connection, or **correlation**, between two sets of data.

A **positive correlation** means that high values of one feature are matched by high values of the other feature.

Scatter diagrams are constructed by plotting points on a graph.

Here are the reaches (or arm spans) and heights of 12 students:

Reach (cm)	148	170	155	160	162	168	165	160	157	152	163	158
Height (cm)	162	180	164	177	176	183	175	179	175	168	181	172

Here is the scatter diagram showing the information. The first student, with a reach of 148 cm and a height of 162 cm, is shown in blue.

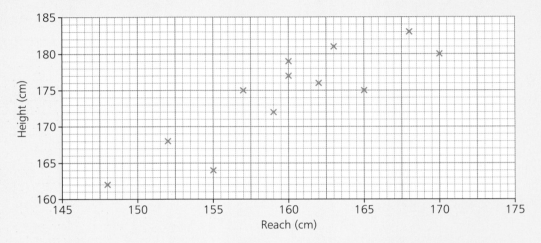

There is a positive correlation between the reach and height; as the height increases, so does the reach. You can see this because the points slope upwards from left to right.

In **negative correlation** points slope downwards from left to right indicating that as one quantity increases, the other decreases.

If the points do not appear to follow a trend, then there is **no correlation**.

Line of best fit

When a scatter diagram shows correlation, a **line of best fit** can be drawn. This is a straight line that goes between the points, passing as close as possible to all of them.

When the points are very close to a line of best fit, it is called a **strong correlation**. If the points are not all close to a line of best fit, it is a **weak correlation**.

A line of best fit can be used to make estimates as shown in the next example.

> **Study tip**
>
> Make sure the line of best fit has approximately equal numbers of points on either side of the line.

Example

The scatter diagram shows the number of hours students spend playing sport and the number of hours they spend watching television in a week.

a Describe the relationship between the hours spent playing sport and the hours spent watching television.

b Draw a line of best fit on the diagram.

c A student plays five hours of sport. Estimate the number of hours of television that he might watch.

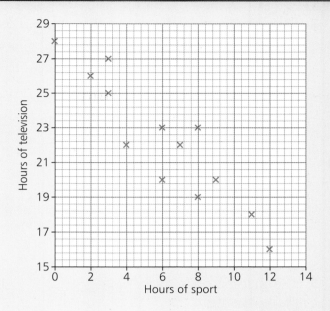

Solution

a As the graph slopes downwards from left to right, it is a negative correlation.

b The black line is a line of best fit.

c The red line shows that a student who plays five hours of sport might watch 23.3 hours of television per week.

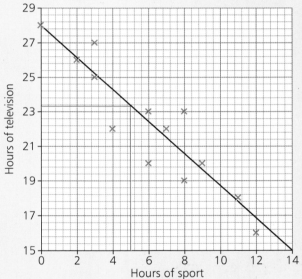

Apply 12.3

1 Karl carried out a survey of the colour of the front doors in his block of flats.

Here are his results.

Colour	Frequency
Red	2
Natural wood	14
White	11
Brown	3

a How many houses are there in Karl's block of flats?

b Show the results of his survey in a pie chart.

2 In a survey of favourite sports, four people chose cricket.

60 people were surveyed altogether.

What angle would represent cricket on a pie chart?

3 In a pie chart showing favourite ice cream, the angle for coconut is 54°.

40 people took part in the survey. How many chose coconut?

4 Describe the correlation shown in each of these diagrams.

a

b

c

5 The table below shows the value of a car according to its age.

Age (years)	1	2	3	4	5	6	7
Value ($)	12 000	9700	8100	6800	5700	4800	4100

a Show this information in a scatter diagram.

b Describe the correlation between age and value.

6 Below are the marks of 20 students in a maths test and a history test.

Student	1	2	3	4	5	6	7	8	9	10	11	12	13	14	15	16	17	18	19	20
Maths test	57	24	45	37	61	43	52	41	48	37	51	49	62	35	61	52	49	38	55	46
History test	56	35	46	38	55	40	45	46	46	33	45	44	57	41	56	50	47	41	51	44

a Show this information on a scatter diagram.

b Describe the relationship between the two sets of scores.

c Draw a line of best fit.

d Another student scored 43 in the maths test, but was absent for the history test. Use your scatter diagram to predict her likely score in the history test.

Assess 12.1–12.3

1 The pictogram shows the colour of 36 shirts in a store.

a Draw a key for the pictogram.

b Show the information in a bar chart.

2 Mona recorded the results of her hockey matches one season.

Here are her results.

Win	Draw	Draw	Win	Lose	Win	Lose	Win	Draw	Lose
Win	Win	Draw	Draw	Win	Lose	Win	Draw	Lose	Win
Lose	Win	Win	Draw	Win	Win	Lose	Win	Win	Draw

a Show this information on a tally chart.

b Draw a pie chart to show the information.

3 The histogram shows the number of seconds taken to complete a puzzle by 40 students.

The column for 45−50 seconds has not been completed.

a How many students completed the puzzle in 25 seconds or less?

b How many students took 40 seconds or less complete the puzzle?

c What should be the frequency for the 45 to 50 second column?

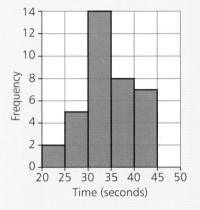

4 a Draw a scatter diagram to show this information about rainfall and average temperature in a holiday resort.

Month	Jan	Feb	Mar	Apr	May	Jun	Jul	Aug	Sep	Oct	Nov	Dec
Average temperature (°C)	5	6	9	12	16	20	24	23	19	14	8	6
Rainfall (cm)	4	3	4.5	4.4	4	2.5	1.5	2	2.5	5.5	4.5	4.8

b Describe the correlation between average temperature and rainfall.

5 In a survey, the number of cars and lorries passing a school were recorded for an hour.

Here are the results.

Time	9:00	9:10	9:20	9:30	9:40	9:50	10:00
Number of cars	15	9	7	14	18	16	
Number of lorries	8	5	5	11	12	13	

a Draw a histogram showing the number of cars passing the school every 10 minutes.

b Draw a scatter diagram showing the number of cars and number of lorries passing the school.

c Describe the correlation.

d Draw a line of best fit.

e Between 10:00 and 10:10, 12 cars passed the school. Use your diagram to estimate the number of lorries that went past the school between 10:00 and 10:10.

6 Three candidates stood in an election.

The table shows the votes each received.

Show this information on a pie chart.

Candidate	Votes received
A	46
B	51
C	23

13 Symmetry

Symmetry in two dimensions

Shapes with symmetry are used in many real contexts such as the patterns on tiles and fabrics and in company logos. This chapter considers two types of symmetry: line symmetry and rotational symmetry.

Learn 13.1 Line symmetry

When a 2-D shape can be folded so that one half fits exactly over the other, the shape is symmetrical and has **line symmetry**.

The fold line is called a line of symmetry.

You can use tracing paper to check that a shape has line symmetry.

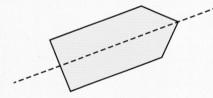
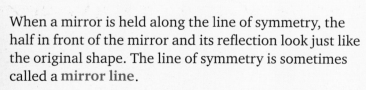
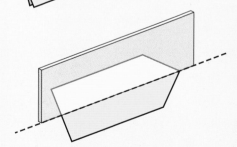

Trace the shape, then fold the tracing paper to see if the halves match.

When a mirror is held along the line of symmetry, the half in front of the mirror and its reflection look just like the original shape. The line of symmetry is sometimes called a **mirror line**.

Some shapes have more than one line of symmetry. Some shapes have no lines of symmetry.

Example

How many lines of symmetry does each shape have?

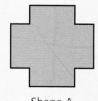
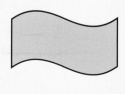

Shape A   Shape B

Solution

Each broken line on the diagram is a line of symmetry.

Shape A has four lines of symmetry.

Shape B has no lines of symmetry.
It is impossible to fold it so that one half fits exactly over the other.

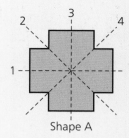

Shape A

Sometimes you may be asked to complete a diagram so that it becomes symmetrical.

Example

Complete the diagram so that the broken line is a line of symmetry.

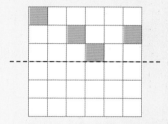

Solution

For each shaded square above the line of symmetry, there must be a matching square an equal distance below the line of symmetry.

The diagram shows the completed pattern.
You can check this answer by tracing and folding it.

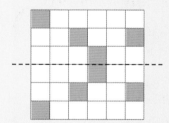

Study tip

Use tracing paper to check your answers.

Apply 13.1

1 For each shape, write down the number of lines of symmetry.

Shape A

Shape B

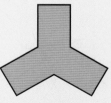

Shape C

Shape D

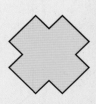

Shape E

2 On a copy of each letter, draw any lines of symmetry.

A D F H N T W X

3 For each road sign, write down the number of lines of symmetry.

No entry   One way   Priority road   Roundabout   Sharp left turn

4 Which of these shapes has:

    a no lines of symmetry   **b** one line of symmetry   **c** two lines of symmetry?

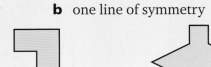

      Shape A   Shape B   Shape C   Shape D

5 Copy each grid onto squared paper.
    Shade more squares so that the broken line is a line of symmetry.

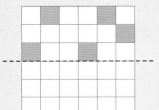   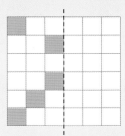   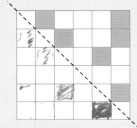

6 For each pattern, write down the number of lines of symmetry.

 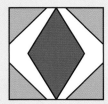 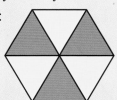 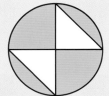

7 Copy each diagram onto squared paper.
    Complete each diagram so that the broken line is a line of symmetry.

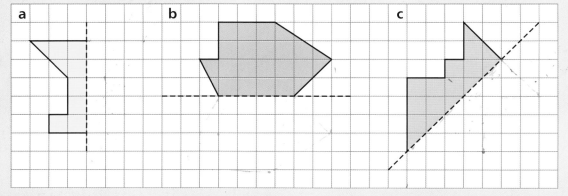

8 Make two copies of the diagram.

On the first copy, shade four triangles so that the result has two lines of symmetry.

On the second copy, shade four triangles so that the result has no lines of symmetry.

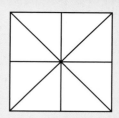

Learn 13.2 Rotational symmetry

All shapes look the same when they are rotated through 360°. When a 2-D shape looks exactly the same after a rotation of *less than* 360° then the shape has **rotational symmetry**. The shape's **order of rotational symmetry** is the number of different positions in which it looks the same during a complete turn.

A square has rotational symmetry of order 4. You can use tracing paper to check this.

1st position   2nd position   3rd position   4th position

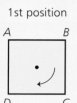 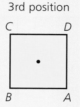 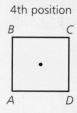

Rotating 90° about the centre gives the next position.   The square looks the same in all four positions.   After another rotation the square is back in its original position.

Example

Which of these shapes has rotational symmetry?

What is the order of rotational symmetry?

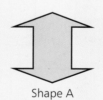 

Shape A   Shape B

Solution

When Shape A is rotated through 180° about its centre, it fits exactly on its original position. It looks the same whether it is in its original position or turned upside down.

Shape A has rotational symmetry of order 2.
Shape B has no rotational symmetry.

Shape B only looks the same in its original position.
(The order of rotational symmetry is 2.)

Sometimes you may be asked to complete a diagram so that it becomes symmetrical.

Example

Complete this diagram so that it has rotational symmetry of order 3 about the point *O*.

O

Solution

A whole turn = 360°. For the diagram to have rotational symmetry of order 3, the angle it will turn through when moving to its next position is 360° ÷ 3 = 120°.

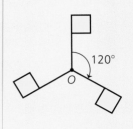

The diagram shows what happens if you rotate the flag by 120° about O, then another 120° about O.

This diagram has rotational symmetry of order 3.

You can check this by tracing the flags and rotating them about O.

> You can use a compass point to keep O in place when rotating the tracing paper.

Study tip

Use tracing paper to check your answers.

Apply 13.2

1 For each shape, write down the order of rotational symmetry.

Shape A

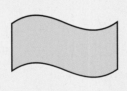

Shape B

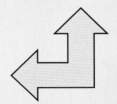

Shape C

Shape D

2 Which of these letters have rotational symmetry. Write down the order of rotational symmetry.

B H I L N S T X Z

3 For each road sign, write down the order of rotational symmetry.

Intersection

Roundabout

No stopping

Give way

No waiting

4 Find the order of rotational symmetry of each shape.

Shape A

Shape B

Shape C

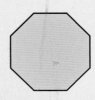

Shape D

5 Write down the order of rotational symmetry of each arrangement of flags.

a 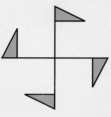 b 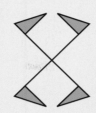 c 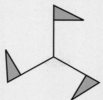 d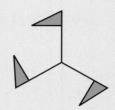

6 For each pattern, write down the order of rotational symmetry.

a 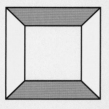 b 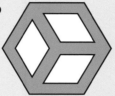 c 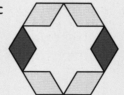 d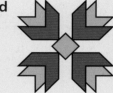

7 Make two copies of the diagram.

  a Add extra arrows to the first copy so that the result has rotational symmetry of order 8.

  b Add extra arrows to the second copy so that the result has rotational symmetry of order 2.

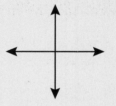

8 Make two copies of the diagram.

  a On the first copy, shade four triangles so that the result has rotational symmetry of order 4.

  b On the second copy, shade two triangles so that the result has rotational symmetry of order 2.

Learn 13.3 Special shapes and their symmetries

The symmetries of some special triangles and quadrilaterals are shown below:

Equilateral triangle

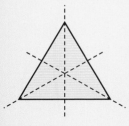

3 lines of symmetry
Rotational symmetry
of order 3

Isosceles triangle

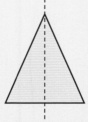

1 line of symmetry
No rotational symmetry
(order 1)

Scalene triangle

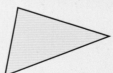

No lines of symmetry
No rotational symmetry
(order 1)

Square

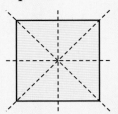

4 lines of symmetry
Rotational symmetry
of order 4

Rectangle

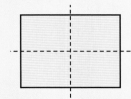

2 lines of symmetry
Rotational symmetry
of order 2

Rhombus

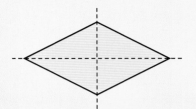

2 lines of symmetry
Rotational symmetry
of order 2

Parallelogram

No lines of symmetry
Rotational symmetry
of order 2

Trapezium

No lines of symmetry
No rotational symmetry
(order 1)

Isosceles trapezium

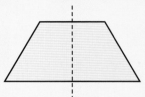

This shape has
two parallel
sides and two
equal sides.

One line of symmetry
No rotational symmetry
(order 1)

Kite

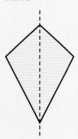

1 line of symmetry
No rotational symmetry
(order 1)

Circle

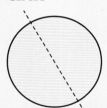

Every diameter of a circle is
a line of symmetry.

It looks the same when
rotated through any angle.

A circle has an infinite number of lines of symmetry.
The order of its rotational symmetry is also infinite.
(order ∞)

order ∞ means that there are an infinite
number of lines of symmetry.

You can sometimes use the symmetry of special shapes to work out other things about them.

Example

BD is a line of symmetry of triangle *ABC*. Use symmetry to find:

a the lengths of

   i *DC*   **ii** *AB*   **iii** the perimeter of triangle *ABC*.

b the size of

   i angle *ABD*   **ii** angle *BCD*   **iii** angle *BDA*.

c What special type of triangle is *ABC*?

To find angle *ABD*,
follow the letters.
This is angle *ABD*.

Solution

a   **i** $DC = AD = 8\,\text{cm}$ **ii** $AB = BC = 17\,\text{cm}$ **iii** Perimeter $= 17 + 17 + 8 + 8 = 50\,\text{cm}$

b   **i**   angle ABD = angle CBD
$= 28°$

   ii   angle BCD = angle BAD
$= 62°$

   iii   angle BDA = angle $BDC = 180° \div 2$
$= 90°$ (a right angle)

> Angles on a straight line add up to 180°, so angle BDA + angle $BDC = 180°$.

c   Triangle ABC is isosceles (because it has just one line of symmetry).

Apply 13.3

1 a   What is the name of the triangle that has no lines of symmetry?

    b   Draw and name the type of triangle that has: **i**   one line of symmetry
                                                             ii   three lines of symmetry.
    On each diagram, show which sides and angles are equal.

2 a   For each part, give the geometrical name of a quadrilateral that fits the description.

      i   It has four lines of symmetry and rotational symmetry of order 4.

     ii   It has one line of symmetry but no rotational symmetry.

    iii   It has rotational symmetry of order 2 but no lines of symmetry.

    b   **i**   Draw and name two special types of quadrilateral that both have two lines of symmetry and rotational symmetry of order 2.

      ii   Mark the sides and angles on each diagram to show which are equal.

3   The diagonal PR is a line of symmetry of kite $PQRS$.

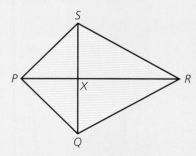

    a   Which side of the kite is equal in length to   **i** PQ?   **ii** SR?

    b   Name an angle that is equal in size to: **i**   angle PSQ **ii**   angle PSR.

        The diagonals PR and QS meet at the point X.

    c   Use symmetry to find angle PXS.

    d   What special type of triangle is QRS?

4 In each triangle below, the broken line is a line of symmetry. Use symmetry to find:
   i the size of lettered angles marked by letters
   ii The perimeter of the triangles.

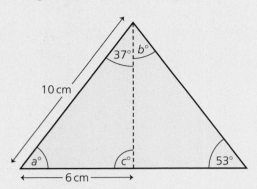

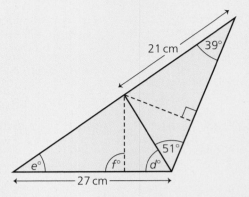

5 Draw each of the quadrilaterals described below on squared paper.

   a *ABCD* has just one line of symmetry, *AC*.

   b *PQRS* has four equal sides and two lines of symmetry, *PR* and *QS*.

   In each case: **i** write down the geometrical name of the shape
               ii state the order of rotational symmetry of the shape
              iii name a pair of equal angles.

Assess 13.1–13.3

1 For each shape, write down: **i** the number of lines of symmetry
                            ii the order of rotational symmetry.

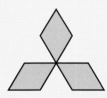

Shape A   Shape B   Shape C   Shape D

2 Copy these symbols.
   In each case draw all the lines of symmetry.

        =

3 a i Draw a sketch to show that it is possible to have a triangle that is both right-angled and isosceles. On your sketch, show the line of symmetry and the right angle.

   ii What is the order of rotational symmetry of this triangle?

   b i Draw and name two special types of quadrilateral that have rotational symmetry of order 2.

   ii On each sketch draw all the lines of symmetry of the quadrilateral.

4 For each pattern, write down **i** the order of rotational symmetry
 ii the number of lines of symmetry.

a   b   c   d

5 Copy and complete the table.

Name of shape	Number of lines of symmetry	Order of rotational symmetry
Isosceles triangle		
Equilateral triangle		
Square		
Rectangle		
Rhombus		
Parallelogram		
Trapezium		
Isosceles trapezium		
Kite		

6 **a** On a square grid, draw a quadrilateral that has exactly one line of symmetry.
Draw the line of symmetry as a broken line.

b On your diagram, show all the pairs of equal sides and angles.

c What is the special name for the quadrilateral that you have drawn?

7 Copy each grid onto squared paper.
Shade more squares so that the result has the symmetry written under the grid.

a 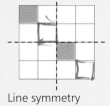 b   c

Line symmetry   Line symmetry   Rotational symmetry
in both broken lines.   in the broken line.   of order 4 about C.

8 **a** For this diagram, write down:

  i the order of rotational symmetry
  ii the number of lines of symmetry.

 b **i** On a copy of the diagram, shade two triangles so that the result
 has just two lines of symmetry.

  ii Write down the order of rotational symmetry of your diagram.

 c **i** On another copy of the diagram, shade two triangles so that the
 result has just one line of symmetry.

  ii Write down the order of rotational symmetry of your diagram.

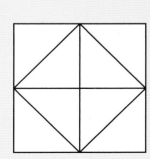

14 Geometry

Learning outcomes:

After this chapter you should be able to:

- use and interpret the geometrical terms: point, line, parallel, right angle, acute, obtuse and reflex angles, perpendicular, similarity, congruence
- use and interpret vocabulary of triangles and quadrilaterals
- calculate unknown angles using:
  - angles at a point
  - angles at a point on a straight line and intersecting straight lines
  - angles formed within parallel lines
  - angle properties of triangles and quadrilaterals.

In this chapter you will use geometrical properties to work out the size of angles.

You will also work out the lengths of sides in some two-dimensional shapes.

Measuring angles and lengths will be covered in a later chapter.

Learn 14.1 Angles

When two or more **lines** meet at a **point**, **angles** are formed.

Angles are measured in **degrees**. They can be used to describe rotations.

A full turn is 360°

A half turn is 180°

A quarter turn is 90°

Line

Point

90° is often called a **right angle** and is shown on diagrams like this:

Two lines at right angles are said to be **perpendicular**.

Other terms that describe the size of angles are given below:

An **acute** angle is less than 90°.

An **obtuse** angle is greater than 90° but less than 180°.

A **reflex** angle is greater than 180° but less than 360°.

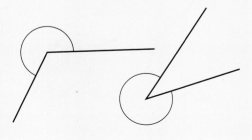

You can sometimes work out the size of angles using the following facts:

Angles at a point add up to 360°	Angles on a straight line add up to 180°	Vertically opposite angles are equal

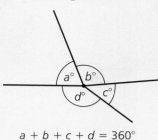

$a + b + c + d = 360°$

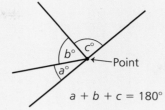

$a + b + c = 180°$

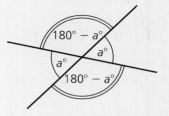

Note that $b = 180 - a$

Note that the equal angles are marked in the same way.

Example

Find the values of a, b, c and d.

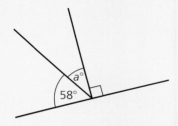

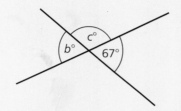

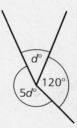

Solution

Adding the two known angles gives $58° + 90° = 148°$

$a + 148 = 180$ Angles on a straight line add up to 180°.

$a = 180 - 148$

$a = 32$

$b = 67$ Vertically opposite angles are equal.

$c = 180 - 67$ Angles on a straight line add up to 180°.

$c = 113$

$5d + d + 120 = 360$ Check: $5d + d + 120 = 200 + 40 + 120 = 360$ ✓

$6d + 120 = 360$ Angles at a point add up to 360°.

$6d = 360 - 120$

$6d = 240$

$d = \dfrac{240}{6}$

$d = 40$

Study tip

Check that your solution agrees with the original information.

For a reminder of solving equations see Learn 9.3.

Parallel lines

Parallel lines never meet. They are the same distance apart everywhere along their length. Arrows are used to show that lines are parallel. (Learn 23.2 shows how to use a set square to draw parallel lines.)

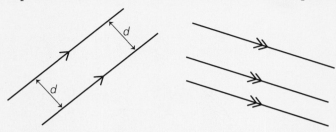

A **transversal** is a line that cuts two or more parallel lines. Some of the angles it makes with the parallel lines are equal.

Alternate angles are equal
$a = c$ and $b = d$

Corresponding angles are equal
$a = e, b = f, c = g$ and $d = h$

Interior angles add up to 180°
$a + d = 180$ and $b + c = 180$

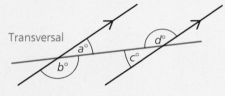

Look for a ⟋ or ⟍ shape

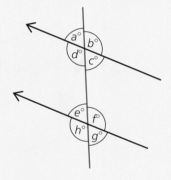

Look for a ⊢ or ⊣ shape

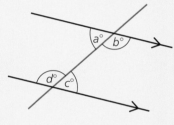

Look for a ⌐ or ⌐ shape

Example

Find the value of each letter. Give a reason for each answer.

a

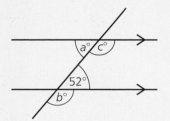

b

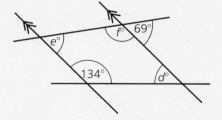

Solution

a $a = 52$ — Alternate angles are equal.

$b + 52 = 180$ — Angles on a straight line add up to 180°.
$\quad b = 180 - 52 = 128$

$c = b = 128$ — Corresponding angles are equal.

b $d + 134 = 180$ — Interior angles add up to 180°.
$\quad\quad d = 180 - 134 = 46$

$e = 69$

$f + e = 180$

$\quad f = 180 - 69 = 111$

> Corresponding angles are equal.

> Interior angles add up to 180°.

> Often there is more than one way to find the answer. Here angles on a straight line could be used instead.

Note that $d°$ and 134° are interior angles, but $e°$ and 134° are not.

Study tip

Take care as you must only use these rules with *parallel* lines.

Apply 14.1

1 Reflex   Right   Acute   Obtuse

Use one of the above terms to describe each of the angles given.

a 120°   **b** 240°   **c** 90°   **d** 190°   **e** 65°

2 Find the size of each angle marked by a letter, giving a reason for each answer.

In each case say whether the angle is acute, obtuse or reflex.

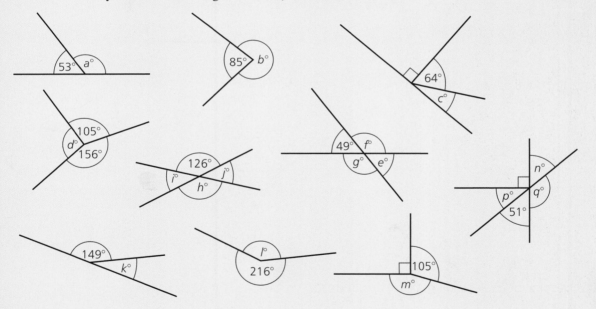

3 Find the value of each letter.

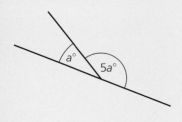 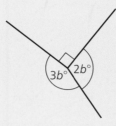 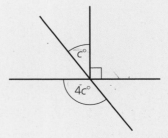

4 **a** Write down an equation in x and y.

   b Find y when $x = 40$.

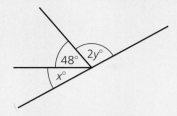

5 **a** Write down an equation in a and b.

   b Find a when $b = 3a$.

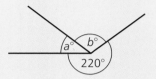

6 Write down the value of each letter. Give a reason for each answer.

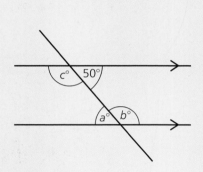
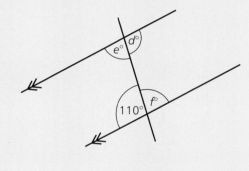

7 Find the value of each letter. Give a reason for each answer.

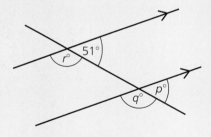
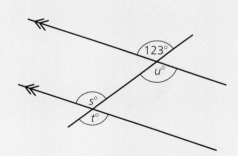

8 Find the size of each angle marked by a letter. Give a reason for each answer.

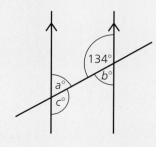
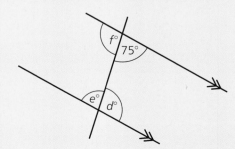

9 Work out the value of each letter. Give a reason for each answer.

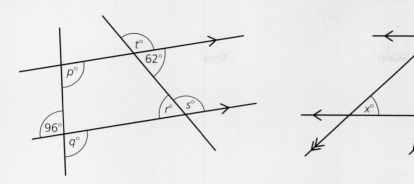

Angles of a triangle

Try this:

- Draw a triangle on paper. Cut it out.
- Shade each angle a different colour.
- Tear off the corners of the triangle and place them next to each other as shown.
- They should lie on a straight line.

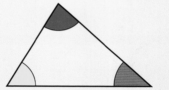

This shows that **the angles of a triangle add up to 180°**.

Angles of a quadrilateral

The diagram shows a quadrilateral, *PQRS*, split into two triangles.

The angles of triangle *PQR* add up to 180° and the angles of triangle *PRS* add up to 180°.
Adding these shows that **the angles of a quadrilateral add up to 360°**.

Example

Work out the size of each angle marked by a letter.

a

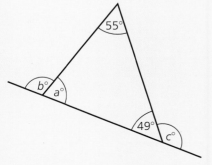

b

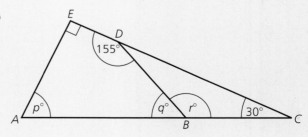

Solution

a $a + 49 + 55 = 180$ | Angle sum of a triangle = 180° |
  $a + 104 = 180$
    $a = 180 - 104 = 76$

  $b + 76 = 180$ | Angles on a straight line = 180° |
    $b = 180 - 76 = 104$

  $c + 49 = 180$ | Angles on a straight line = 180° |
    $c = 180 - 49 = 131$

b $p + 90 + 30 = 180$ | Angle sum of triangle ACE = 180° |
    $p = 180 - 120 = 60$

  $60 + q + 90 + 155 = 360$ | Angles of quadrilateral $ABDE$ = 360° |
    $q + 305 = 360$
      $q = 360 - 305 = 55$

  $55 + r = 180$ | Angles on straight line at B = 180° |
    $r = 180 - 55 = 125$

Apply 14.2

1 Find the size of each angle marked by a letter.

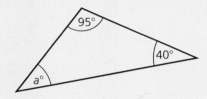

2 Calculate the value of each letter.

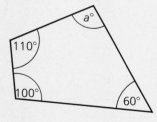
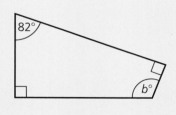
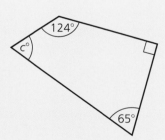

3 Work out the size of each angle marked by a letter. Give a reason for each answer.

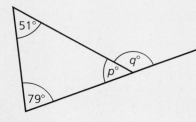
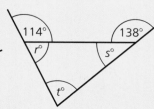
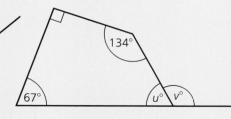

4 Find the value of each letter.

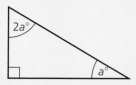
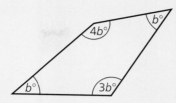
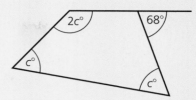

5 Work out the size of each angle marked by a letter. Give a reason for each answer.

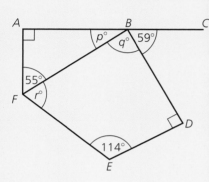
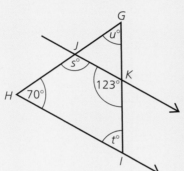
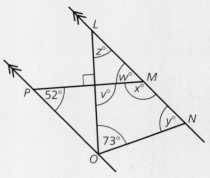

Learn 14.3 Special triangles and quadrilaterals

When all of the angles of a triangle are less than 90°, it is called an **acute-angled triangle**.
When one of the angles of a triangle is 90°, the triangle is called a **right-angled triangle**.
When one of the angles is more than 90°, it is called an **obtuse-angled triangle**.

Some of the other special triangles and quadrilaterals that you have met before are shown below.
This time the diagrams show properties related to the sides and angles of the shapes.
(Compare these diagrams with those in Learn 13.3 that show the symmetries of these shapes.)

Equilateral triangle

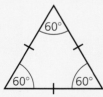

All sides equal
Each angle is 60°

Isosceles triangle

Two equal sides
Two equal angles

Scalene triangle

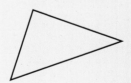

All sides different
All angles different

Square

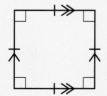

All sides equal
Opposite sides parallel
Each angle is 90°

Rectangle

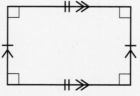

Opposite sides equal
Opposite sides parallel
Each angle is 90°

Rhombus

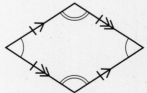

All sides equal
Opposite sides parallel
Opposite angles equal

Parallelogram

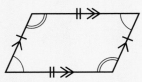

Opposite sides equal
Opposite sides parallel
Opposite angles equal

Trapezium

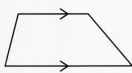

One pair of sides parallel
(In an isosceles trapezium
the non-parallel sides are equal)

Kite

Two pairs of adjacent
sides equal
One pair of equal angles

Congruence and similarity

When two shapes are exactly the same shape and size, they are said to be **congruent**.

When two shapes are the same shape but a different size, they are said to be **similar**.

For example, triangle *PQR* is congruent to triangle *ABC*. The order of the letters tells you which angles and sides are equal.

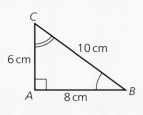

Writing the triangles as $\frac{PQR}{ABC}$ can help you see which angles are equal.

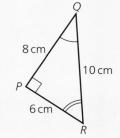

Also $PQ = AB$, $QR = BC$ and $RP = CA$.

Triangles $\frac{XYZ}{ABC}$ are similar.

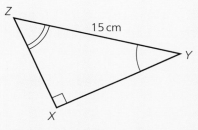

Angle X = angle A, angle Y = angle B and angle Z = angle C.

Corresponding sides are in the same ratio.

This means that $\frac{XY}{AB} = \frac{YZ}{BC} = \frac{ZX}{CA}$ or $\frac{AB}{XY} = \frac{BC}{YZ} = \frac{CA}{ZX}$.

Using the lengths given on the diagram: $\frac{XY}{8} = \frac{15}{10} = \frac{ZX}{6}$ (1)

Knowing one side of triangle *XYZ* means that you can work out the others:

> Using the fractions with the unknown sides in the numerators makes the working easier.

$\frac{XY}{8} = \frac{15}{10}$ simplifies to $\frac{XY}{8} = \frac{3}{2}$

Multiplying by 8 gives $XY = \frac{24}{2} = 12$ cm

> The sides of triangle *XYZ* are all one-and-a-half times as long as the corresponding sides in triangle *ABC*. The sides of triangle *ABC* are all $\frac{2}{3}$ of the corresponding sides in triangle *XYZ*.

Also: $\frac{ZX}{6} = \frac{3}{2}$ so $ZX = \frac{18}{2} = 9$ cm

Example

a What special type of triangle is *ABC*?

b Work out the values of *x*, *y* and *z*.

c Name an obtuse-angled triangle in the diagram.

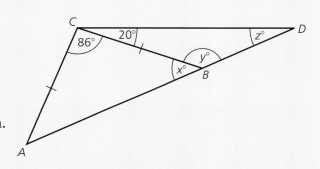

Solution

a Triangle *ABC* is isosceles because two of its sides are equal.

b Angle *CAB* = angle *CBA* = $x°$ | Equal angles of an isosceles triangle |

$$x + x + 86 = 180$$ | Angle sum of a triangle = 180° |
$$2x = 180 - 86$$
$$2x = 94$$
$$x = \frac{94}{2} = 47$$

$$y + 47 = 180$$ | Angles on a straight line = 180° |
$$y = 180 - 47 = 133$$

$$z + 133 + 20 = 180$$ | Angle sum of a triangle = 180° |
$$z = 180 - 153 = 27$$

c Angle *y* is obtuse, so triangle *BCD* is an obtuse-angled triangle.

[Hint: Angle *ACD* = 106°, so triangle *ACD* is also obtuse-angled.]

Example

a Find the size of the angles marked by letters.

b What special type of triangle is *BCD*?

c What special type of quadrilateral is *ABDE*?

d Name a triangle that is congruent to triangle *ABE*.

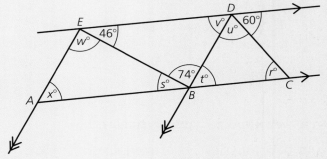

Solution

a $r = 60$ | Alternate angles, since *ED* is parallel to *AC* |

    $s = 46$ | Alternate angles, since *ED* is parallel to *AC* |

    $t + 74 + 46 = 180$ | Angles on a straight line = 180° |
           $t = 180 - 120 = 60$

    $u + 60 + 60 = 180$ | Angle sum of triangle *DBC* = 180° |
           $u = 60$

    $v = t = 60$ | Alternate angles, since *ED* is parallel to *AC* |

    $w = 74$ | Alternate angles, since *AE* is parallel to *BD* |

    $x = t = 60$ | Corresponding angles, since *AE* is parallel to *BD* |

b *BCD* is an equilateral triangle. | All of its angles are 60°. |

c The opposite sides of *ABDE* are parallel, so is *ABDE* is a parallelogram.

d Triangle *DEB* is congruent to triangle *ABE*. Both triangles have equal sides and angles.

Apply 14.3

1 Find the value of each letter. Give reasons for your answers.

 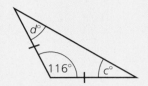 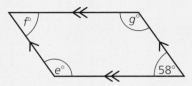 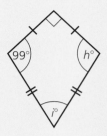

2 All the sides of quadrilateral *ABCD* are equal. Angle *ABC* = 100°.

   a Draw a sketch of *ABCD*.

   b What is the special name of the quadrilateral *ABCD*?

   c Find the size of all the other angles of *ABCD*.

3 **a** What is the special name of the quadrilateral *PQRS*?

   b Name the line of symmetry.

   c **i** Calculate angle *SRQ*.
      ii What is the special name for this size of angle?

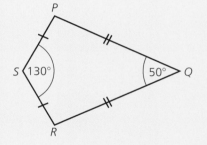

4 **a** What special type of triangle is *BCD*?

   b What special type of quadrilateral is *ABDE*?

   c Work out the size of all the angles in each shape.
     Give a reason for each answer.

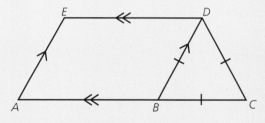

5 **a** What is the special name given to triangle *PQR*?

   b Work out the values of *a*, *b*, *c*, *d* and *e*.
     Give reasons for your answers.

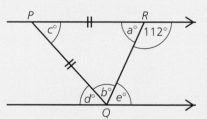

6 *ABCD* is a rectangle. The diagonals *AC* and *BD* intersect at a point *E*.

   a Draw a sketch of *ABCD*.

   b Name a triangle that is congruent to triangle *AED*.

   c Name a triangle that is congruent to triangle *AEB*.

   d Name three triangles that are congruent to triangle *ABC*.

7 a Find the following angles. Give reasons for your answers.

    i Angle *ACB*   **iii** Angle *DEC*

    ii Angle *ABC*   **iv** Angle *CDE*

b Give a reason why triangles *ABC* and *EDC* are similar.

c *AB* = 20 cm, *BC* = 12 cm, *AC* = 16 cm and *DC* = 9 cm.
Calculate the length of *CE* and *DE*.

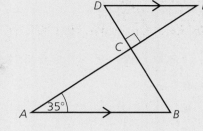

8 a Find the following angles. Give a reason for each answer.

    i Angle *PRQ*   **ii** Angle *PQR*   **iii** Angle *PST*

b Choose one of the following words to complete the statement:

    congruent   equilateral   isosceles   similar

    Triangle *PQR* and triangle *PST* are ………………

c *PR* = 2 cm, *QR* = 3 cm and *RT* = 4 cm.
Calculate the length of *ST*.

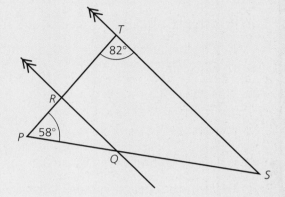

Assess 14.1–14.3

1 Calculate the value of each letter. Give a reason for each answer.

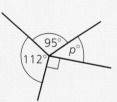

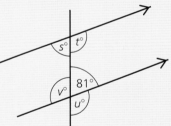

2 Work out the value of each letter. In each case give a reason for your answer.

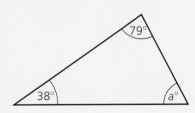

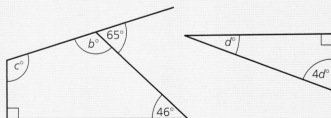

3 Find out the value of each letter. In each case give a reason for your answer.

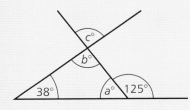

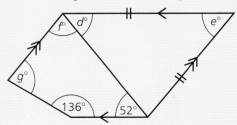

4 a Write down and simplify an equation in x and y.

   b Find x when y = 2x.

   c What type of angles are x° and y°?

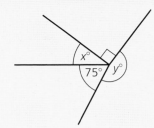

5 a Write down the geometrical name for:

   i a triangle that has two equal sides

   ii a quadrilateral with only one pair of parallel sides.

   b Find the values of x, y and z in the diagram. Give a reason for each answer.

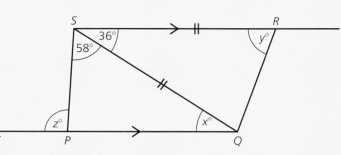

6 AC is a line of symmetry of quadrilateral ABCD.

   a What special type of quadrilateral is ABCD?

   b Find the size of the following angles, giving reasons for your answers:

   i angle ADB

   ii angle DAB

   iii angle BDC.

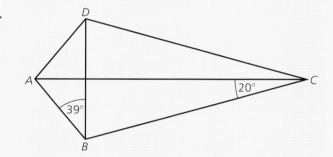

7 PQRS is a parallelogram. The diagonals PR and QS intersect at a point T.

   a Draw a sketch of PQRS.

   b Name a side that is equal in length to side PS.

   c Name an angle that is equal to angle PTQ.

   d Name a triangle that is congruent to triangle PTS.

8 a Find the following angles in the diagram:

   i angle BAC

   ii angle DCE

   iii angle DEC.

   b Copy and complete the following statement:
   Triangle ABC is .... to triangle EDC.

   c Calculate the length of:

   i AC   **ii** DE.

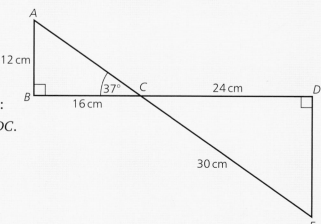

15 Percentages

Learning outcomes:

After this chapter you should be able to:
- calculate a given percentage of a quantity
- express one quantity as a percentage of another
- calculate percentage increase or decrease.

Learn 15.1 Percentage of a quantity

Changing percentages to fractions or decimals

In Learn 8.3 you found out how to change a percentage into a fraction or a decimal.

42% means 42 out of 100.

As a fraction, this is $\frac{42}{100}$.

Cancelling by 2 gives:

$$42\% = \frac{{}^{21}\cancel{42}}{\cancel{100}_{50}} = \frac{21}{50}$$

As a decimal, $42\% = \frac{42}{100} = 42 \div 100 = 0.42$

Units	.	Tenths	Hundredths
0	.	4	2

Example

Change the following percentages into:

i a fraction in its lowest terms **ii** a decimal.

a 4% **b** 12.5%

Solution

a **i** $4\% = \frac{4}{100} = \frac{1}{25}$

  ii $4\% = \frac{4}{100} = 4 \div 100 = 0.04$

Units	.	Tenths	Hundredths
0	.	0	4

b i $12.5\% = \dfrac{12.5}{100}$

$= \dfrac{25}{200}$ Double numerator and denominator to make both into integers.

$= \dfrac{5}{40} = \dfrac{1}{8}$

ii $12.5\% = \dfrac{12.5}{100} = 12.5 \div 100 = 0.125$

$12.5\% = 0.125$

Units	.	Tenths	Hundredths	Thousandths
0	.	1	2	5

Finding a percentage of a quantity

You saw in Learn 8.1 and 8.5 how to multiply by a decimal, and how to find a fraction of a quantity.

To find a percentage of a quantity you can change the percentage to a fraction or a decimal.

For example: find 35% of $24.   Remember that 'of' means 'multiplied by'.

Either use a fraction:

35% of $24 = $\dfrac{35}{100} \times$ $24

$= \$8.40$

Or use a decimal:

35% of $24 = 0.35 \times$ $24

$= \$8.40$

You should be able to work these out on a calculator.

> **Study tip**
>
> Make sure you know how to input fractions into your calculator.

Example

Yusuf has $450.

He spends 35% of it on a present for his mother.

How much does he have left?

Solution 1

He spends 35% of $450.

35% of $450 = $0.35 \times$ $450

$= \$157.50$ Remember that $157.5 on your calculator means $157.50

He has left: $450 − $157.50 = $292.50

Solution 2

He spends 35% of $450.

He has left: 100% − 35% = 65%

65% of $450 = $0.65 \times$ $450

$= \$292.50$

Apply 15.1

1 Change these percentages to fractions in their lowest terms:

   a 25%   **c** 24%   **e** 8%   **g** $3\frac{1}{3}\%$

   b 45%   **d** 80%   **f** 22.5%

2 Change these percentages to decimals:

   a 35%   **c** 20%   **e** 7%   **g** $37\frac{1}{2}\%$

   b 48%   **d** 60%   **f** 35.5%

3 Calculate:

   a 10% of $15   **c** 55% of $670   **e** 5% of $9.60

   b 90% of $20   **d** 15% of $16.20   **f** $7\frac{1}{2}\%$ of $42

4 A test has 120 questions. You need 70% to pass.
How many questions must you get correct?

5 Jill is a salesperson.
She sold a house for $120 000.
Jill earns 6% commission when selling a house.
How much did Jill earn by selling this house?

6 Put these questions into pairs with the same answer:

   a 27% of $40   **d** 90% of $30   **g** 18% of $60   **j** 75% of $20

   b 24% of $15   **e** 11% of $60   **h** 5% of $132   **k** 16% of $50

   c 37.5% of $40   **f** 5% of $540   **i** $8\frac{1}{3}\%$ of $96   **l** 60% of $6

Learn 15.2 Writing one quantity as a percentage of another

To write one quantity as a percentage of another:

- first, write it as a fraction
- then multiply by 100 to get a percentage.

Example

In a class, 18 students are right-handed and 5 are left-handed.
What percentage of the class is left-handed?

Solution

There are 18 + 5 = 23 students in the class.

So $\frac{5}{23}$ are left-handed.

$\frac{5}{23} \times 100\% = 21.7391304...\% = 21.7\%$ (to 1 d.p.)

Example

Dakarai grows tomato plants to sell.

The table shows the heights of his plants:

Height (x cm)	Frequency
$0 < x \leqslant 10$	1
$10 < x \leqslant 20$	4
$20 < x \leqslant 30$	14
$30 < x \leqslant 40$	18
$40 < x \leqslant 50$	17

a What percentage of the plants are more than 10 cm tall but no more than 20 cm tall?

b What percentage of the plants are taller than 30 cm?

c Dakarai can only sell plants that are greater than 20 cm tall.
 i How many plants can he sell?
 ii What percentage of the plants that he can sell are greater than 30 cm tall?

Solution

a There are $1 + 4 + 14 + 18 + 17 = 54$ plants.

 4 plants are between 10 cm and 20 cm tall.

 So $\frac{4}{54}$ are between 10 cm and 20 cm tall.

 $\frac{4}{54} \times 100\% = 7.407\%$
  $= 7.4\%$ (to 1 d.p.)

b $18 + 17 = 35$ plants are taller than 30 cm.

 $\frac{35}{54} \times 100\% = 64.814\%$
  $= 64.8\%$ (to 1 d.p.)

c **i** He has $14 + 18 + 17 = 49$ plants greater than 20 cm tall that he can sell.

 ii He has $18 + 17 = 35$ plants greater than 30 cm tall.

 $\frac{35}{49} \times 100\% = 71.428571\%$
  $= 71.4\%$ (to 1 d.p.)

Study tip

If necessary, round your answer to 1 decimal place.

Apply 15.2

1 What percentage is:
 a 12 students out of 30 students
 b 9 kg out of 20 kg
 c 12 books out of 60 books
 d 34 insects out of 85 insects?

2 Write these as percentages, correct to 1 decimal place:
 a $5 out of $11
 b 7 shells out of 23 shells
 c 400 g out of 3 kg [Hint: Change them to the same unit first.]
 d 19 bananas out of 21 bananas.

3 A bag contains 11 strawberry sweets, 9 chocolate sweets and 5 lemon sweets.
What percentage of the sweets are:

a strawberry   **b** chocolate   **c** lemon?

4 In a week, Una made 12 phone calls that lasted less than 1 minute.
She made 37 calls that lasted between 1 minute and 10 minutes, and 6 that lasted over 10 minutes.

a What percentage of her phone calls lasted less than 1 minute?

b Altogether, 12 of her calls lasted longer than 5 minutes.
What percentage of her calls lasted between 1 minute and 5 minutes?

5 The table below shows information about passengers on a plane:

	Male	Female
Under 20 years old	28	31
Aged 20 or older	77	64

a What percentage of the passengers are male?

b What percentage of the passengers are under 20 years old?

c What percentage of the passengers are males aged 20 or older?

d What percentage of the females are under 20 years old?

e What percentage of the passengers aged 20 or older are females?

Learn 15.3 Percentage increase and decrease

Prices can go up or down. Populations can go up or down.
The price of goods can go up or be reduced in a sale.
When a quantity or amount goes up, it is called an **increase**.
When a quantity or amount goes down, it is called a **decrease**.

Calculating the new amount

If the amount increases, add on the value of the increase.
If the amount decreases, subtract the value of the decrease.

Example

Chen buys an antique clock for $2400.

a During the next year, it increases in value by 8%.
Find the value of the clock after this increase.

b The following year, the value of the clock decreases by 8%.
Find the value of the clock after this decrease.

Solution

a The increase is 8% of $2400

$$= \frac{8}{100} \times \$2400$$

$$= \$192$$

The new value of the clock is $2400 + $192 = $2592

> Note that the two 8% values are not the same because they were of different amounts.

b The decrease is 8% of $2592

$$= \frac{8}{100} \times \$2592$$

$$= \$207.36$$

The new value of the clock is $2592 − $207.36 = $2384.64

Calculating the percentage

All percentage increases and decreases are calculated as percentages of the original value.

You must first calculate the increase or decrease.

Then calculate the increase or decrease as a percentage of the original amount.

Example

The population of a town over a 30-year period is shown in the table:

Year	1980	1990	2000	2010
Population	23 341	28 853	25 567	29 917

Find the percentage increase or decrease between the population in:

a 1980 and 1990 **b** 1990 and 2000 **c** 1980 and 2010.

Solution

a From 1980 to 1990 the population increased from 23 341 to 28 853.

The increase was 28 853 − 23 341 = 5512

As a fraction, this is $\frac{5512}{23\,341} = 0.2361509789...$

$0.2361509789... \times 100\% = 23.6\%$ (to 1 d.p.)

b From 1990 to 2000 the population decreased from 28 853 to 25 567.

The decrease was 28 853 − 25 567 = 3286

As a fraction, this is $\frac{3286}{28\,853} = 0.1138876373...$

$0.1138876373... \times 100\% = 11.4\%$ (to 1 d.p.)

c From 1980 to 2010 the population increased from 23 341 to 29 917.

The increase was 29 917 − 23 341 = 6576

As a fraction, this is $\frac{6576}{23\,341} = 0.2817360010...$

$0.2817360010... \times 100\% = 28.2\%$ (to 1 d.p.)

Apply 15.3

1 A dishwasher costs $320.
  In a sale the price is reduced by 25%.
  Calculate the sale price.

2 There are 40 fish in a pond.

  A disease kills 35% of them.
  How many fish are left?

3 Tak buys a car for $4500.
  She sells it a year later for $3825.
  Calculate the percentage loss.

4 Alayna buys a table for $120.
  She sells it for $144.
  Calculate her percentage profit.

5 Signe collects rainwater to water her garden.
  The table shows the depth of water each day:

Day	Sunday	Monday	Tuesday	Wednesday	Thursday	Friday	Saturday
Depth (cm)	57.4	63.8	68.1	64.0	59.5		56.2

  a Calculate the percentage increase in depth from Sunday to Monday.

  b Calculate the percentage decrease from Tuesday to Wednesday.

  c Calculate the percentage decrease from Monday to Saturday.

  d After heavy rain, there was a 12.3% increase from Thursday to Friday.
     Calculate the depth of water on Friday.

Assess 15.1–15.3

1 Calculate 35% of $56.

2 Toste is cooking.
  He opens a 1 kg bag of flour. He accidentally spills some. He has 745 g left.
  What percentage did he spill?

3 Nissa earns $53 400 per year. She pays $19 546 in tax.
  What percentage of her earnings is paid in tax?

4 A town had a population of 13 600 last year.

The population has increased by 5% this year.

What is the current population?

5 The number of students at a university increased from 2420 to 2783 in one year.
What was the percentage increase?

6 The number of visitors to a website averaged 2310 per day last month.

This month the number had decreased by 30%.

What was the average number of visitors per day this month?

7 Conrad buys a book for $9.20. He wants to sell it for a 20% profit.

How much should he sell it for?

8 A bank pays 3.5% interest.

If you invest $8100 for one year, how much interest will you earn?

9 Miksa has a salary of $55 000.

Her salary is increased by 6%. She has to pay 40% of her salary in taxes.

How much tax will she have to pay on her new salary?

10 The average number of people at a team's football matches last season was 23 465.

This season the average is 21 876.

a Calculate the percentage decrease.

b What percentage increase will the team need next year to reach last year's number?

16 Transformations 2

You need to be able to carry out and recognise four different types of transformation. In Chapter 10 you studied reflections and rotations. In this chapter you will study two other types of transformation: translation and enlargement.

Learn 16.1 Translation

In a **translation** the object moves across the page, but it is not rotated or reflected. Each point on the object has moved the same distance in the same direction.

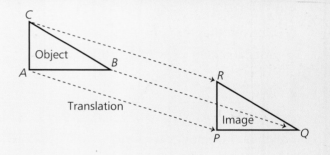

The order of the letters is important. In this case A moves to P, B moves to Q and C moves to R.

Sometimes a **vector** such as $\begin{pmatrix} 3 \\ 5 \end{pmatrix}$ is used to describe a translation.

A translation by vector $\begin{pmatrix} 3 \\ 5 \end{pmatrix}$ moves the object 3 units to the right (in the positive x-direction) and 5 units upwards (in the positive y-direction). The diagram shows flag F and its image, flag G, after this translation.

A translation by $\begin{pmatrix} -3 \\ -5 \end{pmatrix}$ moves the object 3 units to the left (in the negative x-direction) and 5 units downwards (in the negative y-direction). This translation maps flag G onto flag F.

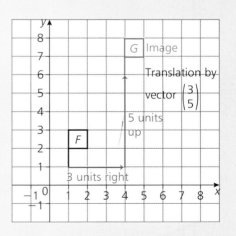

Example

a Plot the points $A(1, 2)$, $B(4, 3)$, $C(6, 2)$, $D(2, -3)$ and draw the quadrilateral $ABCD$.

b Draw the image of $ABCD$ after a translation by the vector $\begin{pmatrix} -7 \\ 4 \end{pmatrix}$.

Solution

a Quadrilateral *ABCD* is shown on the grid.

b Moving each vertex 7 units to the left and 4 units upwards gives the vertices of the image. Joining these vertices gives the image of quadrilateral *ABCD*.

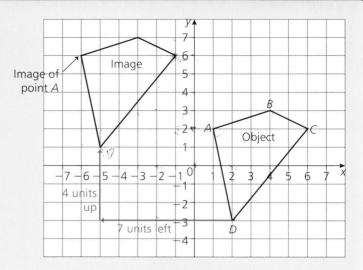

Apply 16.1

1 Copy the triangle *T* onto squared paper.

a On your diagram, draw the image of triangle *T* after translation by the vector $\begin{pmatrix} 5 \\ 3 \end{pmatrix}$.
Label this image *P*.

b On your diagram, draw the image of triangle *T* after translation by the vector $\begin{pmatrix} -4 \\ -2 \end{pmatrix}$.
Label this image *Q*.

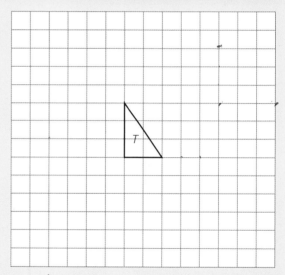

2 Copy these shapes onto squared paper.

a Translate shape *L* using the vector $\begin{pmatrix} -2 \\ 4 \end{pmatrix}$.
Label the image *M*.

b Translate shape *F* using the vector $\begin{pmatrix} 6 \\ -1 \end{pmatrix}$.
Label the image *G*.

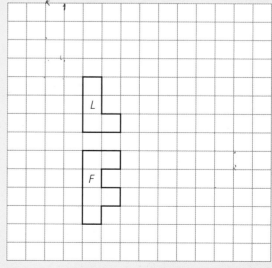

3 Copy the axes and trapezium *T* onto squared paper.

   a On your grid, draw the image of *T* after translation by $\begin{pmatrix} -7 \\ 2 \end{pmatrix}$. Label the image *A*.

   b On your grid, draw the image of *T* after translation by $\begin{pmatrix} 3 \\ -6 \end{pmatrix}$. Label the image *B*.

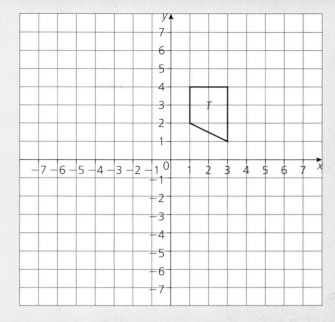

4 Copy the axes and flag *F* onto squared paper.

   a Draw the image of flag *F* after a translation by the vector $\begin{pmatrix} 8 \\ 6 \end{pmatrix}$. Label it *A*.

   b Draw the image of flag *F* after a translation by the vector $\begin{pmatrix} -4 \\ 7 \end{pmatrix}$. Label it *B*.

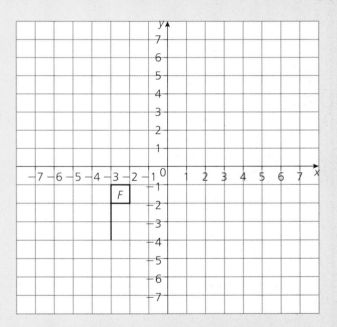

5 Shapes *A*, *B*, *C* and *D* are shown on the grid. Write down the vector that translates:

   a *A* to *B*   **c** *C* to *B*   **e** *D* to *B*

   b *A* to *C*   **d** *C* to *D*   **f** *B* to *A*

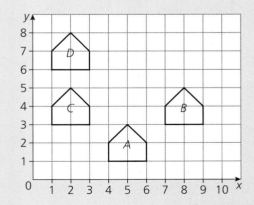

6 Kites K, L, M and N are shown on the grid.
Write down the vector that translates:

a K to L **d** N to M **g** L to N

b L to K **e** M to K **h** K to N

c M to N **f** K to M

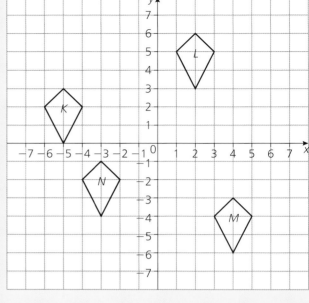

7 a On axes for x and y from -5 to 5, draw the triangle with vertices at $A(-2, 4)$, $B(-5, 2)$ and $C(-1, -1)$.

b A translation maps the triangle ABC onto triangle PQR, where P is the point $(4, 2)$.

  i Draw triangle PQR.

  ii Write down the vector that describes the translation.

  iii Write down the coordinates of the images of Q and R.

Learn 16.2 Enlargement

In an **enlargement**, the shape of an object stays the same, but its size usually changes. To carry out an enlargement you need a **scale factor** and a **centre of enlargement**.

The scale factor tells you how many times bigger the object is than the image. The lines joining each point of the object with its image all meet at the centre of enlargement.

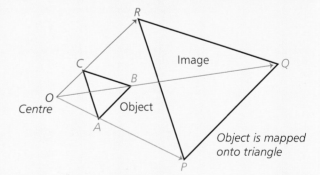

Triangle ABC is mapped onto triangle PQR by an enlargement with scale factor 3 and centre O.

$OP = 3 \times OA$, $OQ = 3 \times OB$ and $OR = 3 \times OC$

Triangles ABC and PQR are similar: their angles are equal and their sides are in the ratio $1 : 3$.

The centre of enlargement O is the point from which all the measuring is done.

When the scale factor of an enlargement is greater than 1, the image is bigger than the object.

When the scale factor of an enlargement is less than 1, the image is smaller than the object.

When the scale factor is 1, the image is the same size as the object.

Example

Points $P(1, 2)$, $Q(9, 2)$, $R(3, 8)$ and $S(1, 8)$ are the vertices of a trapezium.

Draw trapezium $PQRS$ and its image after an enlargement, centre $(3, 4)$, scale factor $\frac{1}{2}$.

Solution

The diagram shows trapezium $PQRS$. The centre of enlargement, labelled C, is inside the object.

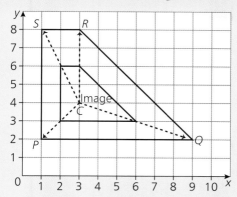

Each vertex of the image is half as far from C as the corresponding vertex of the object.

You can count squares or use a ruler to find the positions of these vertices.
Joining them gives the image.

Each side of the image is half as long as the corresponding side of the object.

When the scale factor of an enlargement is negative, measure from the centre in the opposite direction to find points on the image.

Example

The vertices of a quadrilateral are the points $A(-4, 1)$, $B(-1, 1)$, $C(0, 2)$ and $D(-4, 4)$.

Draw quadrilateral $ABCD$ and its image after an enlargement, scale factor -2, centre the origin.

Solution

The diagram shows the quadrilateral $ABCD$. To find the image:

1. Measure from 0 to A, then measure from 0 twice as far in the opposite direction.

2. Do this for all of the other vertices.

3. Join the images of the vertices to give the image of the quadrilateral.

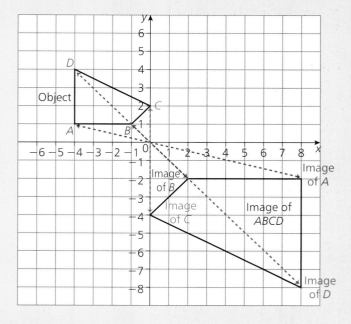

The image is twice as big as the object and upside down.

The next example gives the object and image and asks for a full description of the enlargement.

Example

Points $A(4, 5)$, $B(6, 5)$ and $C(4, 6)$ are the vertices of a triangle.

A transformation maps ABC onto triangle KLM with vertices at $K(1, -1)$, $L(9, -1)$ and $M(1, 3)$.

Give a full description of this transformation.

> **Study tip**
>
> To describe an enlargement you must give *two* pieces of information: the scale factor and the centre of enlargement.

Solution

The diagram shows that the image KLM is 4 times as big as triangle ABC.

The transformation is an enlargement with scale factor 4.

To find the centre of enlargement, draw lines that join each vertex to its image.

These lines meet at the centre of enlargement $(5, 7)$.

So the transformation is an enlargement with centre $(5, 7)$ and scale factor 4.

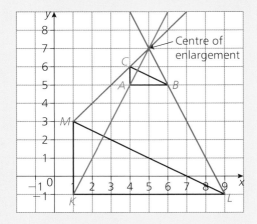

Apply 16.2

1 Copy the diagram onto squared paper.

  a Draw the image of triangle ABC after enlargement with centre O and scale factor 3.

  b Draw the image of trapezium $PQRS$ after enlargement with centre P and scale factor 2.

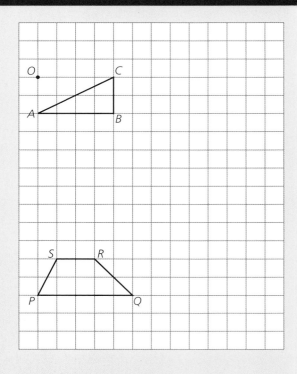

2 Copy the axes and kite *K* onto squared paper.

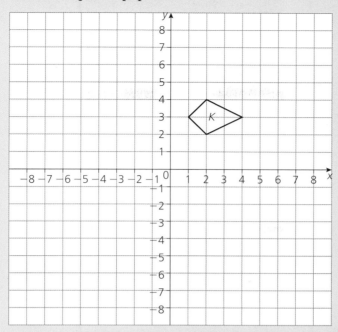

a Draw the image of *K* after enlargement, centre (0, 0), scale factor 2. Label it *A*.

b Draw the image of *K* after enlargement, centre (8, 3), scale factor 2. Label it *B*.

c Draw the image of *K* after enlargement, centre (1, 7), scale factor 2. Label it *C*.

3 Copy the axes and triangle *ABC* onto squared paper.

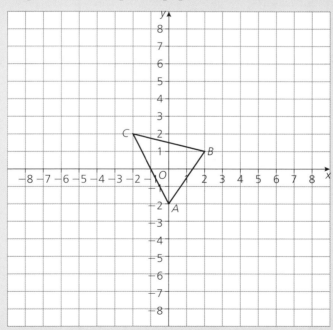

a Draw the image of *ABC* after enlargement, centre *O* and scale factor 4.
Label this image *P*.

b Draw the image of *ABC* after enlargement, centre *A* and scale factor 2.
Label this image *Q*.

4 Copy the diagram onto squared paper.

   a Draw the image of shape *S* after enlargement, centre *O* and scale factor $\frac{1}{2}$. Label it *A*.

   b Draw the image of trapezium *T* after enlargement, centre *O* and scale factor $\frac{1}{3}$. Label it *B*.

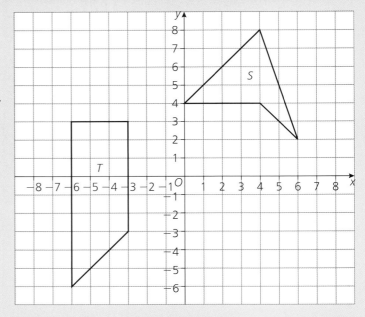

5 Copy the axes and triangle *PQR* onto squared paper.

   a Draw the image of *PQR* after enlargement, centre *O* and scale factor 2. Label this image *A*.

   b Draw the image of *PQR* after enlargement, centre *O* and scale factor −2. Label this image *B*.

   c Draw the image of *PQR* after enlargement, centre *O* and scale factor $\frac{1}{2}$. Label this image *C*.

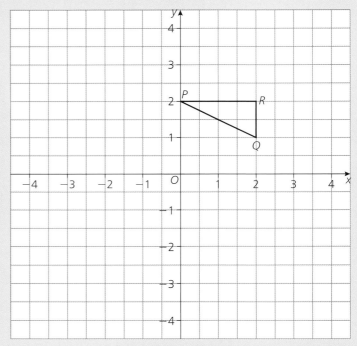

6 **a** On axes for *x* and *y* from −8 to 8, join the points (2, 2), (4, 2), (4, 3), (3, 4) and (2, 3) to give a shape with five sides. Label this shape *A*.

   b Draw the enlargement of *A* with centre (3, 1), scale factor −3. Label this image *B*.

   c Draw the enlargement of *A* with centre (1, 3), scale factor −3. Label this image *C*.

7 Use *x* and *y* axes from −8 to 8 for this question.

   a Points $A(-1, 8)$, $B(-1, 6)$ and $C(1, 5)$ are the vertices of a triangle.
A transformation maps *ABC* onto triangle *XYZ* with vertices at $X(1, 8)$, $Y(1, 2)$ and $Z(7, -1)$.
Give a full description of this transformation.

b Plot and label the following points:

$P(-7, -7), Q(5, -3), R(-3, 1), S(-7, -3), K(-4, -4), L(-1, -3), M(-3, -2), N(-4, -3)$.

A transformation maps quadrilateral *PQRS* onto quadrilateral *KLMN*.

Give a full description of this transformation.

Learn 16.3 Recognising and describing transformations

You have now met four different types of transformation: reflection, rotation, translation and enlargement.

You must be able to recognise and describe the transformation which maps an object onto a given image. It is important to give all the details that are needed to describe the transformation fully.

Transformation	Full description must give:
Reflection	• the position of the mirror line (see Learn 10.1)
Rotation	• the angle of rotation • the direction (clockwise or anticlockwise) • the centre of rotation (see Learn 10.2)
Translation	• the vector (or the distance and direction)
Enlargement	• the scale factor • the centre of enlargement

Study tip

Remember to give a full description of the transformation.

Example

Describe fully the single transformation which maps:

a *S* onto *A*   **c** *S* onto *C*   **e** *S* onto *E*   **g** *S* onto *G*

b *S* onto *B*   **d** *S* onto *D*   **f** *S* onto *F*.

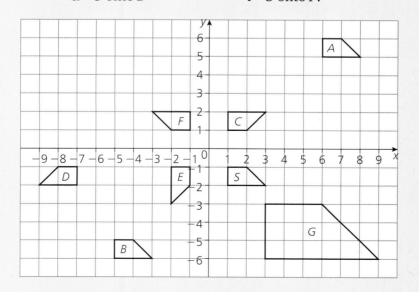

Solution

a When S is mapped onto A, it moves 5 squares to the right (in the positive x-direction) and 7 squares upwards (in the positive y-direction).
The transformation that maps S onto A is a translation by the vector $\begin{pmatrix} 5 \\ 7 \end{pmatrix}$.

b In the mapping from S to B, the shape moves 6 squares to the left (in the negative x-direction) and 4 squares downwards (in the negative y-direction).
The transformation that maps S onto B is a translation by the vector $\begin{pmatrix} -6 \\ -4 \end{pmatrix}$.

c The transformation that maps S onto C is a reflection in the x-axis.

> Remember that to describe a reflection fully you need to give the mirror line.

d The transformation that maps S onto D is also a reflection.
The mirror line must be the same distance from S as it is from D.
The transformation that maps S onto D is reflection in the line $x = -3$.

e The transformation that maps S onto E is a rotation of 90° clockwise about the point $(0, 0)$.

> You can use tracing paper to check that the centre is at the point $(0, 0)$.

Study tip

Remember that a full description of a rotation must include *three* things: the angle, the direction and the centre of rotation.

f The transformation that maps S onto F is also a rotation.
The shape has been turned upside down, so you could give the angle as 180° clockwise or anticlockwise. The centre is again the point $(0, 0)$.
The transformation that maps S onto F is a rotation of 180° clockwise (or anticlockwise) about the origin.

g The sides of shape G are three times as long as those of shape S. The transformation that maps S onto G is an enlargement with scale factor 3.

> To find the centre of an enlargement, draw lines joining each vertex on the object to its image. These lines meet at the centre.

To describe the enlargement fully, you must also give the centre. In this case the centre is the point $(0, 0)$.

The transformation that maps S onto G is an enlargement with scale factor 3 and centre $(0, 0)$.

Study tip

Remember that a full description of an enlargement must include *two* things: the scale factor and the centre of enlargement.

Apply 16.3

1 Describe fully the single transformation that maps triangle *T* onto:

a *A*   **b** *B*   **c** *C*   **d** *D*   **e** *E*   **f** *F*.

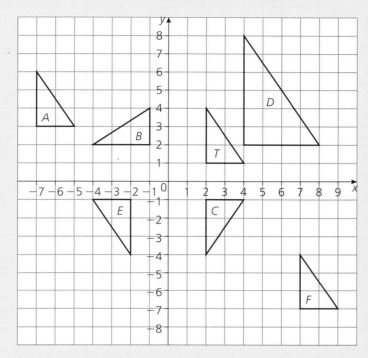

2 Describe fully the single transformation that maps:

a *P* onto *Q*   **c** *P* onto *S*   **e** *R* onto *T*
b *P* onto *R*   **d** *P* onto *T*   **f** *R* onto *S*.

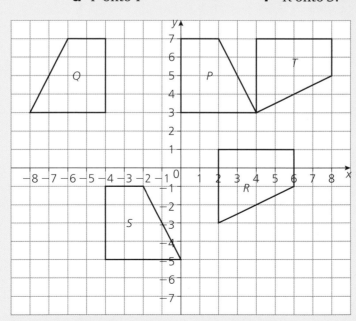

3 Describe fully the single transformation that maps:

  a   *P* onto *Q*   **c**   *F* onto *G*   **e**   *L* onto *M*

  b   *T* onto *U*   **d**   *R* onto *S*   **f**   *J* onto *K*.

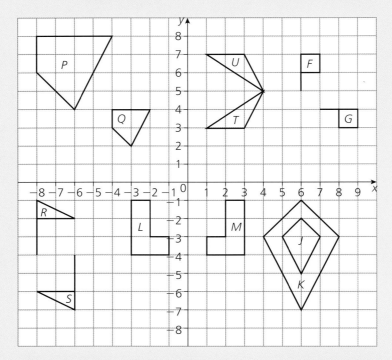

4 Describe fully three different single transformations that map rhombus *A* onto rhombus *B*.

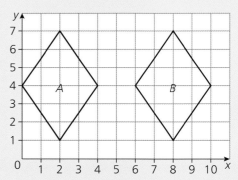

5 Describe fully the single transformation which maps the shaded triangle *ABC* onto:

  a   triangle *EBC*

  b   triangle *IGH*

  c   triangle *AFH*

  d   triangle *ADC*.

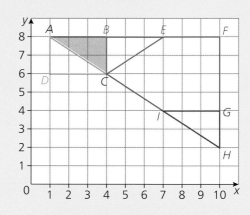

Assess 16.1–16.3

1 Copy flag F onto squared paper.

a Translate F using the vector $\begin{pmatrix} 4 \\ 3 \end{pmatrix}$. Label the image A.

b Translate F using the vector $\begin{pmatrix} -1 \\ -3 \end{pmatrix}$. Label the image B.

c Translate F using the vector $\begin{pmatrix} 5 \\ -2 \end{pmatrix}$. Label the image C.

d Translate F using the vector $\begin{pmatrix} -4 \\ 2 \end{pmatrix}$. Label the image D.

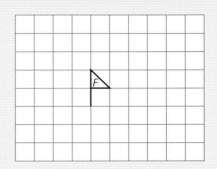

2 Copy triangle PQR onto squared paper.

a Draw the enlargement of triangle PQR, centre O, with scale factor 2. Label the image A.

b Draw the enlargement of triangle PQR, centre C, with scale factor 3. Label the image B.

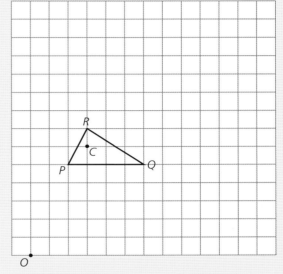

3 Copy the axes and shapes onto squared paper.

a Draw the enlargement of shape T, centre (0, 0), with scale factor $\frac{1}{2}$. Label the image A.

b Draw the enlargement of shape H, centre (6, −2), with scale factor $\frac{1}{3}$. Label the image B.

c Draw the enlargement of shape L, centre (0, 0), with scale factor −2. Label the image C.

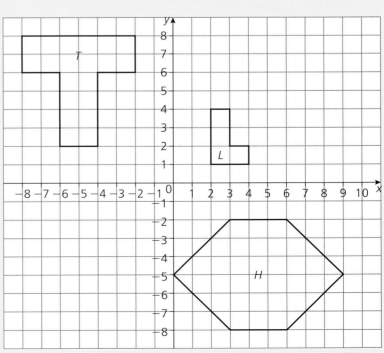

4 Describe fully the single transformation that maps:

  a A onto B
  b C onto D
  c E onto F
  d G onto H.

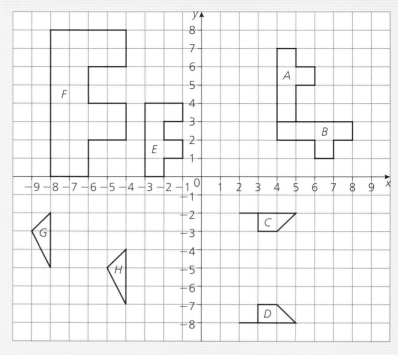

5 Describe fully the single transformation that maps trapezium T onto:

  a A   **f** F
  b B   **g** G
  c C   **h** H
  d D   **i** I.
  e E

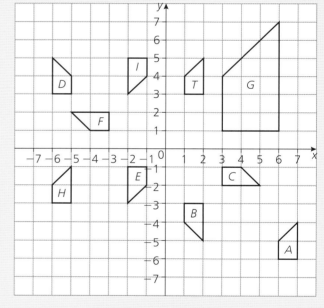

6 Describe fully two different single transformations that map parallelogram P onto parallelogram Q.

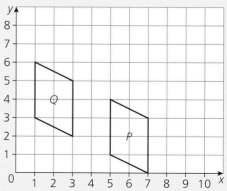

Practice exam questions

1 Marsha plays hockey.

Her team's results for 24 games are shown below:

Win	Win	Draw	Lose	Win	Lose	Draw	Win
Draw	Lose	Win	Win	Win	Lose	Win	Lose
Lose	Draw	Lose	Draw	Lose	Win	Win	Draw

a Complete the frequency table. *(3 marks)*

Result	Tally	Frequency
Win		
Draw		
Lose		

b Show this information in a pie chart. *(3 marks)*

2 Some children take a test. The table below shows the time it took each child to complete the test, and how many correct answers they gave.

Time (minutes)	8	6	1	4	7	2	5	6	2	4	6	4	9	5
Number of correct answers	11	13	19	15	12	17	13	12	15	16	14	13	13	14

a The first seven children's data have been marked on the scatter graph.

Complete the scatter graph. *(1 mark)*

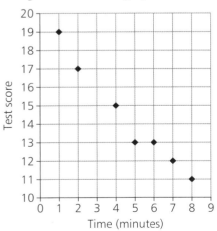

b Describe the correlation. *(2 marks)*

c Draw a line of best fit on your scatter graph.

Use it to estimate the test score of a child who took 3 minutes to complete the test. *(2 marks)*

3 For the shape shown, write down:

    a the number of lines of symmetry   (*1 mark*)

    b the order of rotational symmetry.   (*1 mark*)

4 **a** Write down the order of rotational symmetry of this shape.   (*1 mark*)

    b From the list, write down the numbers which have **two** lines of symmetry.

        0   1   2   3   7   8   (*2 marks*)

5 **a** Winston makes square tiles like the one shown.

    For this tile, write down:

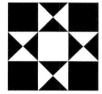

    i the number of lines of symmetry   (*1 mark*)

    ii the order of rotational symmetry.   (*1 mark*)

    b A quadrilateral has rotational symmetry of order 2 and no lines of symmetry.

    Write down the geometrical name of this shape.   (*1 mark*)

6 Copy this diagram.

Complete the diagram accurately so that it has rotational symmetry of order 3 about the point O.   (*2 marks*)

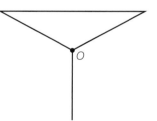

7 Reflex   Right   Acute   Obtuse

Use one of the above terms to describe each of the angles given.

    a $120°$ (*1 mark*)

    b $240°$ (*1 mark*)

8 The diagram shows the side view of the roof of a house.

AB and *DE* are horizontal. *DF* is vertical.

Find the value of

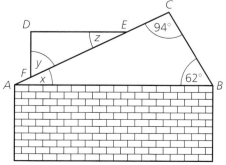

    a x (*1 mark*)

    b y (*1 mark*)

    c z (*1 mark*)

NOT TO SCALE

9 In the diagram *QR* is parallel to *ST*.

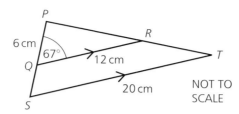

a What special type of quadrilateral is *QRTS*? (*1 mark*)

b Copy and complete the following statement.

Triangle *PQR* is ………………….. to triangle *PST*. (*1 mark*)

c *PQ* = 6 cm, *QR* = 12 cm and *ST* = 20 cm.
Calculate the length of *PS*. (*2 marks*)

d Angle *PQR* = 67°.
Calculate the size of the reflex angle at *S*. (*2 marks*)

10 Peter earns $350 per week.
He pays 22% in tax, and spends $125 on food.

a Calculate the amount of tax he pays. (*2 marks*)

b Calculate the percentage of his earnings that he spends on food. (*2 marks*)

11 Write down three of the numbers below that have the same value.

3% $\frac{3}{10}$ 0.03 $\frac{1}{3}$ 33%   0.3 $\frac{3}{100}$ (*3 marks*)

12 The price of a television is $350.

In a sale it is reduced by 20%.

Calculate the sale price. (*3 marks*)

13 A store has a sign in the window that says

An item that had cost $25.60 is priced
at $22 in the sale.

Kirsty complains to the store owner.

She says that 15% of $25.60 = $\frac{15}{100}$ × $25.60 = $3.84, but the price has only been reduced by $3.60.

The store owner says that it has been reduced by $3.60, which is $\frac{360}{22}$ × 100 = 16.36...%

Who is correct, Kirsty or the store owner? Explain your answer. (*3 marks*)

14   Each diagram below shows a shaded letter and its image.
     In each case describe fully the single transformation which maps the **shaded** figure onto its image.

a

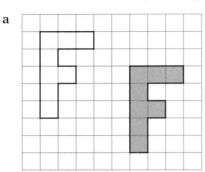

(*3 marks*)

b

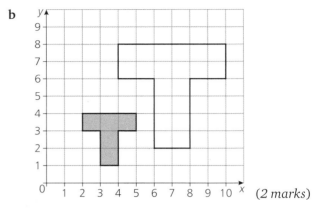

(*2 marks*)

15   The shapes *T*, *A* and *B* are drawn on the grid.

   a   In each case describe fully the single
           transformation which maps

       i   *T* onto *A*   (*3 marks*)

       ii *T* onto *B*.   (*2 marks*)

   b   Copy the grid and *T*. Draw on your grid:

       i   the image of *T* after rotation through
               90° clockwise about (0, 0).

               Label your answer *R*.   (*2 marks*)

       ii the image of *T* after enlargement
               centre (0, 0) with scale factor $\frac{1}{2}$.

               Label your answer *E*.   (*2 marks*)

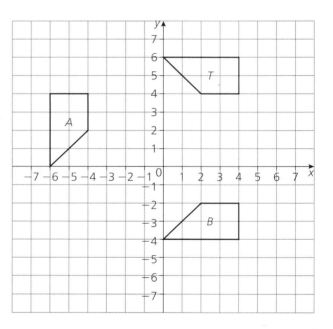

17 Probability

Learning outcomes:

After this chapter you should be able to:

- understand and use the probability scale from 0 to 1
- calculate the probability of a single event as a fraction or decimal
- understand relative frequency.

Probability is the study of chance. It allows you to determine how likely something is.

Probability started with games of chance.

In 1654, a Frenchman, Antoine Gombaud, wanted to see how likely it was to get at least one 'double six' during 24 throws of two dice.

He asked two famous mathematicians, Blaise Pascal and Pierre de Fermat to help, and so they created probability theory.

Learn 17.1 Probability and probability scale

Probability is part of everyday conversation. People say 'I think it's going to rain', 'I have no chance of passing my maths test', or 'I expect I'll win the tennis match'.

Probability is the measure of how likely an **outcome** is.

Something that is **impossible** has a probability of 0.

A **certain** outcome has a probability of 1. All other probabilities lie between 0 and 1.

Probabilities can be represented by marking the position on a **probability scale**.

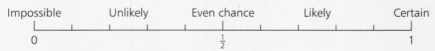

Example

Put arrows on the probability scale to show the probability of these outcomes:

a You will have two birthdays this year.

b You toss a coin and it lands on heads.

Solution

a This is impossible as you cannot have two birthdays.

b This is an even chance, as heads and tails are equally likely.
The arrows show these outcomes on the probability scale:

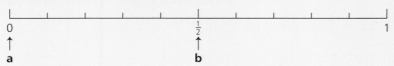

Equally likely outcomes

There are a number of ways of calculating probabilities. When two or more outcomes have the same probability, they are called **equally likely outcomes**.

For example: a **fair** coin is just as likely to land on heads or tails.

A fair dice is just as likely to land on a 1, or a 2, or a 3, or a 4, or a 5, or a 6.

These are equally likely outcomes.

Using equally likely outcomes to calculate probabilities

This spinner has five equal sections:

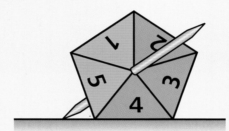

When you spin the spinner, it can stop with any one of the five edges touching the table. All five of these outcomes are equally likely.

Suppose you want to calculate the probability of the **event** that the spinner will stop on a green section.

The spinner has 3 green sections and the total number of sections is 5.

So, the probability of the spinner stopping on a green section is $\frac{3}{5}$. This is how you would write a score of 3 out of 5.

When all the possible outcomes are equally likely,

$$\textbf{probability of an event} = \frac{\textbf{number of outcomes for the event}}{\textbf{total number of outcomes}}$$

You can write probabilities as fractions, decimals or percentages.

For example: you could say the probability is $\frac{3}{5}$, 0.6 or 60%.

The probability of the spinner stopping on an even number is $\frac{2}{5}$, because 2 of the 5 numbers are even (2 and 4).

A short way of writing

'The probability of the spinner stopping on an even number' is P(even) $= \frac{2}{5}$.

The probability of the spinner landing on red, P(red), is $\frac{2}{5}$. This is because there are 2 red sections out of 5.

The other 3 sections are not red, so P(not red) is $\frac{3}{5}$.

Probability of an outcome not happening $= 1 -$ probability of an outcome happening

Example

A bag contains 10 coloured balls.

7 of them are blue.

Dave takes one ball out of the bag at random.

What is:

a P(blue)

b P(not blue)?

Solution

a 7 out of the 10 balls are blue, so the probability of the ball being blue is $\frac{7}{10}$.

P(blue) $= \frac{7}{10}$

b P(not blue) $= 1 - $ P(blue) $= 1 - \frac{7}{10} = \frac{3}{10}$

> **Study tip**
>
> You can write probabilities as fractions, decimals or percentages.

Apply 17.1

1 State whether each of these events is impossible, unlikely, even chance, likely or certain.

   a A newborn baby will be a boy.

   b An athlete will run the 100 m race in less than a second.

   c You will get wet if you stand in the rain.

2 Mark these events on a probability scale:

   a The President of the United States of America will visit this school next week.

   b My teacher will speak in the next 30 minutes.

   c My teacher will jump up in the air three times in the next 30 minutes.

3 A fair coin is tossed.
What is the probability of it landing on heads?

4 The diagram shows a fair square spinner.
What is the probability of it landing on red?

5 A mixed hockey team has 7 girls and 4 boys.
The captain is chosen at random.
Write down the probability that the captain is:

   a a boy   **b** a girl.

6 A box contains 40 pencils. 12 are red, 20 are black and the rest are blue.

   a How many blue pencils are there in the box?

   b If a pencil is chosen at random, what is the probability that the pencil is:

      i red   **ii** black   **iii** blue?

7 Jeffrey has a bag containing red, green, yellow and orange sweets.
The table shows the probabilities of choosing a red, green or yellow sweet:

Colour	Red	Green	Yellow	Orange
Probability	0.3	0.15	0.35	

   What is the probability that Jeffrey chooses an orange sweet?

8 A six-sided dice with sides numbered 1, 2, 3, 4, 5 and 6 is rolled. What is the probability of it landing on:

   a a three

   b an even number

   c a prime number

   d an even number or an odd number

   e an even number or a prime number?

9 Dagmar has a set of 20 cards numbered from 1 to 20.
She picks out a card and then replaces it in the pack.
What is the probability that the number on the card is:

   a a four   **b** even   **c** bigger than 15?

10 The probability that my football team will win its next game is $\frac{3}{8}$. The probability that we will lose is $\frac{1}{8}$. What is the probability that we draw?

Learn 17.2 Experimental probability

Not all outcomes are equally likely. For example, when you drop a drawing pin, the pin may land with the point up or the point down.

To find out whether a drawing pin is more likely to land with the point up or the point down, you need to experiment.

The position on the right is more likely than the position on the left, so these two outcomes are not equally likely

These experiments are called **trials**.

Trials can be used to work out a fraction that is similar to the one used for equally likely outcomes:

relative frequency $= \dfrac{\text{number of successful outcomes}}{\text{total number of trials}}$

If an experiment is repeated a large number of times, the relative frequency becomes the **experimental probability**.

The number of trials that you need to find the experimental probability depends on the number of possible outcomes. It should be about 50 times the number of possible outcomes.

For example, a **biased** coin has only *two* possible outcomes, so 100 trials should be enough. However, a biased dice has *six* possible outcomes, so you would need 300 as trials.

Example

Kris works in a factory testing circuit boards for MP3 players.

Here are his results for last week:

Day	Monday	Tuesday	Wednesday	Thursday	Friday	Saturday
Number tested	220	200	220	130	280	150
Number faulty	11	8	5	8	12	6

a   What is the experimental probability of a circuit board being faulty on Monday?

b   What is the experimental probability of a circuit board being faulty over the whole week?

c   There were 10 000 circuit boards made altogether last week. How many are likely to be faulty?

Solution

a   On Monday, there were 11 faulty circuit boards out of 220, so P(faulty) is $\frac{11}{220} = \frac{1}{20}$

b   Over the whole week, there were 50 faulty out of 1200, so P(faulty) is $\frac{50}{1200} = \frac{1}{24}$

c   You can expect $\frac{1}{24}$ of 10 000 of the circuit boards made last week to be faulty, or 417 to the nearest whole number.

Apply 17.2

1   Astrid throws a dice and records how many times she gets a one.
   After 30 throws, she has scored 4 ones.
   After 60 throws, she has scored 9 ones.
   After 300 throws, she has scored 45 ones.
   After 600 throws, she has scored 104 ones.
   Astrid wants to find out if his dice is fair or biased.

   a   What is the theoretical probability of scoring a one?

   b   What was her experimental probability of scoring a one after:
      i 30 throws   **ii** 60 throws   **iii** 300 throws   **iv** 600 throws?

   c   Do you think her dice is fair or biased? Explain your answer.

2   Jasmine has a bag containing some counters.
   She tries an experiment where she takes a counter, makes a note of its colour and then puts it back in the bag.
   She does this 100 times with these results:

Colour	Yellow	Green	Red	Blue
Frequency	37	25	23	15

   There are 13 counters in the bag.
   How many of each colour is there likely to be?

3 Hamish, Rita and Melissa all did an experiment to find the probability of a spinner landing in a red section.

Here are their results:

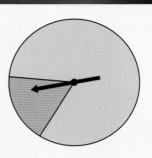

	Red	Green
Hamish	22	120
Rita	35	200
Melissa	7	50

a Whose results are likely to be the most accurate? Give a reason for your answer.

b Find the experimental probability of the spinner landing on red using:

　i the results of the person you chose in part **a**

　ii all the results added together.

4 Tania rolls a dice 500 times. Here are her results:

Score	1	2	3	4	5	6
Frequency	73	103	64	101	63	96

Explain why the experiment suggests that the dice is biased.

Assess 17.1 – 17.2

1 Copy the probability scale and mark the probabilities of these events on it with arrows.

a A rolled dice landing on a number greater than two.

b A tossed coin landing on heads.

c Choosing the yellow counter at random from a bag containing 9 red counters and 1 yellow counter.

2 A dice is rolled. What is the probability of getting:

a a five
b an even number
c a number less than five?

3 A bag contains 1 white, 3 black and 6 blue beads. What is the probability of a bead selected at random being:

a white
b not white
c black or white?

4 Here are six numbered cards:

1　2　2　3　4　5

A card is chosen at random. What is the probability that the number on it is:

a odd
b a 2
c not 2
d prime
e even or prime?

5 A dice is numbered 1, 2, 2, 3, 3, 3.

Abby rolls the dice 100 times with these results:

Score	1	2	3
Frequency	15	36	49

  a What is the theoretical probability of it landing on 1?

  b What is the experimental probability of it landing on 1?

  c What is the theoretical probability of it landing on 2?

  d What is the experimental probability of it landing on 2?

6 A farmer has the choice of buying seed A or seed B.

To help him decide which seed is better, he plants some of each as an experiment.

Here are his results:

Seed	Number that grow	Number that die
A	43	7
B	34	6

  a Based on his experiment, what is the probability of:
    i a type A seed growing
    ii a type B seed growing?

  b Which type of seed is better?

  c Another farmer used type B seed. How many seeds out of 5000 would you expect to grow?

18 Measures

Learning outcomes:

After this chapter you should be able to:

- state the current units of length, mass and capacity
- convert between metric units
- use these units in practical problems
- know and understand how to change between units for area, volume and capacity.

The metric system is used throughout the world.

In this chapter you will use the metric units for length, area, volume, mass and capacity.

You will also learn how to convert from one unit to another.

Learn 18.1 Metric units

Length or distance is measured in:

- kilometres (km)
- metres (m)
- centimetres (cm)
- millimetres (mm).

Mass or weight is measured in:

- tonnes (t)
- kilograms (kg)
- grams (g)
- milligrams (mg).

Capacity is a measure of how much a container can hold.

Capacity is measured in:

- litres (l)
- centilitres (cl)
- millilitres (ml).

When you want to measure something, you must choose the most appropriate or best unit to use.

Example

Which unit of length would you choose to measure the following in?

Choose from the list.

   Kilometres (km)   Metres (m)   Centimetres (cm)   Millimetres (mm)

a The distance from Sydney to Melbourne.

b The length of a cricket bat.

c The length of a football pitch.

d The diameter of a button.

Solution

a Kilometres. It is a long way from Sydney to Melbourne.

b Centimetres. A cricket bat is not large enough to be measured in metres. Think of the length of a ruler, rulers are usually 30 cm long.

c Metres. A football pitch is not large enough to be measured in kilometres.

d Millimetres. Most buttons are quite small.

Converting between metric units

To convert or change from one unit to another, you multiply or divide by a **conversion factor**.

You are expected to know the following conversions between metric units.

Length

1 kilometre = 1000 metres	(1 km = 1000 m)
1 metre = 1000 millimetres	(1 m = 1000 mm)
1 metre = 100 centimetres	(1 m = 100 cm)
1 centimetre = 10 millimetres	(1 cm = 10 mm)

Mass

1 tonne = 1000 kilograms	(1 t = 1000 kg)
1 kilogram = 1000 grams	(1 kg = 1000 g)
1 gram = 1000 milligrams	(1 g = 1000 mg)

Capacity

1 litre = 1000 millilitres	(1 l = 1000 ml)
1 litre = 100 centilitres	(1 l = 100 cl)
1 centilitre = 10 millilitres	(1 cl = 10 ml)

Look at the above lists carefully.

The metric system is based on the number 1000.

Kilo means 1000 as in 1000 m = 1 km and 1000 kg = 1 tonne

Milli means $\frac{1}{1000}$ as in 1 mm = $\frac{1}{1000}$ m, 1 mg = $\frac{1}{1000}$ g and 1 ml = $\frac{1}{1000}$ litre

Centi means $\frac{1}{100}$ as in 1 cm = $\frac{1}{100}$ m and 1 cl = $\frac{1}{100}$ litre

Example

Convert 2500 cl to litres.

Solution

1 litre = 100 cl

So   100 cl = 1 litre | Rearrange so that the unit given in the question is first. |

2500 cl = 25 × 1 litre | Multiply both sides by 25. |

= 25 litres.

Example

Elijah travels 7500 m to school every morning. He travels the same distance home in the afternoon.

He goes to school every weekday, Monday to Friday.

How many kilometres does he travel to and from school in a week?

Solution

In one day, Elijah walks

$$2 \times 7500 \text{ m} = 15\,000 \text{ m}$$

In one week, Elijah walks

$$5 \times 15\,000 \text{ m} = 75\,000 \text{ m}$$
$$1 \text{ km} = 1000 \text{ m}$$

So $\quad 1000 \text{ m} = 1 \text{ km}$ | Rearrange so that the unit given in the question is first.

$$1 \text{ m} = \tfrac{1}{1000} \text{ km}$$
$$75\,000 \text{ m} = 75\,000 \times \tfrac{1}{1000} \text{ km} \quad | \text{ Multiply both sides by 75 000.}$$
$$= 75 \text{ km}$$

You could also work this out by converting 7500 metres to kilometres, and then multiplying the number of kilometres by 2 and then 5.

This will give you the same answer.

Example

A decorator is tiling a kitchen floor.

He is using square tiles 25 cm by 25 cm.

A plan of the floor is shown here.

a How many tiles would he need to completely cover the kitchen floor?

He decides to order an extra 4% of tiles just in case he breaks some whilst laying them.

b How many tiles will he need to order altogether?

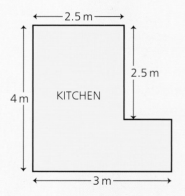

Solution

a **A** is a square 2.5 m by 2.5 m = 250 cm by 250 cm.
$$250 \text{ cm} \div 25 \text{ cm} = 10$$

So 10 tiles will fit along the length and 10 tiles will fit along the width.

Number of tiles needed for **A** = 10 × 10 = 100.

B is a rectangle 3 m by 1.5 m = 300 cm by 150 cm.
$$300 \text{ cm} \div 25 \text{ cm} = 12 \text{ and } 150 \text{ cm} \div 25 \text{ cm} = 6$$

So 12 tiles will fit along the length and 6 tiles will fit along the width.

Number of tiles needed for **B** = 12 × 6 = 72.

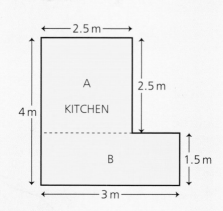

Total number of tiles needed to cover kitchen floor = 100 + 72 = 172.

b Extra tiles needed = 4% of 172

$$= \frac{4}{100} \times 172$$

$$= 6.88 \text{ tiles}$$

He will order an extra 7 tiles.

Total number of tiles needed = 172 + 7 = 179 tiles.

Apply 18.1

1 Which unit of mass would you choose to measure the following in?
Choose from the list.

　　Tonnes (t)　　Kilograms (kg)　　Grams (g)　　Milligrams (mg).

　a The weight of a sack of potatoes.　　**c** The weight of a lorry.

　b The weight of a grain of rice.　　**d** The weight of a banana.

2 Convert these lengths to centimetres.

　a 60 mm　　　　**b** 7 m　　　　**c** 625 mm　　　　**d** 2.004 m

3 Convert these capacities to litres.

　a 300 cl　　　　**b** 272 cl　　　　**c** 15 000 ml　　　　**d** 3754 ml

4 Convert these weights to grams.

　a 8000 mg　　　　**b** 3 kg　　　　**c** 2750 mg　　　　**d** 0.4 kg

5 Copy and complete the following, filling in the missing units.

　a 4000 ___ = 4 kg　　　　　　**e** 0.12 kg = 120 ___

　b 2753 ml = 2.753 ___　　　　**f** 7.1 cl = 71 ___

　c 0.2 m = 200 ___　　　　　　**g** 6 t = 6000 ___

　d 6.2 km = 6200 ___　　　　　**h** 2.7 ___ = 2700 mm

6 A lorry weighs 8 tonnes. How many grams is this?
[Hint: Convert to kilograms first and then to grams.]

7 A truck travels 7 kilometres. How many centimetres is this?

8 Tumo owns a restaurant. He buys a 2.5 kg pack of rice. One serving of rice is 75 g.
How many people can he serve from this pack?

9 How many 65 ml glasses can be filled from a bottle holding 3.25 litres of water?

10 How many 60 mm pieces of wood can be cut from a piece of wood 3.6 metres long?

11 A sweet potato weighs, on average, 190 g. How many whole sweet potatoes do you get in
a 2 kg bag?

Learn 18.2 Changing units of area, volume and capacity

You may also be asked in the examination to convert between units of area.

A square has dimensions
1 metre by 1 metre.

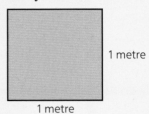

This has the same area as a square
100 cm by 100 cm.

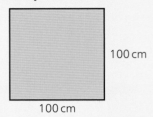

Area = 1 m × 1 m = 1 m²

Area = 100 cm × 100 cm = 10 000 cm²

As these two areas are the same we can write:

$1 \, m^2 = 10\,000 \, cm^2$.

Other conversion factors for area are:

$1 \, cm^2 = 10 \, mm \times 10 \, mm = 100 \, mm^2$

$1 \, km^2 = 1000 \, m \times 1000 \, m = 1\,000\,000 \, m^2$

$1 \, m^2 = 1000 \, mm \times 1000 \, mm = 1\,000\,000 \, mm^2$

Similarly for volume:

A cube 1 m by 1 m by 1 m has a volume of 1 m³.

> **Study tip**
>
> If you find it difficult to remember the conversion $1 \, m^2 = 10\,000 \, cm^2$ then you may find it easier to remember that as there are 100 cm in 1 m, so there are $(100 \times 100) \, cm^2$ in $1 \, m^2$.

This is equivalent to the volume of a cube 100 cm by 100 cm by 100 cm.

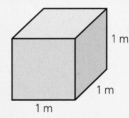   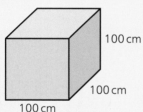

So $1 \, m^3 = 100 \, cm \times 100 \, cm \times 100 \, cm = 1\,000\,000 \, cm^3$

Example

a Convert 12 500 cm² to m².

b Convert 7 m³ to cm³.

Solution

a   1 m = 100 cm

$1 \, m^2 = 100 \, cm \times 100 \, cm = 10\,000 \, cm^2$ 100 × 100 because it is area

$1 \, cm^2 = \dfrac{1}{100 \times 100} \, m^2$ Rearranging

$12\,500 \, cm^2 = 12\,500 \times \dfrac{1}{100 \times 100} \, m^2$ Multiplying both sides by 12 500

$= 1.25 \, m^2$

b 1 m = 100 cm

1 m³ = 100 cm × 100 cm × 100 cm = 1 000 000 cm³ | 100 × 100 × 100 because it is volume |

7 m³ = 7 × (100 × 100 × 100) cm³ | Multiplying both sides by 7 |

     = 7 000 000 cm³

Example

The diagram shows a can of soup.

All dimensions given are internal ones.

Internal dimensions are the inside measurements.

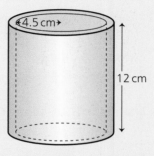

a How many of these cans can be filled from a container holding 12 litres of soup?

The metal used in the making of these cans is 1 mm thick.

b Write down the external diameter of the can in centimetres.

Some of these cans are packed into a rectangular box.
The box measures 0.75 metres by 0.6 metres by 0.4 metres.

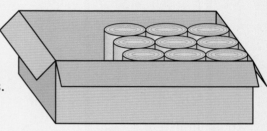

c Find the total number of cans in one box.

Solution

a A cylinder is a prism as it has the same cross-section all the way through.

The cross-section is a circle.

Area of cross-section = πr^2

$\qquad\qquad\qquad = \pi \times 4.5 \times 4.5$ cm²

$\qquad\qquad\qquad = 20.25\pi$ cm²

Volume of a cylinder = Area of cross-section × height

$\qquad\qquad\qquad\quad = 20.25 \times \pi \times 12$ cm³

$\qquad\qquad\qquad\quad = 763.4070...$ cm³

This is the volume of the space inside the can.

1 litre of soup will take up 1000 cm³ of space.

You need to find the capacity of the can in litres.

1 litre = 1000 cm³

So   1000 cm³ = 1 litre

$\qquad\quad$ 1 cm³ = $\dfrac{1}{1000}$ litres

763.4070... cm³ = 763.4070... × $\dfrac{1}{1000}$ litres

$\qquad\qquad\qquad = 0.7634070...$ litres

> ### Study tip
>
> Put this value in the memory of your calculator.
>
> When you want to use this value again, recall it from the memory.
>
> This will give you a more accurate final answer.

Number of cans that can be filled from the container $= \dfrac{\text{Amount of soup in the container}}{\text{Capacity of the can}}$

$= \dfrac{12}{0.7634070}$

$= 15.7190\ldots$ | The answer rounds to 16 cans |

$= 15$ | but there are only 15 full cans. |

The final answer is 15 cans and not 16, because the question asks how many cans can be filled.

As the 16th can is not full, there are only 15 cans that can be filled from the container.

b External diameter = Internal diameter + 0.2 cm

     $= 9 + 0.2 = 9.2$ cm

| 1 mm each side = 2 mm |
| 2 mm = 0.2 cm |

c Number of cans along the length

     $= 0.75$ m $\div$ 9.2 cm $= 750 \div 9.2 = 8.152\ldots$ | You can fit in 8 cans. |

Number of cans along the width

     $= 0.6$ m $\div$ 9.2 cm $= 60 \div 9.2 = 6.521\ldots$ | You can fit in 6 cans. |

So you can fit $8 \times 6 = 48$ cans in one layer of the box.

The box is 0.4 metres high.

Number of layers $= 0.4$ m $\div$ 12 cm $= 40 \div 12 = 3.333\ldots$ | There are 3 layers. |

Total number of cans in the box $= 48 \times 3 = 144$.

Apply 18.2

1 Convert these areas to square centimetres (cm^2).

   a 4590 mm^2 **b** 5.24 m^2 **c** 7.23 mm^2 **d** 0.5 km^2

2 Convert these volumes to cubic centimetres.

   a 6 m^3 **b** 200 mm^3 **c** 0.07 m^3

3 a How many cm^3 are there in 1 m^3?   **b** How many m^3 are there in 1 km^3?

   c Convert 2.3 km^3 to cm^3.

     Give your answer to part **c** in standard form.

4 Jerome is making a sandpit for his son.

He digs a rectangular hole 3 m long, 1.5 m wide and 60 cm deep.

   a Find the volume of the hole in m^3.

   b Write down the volume of the hole in cm^3.

He fills the hole with sand.

Sand is sold in bags which cover 15 m^2 to a depth of 50 mm.

   c Find the volume (in cm^3) of sand in a single bag.

   d How many bags of sand will he need to fill the hole?

5 A bottle of mass 350 grams contains 50 centilitres of water.

   a Write 50 cl in ml   **b** Write 50 cl in litres   **c** Write 350 g in kg.

   d Find the total mass in kilograms of 80 of these bottles.

   e How many litres of water altogether are contained in these bottles?

6 The area of a park on a map is 11 cm^2.
The actual area is 15 000 000 times larger.
Find the actual area of the park in km^2.

7 One cubic metre of metal is melted down to make some coins.
A single coin has a radius of 1.2 cm and a thickness of 3 mm.

   a Find the volume of one coin in mm^3.

   b Write down the volume of the coin in cm^3.

      Give your answers to **a** and **b** correct to 4 significant figures.

   c How many coins are made from metal?

8 Here is a diagram of a swimming pool.

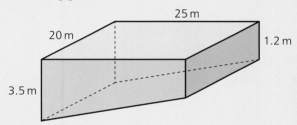

The cross-section of the pool is a trapezium.

   a Use the formula below to find the area of the cross-section in m^2.

      Area of trapezium $= \frac{1}{2}(a + b)h$

      where a and b are the lengths of the parallel sides and h is the perpendicular distance
between the parallel sides.

   b Give the area of the cross-section in cm^2.

   c Find the volume of the swimming pool, and then find the capacity of the swimming pool in
litres.

9 Small sweets are packed into cylindrical tubes of radius 2.4 cm
and height 15 cm.

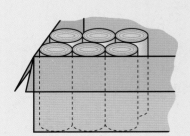

They are to be packed vertically into a box 15 cm high.
The box is 0.9 metres long and 0.5 metres wide.

   a How many tubes can be packed into this box?

When the tubes have been placed in the box, there will be some
empty space around the tubes.

   b What percentage of the box is empty space?
Give your answer correct to the nearest whole number.

Assess 18.1 – 18.2

1 Convert:

  a 0.3 kg to g   **c** 4672 cl to litres   **e** 56.21 m to mm

  b 1700 m to km   **d** 1783 mg to g   **f** 0.31 litres to ml.

2 Convert the following areas and volumes.

  a 350 000 cm^2 to m^2 **c** 0.0004 km^2 to m^2

  b 0.75 mm^3 to cm^3 **d** 7 850 000 cm^3 to m^3

3 Marianne walks 2.5 km to school. She then has to go to the shops which are another 480 m from school. She returns home, the same way.

  a How far does she travel altogether?
     Give your answer in metres.

  Marianne's steps are 40 cm long.

  b How many steps does she make in walking to school, the shops and back home again?

4 A fruit sweet weighs 5 g. The sweets are sold in 1 kg packets. How many of these sweets are in a packet?

5 Jaivyn keeps nine cows. Each cow produces 29 litres of milk per day. Jaivyn needs 11 000 ml of this milk for his family. He sells the rest to the local village shop in 25 litre milk churns. How many churns does he sell?

6 A bedcover is made from stitching together squares. Each square measures 15 cm by 15 cm. The bedcover measures 1.5 metres by 1.2 metres.

  a What is the area of one square in mm^2?

  b How many squares are there in the bedcover?

7 An oil drum is in the shape of a cylinder as shown below.

  a Find the volume of the oil drum in mm^3.

  b Write down the volume in cm^3.

  c How many litres of oil can the drum contain?
     Give all your answers correct to the nearest integer.

850 mm

570 mm

8 A rectangular-based tank contains 40 litres of water.
The base of the tank measures 1.85 m by 1.4 m.
How deep is the water in the tank?
Give your answer correct to the nearest centimetre.

Ratio and proportion

In this chapter, you will be introduced to the ideas of ratio and proportion. You will learn how to write ratios and simplify them. You will study several different types of questions that involve ratios including dividing in a given ratio, direct and inverse proportion and rates of change.

Learning outcomes:

After this chapter you should be able to:

- know the difference between ratio and proportion
- simplify ratios
- solve questions involving direct and inverse variation
- divide a quantity in a given ratio
- use the unitary method
- use scales in practical situations
- solve questions involving the common measures of rate of change.

Learn 19.1 Simplifying ratios

A **ratio** compares two or more quantities with each other.

Fractions also compare two or more quantities, but they compare one quantity with the total of the quantities.

In a class there are 20 boys and 10 girls.

The ratio of boys to girls can be written as:

A colon is used for ratio

This is read as 'twenty to ten' $\longrightarrow$ $20 : 10$

Order matters. The ratio of girls to boys is written as 10 : 20.

Ratios can also be simplified in the same way as for fractions.

Both sides can be multiplied or divided by the same number.

This does not change its value.

$\quad$ 20 : 10

$= 10 : 5$ $\quad$ Dividing both sides by 2.

$= \;\; 2 : 1$ $\quad$ Dividing both sides by 2.

> This could have been done in one stage by dividing by 4.

This ratio is now in its **simplest form**.

A ratio is in its simplest form when it contains the smallest possible whole numbers.

If the ratio given shows units, for example 12 mm : 5 cm. The ratio must first be changed to the same units before it can be simplified.

$$12\,\text{mm} : 5\,\text{cm}$$
$$= 12\,\text{mm} : 50\,\text{mm}$$
$$= 12 : 50$$
$$= 6 : 25 \qquad \boxed{\text{It can now be simplified.}}$$

If you go back to the original problem:

for every girl there are two boys.

Ratio compares one part to another part of a total amount.

- the boys are one part of the class
- the girls are another part of the class.

To compare the number of boys with the total number in the class then you must use **proportion**.

Proportion compares one part to the total amount.

- the boys are one part of the class
- the class is the total amount.

In the ratio 2 : 1 there are $2 + 1 = 3$ parts altogether.

Proportions are written as fractions.

The proportion of boys in the class is $\frac{2}{3}$ (two parts out of three).

Similarly:

The proportion of girls in the class is $\frac{1}{3}$ (one part out of three).

Example

A wall is covered with a mixture, that is 3 parts mortar to 2 parts gravel.

Write down this mix as a ratio of:

a mortar to gravel

b gravel to mortar

Solution

a Ratio of mortar to gravel $= 3 : 2$

b Ratio of gravel to mortar $= 2 : 3$ $\qquad \boxed{\text{Order matters.}}$

Example

Write these ratios as simply as possible.

a $35 : 140$ **b** 3 weeks : 6 days   **c** $3\frac{1}{4} : 6\frac{3}{4}$

Solution

a 35 : 140

= 7 : 20   Dividing both sides by 5

b 3 weeks : 6 days

= 21 days : 6 days

= 7 days : 2 days   Dividing both sides by 3

= 7 : 2

c $2\frac{1}{4} : 6\frac{3}{4}$

= $\frac{9}{4} : \frac{27}{4}$ Changing the mixed numbers to improper fractions

= 9 : 27   Multiplying both sides by 4

= 1 : 3   Dividing both sides by 9

Sometimes ratios compare three or more quantities.

Example

1 kg of breakfast tea was blended from 350 g of Indian tea, 500 g of Indonesian tea and the rest was Chinese tea.

a What is the ratio of Chinese tea to Indian tea?

b Find the ratio of Indian tea : Indonesian tea : Chinese tea.

c What proportion of the tea is Indian?

Solution

a Amount of Chinese tea = 1000 g − (350 g + 500 g)

= 1000 g − 850 g

= 150 g

Ratio of Chinese tea : Indian tea = 150 g : 350 g

= 15 : 35   Dividing both sides by 10

= 3 : 7   Dividing both sides by 5

b Ratio of Indian tea : Indonesian tea : Chinese tea = 350 g : 500 g : 150 g

= 35 : 50 : 15   Dividing each by 10

= 7 : 10 : 3   Dividing each by 5

c The tea is divided into 20 parts (7 + 10 + 3). Seven parts are Indian, 10 are Indonesian and 3 are Chinese.

So:

7 parts out of 20 parts are Indian tea.

The proportion of tea which is Indian is $\frac{7}{20}$.

Apply 19.1

1 Write each of these ratios as simply as possible.

   a 3 : 9   **c** 40 : 5   **e** 18 : 24   **g** 0.6 : 0.8   **i** $\frac{1}{2} : 2\frac{1}{2}$

   b 4 : 16   **d** 60 : 70   **f** 99 : 72   **h** 25% : 70%   **j** 6 : 18 : 12

2 Write each of these ratios as simply as possible.

   a 20 minutes : 1 hour   **f** $1.50 : $1.75

   b 1 kg : 200 g   **g** 4 km : 30 m

   c 70 mm : 140 cm   **h** 240 cm : 9.6 metres

   d 600 ml : 2 litres   **i** 2 hours 15 minutes : 3 hours 30 minutes

   e 4 weeks : 4 days   **j** 1000 ml : 2 litres : 3.5 litres

3 Which of the following ratios is the odd one out?

   12 : 16, $1\frac{1}{2}$: 2,   21 : 35,   32 : 128,   2.4 : 3.2

4 The actual length of a car is 4 m.

   A model is made of this car and the length on the model is 16 cm.

   a Write down the ratio of the actual length to the length on the model.

      Give your answer in its simplest form.

   b Copy and complete the following statements.

      The actual length is ...... times bigger than the length on the model.

      The length on the model is .... times .... than the actual length.

5 An adult male rhino weighs 1 tonne and 250 kg.

   A baby rhino weighs 500 kg.

   Find the ratio of the weight of the baby rhino to the adult rhino.

   Give your answer in its simplest form.

   [Hint: 1000 kg = 1 tonne]

6 A chef spends 1 hour preparing the ingredients, 2 hours 15 minutes cooking and 45 minutes clearing up.

   Find the ratio of the preparation time to the cooking time to the clearing up time. Give your answer in its simplest form.

7 A drink is made by mixing together mango juice and orange juice.

   225 ml of the 500 ml drink is orange juice.

   a How much is mango juice?

   b Find the ratio of orange juice to mango juice.

   c What proportion of the drink is: **i** mango juice   **ii** orange juice?

      Give all answers in their simplest forms.

8 On a map, 1 cm represents 1 km.
Write this scale as a ratio of the map distance to the actual distance.

9 A school has 900 students and 36 teachers.

  a Write down the ratio of students to teachers as simply as possible.

The next school year the number of students has increased by 60 and four teachers have also joined.

  b Find the new ratio of students to teachers.

  c As far as a student is concerned, which of the two ratios is better?

10 The numbers a and b are in the ratio 4 : 5.

  a If a is 8, what is b?   **d** If a is 1, what is b?

  b If b is 50, what is a?   **e** If b is 1, what is a?

  c If a is 2, what is b?   **f** If a and b add up to 27, what are a and b?

Learn 19.2 The unitary method

You can solve ratio and proportion questions by using the **unitary method**.

This is where you find the value of one unit of a quantity.

This method can be used in various types of questions involving ratio, proportion and percentages.

If you know that 10 litres of petrol costs 48 pesos in Argentina, you can find the cost of 1 litre and then from this work out the cost of any number of litres.

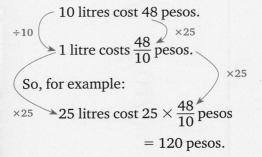

10 litres cost 48 pesos.

$\div 10$ → 1 litre costs $\frac{48}{10}$ pesos. ×25

So, for example:

$\times 25$ → 25 litres cost $25 \times \frac{48}{10}$ pesos ×25

$= 120$ pesos.

Example

A tea plantation employs pickers and sorters in the ratio 5 : 2.

How many sorters are employed if there are 320 pickers?

Solution

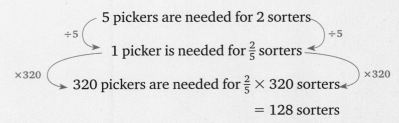

5 pickers are needed for 2 sorters

$\div 5$ → 1 picker is needed for $\frac{2}{5}$ sorters ← $\div 5$

$\times 320$ → 320 pickers are needed for $\frac{2}{5} \times 320$ sorters ← $\times 320$

$= 128$ sorters

This method is also useful for finding the answers to 'best buy' problems.

Example

Two different brands of ground coffee are sold in a supermarket.

Brand A costs $8.50 for a 500 g packet and brand B costs $4.60 for a 200 g packet.

Which brand is the better value for money?

Solution

It is difficult to compare the prices of the brands because they are bought in different amounts.

In order to compare these prices you need to know the cost for the same amount of coffee.

$\div 500$
— 500 g of brand A coffee costs $8.50
$\div 500$
→ 1 g of brand A coffee costs $\dfrac{\$8.50}{500} = \$0.017$

$\div 200$
— 200 g of brand B coffee costs $4.60
$+200$
→ 1 g of brand B coffee costs $\dfrac{\$4.60}{200} = \$0.023$

Comparing these answers shows that brand A coffee is the cheaper per gram and gives the better value for money. It is the better buy.

All the examples given so far involve **direct proportion**.

   As the amount of petrol increased, so did the cost.

   As the number of pickers increased, so did the number of sorters.

Such questions could be shown clearly using a straight-line graph.

For the petrol question, the graph would slope positively.

   As one variable increases, then so does the other.

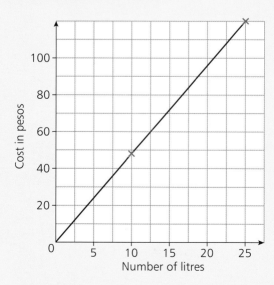

Inverse proportion also involves two variables but:

   as one variable increases then the other decreases.

Example

Two men took a total of five hours to build a wall.

a How long would it have taken five men working at the same speed?

b How many men would have been needed to build it in 1 hr 15 mins?

Solution

a

2 men took 5 hours.
÷2   ×2
1 man would take 10 hours.   ÷5
×5

So   5 men would take $\frac{1}{5} \times 10 = 2$ hours.

[Hint: Notice the arrows].

On the left the first arrow is labelled ÷ 2 and the corresponding arrow on the right is labelled × 2. This is because it takes 1 man two times longer to build the wall.

÷ 2 and × 2 are **inverses** of each other so this is an example of inverse proportion.

b It took

5 hours for 2 men.
×2   ÷2
It would take   10 hours for 1 man
÷10   ×10
1 hour for 10 men.
×1¼   ÷1¼
It would take $1\frac{1}{4}$ hours for $\dfrac{1}{1\frac{1}{4}} \times 10$

$= \frac{4}{5} \times 10$

$= 8$ men.

Apply 19.2

1 A factory produces 660 small cakes in one hour.

How many cakes will it produce in

   a 3 hours   **b** 30 minutes   **c** 8 minutes?

2 50 miles is equal to 80 km.

   a How many kilometres in **i** 40 miles   **ii** 75 miles?

   b How many miles in **i** 72 km   **ii** 140 km?

3 Maja takes $1\frac{1}{2}$ hours to clean a single hospital ward.

   a How many hours will it take her to clean three wards?

Julia is then employed to help her.

   b How many hours will it now take to clean the three wards?

4 **a** Six samosas cost $1.86. How much do 10 samosas cost?

In a special offer, you can buy a large pack of 15 samosas for $4.80.

b Which is the better buy, a large pack or 15 bought separately?

5 A car travels 126 miles on 15 litres of petrol.

a How far would it travel on 25 litres of petrol?

A second car travels 119.6 miles on 13 litres of petrol.

b Which car, the first or the second, has better petrol consumption?

6 It takes six men four days to build a shed.

a How long would it take if eight men were to build a shed?

b If the same shed took 12 days to build, how many men built it?

7 Milk is sold in a Thai supermarket in three different sizes.

The prices are shown in baht.

500ml
16 baht

1 litre
30 baht

$2\frac{1}{2}$ litres
73 baht

Which sized container of milk gives the best value for money?

8 Yoora earns $2096 per month as a teacher in Korea.

Hwang earns $26 508 per year as an engineer.

Who is the better paid?

9 Five musicians play a piece of music in 20 minutes.

How long do eight musicians take to play the same piece?

Learn 19.3 Using ratios to find quantities

You can use ratios to find numbers and quantities.

In the last Learn section, you learnt that there are many ratios that cancel down to give the same simplified ratio.

For example, 4 : 1 is equivalent to 16 : 4,   40 : 10,   2 : 0.5, ...

This equivalence of ratios can be used to find missing quantities.

Example

A large office employs senior and junior staff in the ratio 2 : 13. If there are 12 senior staff, how many junior staff are there?

Solution

You are not given the total number of employees in the office.

But you do know the ratio of senior to junior staff.

There are various methods for solving questions of this type.

One way is to write the details underneath each other.

You are trying to find an equivalent ratio to 2 : 13. Possibilities would be 4 : 26 (multiplying each number by 2) or 6 : 39 (multiplying each number by 3).

However, you need a ratio whose first number is 12.

You could solve this by the unitary method.

There are   2 senior staff for 13 junior staff.

$\div 2$

So   1 senior staff for $\dfrac{13}{2}$ junior staff $\div 2$

$\times 12$

12 senior staff for $12 \times \dfrac{13}{2}$ junior staff $\times 12$

= 78 junior staff.

But you can often miss out a step of working.

This is because $2 \times 6 = 12$.

Therefore, you need to multiply each number in the ratio by 6.

senior staff : junior staff

= $\times 6$ (2 : 13) $\times 6$

= 12 : 78

> Multiply each side of the ratio by the same amount.

So 2 : 13 is equivalent to 12 : 78.

You can now read off the corresponding number of junior staff.

There are 78 junior staff.

Example

Tropical fruit juice is mixed from mango, papaya and orange juice in the ratio 3 : 1 : 4.

Joshua has 400 ml of orange juice.

If he uses it all:

a How much mango and papaya juice will he need?

b How much tropical fruit juice will he make altogether?

Solution

$$\text{mango : papaya : orange}$$

$$= {}_{\times 100}\!\!\left(\begin{matrix} 3 & : & 1 \\ 300 & : & 100 \end{matrix} \;:\; \begin{matrix} 4 \\ 400 \end{matrix}\right)_{\times 100}$$

There are 400 ml of orange juice. $4 \times 100 = 400$.

Multiply every number in the ratio by 100.

a He will need 300 ml of mango juice and 100 ml of papaya juice.

b He will make $300 + 100 + 400 = 800$ ml of tropical fruit juice.

The ratio of the different juices stays the same as 300 : 100 : 400 will cancel down to 3 : 1 : 4.

The juices are in the same **proportion**.

Two quantities are in proportion if their ratio stays the same as the quantities get larger or smaller.

Apply 19.3

1 Calculate the missing numbers in these ratios.

a $1 : 3 = 7 : ?$ **c** $40 : 5 = 8 : ?$ **e** $7\frac{1}{2} : 1\frac{1}{2} = ? : 1$ **g** $0.4 : 8 = 1.6 : ?$

b $5 : 2 = ? : 8$ **d** $108 : 405 = 3 : ?$ **f** $7.25 : 5.5 = ? : 33$ **h** $\frac{1}{3} : \frac{2}{9} = ? : 1\frac{1}{3}$

2 The model of a car is made using a scale of 1 : 50.

This means that 1 cm on the model car is 50 cm on the real car.

a What would a length of 5 cm on the model car be on the real car?

b The length of the roof of the real car is 150 cm.

What would this length be on the model car?

3 Blue and yellow paint is mixed in the ratio 1 : 3 to form a particular shade of green paint.

Sasha has 1 litre of blue paint.

a How much yellow paint will she need?

b How much green paint will this make?

4 The ratio of black and white pages to colour pages in a magazine is 5 : 1.

  a If there are 45 black and white pages, how many colour pages are there?

In a newspaper the ratio of black and white to colour pages is 25 : 2.

  b If there are 16 colour pages, how many black and white pages are there?

5 To take small children out on a school trip, the school says that the ratio of adults to children must be 2 : 5.

Class 3 are going to the local playground.

  a If there are 18 adults, how many children are in Class 3?

Class 4 has 30 children. Both classes are going together to the higher school in the neighbouring town to look around. For this trip they need a ratio of adults to children of 1 : 10.

  b How many adults will they need?

6 A school has paperbacks and hardback books in the school library. There are 54 hardback books.

The ratio of paperbacks to hardback books is 5 : 1.

  a How many paperback books are there?

  b How many books altogether?

7 On a map, a road measures 3 cm. The scale of the map is 1 cm : 4 km.

  a What is the actual length of the road?

  b Rewrite the ratio in the form 1 : n.

  c If a van covers a distance of 80 000 metres, what distance has he covered as shown on the map?

8 Here is a recipe for making Tarator, a pine nut and olive oil sauce from Syria.

These ingredients make enough for six people.

  a List the ingredients you would need for 18 people.

  b List the ingredients you would need for three people.

> **Tarator**
>
> 100 g of pine nuts
> 1 teaspoon of salt
> 2 cloves of garlic, crushed
> 5 tablespoons of olive oil
> Juice of one lemon

9 Adrak ka Raita is a yoghurt dish flavoured with ginger. It is usually served with a dry curry.

This recipe serves four.

  a Rewrite this recipe for eight servings.

  b Bal had 3 litres of yoghurt and plenty of all the other ingredients. If the ingredients were combined in the same proportion how many servings could he make?

> **Adrak ka Raita**
>
> 5 cm piece of fresh ginger
> 600 ml of natural yoghurt
> 1 tablespoon of ghee
> ½ teaspoon of salt
> ½ teaspoon of freshly ground black pepper

Learn 19.4 Dividing quantities in a given ratio

Amounts can be divided into different ratios.

The total number of students in a class is 25.

The ratio of boys to girls = 4 : 1   Total number of parts = 4 + 1 = 5

This means that

$\frac{4}{5}$ of the class are boys and $\frac{1}{5}$ of the class are girls.

If $\frac{1}{5} \times 25 = 5$

Then

No. of boys = $\frac{4}{5} \times 25 = 4 \times 5 = 20$
No. of girls = $\frac{1}{5} \times 25 = 5$

Example

Julienne and Therese are sisters. The ratio of their ages is 3 : 4.

Their parents give them $14 to share in the ratio of their ages.

a How much does each of them receive?

b Write down three different pairs of possible ages for the sisters.

Solution

a

$$3:4$$

Julienne's age
is represented by
3 parts

Therese's age
is represented by
4 parts

There are 3 + 4 = 7 parts altogether

This means that Julienne will receive $\frac{3}{7}$ and Therese will receive $\frac{4}{7}$ of the total amount.

If $\frac{1}{7} \times \$14 = \$2$

Julienne's amount = $\frac{3}{7} \times \$14 = 3 \times \$2 = \$6$

Therese's amount = $\frac{4}{7} \times \$14 = 4 \times \$2 = \$8$

> A useful check is to see that the parts add up to the total amount.
> Here
> $\$6 + \$8 = \$14$ √

b Julienne could be 6 years old and Therese 8 years old.

They could also be any of the following:

12 and 16, 18 and 24, 3 and 4...

These are found by multiplying or dividing both sides of the ratio 3 : 4 by the same amount.

Apply 19.4

1 Divide these amounts in the ratio 4 : 3.

    a 21   **b** 4900   **c** 245   **d** 52.5

2 Divide these amounts in the ratio 1 : 2.

    a $12   **b** 390 cm   **c** $4\frac{1}{2}$ litres   **d** 3.75 kg

3 Divide $144 in the ratio:

    a 1 : 5   **b** 11 : 7   **c** 23 : 25   **d** 8 : 15 : 1.

4 Legaya and Christophene were left $750 by their grandfather in his will. This is shared in the ratio of their ages. They are 8 and 7 years old.

How much do they each get?

5 Solomon is training to take part in a swimming competition. He trains for 4 hours and 45 minutes each day. He divides his training time between speed work and technique in the ratio 3 : 2.

    a How long does he spend on speed work?   **b** How long does he spend on technique?

6 The angles in a triangle add up to 180°.

    a Find the sizes of the three angles in degrees if they are:

        i in the ratio 1 : 3 : 5   **ii** in the ratio 2 : 3 : 3.

    b In **a ii** what sort of triangle is it?

    c What would the ratio of angles be for an equilateral triangle?

7 To make a fresh chilli salsa, tomatoes, onions and chillies are finely chopped and combined in the ratio 22 : 11 : 1. Alonso wishes to make 340 g of the salsa.

How much of each ingredient should he use?

8 Sterling silver can be made from 92.5% silver and 7.5% copper.

    a Find the ratio of silver : copper or another metal. Give your answer in its simplest form.

    b A 200 g bangle is made from sterling silver. Find the amount of each metal in the bangle.

9 Students in India often compete in academic competitions for prizes or scholarships. In a recent technology competition, students could win a scholarship to one of the top universities plus a cash prize depending on whether they came first, second or third.

    a The total prize was 450 000 Indian Rupees (INR).

        This prize was divided in the ratio of $3 : 1 : \frac{1}{2}$.

        Find the amount awarded for 1st, 2nd and 3rd prize.

    b In India there is another unit of currency called the lakh.

        One lakh = 100 000 INR

        Write down the ratio of the prizes in lakhs.

10 Two brothers, Kibou and Satoshi went into business. Kibou invested $135 000 and Satoshi invested $95 000.

a Write down and simplify the ratio of Kibou's investment to Satoshi's investment.

b In the first year they made a profit of $17 955. The profit was divided in the same ratio as their investments. How much did each of them receive?

c In the second year, their profit was $26 932.50. Compare this with their first year's profit. Find the percentage increase in the profit from the first year to the second year.

d How much did Kibou and Satoshi receive in the second year?
Give your answers to the nearest dollar.

Learn 19.5 Compound measures

Compound measures combine the measurements of two or more different types.

For example, speed is a measurement of how distance changes in relation to time.

$$\text{Speed} = \frac{\text{distance}}{\text{time}}$$

Speed can also be defined as the **rate of change** of distance with respect to time.

The units are also given as a rate. Speed is measured in kilometres per hour (km/hr).

$$\text{Speed} = \frac{\text{distance (km)}}{\text{time (hours)}}$$

It is very unlikely that the speed would be constant for the whole journey.

So **Average speed** $= \dfrac{\text{distance (km)}}{\text{time (hours)}}$

Example

Car A travels a distance of 174 km in three hours.
Car B travels a distance of 200 m in 12 seconds.
On average, which car is the faster?

Solution

To be able to compare the two cars, the speed should be in the same units.

For Car A Average speed $= \dfrac{\text{distance (km)}}{\text{time (hours)}}$

$= \dfrac{174\,\text{km}}{3\,\text{h}}$

$= 58\,\text{km/h}$

For Car B Average speed $= \dfrac{\text{distance (km)}}{\text{time (hours)}}$

$200\text{ metres} = \dfrac{200}{1000}\text{ km} = \tfrac{1}{5}\text{ km}$

$12\text{ sec} = \dfrac{12}{60 \times 60}\text{ h}$

$\text{Average speed} = \tfrac{1}{5} \div \dfrac{12}{60 \times 60}$

$= 60\,\text{km/h}$

> Divide by 60 × 60 because
> 60 sec = 1 min, 60 min = 1 hour

Car B has the greater average speed, so it is the faster.

The average speed formula can also be used to find the distance travelled and the time taken.

Rearranging the formula gives

> **distance = speed × time**

and

> $$\text{Time} = \frac{\text{distance}}{\text{speed}}$$

Notice that for shortness **average speed** is often written as just speed.

Study tip

There is an easy way of remembering this formula.
If you cover S with your finger, you will get $\frac{D}{T}$, which gives the formula for speed.

If you cover D, you will get S T, which gives S × T, the formula for distance.

If you cover T, you will get $\frac{D}{S}$, which gives the formula for time.

Example

A person walks at 3.5 km/h for 90 minutes. What is the distance travelled?

Give your answer in kilometres.

Solution

Begin by checking the units. | Minutes must be changed to hours. |

90 minutes = 1 hour and 30 minutes = 1.5 hours

> Distance = speed × time
> = 3.5 × 1.5 km
> = 5.25 km

Example

A plane flies at an average speed of 500 km/h.

It travels a distance of 2725 km.

How long does it take?

Give your answer in hours and minutes.

Solution

$$\text{Time} = \frac{\text{distance}}{\text{speed}}$$

$$= \frac{2725}{500}$$

$$= 5.45 \text{ hours}$$

The decimal part of an hour needs to be changed to minutes.

- Subtract the whole number. 5.45 (−) 5 = 0.45
- Multiply by 60 as there are 60 minutes in an hour. 0.45 × 6 0 = 27

The time in hours and minutes is 5 hours and 27 minutes.

Other common compound measures or rates of change include density and fuel consumption.

Density is usually measured in grams per cm cubed (g/cm^3).

Fuel consumption (the rate at which fuel is used up), is usually measured in kilometres per litre (km/litre) or miles per gallon (mpg). You might want to learn these diagrams.

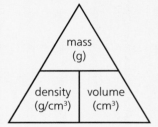 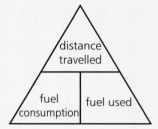

Apply 19.5

1 Work out the average speed for each of the following.
State the units of your answers.

  a A car travels 140 kilometres in 2 hours.

  b A car travels 300 metres in 10 seconds.

  c A plane travels 720 miles in 1 hour and 30 minutes.

2 Express each of these times as decimal fractions of an hour.

  a 15 minutes   **b** 24 minutes   **c** 42 minutes

3 Write each of these times as hours and minutes.

  a 3.75 hours   **b** 2.35 hours   **c** 1.625 hours

4 A cyclist travels for $2\frac{1}{2}$ hours and covers a distance of 40 km.

  a Find his average speed for the journey.

  Later on, he returns home but this time he takes an hour longer.

  b Find his average speed for the journey home.
  Give your answer correct to one decimal place.

5 Work out the time taken for each of these journeys.
Write your answer in hours and minutes.

  a A train travels 425 km at an average speed of 170 km/h.

  b An athlete runs 810 metres at an average speed of 300 metres per minute.

  c A lorry travels 350 km at an average speed of 80 km/h.

6 Work out the distance travelled for each of these journeys.

   a A car travelling at 90 km/h takes 2 hours 15 minutes.

   b A snail crawling at 0.5 cm per second takes 48 minutes.

   c A child walking at 2 km/h takes 1 hour 50 minutes.
      Give the answer to part **c** correct to 1 decimal place.

7 A racing car completes a 7.4 km lap in 1 minute 23.4 seconds.
   Find the average speed in:

   a m/s   **b** km/h.

   Give your answers correct to 2 decimal places.

8 A boat sails at an average speed of 11 knots. One knot is equivalent to one nautical mile per hour.

   a How long will it take for it to travel 88 nautical miles?

   The boat then continues travelling at 10 knots for another three hours.

   b Find the average speed in knots for the total journey.
      State your answer correct to 1 decimal place.

9 Mr Khan set out on a business trip with a full tank of petrol. He travelled 560 km. When he arrived at his destination his petrol tank was $\frac{1}{5}$ full. A full tank of petrol holds 50 litres.

   a How much petrol did it take to complete the journey?

   b What was his average fuel consumption?

   c How much further could he travel before he runs out of petrol?
      Assume that the fuel consumption remains at its average.

Assess 19.1–19.5

1 Simplify the following ratios.

   a 25 : 45   **c** 1 kg : 128 g   **e** 1 week : 2 days : 12 hours

   b 104 mm : 7.8 cm   **d** 0.3 : 30

2 Copy and complete the following ratios.

   a 2 : 7 = ? : 21   **c** $3\frac{1}{4} : 2\frac{3}{4} = 13$: ?   **e** 4 : 0.004 = ? : 1

   b 3.6 : 5.6 = 9 : ?   **d** 0.2 : 12 = 1 : ?

3 A model of a train is built to a scale of 1 : 200.
   The length of the model train is 17 cm.

   a Calculate in metres the length of the real train.

   The height of a door on the real train is 1.8 metres.

   b Find the height of the train door on the model.

4 Gerome is going on a business trip. His plane fare, accommodation and food are in the ratio

$7 : 4 : 2$

He spends $952 on his plane fare.

How much does he spend:

a on his food   **b** in total?

5 A plan is made of a hockey pitch. The length is to be 90 metres.

Where length : width $= 18 : 11$.

Find the width of the hockey pitch.

6 Juan is trying to eat healthily. When shopping he spends according to the following ratio.

Meat : Fish : Fruit.

$= \quad 2 \quad : \quad 5 \quad : \quad 9$

He spends $42.50 on fish.

How much does he spend altogether?

7 In one week Augustus was paid $27 for helping his neighbour with small jobs around his garage.

In that week he worked for 18 hours.

How much would he be paid if he worked for 23 hours?

8 Three men can dig a field in 10 hours.

How long would it take five men?

9 A particular brand of washing powder comes in two different sizes; 2 kg and 0.75 kg.

In South Africa, a 2 kg box costs 65 rand.

A 0.75 kg box costs 35 rand.

Which is the better value for money?

10 Aki runs 9 km in 45 minutes and 21 seconds.

Find his average speed in m/s.

Give your answer correct to 1 decimal place.

Real-life graphs

Graphs in practical situations

Real-life graphs are a useful way of showing how two quantities vary.

This chapter shows you how to draw some real-life graphs and how to use them to find further information.

Learn 20.1 Cartesian coordinates

Plotting points

Cartesian coordinates use two **axes** (singular: **axis**) at right angles as shown below.

The point where the axes cross is called the **origin**.

At the origin, both coordinates are zero. The origin is the point (0, 0).

The point P is (3, 4).

P is 3 units from the origin in the **horizontal** direction and 4 units in the **vertical** direction.

3 and 4 are the coordinates of the point.

The point Q is (−4, −2).

The point R is (0, −3).

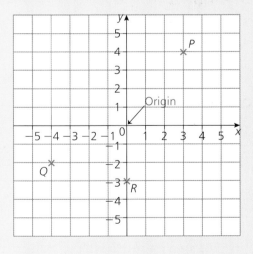

> Always write the horizontal coordinate first and the vertical coordinate second.

Apply 20.1

1

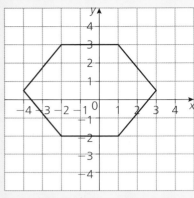

Write down the coordinates of:

a the top right-hand corner of the hexagon

b the top left-hand corner of the hexagon

c the mid-point of the base of the hexagon.

For each of questions **2** to **10**, you will need to draw a pair of axes numbered from −6 to 6, on squared paper.

2 Plot the points: $A(2, 1), B(2, 5), C(6, 5), D(6, 1)$.
What is the mathematical name of the shape ABCD?

3 Plot the points: $E(−4, 0), F(−2, 4), G(0, 0)$.
What is the mathematical name of the shape EFG?

4 Plot the points: $J(−3, −1), K(−3, −3), L(3, −4), M(3, 3)$.
What is the mathematical name of the shape JKLM?

5 Plot the points: $P(−3, 2), Q(5, 2), R(4, −2), S(−4, −2)$.
What is the mathematical name of the shape PQRS?

6 Plot the points $A(−4, 3), B(2, 3), C(2, −3)$.
Plot a point D such that $ABCD$ is a square.
Write down the coordinates of D.

7 Plot the points $E(2, 4), F(1, −1), G(−2, −1)$.
Plot a point H such that $EFGH$ is a parallelogram.
Write down the coordinates of H.

8 Annie, Billy and Cara are trying to find the third vertex, R, of an isosceles triangle PQR.
They know that P is $(1, 0)$ and Q is $(3, 0)$.
Annie places R at $(3, 6)$. Billy places it at $(2, −1)$. Cara places it at $(2, 5)$.
Who has found a correct place for R?

9 Plot the points $S(−2, 4), T(−4, 1), U(−2, −2)$.
V is the point $(5, a)$ and $STUV$ is a kite.
Plot V and write down the value of a.

10 a $A(0, 3)$ and $B(0, −1)$ are two corners of a square $ABCD$.
Write down the coordinates of C and D.
[Hint: There are two possible answers to this question].

b AB is a diagonal of the square $APBQ$.
Write down the coordinates of P and Q.

Learn 20.2 Conversion graphs

Conversion graphs are used to convert from one unit to another.

They are drawn on graph paper so that you can read off intermediate values.

Reading from a conversion graph
Example

This is a conversion graph for converting miles to kilometres.

To convert 10 miles to kilometres, you first find 10 miles on the horizontal axis.

Draw a ruled vertical line from this point until you reach the graph.

From the graph now draw a horizontal line across to the vertical axis.

You reach the vertical axis at 16 kilometres, so 10 miles = 16 kilometres.

> You could also use this graph to convert kilometres to miles.

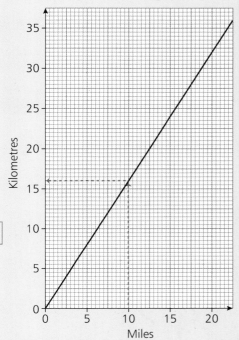

Drawing a conversion graph
Example

Jenny knows that 100 US dollars are equal to 72 euros.

Using this information, she can draw a graph to convert US dollars to euros.

She labels the horizontal axis US dollars and numbers it from 0 to 100.

She labels the vertical axis euros and numbers it from 0 to 80.

One point on the graph will be (100, 72).

The point (0, 0) will also be on the graph because no money is zero in both currencies.

Jenny plots these points and joins them with a ruled line.

To convert 44 US dollars to euros, start from 44 on the horizontal axis.

Draw a ruled vertical line from this point until you reach the graph.

From the graph now draw a horizontal line across to the vertical axis.

You reach the vertical axis at 32 euros, so 44 US dollars = 32 euros.

> Jenny could also use this graph to convert euros to US dollars.

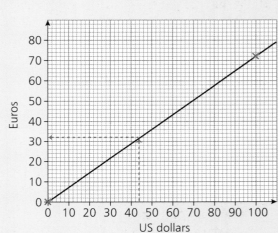

Apply 20.2

1 This graph can be used to convert UK gallons to litres.

    a Jamal says that 6 UK gallons are equal to 23.5 litres.
Explain why Jamal is wrong.

    b Use the graph to convert 11 UK gallons to litres.

    c Use the graph to convert 78 litres to UK gallons.

    d Convert 30 UK gallons to litres.

> **Study tip**
>
> Always check the scales used on the axes
> − they may not be the same.

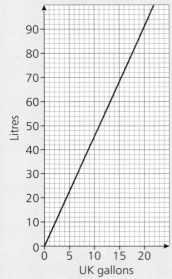

2 This graph can be used to convert Hong Kong dollars to Japanese yen.

    a Use the graph to convert 35 Hong Kong dollars to Japanese yen.

    b Use the graph to convert 170 Japanese yen to Hong Kong dollars.

    c Convert 70 Hong Kong dollars to Japanese yen.

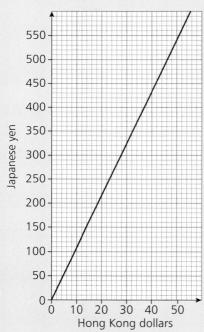

3 5 kg are equivalent to 11 lb.

Use this information to draw a conversion graph.

Use your graph to:

    a convert 2.4 kg to lb

    b convert 7.4 kg to lb.

    c Elena's baby weighed $7\frac{1}{2}$ lb when he was born.

      Juana's baby weighed 3.3 kg when she was born.

      Which baby was heavier?

      Show how you worked this out.

4 Thiago has a mobile phone.

The graph shows his monthly charges for calls up to 300 minutes.

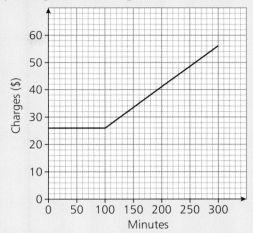

a What is his basic monthly charge?

b How many minutes of calls are included in his monthly charge?

c What does he pay for: **i** 150 calls   **ii** 250 calls?

d What is the rate per minute for excess calls?

5 | 60 °C is equivalent to 140 °F and −40 °C is equivalent to −40 °F. |

a Use the given information to draw a graph to convert degrees Celsius to degrees Fahrenheit.
Draw a horizontal axis labelled from −100 to 100 (Celsius temperatures).
Draw a vertical axis from −100 to 240 (Fahrenheit temperatures).
Use a scale of 1 cm to represent 20 units on each axis.

b Use your graph to convert these temperatures to degrees Fahrenheit.
i 80 °C   **ii** −60 °C   **iii** 0 °C   **iv** 100 °C

c Normal human body temperature is 37 °C.
Find normal human body temperature in °F.

d The highest temperature recorded in Bogota was 25 °C.
Express this temperature in °F.

Learn 20.3 Travel graphs

A travel graph plots distance against time.

It is sometimes called a distance–time graph.

The vertical axis is always distance. The horizontal axis is always time.

The distance is measured from a particular point – which is usually the starting point.

The time on the horizontal axis may be shown as actual time, e.g. 0900, 0930, 1000, etc.

It could be measured in hours from the start of the journey.

Example

This travel graph shows the journey of a bus dropping passengers at two villages.

Describe the journey.

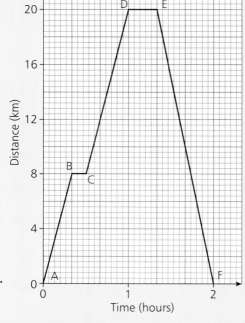

Solution

From A to B, the bus travels 8 km in 20 min.

3×20 min $= 1$ h, so the speed of the bus is $3 \times 8 = 24$ km/h.

After 20 min, the bus stops for 10 min (BC).

It then goes on at the same speed.

> The gradient from C to D is the same as the gradient from A to B, so the speed is the same.

One hour after the start of its journey, the bus stops again for 20 min (DE).

Then the bus returns to its starting place (EF).

From E to F, the bus travels 20 km in 40 min.

This is equivalent to 10 km in 20 min and 30 km in 60 min.

The speed of the bus on its return journey is 30 km/h.

Apply 20.3

1 The graph shows the journeys of three people: Asha, Benson and Clara.

Distances on the graph are measured from Barcelona.

a Where did Asha start from and how fast is she moving?

b How far is Benson from Barcelona?

c What else does this graph tell you about Benson?

d How far from Barcelona do Asha and Clara meet?

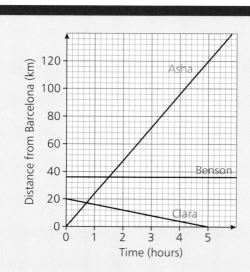

2 The distance–time graph shows Kim's journey by car from London.

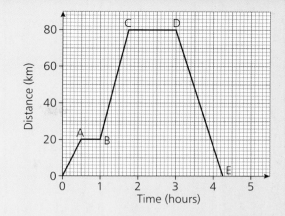

   a How long does Kim stay at her destination?

   b Work out Kim's speed:

      i from the start to A

      ii from B to C

      iii from D to E.

3 Oliver went on a mountain bike trail.
This travel graph shows his journey.

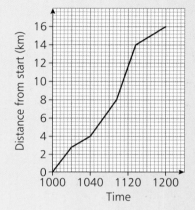

   a At what time had Oliver travelled 10 km?

   b What was his average speed between 1000 and 1020?

   c What happened between 1020 and 1040?

   d Between what times was he travelling the fastest?

   e What was his average speed over the whole journey?

4 Nikki drives from Pyetown (P) to Quintao (Q).
The graph shows her journey.

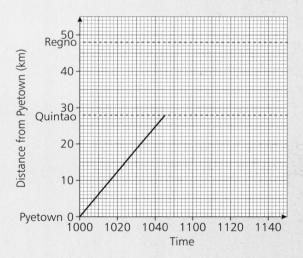

   a How far is it from Pyetown to Quintao?

   b At what time does Nikki arrive at Quintao?

   c Nikki stays at Quintao for 15 min, then she drives on to Regno at the same speed as before.

      i Copy the graph and draw on it the rest of her journey.

      ii At what time does she arrive at Regno?

5 Mary walked to her grandmother's house for 15 min at 4 km/h.
She stayed there for 20 min and then walked home at 3 km/h.
Draw a distance–time graph to show Maria's journey.

6 Luca travels by train from Cologne to Munich via Frankfurt.
The distance from Cologne to Frankfurt is 190 km.
The distance from Frankfurt to Munich is 400 km.

He leaves Cologne at 0950 and arrives at Frankfurt at 1210.

His next train leaves Frankfurt at 1250 and gets to Munich at 1600.

a Draw a distance–time graph to show Luca's journey, using axes as shown.

b Work out the average speed over his whole journey.

$$\left(\text{Average speed} = \frac{\text{total distance}}{\text{total time}}\right)$$

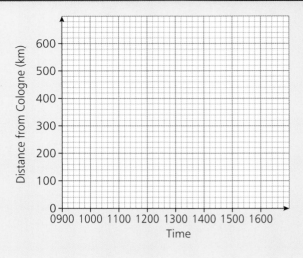

7 The graph shows Joe's journey as he walks the 8 km from his home to Klaus's house.

Klaus leaves home at 1045 and cycles to meet him at 16 km/h.

a Copy the graph and show Klaus's journey on it.

b At what time do they meet?

c How far are they from Joe's house when they meet?

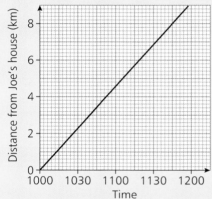

Assess 20.1–20.3

1

Write down the coordinates of each of the points A to F.

2 Draw a pair of axes like those shown in question **1**.

Plot the points $P(-3, -2)$, $Q(3, 0)$, $R(4, -2)$ and $R(3, -4)$.

What is the name of quadrilateral $PQRS$?

3 Draw a pair of axes like those shown in question **1**.
Plot the points $T(0, -2)$, $U(1, 3)$, $V(6, 4)$, $W(5, -1)$.
Jazmin says $TUVW$ is a rhombus.
Is this correct? Give a reason for your answer.

4 Joy says it is further from $(3, -4)$ to $(4, 1)$ than it is from $(3, 4)$ to $(4, -1)$.
Nicola says it is further from $(3, 4)$ to $(4, -1)$ than it is from $(3, -4)$ to $(4, 1)$.
Valentina says these points are the same distance apart.
Plot the points on a grid and measure the distance to find who is correct.

5 This graph is used to convert UK pints to litres.

   a Use the graph to convert 12 pints to litres.

   b Use the graph to convert 30 pints to litres.

   c Use the graph to convert 2 litres to pints.

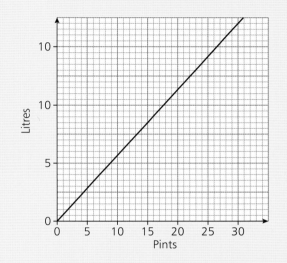

6 James knows that £25 (pounds sterling) is equivalent to 41 US dollars.
Use this information to draw a graph to convert sterling to US dollars.
From your graph:

   a convert £12 to US dollars

   b convert £45 to US dollars

   c convert 18 US dollars to pounds sterling.

7 The graph shows the charges for hiring a bike
from two different stores.

   a Store A has a daily charge for each day of hire.
What is this daily charge?

   b Store B has a basic charge plus a lower
daily charge.

     i What is the basic charge?

     ii What is the daily charge?

   c Which store is cheaper for seven days' bike hire
and how much would you save?

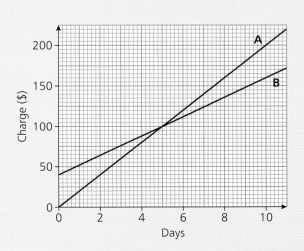

8 Gary knows that £20 (pounds sterling) equals AUD$31 (Australian dollars).
Use this information to draw a graph to convert sterling to dollars.

  a Use your graph to:
    i convert £6 to AUD$ **iii** convert AUD$15 to £
    ii convert £35 to AUD$ **iv** convert AUD$75 to £.

  b Gary is staying with friends in Australia.
    He sends a postcard to his parents in the UK.
    The charge for postage is AUD$1.50.
    The charge for sending a postcard from the UK to Australia is £1.65.
    Which is cheaper?
    Show how you worked this out.

9 The graph shows a train journey.

  a What is the speed of the train on the outward journey?

  b How long does it stop on the return journey?

  c What is the speed of the train on the second part of its return journey?

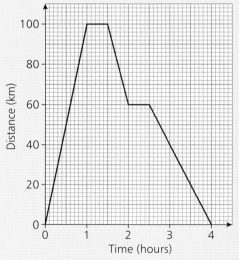

10 This graph shows Roberto's car journey from home to the superstore.

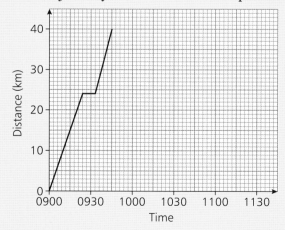

  a Roberto joined a traffic jam at 0924.
    How long was he at a standstill?

  b What was Roberto's average speed before he stopped in the traffic jam?

  c Roberto stayed at the superstore for three-quarters of an hour.
    Then he drove home at 50 km/h.
    Copy the graph above and show the rest of his journey on your grid.

11 Part of a coach timetable is shown below.

Abrada	dep	1420
Bourkish	arr	1510
	dep	1530
Chitto	arr	1610
	dep	1620
Douras	arr	1700

The first leg of the journey is shown on the grid.

a Copy and complete the graph for this journey.

b What is the average speed of the coach between Abrada and Bourkish?

c Use the graph to decide in which part of the journey the coach travels at the fastest speed. Explain how you decided.

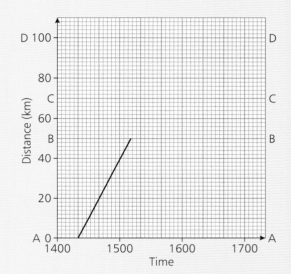

12 Ana lives 5 km from her friend Maria.

She sets out at 1130 to walk to Maria's house at 3 km/h.

Maria leaves home at 1215 and walks to meet her at 3.5 km/h.

Show their journeys on a grid like the one here to find where and when they meet.

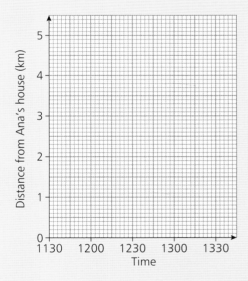

21 Personal finance

Money

If you want to look after your money, it is important to understand best value when shopping, and how to invest wisely or borrow cheaply.

Learn 21.1 Earnings

Wages and salaries

Some people are paid a **weekly wage** for the work they do. Others are paid an **annual salary**.

Wages

People on a weekly wage usually have an **hourly rate of pay**, and a number of hours a week they have to work.

Any extra hours worked are called **overtime** and those hours are usually paid at a higher hourly rate.

It may be $1\frac{1}{2}$ times the hourly rate. This is called **time-and-a-half**.

Or it may be paid at **double time** or twice the normal hourly rate.

Example

Melissa earns $9 per hour for a basic 35-hour week. Overtime is paid at time-and-a-half.

Last week she worked a total of 41 hours.

Calculate her total weekly wage.

Solution

Her weekly wage is calculated as follows:

for the basic week: 35 hours at $9 per hour = $315

overtime: 41 − 35 = 6 hours

rate for overtime = $9 × 1.5 = $13.50

overtime = 6 hours at $13.50 = $81

total weekly wage = $315 + $81 = $396

> Time-and-a-half means getting paid 1.5 times the usual rate.

Salaries

People who earn a salary get a fixed amount of money for a year's work. The money is paid monthly, so the annual salary is divided by 12 and that amount is paid every month.

People on salaries are not paid overtime.

They sometimes get a **bonus** at the end of the year. This is an extra payment, which is usually a percentage of the company's profits.

Example

Peter is the managing director of a company. He has an annual salary of $75 000.

He receives an annual bonus of 1% of the company's profits.

Last year the company made a profit of $1 240 000.

Calculate his total earnings last year.

Solution

Peter's bonus was 1% of $1 240 000 = $12 400

Total earnings for the year = $75 000 + $12 400 = $87 400

Taxes

People pay taxes to the government. The government uses this money to pay for public services. The amount of tax you pay depends on which country you live in.

Income tax is the tax paid on the money you earn. In most countries, you are allowed some tax-free earnings and then you pay income tax on the rest.

Example

Jamaal is allowed to earn $6000 tax free. He then pays income tax of 20% on the next $25 000 and 40% on any earnings over $31 000.

Jamaal's annual salary is $38 000. How much does he receive each month after tax?

Solution

Jamaal's income tax is:

$6000 at 0% = $ 0

$25 000 at 20% = $5000

$7000 at 40% = $2800

Total tax = $7800

Annual salary after tax = $38 000 − $7800 = $30 200

Monthly salary after tax = $30 200 ÷ 12 = $2516.66

Apply 21.1

1 Neil works a 35-hour week at $8.50 per hour, with overtime paid at time-and-a-half.

He works 40 hours every week.

How much does he earn per week?

2 Mona earns $243 per week for a 36-hour week.

What is her hourly rate of pay?

3 Henry is paid $7.20 per hour for a 38-hour week, with overtime paid at double time.

Last week he earned $316.80.

How many hours did Henry work last week?

4 José has a salary of $72 000.

He earns $20 000 tax free. He then pays 18% tax on earnings up to $51 000 and 35% tax on earnings over $51 000.

   a How much tax does José pay per year?

   b What are José's monthly earnings after tax?

5 Luigi has a salary of $56 000. He also receives a bonus of 2% of the company's profits.

Last year, the company made a profit of $245 000.

Calculate Luigi's total earnings last year.

6 The table shows how much tax Navarro pays on his earnings:

Earnings	Up to $5000	Next $22 000	Over $27 000
Tax	No tax paid	20%	40%

Navarro has a salary of $32 000 and receives a bonus of 2% of the company's profits.

The company made a profit of $140 000.

   a Calculate Navarro's total earnings.

   b Calculate the amount of tax he pays.

Learn 21.2 Buying and selling

Profit and loss

If you sell something for more than you paid for it, you make a **profit**.

If you sell it for less than you paid for it, you make a **loss**.

Selling price = cost price + profit

 Selling price = cost price − loss

Profit and loss are expressed as percentages of the cost price.

> **Study tip**
>
> Whenever a value changes, the change is given as a percentage of the *original value*.

Example

Harry buys a car for $12 000 and sells it later for $10 000.

He buys a motorbike for $2500 and sells it to make a 15% profit.

a Calculate the percentage loss Harry makes on the car.

b Calculate the selling price of the motorbike.

Solution

a Harry's loss on the car is $2000 out of $12 000.

This is $\frac{2000}{12\,000} = 0.16666\ldots = 16.7\%$ (to 1 dp)

b His profit on the motorbike is 15% of $2500.

$$15\% \text{ of } £2500 = \frac{15}{100} \times \$2500$$
$$= \$375$$

Harry must sell the motorbike for $2500 + $375 = $2875.

Discount

Stores sometimes offer a **discount**. This is a percentage that they take off the price, for example, in a sale. As with profit and loss, discounts are a percentage of the cost price.

Example

Olivia sees some shoes in the sale. They normally cost $70 but there is a 20% discount.

How much does Olivia pay for the shoes?

Solution

The discount is:

$$20\% \text{ of } \$70 = \frac{20}{100} \times \$70 = \$14$$

The shoes cost $70 − $14 = $56

GST (General Sales Tax) or VAT (Value Added Tax)

Many countries charge **GST** or **VAT**, sales or consumption tax on goods. The level of these taxes varies, but they are usually around 15%.

This is added on to the price that you pay for the goods in the shop.

Example

A painting costs $28 plus 15% GST.

Find the cost of the painting including GST.

Solution

$$GST = 15\% \text{ of } \$28$$
$$= \frac{15}{100} \times \$28$$
$$= \$4.20$$

The painting costs $28 + $4.20 = $32.20

> **Study tip**
>
> Find out the level of sales or consumption tax in your country.

Hire purchase

Sometimes you can buy goods on **hire purchase**. This is a useful way of buying items and paying for them over a number of months. You pay some money to start with, called a **deposit**, followed by a number of equal monthly payments, called **instalments**. Buying by hire purchase usually costs more than paying the whole price as a single payment.

Example

Petra wanted to buy a $900 television. She pays a deposit of $200 followed by 24 monthly instalments of $35.

a How much extra does she pay by using hire purchase?

b What percentage of the cash price of $900 is this?

Solution

a
$$\text{Deposit} = \$\ 200$$
$$24 \text{ instalments of } \$35 = \underline{\$\ 840}$$
$$\text{Total} = \$1040$$

Petra paid an extra $1040 − $900 = $140

b As a fraction, she paid an extra $\dfrac{140}{900} = 0.15555\dot{}\ldots = 15.6\%$ (to 1 dp)

Appreciation and depreciation

When an item gains in value, we say it appreciates. The increase in value is called **appreciation**.

When an item loses value, we say it depreciates. The decrease in value is called **depreciation**.

Jewellery and antiques are examples of items that appreciate.

The value of an item may become less every year, for example, a car. This is also called depreciation.

Again, the change is given as a percentage of the original value.

Example

A car dealer buys a car for £2600. He sells it to Marcus, making a profit of 20%.

Two years later, Marcus sells the car. It has depreciated by 20%.

a How much did Marcus pay for the car?

b For how much did Marcus sell the car?

Solution

a The dealer sold it for $2600 + 20% of $2600

$$= \$2600 + \tfrac{20}{100} \times \$2600$$

$$= \$2600 + \$520$$

$$= \$3120$$

b Marcus sold it for $3120 − 20% × $3120

$$= \$3120 - \tfrac{20}{100} \times \$3120$$

$$= \$3120 - \$624$$

$$= \$2496$$

Apply 21.2

1 Jacob buys a guitar for $240.
He sells it at a profit of 20%.
Calculate the selling price.

2 Josie buys a car for $12 000.
Two years later she sells it at a loss of 35%.
How much did she sell it for?

3 Daisy buys two cameras for $135 each.
She sells one for a 15% profit and the other for a 12% loss.
How much money does she receive altogether?

4 A necklace is priced at $75.
In a sale, it is reduced by 30%.
Calculate the price in the sale.

5 A drum kit costs $700.
VAT of 15% has to be added to the price.
Calculate the price including VAT.

6 Maurice needs to buy a new multi gym.
He can choose one of three ways to pay:
Method A: buy it with one payment of $600
Method B: pay a deposit of $200 followed by six monthly payments of $75
Method C: pay a deposit of $150 followed by twelve monthly payments of $45.
  a How much more does method B cost than method A?
  b How much more does method C cost than method A?
  c By what percentage is the price increased under method C?

7 Sheila's car insurance is $620 per year.
She can pay it all at once or in 12 monthly instalments.
If she pays in instalments, the insurance company adds 8% to the price.
Calculate the value of each monthly instalment.

8 A car costs $16 000.
It depreciates by 20% in the first year.
  a Find the value of the car after one year.
  b In the next year, it depreciates by 15% of its value at the start of that year.
  Find the value of the car after the second year.

9 An antique watch has a value of $350.
Over a year it appreciates in value to $413.
By what percentage has it appreciated?

Learn 21.3 Interest

Simple interest

When you invest money in a bank, they usually pay you **interest**.

Interest is the extra money the bank gives you for investing with them.

They pay you a percentage of what you invest **per annum** (every year).

This percentage is called the **rate** of interest.

The amount of money you invest is called the **principal**.

Suppose you invest $300 at 4% **simple interest** for 5 years.

Every year you would receive 4% of $300 as interest.

$\qquad$ 4% of $300 $= \frac{4}{100} \times \$300$

So, in 5 years you would receive $\frac{4}{100} \times \$300 \times 5$ interest, or $60.

The amount of interest that you receive, I, is given by the formula:

$$I = \frac{PRT}{100}$$

where P is the principal, R is the rate of interest per year and T is the time in years that you invest the money.

Example

Yusuf invested $2000 for 3 years and received $180 simple interest.

Calculate the rate of interest.

Solution

Use the formula for simple interest:

$$I = \frac{PRT}{100}$$

$P = 2000, I = 180$ and $T = 3$:

$\qquad 180 = \dfrac{2000 \times R \times 3}{100}$

$\qquad 180 = 60R$

$\qquad\ \ R = 3\%$

Compound interest

In reality, most banks pay **compound interest**.

With compound interest, the first year's interest is added to the principal.

So the second year's interest is calculated on a bigger principal.

If you invest $2000 at 3% per annum (per year), at the end of the first year you receive interest:

$\qquad$ 3% of $2000 $= \frac{3}{100} \times \$2000 = \$60$

You now have a total of $2060.

In the second year, you earn an extra 3% of $2060:

$$\frac{3}{100} \times \$2060 = \$61.80$$

so you then have $2121.80.

In the third year, you receive 3% of $2121.80 = $63.65, giving a total of $2185.45, or interest of $185.45.

You also pay compound interest on loans, including credit cards.

Example

Leroy invested $6000 at 4% compound interest.

Calculate the value of the investment after three years.

Solution

Year 1:

Interest = 4% of $6000

$$= \frac{4}{100} \times \$6000$$

$$= \$240$$

Investment value after year 1 = $6000 + $240 = $6240

Year 2:

Interest = 4% of $6240

$$= \frac{4}{100} \times \$6240$$

$$= \$249.60$$

Investment value after year 2 = $6240 + $249.60 = $6489.60

Year 3:

Interest = 4% of $6489.60

$$= \frac{4}{100} \times \$6489.60$$

$$= \$259.584$$

Investment value after year 3 = $6489.60 + $259.584 = $6749.18 (to the nearest $0.01)

Apply 21.3

1 Calculate the simple interest payable on $300 at 6% per annum over four years.

2 Kane invests $2000 at 3% simple interest per annum.
    After a few years, his investment is worth $2360.
    For how many years was the money invested?

3 Hugo borrows $2000 to finance a new kitchen.
    He is charged 3% compound interest.
    If he makes no repayments, how much does he owe after three years?

4 Malinda invests $4000 at 4% compound interest.
She wants it to appreciate to $4500.
Will it take more or less than three years to reach this value?

5 Hattie invests a sum of money at 4% simple interest for five years.
The interest amounts to $450.
How much did Hattie invest?

6 Chilton needs to borrow $6000 for three years.
He can borrow it at either 3.5% compound interest or 3.7% simple interest.
Which method will charge the least interest?

7 The table below shows how much $100 amounts to with compound interest.
For example, after five years at 2.3% compound interest, $100 increases to $112.04.

Principal $100	Number of years									
Annual rate of compound interest	1	2	3	4	5	6	7	8	9	10
2.0%	102.00	104.04	106.12	108.24	110.41	112.62	114.87	117.17	119.51	121.90
2.1%	102.10	104.24	106.43	108.67	110.95	113.28	115.66	118.09	120.57	123.10
2.2%	102.20	104.45	106.75	109.09	111.49	113.95	116.45	119.02	121.63	124.31
2.3%	102.30	104.65	107.06	109.52	112.04	114.62	117.25	119.95	122.71	125.53
2.4%	102.40	104.86	107.37	109.95	112.59	115.29	118.06	120.89	123.79	126.77
2.5%	102.50	105.06	107.69	110.38	113.14	115.97	118.87	121.84	124.89	128.01
2.6%	102.60	105.27	108.00	110.81	113.69	116.65	119.68	122.79	125.99	129.26
2.7%	102.70	105.47	108.32	111.25	114.25	117.33	120.50	123.76	127.10	130.53
2.8%	102.80	105.68	108.64	111.68	114.81	118.02	121.33	124.72	128.21	131.80
2.9%	102.90	105.88	108.95	112.11	115.37	118.71	122.15	125.70	129.34	133.09

a What is the value of $100 invested for six years at 2.6% compound interest?
b Yaakov invests $100 at 2.7% compound interest for seven years.
Lanika invests $100 at 2.7% simple interest for seven years.
How much more does Yaakov receive than Lanika?
c How much would $500 amount to after eight years at 2.6% compound interest?

Assess 21.1–21.3

1 Samira works a 36-hour week at $8.40 per hour, with overtime paid at time-and-a-half.
She worked 40 hours last week.
How much did she earn?

2 Marguerite is paid $9.20 per hour for a 32-hour week, with overtime paid at time-and-a-half.
Last week she earned $335.80
How many hours did Marguerite work last week?

3 Nigel has a salary of $76 500.
He earns $25 000 tax free. He then pays 20% tax on earnings up to $54 000 and 45% tax on earnings above $41 000.
   a How much tax does Nigel pay per year?
   b What are Nigel's monthly earnings after tax?

4 Marcy has a salary of $75 000 and also receives a bonus of 1.5% of the company's profits.
Last year the company made a profit of $954 000.
Calculate Marcy's total earnings last year.

5 Joshua buys an MP3 player for $20.
He sells it at a profit of 12%.
Calculate the selling price.

6 Lily buys 12 shirts to sell in her store.
She pays $7 each for them.
She adds on 30% for her profit.
She sells nine of them.
To sell the remaining three, she puts them in a sale at 50% off.
Calculate:
   a the selling price of a shirt
   b the sale price of a shirt
   c how much Lily receives altogether
   d Lily's percentage profit or loss.

7 A bracelet costs $45.
VAT at 15% has to be added to the price.
Calculate the price including VAT.

8 Dermot needs to buy a washing machine. The cost is $240.
He can buy it on hire purchase with a $50 deposit and 12 monthly payments of $19.50.
   a Calculate the total cost of buying the washing machine on hire purchase.
   b Calculate the percentage interest he pays by using hire purchase.

9 A cellphone costs $200.
It depreciates by 40% in the first year.
Find the value of the phone after one year.

10 A rare book has a value of $55.

Over a year it appreciates in value to $63.80.

By what percentage has it appreciated?

11 Calculate the simple interest payable on $450 at 3% per annum over five years.

12 Lucas borrows $6000 for home improvements.

He is charged 4% compound interest.

How much does he owe after two years?

13 George has $8000 to invest.

He has a choice of three accounts:

- account A pays 4.3% simple interest per annum
- account B pays 4% compound interest per annum
- account C pays 3% compound interest in the first year and 5% compound interest after that.

George wants to invest his money for three years.

Which account will earn him the most interest?

Practice exam questions

1 The diagram shows a probability scale:

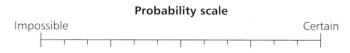

Mark on the scale the probability of:

a flipping a coin and it landing on heads

b choosing a red counter at random from a bag containing 5 red counters, 4 blue counters and 3 black counters. *(2 marks)*

2 The table below shows whether students are left-handed or right-handed, and whether they are wearing a watch.

	Wearing a watch	No watch
Left-handed	4	2
Right-handed	36	18

A student is selected at random.
What is the probability that the student is:

a left-handed   **b** wearing a watch   **c** left-handed and wearing a watch?

(3 marks)

3 **a** Change 230 000 centilitres into litres.

  b Change 0.4 kilogram into grams.

  c Change 15.3 metres into millimetres

  d Change 5.67×10^4 kilograms into tonnes.

  e Give your answer to part **c** in standard form. *(5 marks)*

4 The cylindrical base of a trophy has radius 7 cm and height 5 cm.

  a Find the volume of the base in cm^3. *(2 marks)*
    Give your answer correct to 1 decimal place. *(4 marks)*

  b Convert this volume to:
    i mm^3 **ii** m^3.
    Write your answers to parts **i** and **ii** in standard from and correct to 1 decimal place. *(3 marks)*

5   Jerome is bricking up two windows in his house.

The windows measure 60 cm by 90 cm.

Each brick is 215 mm long and 100 mm high. Several bricks will need to be cut.

a   Estimate the number of bricks needed for the job.

He is also painting the walls in the same room.
The dimensions of the room, ignoring doors and windows,
are shown on the diagram.

b   Find the total area of the four walls to be covered in m².

Each litre tin of paint covers 12.5 square metres of surface
and the walls will need two coats of paint.

c   How many litre tins of paint should he buy?   (*6 marks*)

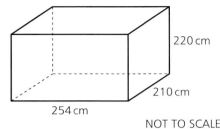

220 cm

210 cm

254 cm

NOT TO SCALE

6   The largest statue of Buddha in Japan is 100 metres high. A student made a model of this. The ratio of the model to the statue itself is 1 : 250.

a   How high, in centimetres, is the model of the statue?

The statue stands on a combined lotus flower and platform. On the model, this is 8 cm high.

b   Find the height of this platform on the real statue. Give your answer in metres.

c   What is the total height of the real statue?   (*3 marks*)

7   In India, a brand of washing powder is sold in three sizes − small, medium and large.

a   Which of these sizes is the best buy?

b   When buying this size, what is the cost for 1 g of powder?
Give your answer correct to 3 decimal places.
(*4 marks*)

500 g
Rs 72.50

750 g
Rs 100.75

1 kg
Rs 139.25

8   A businessman travels from Kuala Lumpur to the island of Lombok, in Indonesia. To do this he has to land at Bali on the way.

It takes 3 hours and 12 minutes to fly from Kuala Lumpur to Bali, which is a distance of 1970 km.

a   Find the average speed of the aeroplane for this part of the journey.
Give your answer in km/h correct to the nearest whole number.

He then has to wait for 24 minutes at Bali airport.

A smaller aeroplane, travelling at an average speed of 200 km/h takes him to Lombok. This is a distance of 130 km.

b   How long in minutes does the journey take?

c   By considering the total distance travelled and the total time taken to travel from Kuala Lumpur to Lombok, find the average speed for the whole journey in km/h.
Give your answer correct to the nearest whole number.   (*6 marks*)

9 The travel graph shows part of Garcia's journey to deliver pots to a store.

He drives from the factory to the store, unloads the pots and then drives back.

  a How far is it from the factory to the store?
  (1 mark)

  b How long does Garcia stay at the store?
  (1 mark)

  c What is his speed on the way from the store to the café? *(2 marks)*

  d He stops at the café for an hour, then drives back to the factory at 40 km/h.
  Complete the travel graph. *(3 marks)*

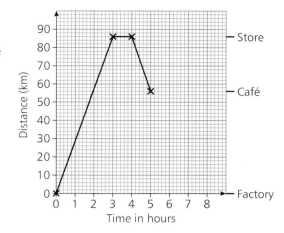

10 Lester earns $8.40 per hour for a 36-hour week.
Overtime is paid at time-and-a-half.
Lester works 39 hours in a week.
Calculate his wage for that week. *(2 marks)*

11 Kofi buys a coat for $72.
He sells it for $63.

  a Calculate the loss he makes.

  b Calculate this loss as a percentage of the original cost. *(3 marks)*

12 Philippe buys a car which is valued at $9000.
He pays a deposit of 20%.
He pays the rest in 24 monthly instalments of $320.

  a Calculate the deposit that Philippe pays.

  b After 24 months Philippe has paid more than the $9000 value of the car.

  Calculate how much more he has paid. *(3 marks)*

13 Juanita invests $6400 in a bank account.
The bank pays 3% compound interest.

  a Calculate the interest after one year.

  b Calculate how much money is in Juanita's account after two years. *(3 marks)*

14 Perla has $4000 to invest for two years.
She can invest it at 4.1% per annum simple interest or 4% per annum compound interest.

  a Calculate the interest she is paid after two years at 4.1% per annum simple interest.

  b Calculate the interest she is paid after two years at 4% per annum compound interest. *(5 marks)*

22 Estimation and accuracy

It is not always necessary to work out the answer to a calculation accurately. Sometimes a rounded answer is all that is needed.

In this chapter you will learn how to round answers to the nearest 10, 100, 1000, etc., as well as learning how to round to a specified number of decimal places or significant figures.

You will also learn how to use rounded numbers to estimate the answers to calculations, and how to work backwards to calculate the range of original possible values for amounts that have already been rounded.

Learn 22.1 Rounding

Answers do not always need to be given exactly.

This could be because an approximate answer is all that is needed or an approximate answer is easier to understand.

This approximate answer can be found by **rounding**.

Numbers can be rounded to the nearest integer or to the nearest power of 10, e.g. 10, 100 or 1000.

Example

A large rock has a mass of 15.6 kilograms.
Round this number to the nearest kilogram.

Solution

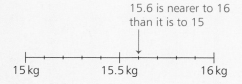

15.6 is nearer to 16 than it is to 15

15 kg   15.5 kg   16 kg

So 15.6 kg rounded to the nearest kg is 16 kg.

Example

Round the number 24 651 to:

   a the nearest 10   **b** the nearest 100.

Solution

a Look at the tens column.

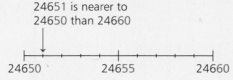

So 24 651 = 24 650 (to the nearest 10).

b Look at the hundreds column.

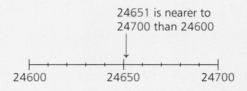

24 651 lies between 24 600 and 24 700.

24 651 is nearer to 24 700.

So 24 651 = 24 700 (to the nearest 100).

If a number lies exactly mid-way between two numbers, then it is usual to round it up to the higher one.

So 675 would round up to 680, not down to 670.

> **Study tip**
>
> - If you are rounding to, say, the nearest 10, then look at the number in the next place value (units) column. You round up only if this number is 5 or more. If not, you round down.
> - Similarly, to round to the nearest 100, look in the tens column, and to round to the nearest 1000, look in the hundreds column.

Apply 22.1

1 Round each of the following to the nearest whole number:

    a 14.2   **c** 5.5   **e** 19.92   **g** 402.38   **i** 1.098

    b 3.8   **d** 7.07   **f** 301.3   **h** 1.98   **j** 0.85

2 Round each of the following numbers to the nearest ten:

    a 13   **c** 11   **e** 399   **g** 7075   **i** 44.23

    b 67   **d** 289   **f** 4023   **h** 90 951   **j** 2.5

3 Round each of the following numbers to the nearest hundred:

a 436	**c** 3450	**e** 1954	**g** 567 129	**i** 98 949
b 198	**d** 7299	**f** 1923	**h** 43 256	**j** 99 950

4 Georgie measures his height to be 1364 mm tall.

    a What is his height to the nearest centimetre?

    b What is his height to the nearest metre?

5 The Mariana Trench is the deepest ocean trench in the world. It is situated in the Pacific Ocean to the south of Japan. The trench is approximately 2542 kilometres long and its maximum depth is 10.91 kilometres.

    a What is its length to the nearest 100 km?

    b What is its maximum depth to the nearest kilometre?

6 Many of the highest mountains in the world are in Asia.

The table below shows the highest mountains in five different countries:

Mountain	Country	Height (in metres)
Mowdok Taung	Bangladesh	1052
Anamudi	India	2675
K2	Pakistan	8611
Mount Everest	Nepal	8848
Gangkhar Puensum	Bhutan	7570

Rewrite each of these heights to:

    a the nearest 100 metres   **b** the nearest 10 metres.

7 The population of the city of Rio de Janeiro in Brazil in 2010 was 6 323 037 people. Round this figure to:

    a the nearest million   **b** the nearest 10 thousand   **c** the nearest 10.

8 Sharia says that 24 578 rounded to the nearest hundred is 246.

What has she done wrong?

9 Give an example of a number that has the same answer when rounded to the nearest 10 as when rounded to the nearest 100.

10 A carpenter is building some shelves and needs to fill a space that measures 1004 mm.

The wood is sold in 100 m, 200 cm and 300 cm lengths.

The carpenter buys a 1 metre piece of wood. Does he buy the right size?

Explain your answer.

Learn 22.2 Decimal places

Numbers can be rounded to a given number of decimal places.

Decimal places are counted from the right of the decimal point.

$$3 \cdot 1 \ 7 \ 8$$

         ↑   ↑   ↑
       1st   2nd   3rd
  decimal decimal decimal
   place   place   place

To round 3.178 to 2 decimal places, draw a line straight after the second decimal place.

Now look at the 3rd decimal place (the digit to the right of the line).

If this digit is 5 or more, the digit before the line (to the left) goes up by 1.

$$3 \cdot 1 \ 7 \,|\, 8$$

         ↑   ↑   ↑
       1st   2nd   3rd
  decimal decimal decimal
   place   place   place

So the figure 3.178 rounds to 3.18, correct to 2 decimal places.

This is because 3.178 is nearer to 3.18 than it is to 3.17.

If the number had been 3.172, then the answer would be rounded down to 3.17.

The following rules can be used.

If the number after the line is 5 or more, round up.

If the number after the line is less than 5, round down.

Example

Round the number 4.8036 to:

a 1 decimal place   **b** 2 decimal places   **c** 3 decimal places.

Solution

a

$$4 \cdot 8 \,|\, 0 \ 3 \ 6$$

If the number after the
line is less than 5,
round down.

4.8036 = 4.8 (to 1 d.p.)

b

$$4 \cdot 8\, 0\, |\, 3\, 6$$

If the number after the
line is less than 5,
round down.

4.8036 = 4.80 (to 2 d.p.)

Even though 4.8 is equivalent to 4.80, the answer must be 4.80 to show that you have rounded to 2 decimal places.

c

$$4 \cdot 8\, 0\, 3\, |\, 6$$

If the number after the
line is less than 5,
round down.

4.8036 = 4.804 (to 3 d.p.)

Study tip

- Rounding to 1 decimal place is the same as rounding to the nearest tenth.
- Rounding to 2 decimal places is the same as rounding to the nearest hundredth.
- Rounding to 3 decimal places is the same as rounding to the nearest thousandth.

Apply 22.2

1 Round each of the following numbers to 1 decimal place:

a 7.81	**c** 3.96	**e** 56.251	**g** 0.58	**i** 0.09
b 4.52	**d** 4.05	**f** 682.824	**h** 0.4999	**j** 0.039

2 Round each of the following numbers to 2 decimal places:

a 5.473	**c** 78.046	**e** 2.005	**g** 0.0175	**i** 0.0574
b 9.089	**d** 123.904	**f** 0.175	**h** 0.574	**j** 0.9966

3 Round these numbers to the degree of accuracy given in brackets:

a 4.7 (to the nearest whole number)   **f** 2472.472 (to the nearest ten)

b 0.894 (to the nearest hundredth)   **g** 2472.472 (to the nearest tenth)

c 8160.076 (to the nearest hundredth)   **h** 2526.2728 (to the nearest thousandth)

d 172.278 (to the nearest tenth)   **i** 2526.2728 (to the nearest thousand)

e 0.090909 (to the nearest thousandth)   **j** 1919.1919 (to the nearest hundredth).

4 A car is 5.279 metres long.

a Write this length correct to 2 decimal places.

b Rewrite your answer to part **a** in another way.

5 A doctor takes the temperature of one of his patients. The patient has a temperature of 36.94 degrees Celsius. Write this temperature to:

   a the nearest degree   **b** the nearest 0.1 of a degree.

6 It takes the Earth approximately one day to complete a single rotation on its own axis. This is known as the rotation period.

The table below shows the rotation period for five of the planets in our solar system:

Planet	Rotation period (in days)
Mercury	58.646225
Venus	243.0187
Earth	0.99726968
Mars	1.02595675
Jupiter	0.41354

   a Round each rotation period correct to 2 decimal places.

   b Which two planets have very similar rotation periods?

7 Sayed works out $\frac{2}{3}$ on his calculator. The calculator gives him the answer 0.66666667.

   a Give this answer correct to 3 decimal places.

   b The calculator's answer has already been rounded. To how many decimal places has it been rounded?

8 The table shows the five fastest times ever run by men in the 5000 metres.

The time is given in minutes and seconds. For example, 12:37.35 means 12 minutes and 37.35 seconds. Round each of the times to the nearest second.

Name	Country	Time
Kenenisa Bekele	Ethiopia	12:37.35
Haile Gebrselassie	Ethiopia	12:39.36
Daniel Komen	Kenya	12:39.74
Eliud Kipchoge	Kenya	12:46.53
Sileshi Sihine	Ethiopia	12:47.04

9 Using your calculator, work out:

$$(4.1^2 + 3.2^2)^3$$

   a Give your answer as the exact number displayed on the calculator.

   b Give your answer correct to 1 decimal place.

10 Using your calculator, work out $\dfrac{10.23 \times 0.75}{7.64}$.

   a Give your answer as the exact number displayed on the calculator.

   b Give your answer correct to 1 decimal place.

Learn 22.3 Significant figures

Numbers can also be rounded to a given number of **significant figures**.

Significant figures are counted from the first non-zero digit.

$$3\ 4\ \cdot\ 7\ 0\ 2$$

1st sig. fig.   2nd sig. fig.   3rd sig. fig.   4th sig. fig.   5th sig. fig.

The number 3 is the most significant figure as it is worth 30. The next most significant figure is the 4 as it is worth 4 units. The least significant figure is 2 because it is only worth 2 thousandths (0.002).

The zeros at the front of the number are not significant:

$$0\ \cdot\ 0\ 1\ 2\ 7$$

1st sig. fig.   2nd sig. fig.   3rd sig. fig.

Example

Round each of these numbers to 2 significant figures:

a 656   **b** 4.0356   **c** 0.00347

Solution

a

$$6\ 5\ |\ 6$$

If the number after the line is 5 or more, round up.

656 = 660 (to 2 s.f.)

Notice here that a zero has been added to make the number the right size.

656 cannot round to 66. It rounds to 660, which is much nearer.

b

$$4\ \cdot\ 0\ |\ 3\ 5\ 6$$

If the number after the line is 5 or more, round up.

4.0356 = 4.0 (to 2 s.f.)

c

0·0034|7

If the number after the line is 5 or more, round up.

Ignore the zeros at the front of the number as they are not significant.

0.00347 = 0.0035 (to 2 s.f.)

Estimating

When using a calculator to find the answers to calculations, it is often useful to estimate your answer first.

This is usually done by rounding each number to one significant figure.

Example

By rounding each number to one significant figure, find an estimate to:

5452 × 574

Solution

Draw in the lines after the first significant figure.

5|452 × 5|74

Using the rules for rounding, the estimate is:

$$5000 \times 600 = 5 \times 6 \times 1000 \times 100$$
$$= 30 \times 100\,000$$
$$= 3\,000\,000$$

The actual answer is 3 129 448, which is close to 3 000 000.

Example

$$\frac{432 \times 256}{96}$$

a Write all the numbers in the above calculation correct to 1 significant figure.

b Use your answers to estimate the value of the calculation.

c Use your calculator to find the value of the original calculation correct to 3 significant figures.

Solution

a $\dfrac{4|32 \times 2|56}{9|6} = \dfrac{400 \times 300}{100}$

c $\dfrac{432 \times 256}{96} = 115|2 = 1150$ (to 3 sf)

b $\dfrac{400 \times 300}{100} = \dfrac{120\,000}{100} = 1200$

The rounded answer of 1200 is close to the accurate answer of 1152.

Example

$0.5178 \times (3.16 + 6.932)^2$

a Write all numbers in the above calculation correct to one significant figure.

b Use your answers to estimate the value of the calculation.

c Use your calculator to find the value of the original calculation correct to 3 significant figures.

Solution

a $0.5|178 \times (3|.16 + 6|.932)^2$

$= 0.5 \times (3 + 7)^2$

b $0.5 \times (3 + 7)^2 = 0.5 \times 10^2 = 0.5 \times 100 = 50$

c $0.5178 \times (3.16 + 6.932)^2 = 52.7|3713466 \ldots = 52.7$ (to 3 s.f.)

Study tip

When asked to calculate something, always do a quick estimate to make sure that you entered the numbers correctly in the calculator. Your estimate should be close to your accurate answer.

Apply 22.3

1 Round these numbers to 1 significant figure:

| **a** 38 | **c** 134 | **e** 128.1 | **g** 0.037 | **i** 0.006767 |
| **b** 8723 | **d** 45.9 | **f** 23 450.6 | **h** 0.72 | **j** 0.1987 |

2 Round these numbers to 3 significant figures:

a 45 723	**e** 4050.7	**i** 1.0101
b 2 398 000	**f** 4.076	**j** 0.000056765
c 12.7282	**g** 0.3545	
d 321.936	**h** 0.00070707	

3 Round each of these to the number of significant figures given in brackets:

a 188 m (to 1 s.f.)	**e** 784.728 km (to 4 s.f.)	**i** 0.007945 m (to 2 s.f.)
b 776 g (to 2 s.f.)	**f** 3.5026 litres (to 3 s.f.)	**j** 0.03985 kg (to 2 s.f.)
c 28 643 miles (to 3 s.f.)	**g** 0.89 mm (to 1 s.f.)	
d 58.44 minutes (to 2 s.f.)	**h** 0.00708 km^2 (to 1 s.f.)	

4 Estimate the answer to these calculations, by rounding each number to 1 significant figure:

a $2.95 + 4.52$ **b** $1027.5 + 235.4$ **c** $47.84 - 9.23$ **d** $2564.3 - 1632.4$

Now use your calculator to find the accurate answers. Compare each answer with its estimate.

5 Estimate the answer to these calculations, by rounding each number to 1 significant figure:

    a 47.9×24.6 **b** 6.2×166 **c** $124.1 \div 36.5$ **d** $360.75 \div 19.5$

    Now use your calculator to find the accurate answers. Compare each answer with its estimate.

6 $\dfrac{32.6 + 15.2}{9.91}$

    a Write all the numbers in the above calculation correct to 1 significant figure.

    b Use your answers to estimate the value of the calculation, correct to 1 significant figure.

    c Use your calculator to find the value of the original calculation, correct to 2 significant figures.

7 $\dfrac{180.2 + 142.5}{245.4 - 98.7}$

    a Write all the numbers in the above calculation correct to 1 significant figure.

    b Use your answers to estimate the value of the calculation, correct to 1 significant figure.

    c Use your calculator to find the value of the original calculation, correct to 3 significant figures.

8 $89.59 - 6.35 \times 0.48$

    a Write all the numbers in the above calculation correct to 1 significant figure.

    b Use your answers to estimate the value of the calculation, correct to 1 significant figure.

    c Use your calculator to find the value of the original calculation, correct to 2 significant figures.

9 Give an example of a number that when rounded to 2 significant figures or to 3 significant figures is 2300.

10 Give an example of a number that gives the same answer when rounded to the nearest 10 as it does when rounded to 1 significant figure.

Learn 22.4 Upper and lower bounds

When a number has already been rounded, you can work backwards to find the numbers it could have been before rounding.

A length is measured as 8 cm (to the nearest cm).

Any length between 7.5 cm and 8.5 cm, but not exactly equal to 8.5 cm, would round to 8 cm (to the nearest cm).

The **upper bound** is 8.5 cm.

The **lower bound** is 7.5 cm.

The length was rounded 'to the nearest cm'.

So the upper and lower bounds are found by adding and subtracting exactly half of this amount to 8 cm, i.e. the upper and lower bounds are found 0.5 cm to each side of 8 cm.

7.5 cm   8 cm   8.5 cm

The measured value could be anywhere in this region

The measured value cannot be 8.5 cm or any value above this as such values would round to 9 cm. The upper bound 8.5 cm is a value that cannot be used.

This is easily shown as an **inequality**.

$$7{\cdot}5\,\text{cm} \leqslant \text{length} < 8{\cdot}5\,\text{cm}$$

is less than
or equal to

is less than

This reads as '7.5 centimetres is less than or equal to the length, which is less than 8.5 centimetres.'

Example

At a recent football match, there were 25 000 spectators (to the nearest thousand).

Copy and complete the following statement about the limits:

___ $\leqslant$ number of spectators $<$ ___

Solution

The number has been rounded to the nearest thousand.

So the upper and lower bounds are found to be half of one thousand, i.e. 500, to each side of 25 000.

The upper bound is 25 500.

The lower bound is 24 500.

So

    24 500 $\leqslant$ number of spectators $<$ 25 500

Example

An answer of 14.8 cm has been rounded to the nearest mm.

Copy and complete the following statement:

___cm $\leqslant$ length $<$ ___cm.

Solution

14.8 cm has been rounded to the nearest mm.

14.8 cm has been rounded to 1 decimal place.

So the upper and lower bounds are found to be 'half of 0.1', i.e. 0.05, to each side of 14.8.

The upper bound is 14.8 + 0.05 = 14.85 cm.

The lower bound is 14.8 − 0.05 = 14.75 cm.

So 14.75 cm $\leqslant$ length $<$ 14.85 cm

Apply 22.4

1 Julio lives in Chipiona in Spain. He goes to school in Sanlucar de Barrameda which is 10 km away, correct to the nearest kilometre.

   a What is the largest possible distance from his home to school?

   b What is the smallest possible distance from his home to school?

2 A baby weighs 3.0 kg to the nearest kilogram.

   a What is the heaviest that the baby could weigh?

   b What is the lightest that the baby could weigh?

   c What is the difference in weight between these two figures?

3 The attendance figures at a Sydney Swans Australian Football match are 62 300, correct to the nearest hundred.

   a What is the largest possible attendance figure?

   b What is the smallest possible attendance figure?

4 A bridge is 3.7 metres high. A lorry is 3.62 metres high, correct to the nearest 1 cm.

   a What is the maximum height of the lorry?

   b What is the minimum height of the lorry?

   c Can the lorry pass under the bridge?

5 **a** The weight of a packet of rice is measured to the nearest gram. The packet weighs 500 g. Find the upper and lower bounds for the weight.

   b You are now told that the measurement of 500 g is correct to the nearest half gram. Find the new upper and lower bounds for the weight.

6 Yoora measures herself to be 139 cm tall, correct to the nearest centimetre.

Copy and complete the following statement about the upper and lower bounds for her height:

   ___ cm $\leqslant$ height $<$ ___ cm

7 State Highway 1 is the longest motorway in New Zealand. It is so long that it crosses the North Island and then continues with the same name across the South Island.

State Highway 1 is 2050 kilometres long, correct to the nearest 10 kilometres.

Copy and complete the following statement about the upper and lower bounds for the distance:

   ___ km $\leqslant$ distance $<$ ___ km

8 Damerae is selling melons in the market. A particular melon weighs 2.9 kg to the nearest tenth of a kilogram.

Complete the following statement about the limits for the weight:

   ___ kg $\leqslant$ weight $<$ ___ kg

9 Two pieces of rope are to be joined together.

The first is 52 metres long, correct to the nearest metre.

The second is 45 metres long, correct to the nearest half metre.

   a Complete a statement similar to the one below for each rope:

        ___ m ⩽ length of rope < ___ m

The ropes are joined.

   b Find the largest and the smallest possible lengths for the new rope.

10

       15.4 cm

       9.8 cm

The dimensions of the rectangle are given to the nearest millimetre.

   a Find the maximum and minimum possible values for:

       i the length   **ii** the width.

   b Use your answers to part **a** to find the maximum and minimum values for the area of the rectangle.
Give each answer correct to 2 decimal places.

Assess 22.1–22.4

1 Round these numbers to the degree of accuracy given in brackets:

   a 6438 (to the nearest thousand)   **e** 43 568 (to the nearest hundred)

   b 732.9 (to the nearest whole number)   **f** 896 439 (to 1 s.f.)

   c 23.74 (to the nearest 10)   **g** 896 439 (to the nearest thousand)

   d 43 568 (to 2 s.f.)   **h** 1 302 075 (to 5 s.f.).

2 Round these numbers to the degree of accuracy given in brackets:

   a 0.67 (to 1 d.p.)   **e** 0.00435 (to 1 s.f.)

   b 0.03546 (to 2 s.f.)   **f** 0.0720563 (to 3 s.f.)

   c 0.03546 (to 2 d.p.)   **g** 0.0459 (to the nearest thousandth)

   d 0.00005769 (to 3 s.f.)   **h** 0.009568 (to the nearest hundredth).

3 In 2010, 1 799 601 pilgrims went to Mecca in Saudi Arabia to perform the Hajj.
Round the number of pilgrims to:

   a the nearest million   **c** the nearest 1000

   b the nearest hundred   **d** the nearest 100 000.

4 Susie worked out the area of a triangle in cm^2.

Her calculator showed the answer as: $\boxed{\text{87.204569}}$

Round this number to:

a the nearest 10

b the nearest tenth

c four decimal places

d three significant figures.

5 Use a calculator to find the answer to:

$$5.2 \times 9.4 \div (21.4 - 20.6)$$

Give your answer:

a as shown on your calculator

b to one significant figure.

6 $\dfrac{12.8 + 25}{8.6 - (63 \div 28)}$

a Write all the numbers in the above calculation correct to 1 significant figure.

b Use your answers to estimate the value of the calculation, correct to 1 significant figure.

c Use your calculator to find the value of the original calculation, correct to 4 significant figures.

7 Approximately 32 000 people attend a rock festival in Ishikari, Japan.

This figure has been rounded to the nearest thousand.

a Copy and complete the statement:

___ $\leqslant$ number of people $<$ ___

b If the number of people is rounded to the nearest 500 people, rewrite the statement showing the new upper and lower bounds.

8 The density of silicon is 2.33 g/m^3, correct to 2 decimal places.

Copy and complete the statement:

___ g/m^3 $\leqslant$ density of silicon $<$ ___ g/m^3

9 In 1610, Galileo discovered the largest four of Jupiter's moons.

The table shows their names together with the radius in kilometres.

Name of moon	Radius in km
Io	1820
Europa	1560
Ganymede	2630
Callisto	2410

These figures have been rounded to the nearest 10 kilometres.

Calculate the upper and lower bounds for the radius of each of the four moons.

10 Nijah and Talal measure their heights to be 149 cm and 157 cm, correct to the nearest centimetre.

By considering the upper and lower bounds for each of their heights, find the smallest possible difference between their heights.

Constructions

Types of construction

Constructions are accurate drawings. You can take measurements from your drawing.

You must take care to be as accurate as possible.

Always use a sharp pencil.

Learn 23.1 Measuring and drawing lines and angles

Measuring and drawing lines

When measuring a line, make sure you line up the 0 on your ruler with the beginning of the line.

This ruler does not mark the beginning with 0, but it is clear where it should be.

The line is 10.6 cm long.

To draw a line, always start drawing from the 0 mark on your ruler.

Measuring and drawing angles

An **angle** is a turn, or change in direction.

You measure angles with a protractor.

Protractors have two scales, one numbered clockwise and the other anticlockwise.

To measure an angle, the cross at the centre of the protractor must be placed on the vertex.

One of the zero lines must be placed on one of the lines making the angle.

Look at the top angle.

The scale starting at zero is numbered anticlockwise. The angle is 30°.

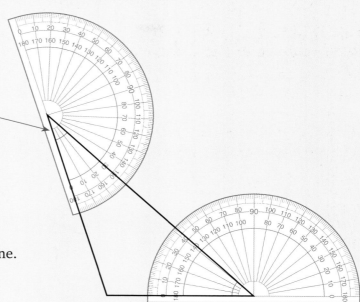

Now look at the bottom angle.

The scale starting at zero is numbered clockwise.

The angle is 42°.

To draw an angle, you must first draw a line.

> Put the protractor on the line with the centre cross on the end of the line.
>
> A zero line on the protractor must cover the line you have drawn.
>
> Follow the scale that starts at zero.

Example

Draw an angle of 132°.

Solution

Draw a line.

Position the protractor with the centre cross on the end of the line.

A zero line of the protractor covers the drawn line.

Follow the zero scale round anticlockwise to 132° and make a mark.

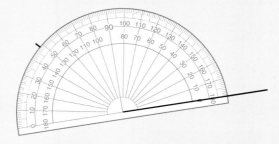

To complete the angle, remove the protractor and join the end of the line to the 132° mark.

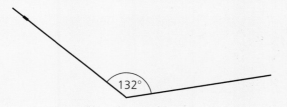

Apply 23.1

1 Measure these lines:

a _____

c

b

2 Measure these angles:

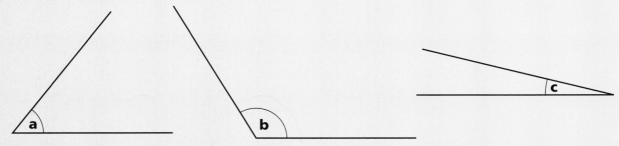

a　　　　**b**　　　　**c**

3 Draw a triangle.
Measure all three sides.
Measure all three angles.

4 Draw a line AB, 11.4 cm long.
At A, measure an angle of 53° and make a mark.
Draw a line from A through this mark.
Mark a point C on this line so that AC measures 9.2 cm.
Join and measure the length of BC.
Measure the angles at B and C.

Learn 23.2 Constructing triangles

You can construct a triangle given three pieces of information:

- the length of two sides and the size of the angle between them (SAS); or
- the length of all three sides (SSS); or
- the length of two sides and the size of an angle that is not in between them (SSA); or
- the length of one side and the size of two angles (ASA).

Constructing an SAS triangle

The angle between two given sides is called the **included angle**.

This is probably the easiest type of triangle to construct, as shown in the example.

Example

Draw a triangle *ABC* with *AB* = 8 cm, *AC* = 6 cm and angle *BAC* = 56°.

Solution

Draw the longer side (*AB*) first, and then use a protractor to measure an angle of 56° at *A*.

Extend this line to 6 cm (shown in blue) to point *C* and then draw *BC* (shown in green) to complete the triangle.

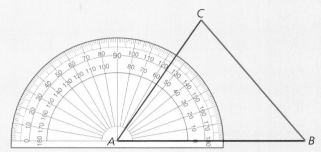

Constructing an SSS triangle

If you are given the length of all three sides, you need to use a pair of compasses to construct the triangle.

This is because you do not know the angles between the sides. The example below demonstrates the method.

Example

Draw a triangle with sides of 8 cm, 7 cm and 6 cm.

Solution

Draw the longest side first: 8 cm (shown in black).

With compasses open to 7 cm, put the point on one end of the 8 cm line and draw an arc (shown in blue).

With compasses open to 6 cm, put the point on the other end of the 8 cm line, and draw an arc to cross the first arc (shown in green).

Finally, connect the two ends of the 8 cm line to the intersection of the arcs (shown in red).

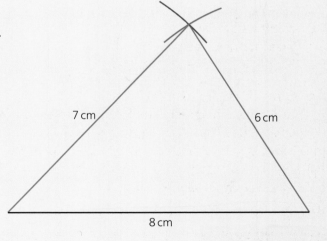

Constructing an SSA triangle

The steps are:

- draw the side that is attached to the given angle
- measure the angle
- use compasses to find the third vertex.

The following example demonstrates the method.

Example

Construct a triangle ABC with $AB = 7$ cm, $AC = 6$ cm and $ABC = 50°$.

Solution

AB forms part of the given angle ABC, so draw AB 7 cm long.

Draw an angle of 50° at B (shown in blue).

With compasses open to 6 cm and the point on A, draw an arc to cross the 50° line (shown in green).

The arc crosses at two points (labelled C_1 and C_2). Joining either of these to A gives a triangle that matches the description.

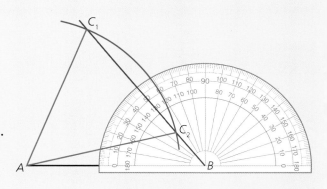

This construction is known as the **ambiguous case**, as it can have two different possible answers.

Constructing an ASA triangle

If you know two angles of a triangle, you can calculate the third as the sum of the angles in a triangle is 180°.

Example

Construct a triangle ABC with $AB = 7$ cm, angle $BAC = 42°$ and angle $ACB = 86°$.

Solution

Draw the line AB, 7 cm long.

Measure an angle of 42° at A (shown in blue).

The angle at $B = 180° - 42° - 86° = 52°$, as the angles in a triangle add up to 180°.

Draw angle $ABC = 52°$ (shown in green).

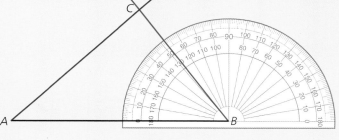

Extend the lines if necessary so they intersect at C.

Check you have constructed the triangle accurately: angle ACB should measure 86°.

Apply 23.2

1 a Make an accurate construction of the triangle PQR.

  b Measure the length of QR.

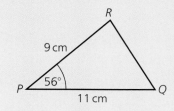

2 a Construct a triangle *ABC*, where *AB* = 9 cm, angle *BAC* = 52° and *ABC* = 64°.

  b Measure the lengths of *AC* and *BC*.

3 Construct an isosceles triangle with two sides of 12 cm and one side of 9 cm.
Measure the size of all three angles.

4 Construct an equilateral triangle with sides of 11 cm.
Check that each angle is 60°.

5 A triangle *ABC* has *AB* = 10 cm, *AC* = 9 cm and angle *ABC* = 49°.
Draw both possible triangles. Measure angle *BAC* in each case.

6 Construct a triangle *ABC* with *AB* = 10.3 cm, *AC* = 6.4 cm and *BAC* = 127°.
Measure the length of *BC*.

Learn 23.3 Constructing parallel lines

Squares, rectangles, rhombuses, parallelograms and trapezia
all have parallel lines.

You can use a ruler and set square to construct parallel lines.

Place a set square on a straight line.

Put a ruler against the **hypotenuse** (long side) of the set square.

Hold the ruler in position and slide the set square along the ruler.

You can draw a line parallel to the first line.

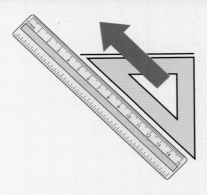

Example

Construct a trapezium *ABCD*, with *AB* parallel to *DC*. *AB* = 7 cm, *AD* = 4 cm, *CD* = 3 cm and *BAD* = 52°.

Solution

First, draw and label a rough sketch.

Draw the base, *AB*, 7 cm long.

Measure angle *BAD* = 52°.

Draw *AD*, 4 cm long.

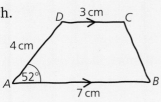

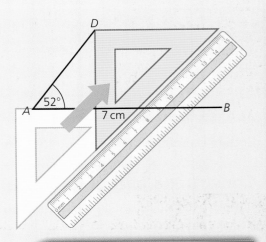

Place the set square along AB.

Put the ruler along the hypotenuse of the set square.

Slide the set square until it passes through *D*.

Draw *CD*, 3 cm long.

Join *BC*.

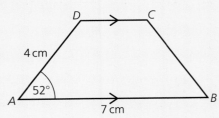

Apply 23.3

1 Construct a rhombus *ABCD* by following these instructions:

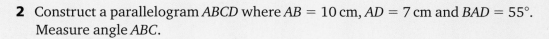

Draw *AB*, 9 cm long.

Measure angle *DAB* = 57°.

Draw *AD* = 9 cm.

Construct a line through *D* parallel to *AB*.

Construct a line through *B* parallel to *AD*.

Label the intersection of these lines *C*.

2 Construct a parallelogram *ABCD* where *AB* = 10 cm, *AD* = 7 cm and *BAD* = 55°.
Measure angle *ABC*.

3 Construct a trapezium *PQRS* with *PQ* parallel to *SR*. *PQ* = 11.5 cm, *PS* = *SR* = 7.1 cm, and *QPS* = 70°.
Measure the length of *QR*.

4 *ABCDE* is a pentagon with dimensions as shown.
AB is parallel to *EC*.
Construct the pentagon *ABCDE*.
Measure the length of *BC* and the size of angle *EDC*.

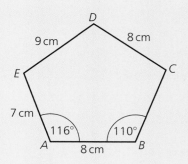

Learn 23.4 Bisectors and scale drawings

To **bisect** means to cut in half.

A **perpendicular bisector** cuts a line in half at right angles.

An **angle bisector** cuts an angle in half.

Both of these bisectors can be constructed using a pair of compasses and a straight edge.

Construct a perpendicular bisector

The perpendicular bisector of a line AB joins all the points which are **equidistant** (the same distance) from *A* and *B*.

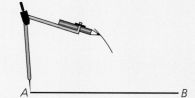

A————————B

Open the compasses more than half the length of *AB*.

Put the point on *A* and make two arcs, one on each side of the line.

Now move the compass point to *B* and repeat.

The arcs must cross the first two arcs.

The line passing through the intersections (shown in blue) is the perpendicular bisector of *AB*.

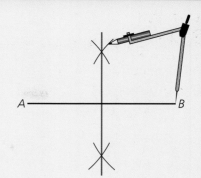

Construct an angle bisector

The bisector of an angle joins all the points which are equidistant from two lines.

The bisector of angle *BAC* joins all the points equidistant from *AB* and *AC*.

To bisect (or cut exactly in half) an angle *BAC*, put the compass point on the vertex, *A*, and make equal marks at *B* and *C* along each arm of the angle.

Using *B* and *C* as centres, draw two arcs to cross inside the angle at *D*.

Draw the angle bisector from *A* through *D*.

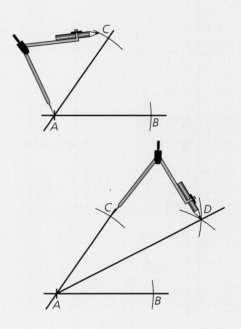

Scale drawings

A **scale drawing** is an accurate drawing that shows the exact shape but does not use the actual size.

Maps and architects' plans are examples of scale drawings.

In a scale drawing, a scale is often represented in words, for example, '1 cm represents 100 m'.

On other occasions, a scale is written as a ratio.

For example, a map might have a scale of 1 : 1000.

This means that the real world is 1000 times greater than the drawing, so 1 cm on the drawing represents 1000 cm or 10 m in the real world.

Example

The map of an island shows three towns, *A*, *B* and *C*.

a Measure the distance of *A* from *B* on the map.

b Calculate the real distance between *A* and *B*.

c *A*, *C* and *D* lie on a straight line. *D* is 1.6 km from *C*.

On the map, mark the two possible positions of *D*.

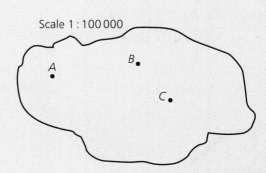

Scale 1 : 100 000

Solution

a Draw the line *AB*. It measures 2.3 cm.

b The real distance is:

$2.3 \times 100\,000$ cm $= 230\,000$ cm

$= 2300$ m $= 2.3$ km.

c 1.6 km $= 160\,000$ cm.

On the map, this is represented by $\dfrac{160\,000}{100\,000} = 1.6$ cm.

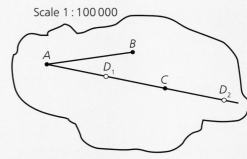

Scale 1 : 100 000

D could be on either side of *C*, so draw a line from *A* to *C* and extend it.

Measure 1.6 cm either side of *C* and mark two points. Label the points D_1 and D_2.

D_1 and D_2 are the two possible positions of *D*.

Apply 23.4

1 Draw a line *AB*, 12 cm long. Construct the perpendicular bisector of *AB*.
Check, by measuring, that *AB* has been bisected.

2 Draw an angle *ABC* = 72°. Bisect angle *ABC*.
Check, by measuring, that *ABC* has been bisected.

3 a Construct a triangle *ABC* with *AB* = 10 cm, *AC* = 6 cm and *BC* = 8 cm.
b Construct the perpendicular bisector of *AC*.
c Construct the perpendicular bisector of *BC*.

4 a Construct a rhombus *ABCD* with sides of 9 cm and angle *DAB* = 58°.
b Construct the bisector of angle *DAB*.
c Construct the bisector of angle *ABC*.

5 Here is a scale drawing of a bungalow.
1 cm represents 2 m.
  a Write the scale as a ratio.
  b By taking measurements from the plan, calculate:
  i the length and width of the living room
  ii the area of bedroom 1
  iii the perimeter of the bungalow.

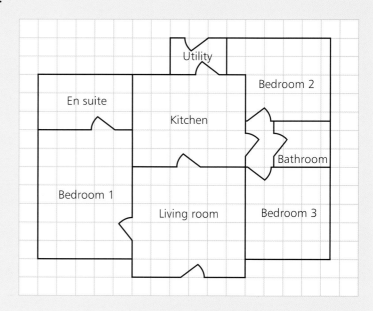

Assess 23.1–23.4

1 Construct a triangle *ABC* such that:

  a *BC* = 6 cm, *AC* = 4 cm, *AB* = 5 cm.
    Measure angle *ABC*.

  b *CAB* = 40°, *ABC* = 60°, *AB* = 7 cm.
    Measure the length of *AC*.

  c *BAC* = 30°, *ABC* = 45°, *AC* = 6 cm.
    Measure the length of *AB*.

  d *BC* = 8 cm, *AC* = 6 cm, *ACB* = 50°.
    Measure the size of angle *ABC*.

  e *BC* = 7 cm, *AC* = 6 cm, *ABC* = 45°.
    Measure the size of angle *ACB*.

2 **a** Make an accurate drawing of the quadrilateral *ABCD*.

  b Construct the bisector of angle *DAB*.

  c Construct the perpendicular bisector of *AB*.

  d Label the point *E* where the bisectors meet.

  e Measure the length of *AE*.

3 Nell makes a scale drawing of a caravan.

  a What length is represented by
    1 cm on the scale drawing?

  b What length on the drawing
    would represent 5 m?

Scale 1 : 50

  c Complete the table below.

	Scale drawing	Real caravan
Overall length from tow bar to back		
Height from ground to roof		
Caravan body length		
Height of door		
Diameter of wheel		

4 A 10-metre ladder rests against a wall with its foot 3 metres away from the wall.

  a Construct a scale drawing using 1 cm to represent 1 m.

  b Use a ruler and protractor to measure as accurately as possible:

    i how far up the wall the ladder reaches

    ii the angle between the ladder and the ground.

5 Draw a triangle *ABC* with sides at least 12 cm long.

  a Bisect *AB*.

  b Bisect *AC*.

  c Label the point *D* where the
    bisectors meet.

  d Draw a circle with *D* as the centre and the
    radius equal to *AD*.

  e What do you notice about the circle?

24 Loci

Learning outcomes:

After this chapter you should be able to:

- use loci to find sets of points which are:
  - at a given distance from a given point
  - at a given distance from a given straight line
  - equidistant from two given points
  - equidistant from two given intersecting straight lines.

A locus is the path followed by a moving point. The plural of locus is loci.

When you drop a ball, the locus (or path it follows) is a straight, vertical line.

The constructions you learned in Chapter 23 will be used again in this chapter.

Learn 24.1 Describing a locus

A grounds person has to mark a centre circle on a football pitch.

He ties a rope to his marker, and stakes the rope to the centre spot.

As he marks the circle, he keeps the rope tight.

The marker goes round in a circle.

The path of the marker is called a **locus (plural: loci)**.

A locus is a path that follows a rule.

A **circle** is the locus of a point moving at a given distance from a fixed point.

Example

Mark a point on the edge of a coin.

Roll the coin along a ruler.

Draw the locus of the marked point.

Solution

The edge of the coin follows the path shown.

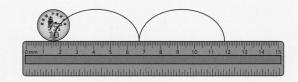

Apply 24.1

1 A child is sitting on a roundabout. Describe the locus of the child when the roundabout turns.

2 Cut a square from card.

Mark a corner of the square.

Rotate the square along a ruler.

Draw the locus of the marked corner.

3 Jesse throws a ball down the path.

Which of these is the locus of the bouncing ball?

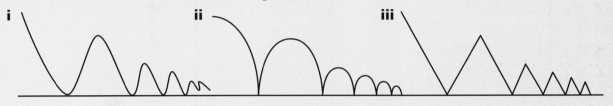

i   ii   iii

Learn 24.2 Constructions and loci

There are some standard constructions that deal with loci.

Points at a given distance from a fixed point

You saw in Learn 24.1 that a circle is the locus of a point moving at a given distance from a fixed point.

Points at a given distance from a straight line

If you are asked to find the distance from a point to a line, you should measure the shortest distance.

This is the distance perpendicular to the line.

A point moving 2 cm from a straight line follows a line parallel to that line.

The locus is shown in red.

The locus consists of two parallel lines, one on either side of the original line.

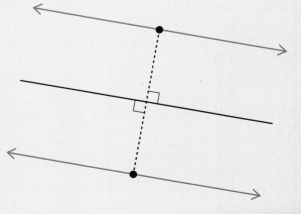

If the line does not continue for ever (this is called a **line segment**), then the parallel lines are joined by semicircles. The complete locus is shown in red below.

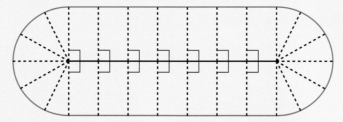

The locus of points less than 2 cm from the line is the area inside the red line, shaded yellow:

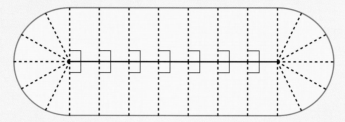

Example

Shade all the points that are within 2 cm of the lines shown.

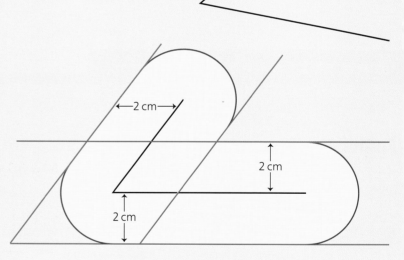

Solution

First, construct parallel lines 2 cm from the original lines (shown in red).

Then, draw arcs with a 2 cm radius with centres at the vertices (arcs shown in blue).

Shade the region inside the parallel lines and arcs.

Points equidistant from two given points

All the points **equidistant** (the same distance) from A and B lie on the perpendicular bisector of AB.

You learned how to construct the perpendicular bisector in Chapter 23.

The dotted lines show that points on the perpendicular bisector are equidistant from A and B.

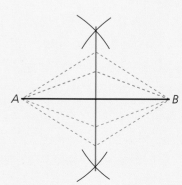

Points equidistant from two intersecting lines

All the points equidistant from two lines *AB* and *AC* lie on the bisector of angle *BAC*.

You learned how to construct the angle bisector in Chapter 23.

The dotted lines show that points on the bisector of angle *BAC* are equidistant from *AB* and *AC*.

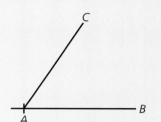

Example

Find:

a the locus of points equidistant from *A* and *B*.

b the locus of points equidistant from *AB* and *AC*.

c the locus of points that are closer to *A* than *B*, and equidistant from *AB* and *AC*. Label the locus *D*.

Solution

a This is the perpendicular bisector of *AB* (constructed in red).

b This is the angle bisector of *CAB* (constructed in blue).

c This is the segment of the angle bisector to the left of the perpendicular bisector, marked in a thicker blue line.

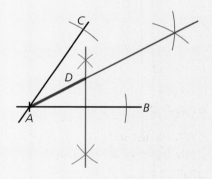

Apply 24.2

1 a Draw a line *AB*, 7 cm long.

   b Shade the locus of points no more than 2 cm from *AB*.

2 a Draw a line *CD*, 9 cm long.

   b Shade the locus of all points no more than 7 cm from *C* and no more than 3 cm from *D*.

3 a Draw a line *EF*, 8 cm long.

   b Shade the locus of points no more than 5 cm from *E* and closer to *F* than *E*.

4 a Draw an angle *ABC* of 56°.

   b Shade the locus of points closer to *BC* than *AB* that are no more than 4 cm from *B*.

5 a Construct a triangle *ABC* where *AB* = 9 cm, *AC* = 7 cm and *BC* = 10 cm.

   b Label the point *P* that is equidistant from *A* and *B*, and also equidistant from *AB* and *AC*.

Learn 24.3 Loci and scale drawing

Many problems require you to apply the skills of constructions, loci and scale drawing.

Example

The map shows an island.

A radio mast is to be placed on the island.

It must be equidistant from *A* and *B*, and no more than 6 km from *C*.

Mark the points where the mast can be built.

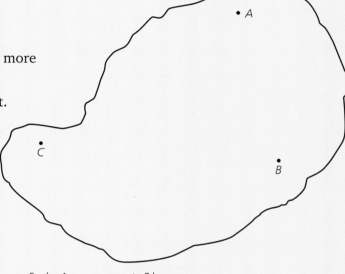

Scale: 1 cm represents 2 km

Solution

The locus of points equidistant from *A* and *B* is the perpendicular bisector of *AB*.

The construction is shown in red.

The locus of points 6 km from *C* is shown as a blue circle, centre *C*.

The radius is 3 cm, as each cm represents 2 km.

The mast can be built anywhere along the thick line *XY*.

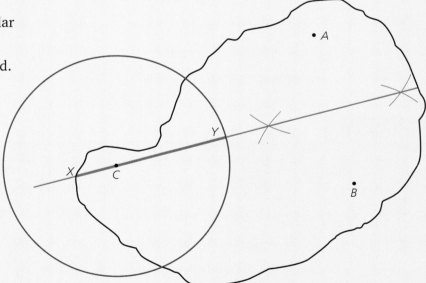

Scale: 1 cm represents 2 km

Study tip

- Leave in your construction lines to show how you answered the question.
- Use shading to mark the answer region clearly.

Apply 24.3

1 The diagram shows a plan of a gorilla in a cage.

The cage is 12 m long and 8 m wide.

a What scale has been used for the drawing?

b A fence is to be built outside the cage.

The fence is 2 m from the cage at all points.

Copy the plan then draw the fence on the plan.

2 A rectangular lawn is 12 m long and 10 m wide.

A gardener places three sprinklers on the lawn.

A and *B* are 3 m from the wall, and 3 m from the edge.

C is 3 m from the house and 6 m from the left edge.

Each sprinkler sprays water in a circle with a radius of 3 m.

Make a scale drawing of the lawn and shade the part that gets watered by the sprinklers.

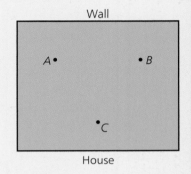

3 A field measures 24 m long and 16 m wide.

In one corner is a shed, 8 m long and 6 m wide.

a Use a scale of 1 cm to 2 m to make a scale drawing of the field and the shed.

b A goat is tethered to corner *A* with a rope 14 m long.

Shade the area that the goat can reach.

c After a week, the goat is tethered to point *B*.

Shade the area the goat can reach from point *B*.

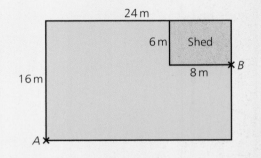

4 *A* and *B* are two points on the coast.

B is 10 km east and 2 km north of *A*.

a Using a scale of 1 cm to represent 2 km, make a scale drawing of the coast.

b A boat is within 6 km of *A* and 7 km of *B*.

Shade the possible area where the boat could be.

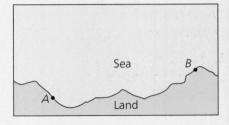

5 Three towns, *X*, *Y* and *Z* are situated so that *XY* = 12 km, *YZ* = 11 km and *XZ* = 7 km.

a Using a scale of 1 cm to represent 1 km, make a map of the three towns.

b A large store is to be built between the towns.

It must be:

i closer to *Y* than *X*, and   **ii** within 4 km of *Z*.

Shade the possible positions of the store.

Assess 24.1–24.3

1 a Draw a rectangle *ABCD* with *AB* = *CD* = 7 cm and *BC* = *AD* = 4 cm.

  b Mark the locus of points that are less than 3 cm from *A* and less than 2 cm from *CD*.

2 Which of these diagrams shows the correct red locus of points exactly 1 cm from *ABCD*?

a
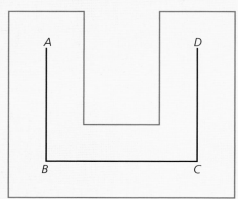

b
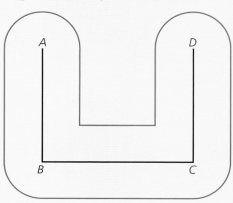

c
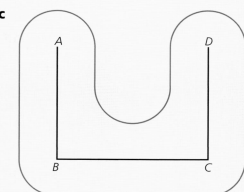

3 *AB* = 7 cm, *BC* = 5 cm and *ABC* = 90°.

Make **three** copies of the diagram to mark these loci:

  a Points exactly 1 cm from *BC* but more than 2 cm from *AB*.

  b Points within 4 cm of *C* and within 5 cm of *A*.

  c Points closer to *AB* than *BC* but within 2 cm of *B*.

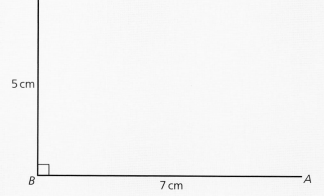

4 a Construct a triangle *ABC* with *AB* = 9 cm, *AC* = 7 cm and *BC* = 5 cm.

  b Shade the locus of points closer to *AB* than *AC* that are within 3 cm of *C*.

25 Statistical measures

Learning outcomes:

After this chapter you should be able to:

- calculate the mean, median and mode for discrete data
- calculate the mean, median and mode from frequency tables
- know when to use each average
- calculate the range.

When you collect a large amount of data, you can display it in graphs or charts. You covered this in Chapter 12.

When comparing two sets of data, it helps to have some summary statistics.

You might use an average, such as the mean, median or mode.

An average is a single number that represents all the data.

You might also discover how spread out the data is by using the range.

Learn 25.1 Mean, median and mode

There are three commonly used **averages**; the **mean**, the **median** and the **mode**. Each has its advantages and disadvantages.

The mean

The most commonly used average is the mean.

The mean is a way of calculating how much each value would be if they were shared out equally.

To find the mean, you add all the values together, and then share them out equally by dividing.

$$\text{Mean} = \frac{\text{sum of all the values}}{\text{total number of values}}$$

When you find a mean, you use every piece of data.

The median

Another way of finding a number that represents a set of data is to find the middle value, or median.

The median can be a useful average because it has the same amount of data on either side.

To find the median, you must put the data in order.

The position of the median, m, is given by $m = \frac{n+1}{2}$, where n is the size of the data set.

If there is an even number in the data set, then there will be a middle pair.

The median is the mean of the middle pair.

The mode

When you take a maths test, there are usually a few people who do very well, a few who do not do well, and a large group in the middle with similar or the same marks.

A quick way to find a score that is a typical score (or average) is to find the most common score, or the mode. The mode is the score with the highest frequency.

The mode can be called the **modal** number.

Example

Find **a** the mean, **b** the median and **c** the mode of 23, 26, 23, 27, 21, 28, 24, 20.

Solution

a The mean is found by adding all the data and dividing by the number of values, 8.

$$\text{Mean} = \frac{23 + 26 + 23 + 27 + 21 + 28 + 24 + 20}{8} = \frac{192}{8} = 24$$

b The median is the middle number.
Put the data in order:
20, 21, 23, 23, 24, 26, 27, 28
There are 8 numbers, so the middle one is the $\frac{8+1}{2} = 4.5$th number.
This is halfway between the 4th and 5th numbers.
The mean of 23 and 24 is 23.5

c The mode is the most common.
23 is there twice, so it is the mode.

Apply 25.1

1 Find **a** the mode and **b** the median of 3, 6, 7, 4, 5, 2, 6, 8, 9.

2 Find the mean of 4, 6, 5, 7, 8, 4, 5, 6, 7.

3 Griselda carried out a survey of the number of people living in each house in a street.
Her results were:
2, 4, 1, 4, 2, 5, 5, 4, 2, 4, 5, 3, 5, 4, 5, 6, 2, 3, 1, 4.
Find **a** the mean, **b** the median and **c** the modal number of people in each house.

4 Three numbers have a mean of 4.
What is the sum of the three numbers?

5 The mean age of four people in a restaurant is 23.
A friend joins them, and the mean increases to 24.
Find the age of the friend.

6 A set of data has a mean of 6, a mode of 7 and a median of 6.5
The largest number is changed from 9 to 10.
Which of the mean, median and mode will change?

7 Five positive integers have a median of 6, a mode of 8 and a mean of 5.
Find the five numbers.

Learn 25.2 Using frequency tables

For large groups of data, the information is often presented in **frequency tables**.

A frequency table is a short way of writing a large list.

For example, you might make a note of how many people there are in each car as it passes the school.

Your list might look like this:

1, 1, 1, 2, 2, 1, 3, 1, 2, 3, 2, 1, 1, 1, 2, 3, 3, 1, 3, 1, 5, 2, 2, 2, 3, 1, 1, 2, 2, 1, 4, 1, 3, 4, 1, 1, 2, 1, 1, 3, 2, 1, 3, 1, 2, 1, 3, 4, 2, 2, 1, 2, 1, 1, 2, 1, 1, 1, 2, 1, 4, 1, 2, 1, 1, 3, 1, 1, 3, 1, 1, 4, 2, 3, 1, 5, 1, 3, 3, 1, 2, 4, 1, 1, 2, 2, 2, 5, 2, 4, 2, 2, 2, 4, 2, 2, 2, 2, 2, 3, 3, 1, 2, 3, 4, 1, 2, 1, 1, 3

The number of people in cars passing a school could be recorded in a frequency table:

Number of people in the car	Frequency
1	44
2	35
3	19
4	9
5	3

To find the mean, you must divide the total number of occupants by the sum of all the cars.

There were 44 cars with 1 person. These cars contained 44 people.

There were 35 cars with 2 people. These cars contained $2 \times 35 = 70$ people.

You can extend the table to help work out the totals:

Number of people in the car	Frequency	Number of people × frequency
1	44	44
2	35	70
3	19	57
4	9	36
5	3	15
Total	110	222

> **Study tip**
>
> You must find the mean of all the data.

The mean is $\frac{222}{110} = 2.02$ (to 2 decimal places)

This table is a short way of writing 1, 1, 1, 1, 1, 1, 1, 1, 1, 1, 1, 1, 1, 1, 1, 1, 1, 1, 1, 1, 1, 1, 1, 1, 1, 1, 1, 1, 1, 1, 1, 1, 1, 1, 1, 1, 1, 1, 1, 1, 1, 1, 1, 1, 2, 2, 2, 2, 2, 2, 2, 2, 2, 2, 2, 2, 2, 2, 2, 2, 2, 2, 2, 2, 2, 2, 2, 2, 2, 2, 2, 2, 2, 2, 2, 2, 2, 2, 2, 3, 3, 3, 3, 3, 3, 3, 3, 3, 3, 3, 3, 3, 3, 3, 3, 3, 3, 3, 4, 4, 4, 4, 4, 4, 4, 4, 4, 5, 5, 5.

The median is the middle number.

There were $44 + 35 + 19 + 9 + 3 = 110$ cars.

The median is the $\frac{110 + 1}{2} = 55.5$th number.

The middle numbers are in positions 55 and 56.

The first 44 cars all had one person. You can see this from the table without looking at the list.

The next 35 had two people.

These are in positions 45 to 79.

So the 55th and 56th had two people.

The median is 2.

The mode is the most common number.

There were more cars with just one person than any other number.

The table tells you this because 1 has the highest frequency.

So the mode is 1.

Apply 25.2

1 The age of second-hand books in a shop is shown in the table below.

Age (years)	Frequency
1	56
2	35
3	27
4	25
5	11

Find:

a the mean age   **b** the median age   **c** the modal age.

2 In a football league there were 36 matches played one weekend.

The table shows the number of goals scored in each game.

Number of goals scored	0	1	2	3	4	5	6
Frequency	6	10	9	4	4	1	2

Calculate:

a the mean number of goals per game   **b** the median   **c** the mode.

3 On a box of paper clips was printed 'Average contents 80'.

An office worker had 60 boxes of these paper clips and decided to count the number of clips in each box.

Her results are shown below.

Number of clips in box	Frequency (number of boxes)
77	4
78	3
79	17
80	15
81	11
82	9
85	1
Total	60

a Calculate the mean number of paper clips per box.

b What is the median number of clips in a box?

c What is the modal number of clips in a box?

d Was the statement 'Average contents 80' accurate?

4 A company employs 30 people.

The job title, number of employees and salary are shown in the table.

Job title	Number employed	Annual salary
Chairman	1	$92 000
Managing director	1	$81 000
Supervisor	2	$35 000
Skilled worker	12	$27 000
Non-skilled worker	14	$20 000

The shop floor workers asked for a pay rise, claiming the average salary was $20 000.

The management said the average salary was $28 233.

The story went to the press, who quoted the average salary as $27 000.

a Which average were the shop floor workers using?

b Which average was the management using?

c Which average was the press using?

d Which do you think is the best average? Give a reason for your answer.

Learn 25.3 Comparing sets of data

The range

Vairaja and Firaki went fishing.

They each caught six fish.

The lengths of Vairaja's fish, in cm, were 7, 9, 9, 9, 10, 10.

The lengths of Firaki's fish, in cm, were 3, 4, 9, 9, 14, 15.

The first set of numbers has a mean, median and mode of 9.

The second set of numbers also has a mean, median and mode of 9.

You should notice that the second set is more spread out.

For Vairaja's fish, the longest fish is 3 cm longer than the shortest fish.

Firaki's longest fish is 12 cm longer than the shortest.

This is called the **range**.

The range is not an average. It is a measure of how spread out the data is.

The range is calculated by subtracting the smallest number from the largest.

The range of Vairaja's fish is $10 - 7 = 3$.

The range of Firaki's fish is $15 - 3 = 12$.

This tells you that the second set is more spread out as it has a larger range.

Example

Find the range of 5, 7, 10, 4, 2, 6, 12, 5.

Solution

The largest number is 12, the smallest number is 2.

So the range is $12 - 2 = 10$.

> **Study tip**
> - Remember that the range is not an average.
> - The range is a single value.

Choosing the best average

The mean, median and mode all have strengths and weaknesses.

Strength of the mean

A strength of the mean is that it uses all of the data. You can also use it for other calculations:

The mean $= \dfrac{\text{sum of all the values}}{\text{total number of values}}$, so

The mean $\times$ total number of values $=$ the sum of all the values.

If the mean age of six children is 13, you can calculate the sum of their ages.

$13 \times 6 = 78$.

Weakness of the mean

If a few pieces of data are much larger or smaller than the rest, the mean can be affected.

For example, a teacher takes eight children on a visit.

Their ages are 53, 8, 8, 8, 9, 9 and 10.

The mean age is $\dfrac{53 + 8 + 8 + 8 + 9 + 9 + 10}{7} = \dfrac{105}{7} = 15$

The mean is not useful as all the children are below the mean and the teacher is much older.

Strength of the median

It is not affected by a very large value or a very small value.

Weakness of the median

It does not use all the values and so can be misleading.

Gopal and Werner are cricketers.

In six innings, Gopal scores 0, 11, 14, 16, 18 and 19.

His median score is 15.

Werner's six scores are 9, 13, 15, 15, 24 and 26.

His median score is also 15.

The mean is a better average in this case. Gopal's mean is 13 and Werner's is 17.

Strength of the mode

The mode is always one of the numbers in the data set.

The mode can be used for **qualitative** data. For example, you could find the modal car colour in a car park.

Weakness of the mode

There may be more than one mode, or none.

It is not useful with only a small amount of data.

Example

The children in class A and class B were asked how many days they had been absent from school in the last month. Here are the results.

Number of days absent	Class A frequency	Class B frequency
0	7	12
1	9	4
2	11	2
3	3	7
4	0	3
5	0	2

a Work out the mean, median, mode and range for each class.

b Which average is the best in this situation?

c Compare the two sets of data.

Solution

a Mean, there are 30 children in each class:

Number of days absent	Class A frequency	Class A: Number of days × frequency	Class B frequency	Class B: Number of days × frequency
0	7	0	12	0
1	9	9	4	4
2	11	22	2	4
3	3	9	7	21
4	0	0	3	12
5	0	0	2	10
Total	30	40	30	51

$$\text{Mean} = \frac{\text{sum of all the values}}{\text{total number of values}}$$

Class A mean $= \frac{40}{30} = 1.\dot{3}$ Class B mean $= \frac{51}{30} = 1.7$

Median, the middle of 30 numbers is number $\frac{30 + 1}{2} = 15.5$

The median for class A is 1.   The median for class B is 1.

Mode, the most common number has the highest frequency.

The mode for class A is 2.   The mode for class B is 0.

b The best average is the mean, as it takes account of all the data.

For class B, the mode is the smallest number, which is not representative.

The medians are equal.

c The range is the largest − the smallest.

The range for class A is $3 - 0 = 3$.
The range for class B is $5 = 0 = 5$.

> **Study tip**
>
> When comparing data, make use of averages and range.

The numbers of absences in class B were more spread out, as shown by the larger range.

On average, children in class B had more absences, shown by the higher mean.

Apply 25.3

1 Decide which average you would use for the following, giving a reason for your answer.

a The average shoe size for students in your class.

b The average height of the students in your class.

c The most common hair colour of the students in your class.

d The average mark in a maths exam for the students in your class.

2 a For each set of data, find the mean, the median and the mode.

    i 5, 4, 10, 3, 7, 4, 5, 4, 11, 7

    ii 16, 12, 20, 12, 18, 12, 20, 12, 16, 12

    iii 5, 2, 3, 1, 26, 6, 0, 2, 8, 7

b For each set of data, say which average best represents the data, giving a reason for your answer.

3 Winston, Luke, Rob and Steve play cricket for the same club.

Here are their scores in their last six innings.

Winston	45	46	23	18	23	101
Luke	23	43	66	74	23	22
Rob	33	59	33	92	20	19
Steve	22	55	70	18	54	34

a Which two cricketers have the same mode?

b Which two cricketers have the same median?

c Which two cricketers have the same mean?

d Which two cricketers have the same range?

4 Karl uses his phone to send texts.

Here are the number of texts he sends in a week.

Monday	Tuesday	Wednesday	Thursday	Friday	Saturday	Sunday
14	12	16	11	12	60	54

a Calculate the mean, median and mode.

b Which do you think is the best average? Give a reason for your answer.

5 Molly, Julia and Philippa belong to an athletics team.

They all want to be selected to run the 100 metres.

They run six trial races.

Here are their times, in seconds.

	Race 1	Race 2	Race 3	Race 4	Race 5	Race 6
Molly	12.6	12.2	12.2	12.8	12.7	12.1
Julia	12.7	12.3	12.3	12.2	12.1	12.8
Philippa	12.4	12.1	12.5	12.3	12.5	12.2

a Who had the best mean time?

b Who had the best median time?

c Who had the best modal time?

d Who won the most races?

e Who should be chosen to represent the team?

Assess 25.1–25.3

1 Find the median of 3, 6, 4, 7, 5, 2, 10.

2 Find **a** the mean, **b** the median, **c** the mode and **d** the range of 24, 33, 35, 23, 33 32, 41, 30.

3 A restaurant carries out a survey of the size of each group having a meal.
The results are shown in the table.

Size of group	1	2	3	4	5	6	7	8
Frequency	1	21	31	32	7	8	1	3

Calculate:

a the mean

b the median

c the mode.

4 Kristin, Petra and Jon are playing a game.
They keep a record of their scores when they roll a dice.

Kristin	3	2	6	2	5	2	3	5	3	1	1	3	5	4	6	5	2	3	4
Petra	1	3	4	6	1	3	3	4	3	5	5	1	4	2	5	6	6	2	2
Jon	2	4	3	1	5	3	6	2	4	1	4	6	2	5	4	3	1	6	2

Next, Kristin rolls a 4.

a After Petra's next roll, she has the same mode as Kristin.
What score did she roll?

b After his next roll, Jon has the same mean score as Petra.
What score did he roll?

5 Four numbers have a mean of 6, a median of 7 and a mode of 8.
Find the four numbers.

6 Irma and Corrine both want to represent the school in the 100 metres.
Here are their times in the last six races, in seconds.

Irma	12.8	12.4	12.3	13.0	12.6	12.3
Corrine	12.4	12.4	12.9	12.5	12.4	12.8

Who would you choose to represent the school? Give your reasons.

7 Jake says, 'I have a higher than average number of legs!'

a Which average is he using?

b Is this the best average to use?

26 Straight line graphs

Equations such as $y = 2x + 3$ are called linear equations because they can be represented by straight lines on a graph. The values of x and y can be negative as well as positive.

Learn 26.1 Introduction to straight line graphs

You have already used coordinates for practical graphs in Chapter 20.

In this chapter, points on the grid are defined by their **x-coordinates** and **y-coordinates**.

The axes divide the grid into four **quadrants**.

P is in the fourth quadrant. Its x-coordinate is 2 and its y-coordinate is -4.

P is the point $(2, -4)$.

> Note that the x-coordinate is written first, then the y-coordinate.

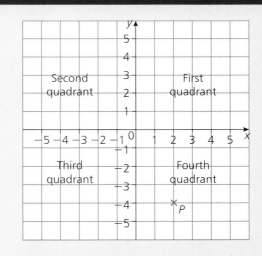

Vertical lines

The points $(2, 4)$, $(2, 1)$, $(2, -2)$ and $(2, -4)$ are marked on the grid.

Any point on the vertical line through these points will have an x-coordinate of 2.

The equation of this line is $x = 2$.

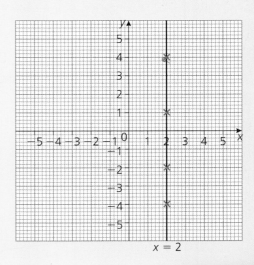

Horizontal lines

The points $(-4, -4)$, $(-2, -4)$, $(0, -4)$, and $(3, -4)$ are marked on the grid.

Any point on the horizontal line through these points will have a y-coordinate of -4.

The equation of this line is $y = -4$.

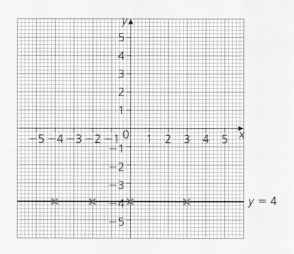

> **Study tip**
>
> The x-axis is the line $y = 0$.
> The y-axis is the line $x = 0$.

Other straight lines

An equation such as $y = 3x - 2$ can be shown on a graph.

The graph will be a straight line and $y = 3x - 2$ is called a **linear equation**.

A linear equation does not contain any powers or roots of x or y such as x^2 or $\sqrt{y}$.

To draw the graph you need to plot the coordinates of three points on the line.

> Two points would be enough to draw the line. The third point is a check to make sure you have worked out the values correctly.

You may be given a table of values to use.

If not, choose any three values of x that lie within the range you have been given.

Substitute each value of x in the linear equation to find the value of y.

Plot the points. Draw the straight line through all three points.

The line must go across the full range of values for x.

> **Study tip**
>
> It is a good idea to use zero as one of your x values as it is easy to substitute this into the equation.

Example

Draw the graph of $y = 3x - 2$ for values of x from -2 to 4.

Solution

Choose three values, for example: $x = 0$ and $x = -2$ and 4, the end values.

Work out the y values and put them in a table.

x	-2	0	4
y	-8	-2	10

Plot the points. (In the exam the axes will be drawn for you.)

Draw the line through the plotted points, making sure it goes from $x = -2$ to $x = 4$.

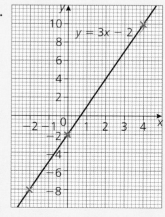

> Note that different scales have been used on the two axes, because the range of values for y is large.

Example

Draw the graph of $x + 2y = 6$ for values of x from -2 to 6.

Solution

Choose three values of x, substitute them in the equation and make a table of values.

x	−2	0	6
y	4	3	0

Plot the points.

Draw the line through the points you have plotted.

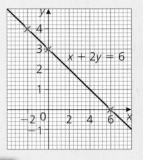

> ### Study tip
>
> When you are asked to draw a straight line graph, always work out the coordinates for *three* points on the line. If you cannot draw a straight line through your three points, go back and check your working as at least one of them must be wrong.

Apply 26.1

1 Write down the equations of:

  a the line *AB*

  b the line *CD*

  c the line *EF*.

2 Write down the coordinates of three points on the line $x = 5$.

3 Write down the coordinates of three points on the line $y = 0$.

4 The line $y = 1$ crosses the line $x = -3$ at the point *P*. Write down the coordinates of *P*.

5 Write down the coordinates of three points on the line $y = x$.

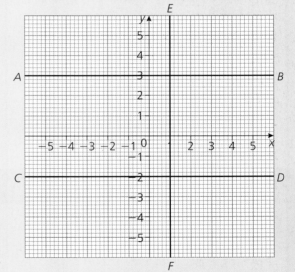

6 a At what point does the line $y = 1$ cross the y-axis?

  b Explain why the line $y = 1$ does *not* cross the x-axis.

7 a Draw a set of axes labelled from -3 to 4 on the x-axis and from -1 to 6 on the y-axis.

  b On these axes draw the graph of $y = x + 2$ for values of x from -3 to 4.

  c Write down the coordinates of the point where this graph crosses the x-axis.

8 a Draw a set of axes labelled from -3 to 3 on the x-axis and from -10 to 8 on the y-axis.

  b On these axes draw the graph of $y = 3x - 1$ for values of x from -3 to 3.

  c Write down the coordinates of the point where this graph crosses the line $y = 4$.

9 **a** Complete this table of values for $x + 3y = 6$.

x	0	3	
y			0

b Draw the graph of $x + 3y = 6$ for values of x from 0 to 6.

c Write down the coordinates of the point on your graph where $x = 2$.

10 **a** Complete this table of values for $x - 2y = 1$.

x	−3	0	3
y	−2		

b Draw the graph of $x - 2y = 1$ for values of x from −3 to 3.

c Write down the coordinates of the point on your graph where $y = 0.4$

11 Which of these equations represent straight line graphs?

A $y = 5x + 1$ B $y^2 = 5x - 1$ C $y = 5x^2 + 1$ D $y + 5x + 1 = 0$

12 Which of these points lie on the line $4x + 3y = 12$?

$P(0, 4)$ $Q(2, 3)$ $R(3, 2)$ $S(0, 3)$ $T(1.5, 2)$ $U(3, 0)$

Show how you found your answers.

13 $A(3, -6)$, $B(0, 0)$ and $C(-2, 4)$ are three points on a straight line graph.

Which of these is the equation of the line?

$x + y + 3 = 0$ $2x + y = 0$ $x + 2y = 0$

Show how you decided.

14 Here are the equations of three straight lines.

$y = 2x - 1$ $x + y + 4 = 0$ $2x - y = 1$

Which of these points: $D(1, 1)$, $E(0, -1)$, $F(-1, -3)$ or $G(2, 3)$ lies on all three lines?

Show your working.

Learn 26.2 Gradients of straight line graphs

The **gradient** of a straight line graph is a measure of how steep the line is.

A line that goes from bottom left to top right has a positive gradient because y increases as x increases.

The gradient can be found from the graph of the line.

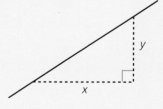

$$\text{Gradient} = \frac{\text{change in vertical distance}}{\text{change in horizontal distance}} = \frac{y}{x}$$

To find the gradient, draw a line parallel to the x-axis and a line parallel to the y-axis to make a right-angled triangle under the line.

This right-angled triangle can be drawn anywhere on the graph.

Study tip

Choose a triangle that gives you a horizontal distance that is easy to divide by.

Example

Find the gradient of the graph.

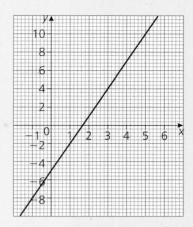

Solution

From the triangle, you can see that the increase in the vertical distance is 12 and the increase in the horizontal distance is 4.

$$\text{Gradient} = \frac{12}{4} = 3$$

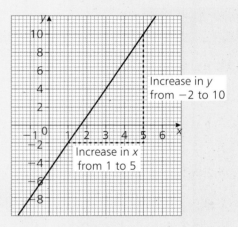

Increase in y from -2 to 10

Increase in x from 1 to 5

Study tip

Take careful note of the scales used on the graph. They may not be the same on both axes so make sure you think of the **units** in both directions and do not just count the squares.

A line that goes from top left to bottom right has a negative gradient because y decreases as x increases.

$$\text{Gradient} = -\frac{y}{x}$$

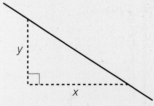

Finding the gradient from the equation of the line

To find the gradient, write the equation in the form $y = mx + c$.

y and x are the **variables** in the equation because they vary, which means they take different values.

m and c are fixed numbers.

The number in front of x (m, which is called the **coefficient** of x) is the gradient of the line.

c is the value of y when $x = 0$, so it tells you where the line crosses the y-axis.

Example

What is the gradient of $y = 6x - 1$?

Solution

The coefficient of x is 6 so the gradient is 6.

Example

What is the gradient of $y + 3x = 5$?

Solution

You have to change the equation to start $y = \ldots$

$$y + 3x = 5$$
$$y + 3x - 3x = 5 - 3x \qquad \boxed{\text{Subtract } 3x \text{ from both sides.}}$$
$$y = 5 - 3x$$

The coefficient of x is -3, so the gradient is -3.

Apply 26.2

1 Find the gradient of each line.

a

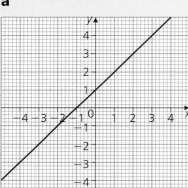

b

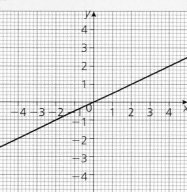

c

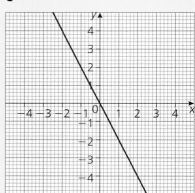

2 Find the gradient of each line.

[Hint: The scales are not the same on both axes.]

a

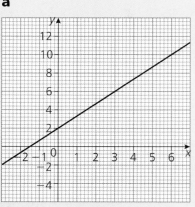

b

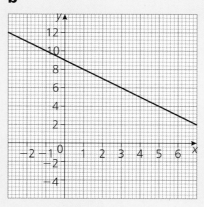

c

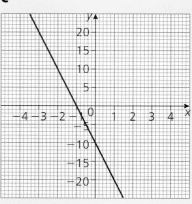

3 Juana says that the lines $y = 3 - 2x$ and $y = 3 - 5x$ have the same gradient.

Explain why Juana is wrong.

4 Work out the gradient of each of these straight lines.

a $y = 4x + 5$ **c** $y = 8 - 2x$ **e** $2y + 1 = 5x$

b $y = x - 2$ **d** $y - 2 = 3x$ **f** $x + y = 7$

5 The diagram shows four lines labelled AB, CD, EF, GH.

  a Which line has a gradient of $\frac{3}{4}$?

  b Which line has the steepest gradient?

    What is this gradient?

  c Which lines have negative gradients?

  d What is the gradient of the line EF?

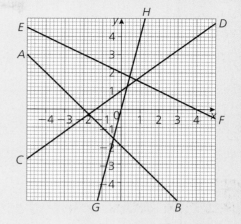

6 Find the three pairs of parallel lines in these equations:

$y = 4x$	$y = 1 + 3x$	$x + y = 8$	$x = \frac{1}{4}y + 2$
$y - 5x = 4$	$2x - y = 7$	$2y - 6x = 5$	$3x + y = 10$
$3y + x = 8$	$4x + y = 2$	$y = 3 - x$	$5y - x = 2$

[Hint: Start by changing each equation to the form $y = mx + c$.]

7 Draw a set of axes labelled from -8 to 8 on both axes.

On your axes draw these straight line graphs:

a $y = 2x - 3$ **b** $y = 2x + 1$ **c** $y = 2x$

What do you notice?

What is the same in the equations of the lines?

Learn 26.3 Finding the equation of a straight line graph

The equation of a straight line graph can always be written in the form $y = mx + c$.

When you are given the graph, first find the gradient (m).

Where the graph crosses the y-axis you can read off the value of c.

Or you can substitute one pair of coordinates to find c.

Use a similar method to find the equation of a line parallel to a given line.

Parallel lines will have the same gradient.

Example

Find the equation of the line joining the points $A(1, 3)$ and $B(4, 9)$.

Solution

Draw a sketch graph to show the positions of A and B.

The gradient of the line is $\frac{9-3}{4-1} = 2$.

The equation of the line is $y = 2x + c$.

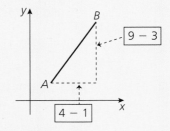

The line goes through $(1, 3)$ so when $x = 1, y = 3$.

$$3 = 2 \times 1 + c \qquad \boxed{\text{Substitute } x = 1 \text{ and } y = 3 \text{ in the equation.}}$$

$$c = 1$$

The equation of this line is $y = 2x + 1$.

You can check your answer by substituting the coordinates of $B(4, 9)$ in this equation.

Study tip

Always draw a diagram to help you to understand the relative positions of the points.

Example

Find the equation of the line through the point $(2, -3)$ that is parallel to the line $y = 3 - 5x$.

Solution

The gradient of $y = 3 - 5x$ is -5, so the new line has the same gradient.

The equation will be $y = -5x + c$.

The new line goes through $(2, -3)$ so when $x = 2, y = -3$.

Substitute these numbers in $y = -5x + c$.

$$-3 = -5 \times 2 + c$$

$$c = 7$$

The new line is $y = -5x + 7$.

Apply 26.3

1 Find the equations of the lines shown below.

a

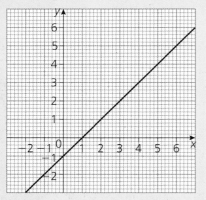

b

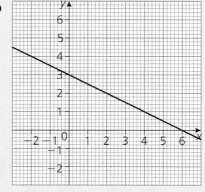

2 Find the equation of the line through $A(0, 1)$ and $B(4, 3)$.

3 Find the equation of the line through $C(1, 1)$ and $D(3, 5)$.

4 Find the equation of the line through $(0, 4)$ that is parallel to $y = 3x - 1$.

5 Find the equation of the line through $(-2, -5)$ that is parallel to $y = 4x + 7$.

6 Find the equation of the line through $(3, -1)$ that is parallel to $x + y = 8$.

7 Find the equation of the line through $(-4, 2)$ that is parallel to $3x + 2y = 6$.

8 Find the equation of the line through $K(-5, 3)$ and $L(1, -1)$.

9 M is the point $(-1, 6)$ and N is the point $(5, 3)$.
Find the equation of the line MN.

10 $P(-4, 2)$, $Q(4, 4)$, $R(6, 0)$ and $S(-2, -2)$ are the vertices of a quadrilateral.
Use gradients to show that $PQRS$ is a parallelogram.

Assess 26.1–26.3

1 Write down the coordinates of three points on the line $y = -5$.

2 Write down the equation of the line through the points $(3, 1)$ and $(3, 5)$.

3 Write down the coordinates of the point where the line $x = -7$ crosses the line $y = 2$.

4 a Draw a set of axes labelled from -1 to 4 on the x-axis and from -9 to 9 on the y-axis.

  b On these axes draw the graph of $y = 4x - 5$ for values of x from -1 to 4.

  c Write down the coordinates of the point on the graph where $y = 4$.

5 a Complete this table of values for $2x + 5y = 10$.

x	−2	0	5
y	2.8		

  b Draw the graph of $2x + 5y = 10$ for values of x from -2 to 5.

  c If this graph was extended, would it go through the point $(10, -3)$?
Show how you decided.

6 Work out the gradient of each of these lines.

a   **b**   **c**

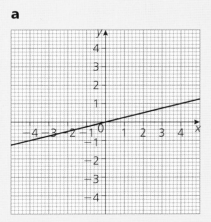
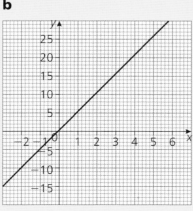
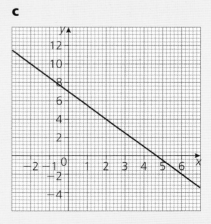

7 Show that the lines $5x + y = 15$ and $y = 3 - 5x$ have the same gradient.

8 Find the three pairs of parallel lines in these equations.

$y = 7 - x$ $2y + 5x = 3$ $5y - x = 2$ $5x = 7 - 2y$

$x - y = 3$ $x + y = 2$ $7 - x = 5y$ $3y + 5 = 3x$

$y + 5x = 1$ $3y - 5x = 5$

9 Draw a set of axes labelled from -4 to 4 on the x-axis and from -4 to 8 on the y-axis. On your axes draw these straight line graphs:

    a $2x + y = 8$ **b** $2x + y = 5$ **c** $2x + y + 4 = 0$

    What is the same for all the lines and what is different?

10 Find the equations of the lines shown below

    a
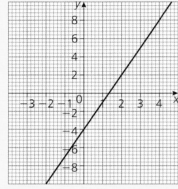
    b
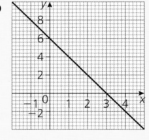

11 Find the equation of the line through $P(0, -5)$ and $Q(2, 1)$.

12 Find the equation of the line through $R(-6, 5)$ and $S(3, 2)$.

13 Find the equation of the line through $(4, 5)$ that is parallel to $y = 7 - 2x$.

14 Find the equation of the line through $(7, -2)$ that is parallel to $x + 4y = 11$.

15 $A(-2, 3)$, $B(3, 2)$, $C(0, -4)$ and $D(-4, -1)$ are the vertices of a quadrilateral. Show that $ABCD$ is a trapezium.

Practice exam questions

1   **a**   The diameter of a particular red blood cell is 0.00753 mm.
        Write this number:
        i correct to 3 dp   **ii** correct to 2 sf   **iii** in standard form.

   b   By writing each number correct to 1 significant figure, find an approximate answer for:
        $96.89 - (6.43 \times 0.494)^2$
        by rounding each number to 1 significant figure.

   c   Use your calculator to find an accurate answer to the calculation.   (*5 marks*)

2   **a**   Find an estimate to the following calculation by rewriting each number correct to
        1 significant figure:

$$\frac{12.14 + 2.98}{7.22 - (8.32 \div 3.64)}$$

   b   Using your calculator, find the exact answer to the original calculation as shown on your
        calculator.

   c   Round this answer to 4 significant figures.   (*3 marks*)

3   **a**   The highest mountain in Bolivia is the Nevado Sajama which is 6542 metres high.
        This height is correct to the nearest 20 metres.
        Copy and complete the statement about the height, h, for this mountain.
        .... $\leqslant h <$ ....

   b   The lowest point in Bolivia is at the Rio Paraguay which is at 90 metres above sea level.
        The upper and lower bounds for this measurement are:
        87.5 metres $\leqslant$ height above sea level < 92.5 metres
        To what degree of accuracy has this been rounded?   (*6 marks*)

4   **a**   Make an accurate drawing of the triangle *ABC*.

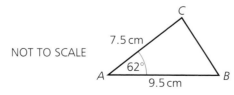

   b   Measure the size of angle *ACB*.   (*4 marks*)

5   **a**   Using your ruler and compasses only construct the triangle *ABC*, with *AB* = 9 cm,
        AC = 8 cm and *BC* = 7 cm.

   b   Using your ruler and compasses only construct the bisector of angle *ACB*.   (*5 marks*)

6 **a** Using ruler and compasses only construct
    i a triangle ABC with $AB = 11$ cm, $BC = 10$ cm and $AC = 7$ cm
    ii the locus of points equidistant from A and B
    iii the locus of points equidistant from AB and BC.

  b Mark the point P that is equidistant from A and B and equidistant from AB and BC. *(6 marks)*

7 **a** Construct a triangle ABC with $AB = 8$ cm, $AC = 7$ cm and angle $BAC = 75°$.

  b Construct the locus of points equidistant from A and B and less than 5 cm from C.

  c Draw the locus of points which are 5 cm from C. *(5 marks)*

8 Three towns A, B and C are situated so that A is 24 km from B and 32 km from C, and B is 26 km from C.

  a Use a scale of 1 cm to 4 km to make a scale drawing of the three towns.

  b An airport is equidistant from AB and AC and is 14 km from B.
    Find the two possible locations of the airport. Label them P and Q. *(5 marks)*

9 Here are the lengths of 10 pencils, in centimetres.

    9.2 7.6 12.2 13.4 12.6 11.9 10.5 13.8 12.3 12.2

  Find:

  a the mean length   **c** the modal length

  b the median length   **d** the range. *(6 marks)*

10 Jolene and Marsha both swim.
Here are their times, in seconds, in five races.

	Race 1	Race 2	Race 3	Race 4	Race 5
Jolene	23.6	26.1	23.7	24.5	26.2
Marsha	25.2	24.5	24.8	24.7	24.9

  a Calculate Jolene's:
    i mean time   **ii** median time   **iii** range.

  b Calculate Marsha's:
    i mean time   **ii** median time   **iii** range.

  c Who do you think is the faster swimmer? Give your reasons. *(7 marks)*

11 The mean height of four girls is 150 cm.
The mean height of five boys is 168 cm.
Calculate the mean height of all nine children. *(4 marks)*

12 Malinda counted the number of peas in a pod. There were 30 pods.
Here are her results:

Number of peas in a pod	Frequency
3	3
4	9
5	
6	7
7	3

   a How many pods had 5 peas?

   b What was the modal number of peas?

   c Find the mean number of peas in a pod.   *(3 marks)*

13 **a** Copy and complete the table for $y = 5 - 3x$:

x	-3	0	3
y	14		

   b Draw the graph of $y = 5 - 3x$ for values of x from -1 to 2.   *(4 marks)*

14 **a** Write down the gradient of the line $y = 5x - 7$.

   b Write down the equation of a line through $(0, 0)$ parallel to $y = 5x - 7$.   *(2 marks)*

15 Write down the equation of the straight line through $(2, 2)$, which is parallel to
$$y = 5 - 3x.$$ *(2 marks)*

16 **a** Copy the grid and draw the straight line joining
the points $(4, 5)$ and $(-1, -2.5)$.

   b Find the gradient of this line.

   c Write down the equation of this line in the form $y = mx + c$.
    (5 marks)

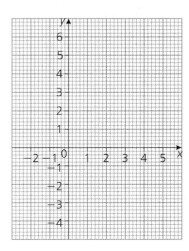

27 Angle properties

In this chapter you will use some of the geometrical properties of polygons and circles to work out the sizes of angles.

Learning outcomes:

After this chapter you should be able to:

- use and interpret vocabulary of circles and polygons
- calculate unknown angles using:
  - angle properties of regular polygons
  - angle in a semicircle
  - angle between tangent and radius of a circle.

Learn 27.1 Regular polygons

A **polygon** is a two-dimensional shape with straight sides.

The table gives the names of the polygons that you need to know.

Name of polygon	Number of sides
Triangle	3
Quadrilateral	4
Pentagon	5
Hexagon	6
Heptagon	7
Octagon	8
Nonagon	9
Decagon	10

A **regular** polygon has all its sides equal and all its angles equal.

A regular triangle is also called an equilateral triangle. (See Learn 14.3.)

The angle sum of any triangle is 180°. So each angle in an equilateral triangle = 180° ÷ 3 = 60°.

A regular quadrilateral has 4 equal sides.

The angle sum of any quadrilateral is 360°. (See Learn 14.2.)

So each angle in a regular quadrilateral = 360° ÷ 4 = 90°.

This is a right angle, so a regular quadrilateral is a square.

Exterior and interior angles of a polygon

Imagine that you are walking around the outside of any large polygon.

(You can walk around either way as long as you are consistent.)

The angle you turn through at each vertex is called an **exterior angle** of the polygon.

The angle inside the polygon at each vertex is called an **interior angle**.

The interior angle and exterior angle at the vertex lie on a straight line.
So at each vertex: *interior angle + exterior angle = 180°*.

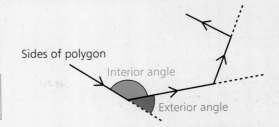

Sides of polygon

Interior angle

Exterior angle

> You can go around the shape in a clockwise or anticlockwise direction.

In walking around the outside of the polygon once, you turn through 360°.

Therefore *the sum of the exterior angles of any polygon = 360°*.

Example

a Find the interior angle of a regular pentagon.

b A regular polygon has interior angles of 135°.
  i Find the number of sides of the polygon.
  ii Write down the name of the polygon.

Solution

a A regular pentagon has five equal sides and five equal exterior angles.

The first diagram shows the exterior angles that you get by going around the outside of the polygon in a clockwise direction. The second diagram shows the exterior angles you get by going around the polygon in an anticlockwise direction.

In each case the sum of the five exterior angles is 360°.

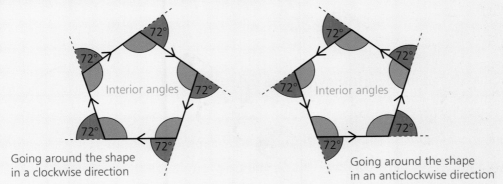

Going around the shape in a clockwise direction

Going around the shape in an anticlockwise direction

Each exterior angle = 360° ÷ 5 = 72°
Each interior angle = 180° − 72° = 108°
The interior angle of a regular pentagon is 108°.

b **i** Exterior angle of this polygon = 180° − 135° = 45°
    Number of exterior angles = 360° ÷ 45° = 8
    Number of sides of polygon = 8

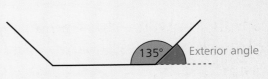

135°   Exterior angle

  ii A polygon with eight sides is called an octagon.

Apply 27.1

1 a i Work out the size of each exterior angle of a regular hexagon.
   ii Use your answer to part **i** to find the size of each interior angle of a regular hexagon.

   b Repeat part **a** for a regular decagon.

2 A regular polygon has 12 sides. Work out the size of:

   a the exterior angle of this polygon

   b the interior angle of this polygon.

3 Work out the number of sides of a regular polygon that has exterior angles of:

   a 20°   **b** 18°   **c** 15°   **d** 12°

4 The diagram shows part of a regular polygon.
Each interior angle of the polygon is 156°.
Calculate the number of sides of the polygon.

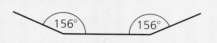

5 A regular polygon has interior angles of 140°.

   a Find the number of sides of the polygon.

   b Write down the name of the polygon.

6 The diagram shows a regular hexagon and a square.
   Calculate the values of a and b.

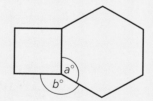

7 The formula for finding the interior angle of a regular polygon with n sides is given below.

$$\text{Interior angle} = \frac{180(n-2)}{n}$$

   a Use the formula to find the size of the interior angle of a regular polygon with 20 sides.

   b Use your answer to part **a** to find the size of the exterior angle of this polygon.

   c Check your answer to part **b** by finding the sum of the exterior angles of this polygon.

8 *ABCDEFGH* is a regular octagon.
   Find: **a** angle *ABC*   **b** angle *ACB*   **c** angle *ACD*.

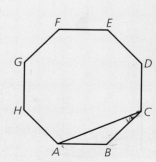

9 The diagram shows a regular nonagon drawn in a circle, centre O.

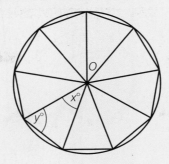

The nonagon is split into nine triangles.

a Choose *three* of the following words that apply to these triangles:

  acute-angled   obtuse-angled   similar
    congruent   isosceles   equilateral

b Work out the values of x and y.

c Use your answer to part **b** to find the size of the interior angle of a regular nonagon.

Learn 27.2 Angle properties of circles

In the diagram, AB is a diameter of a circle, centre O.

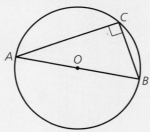

> You can check this by drawing and measuring some angles in semicircles.

Angle ACB is called an angle in a semicircle. An angle in a semicircle is always equal to $90°$.

A **tangent** is a straight line that touches a circle at only one point. The tangent is always perpendicular to the radius drawn at the point where the tangent touches the circle.

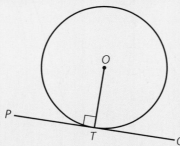

> You can check this by drawing and measuring angles between tangents and radii.

The diagram shows tangent PQ touching the circle, centre O, at point T.

Angle $PTO = 90°$ and angle $QTO = 90°$.

Example

Find the value of each letter in the diagrams. Give a reason for each answer.

a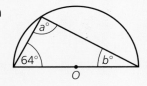

b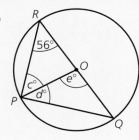

Note: $OP = OQ = OR$ because they are all radii of the circle.

Solution

a $a = 90$ (angle in a semicircle)

$64 + 90 + b = 180$ (angle sum of triangle is 180°)

$b = 180 - 154 = 26$

b $c = 56$ (equal angles of isosceles triangle OPR)

$c + d = 90$ (RPQ is an angle in a semicircle)

$d = 90 - 56 = 34$

angle $OQP = d = 34$ (equal angles of isosceles triangle OPQ)

$e = 180 - 68 = 112$ (angle sum of triangle is 180°)

> Often there is more than one way to find an angle. In this example, e could also be found by working out angle POR, then using angles on a straight line.

Study tip

Remember that the equal radii of a circle often give isosceles triangles.

Example

AB and BC are both tangents to the circle, centre O. Angle $AOC = 126°$.
Find angle ABC.

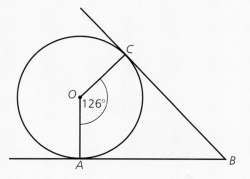

Solution

Angle $OAB = 90°$ (angle between tangent AB and radius OA).

Angle $OCB = 90°$ (angle between tangent BC and radius OC).

Angles of quadrilateral $OABC$ add up to 360°.

So angle $ABC = 360° - 90° - 90° - 126°$

$= 360° - 306° = 54°$

Angle $ABC = 54°$

> Remember to give a reason for each step.

> This is the quickest way to work out angle ABC, but there are other ways. For example: you could draw the line OB and use triangles OAB and OBC.

Apply 27.2

1 Write down the value of each letter in the diagrams. Give a reason for each answer.

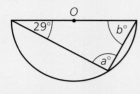 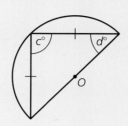 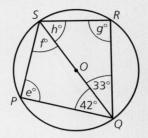

2 Find the value of each letter in the diagrams. Give reasons for each answer.

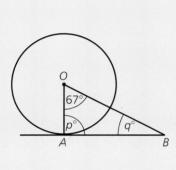 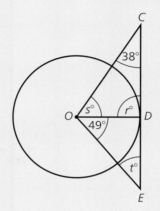 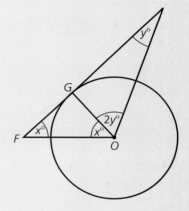

3 In the diagrams, calculate the value of each letter. Give reasons for your answers.

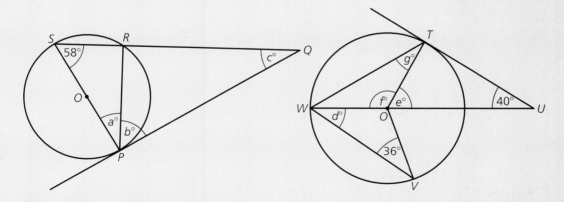

4 *AB* is a diameter of a circle, centre *O*.
CD is a tangent to the circle at *C*. Angle *AOC* = 98°.

Calculate, giving reasons for your answers:

a angle *ACO*

b angle *OCB*

c angle *BCD*.

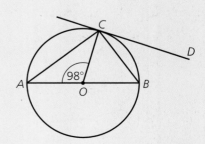

5 *AC* and *BD* are diameters of a circle, centre *O*. *AE* is a tangent to the circle at *A*. Angle *CDB* = 31°.

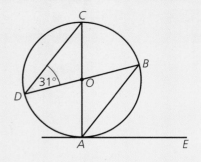

  a Calculate: **i** angle *COD*

              ii angle *OAB*

              iii angle *BAE*.

  b Which of the following words apply to triangles *COD* and *AOB*?

        acute-angled   obtuse-angled   similar

          congruent   isosceles   equilateral

6 *ABC* and *CDE* are tangents to the circle, centre *O*. Angle *OBF* = 24°. *OFC* and *BFD* are perpendicular lines.

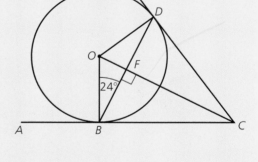

  a Find: **i** angle *FBC*   **iv** angle *FDC*

          ii angle *BCF*   **v** angle *DCF*.

         iii angle *ODF*

  b Name a triangle that is congruent to:
    i triangle *OBF*   **ii** triangle *OBC*.

  c What special kind of triangle is triangle *BDC*?

  d Name six right-angled triangles that are present in the diagram.

7 The points *A*, *B* and *C* lie on a circle, centre *O*. *AOC* is a straight line and *DA* is a tangent to the circle at *A*. Angle *ADO* = 23°.

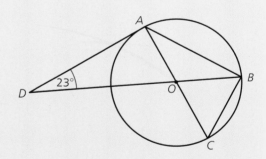

  a Write down the size of angle *DAO*, giving a reason for your answer.

  b Find, giving reasons:

    i angle *DOA*   **iii** angle *OBC*

    ii angle *BOC*   **iv** angle *OBA*.

8 *PTQ* is a tangent to the circle, centre *O*. *RS* is parallel to *PTQ* and angle *PTR* = 59°.
Calculate the size of the following angles.
Give a reason for each answer.

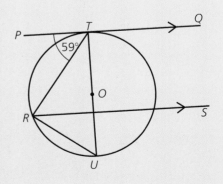

  a angle *RTU*   **d** angle *TRS*

  b angle *TRU*   **e** angle *URS*

  c angle *RUT*

Assess 27.1–27.2

1 A regular polygon has 15 sides. Work out the size of:

  a the exterior angle of this polygon

  b the interior angle of this polygon.

2 The diagram shows part of a regular polygon. Each interior angle of the polygon is 170°. Calculate the number of sides of the polygon.

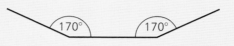

3 A regular polygon has interior angles of 144°.

  a Find the number of sides of the polygon.

  b Write down the name of the polygon.

4 Calculate the value of each letter. Give a reason for each answer.

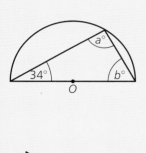
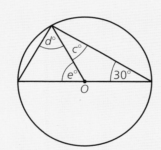
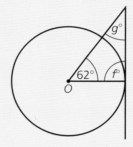

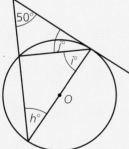
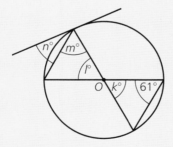
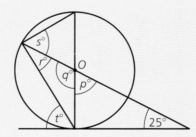

5 *PS* and *PT* are both tangents to the circle, centre *O*. Angle *SPT* = 58°. Find angle *SOT*.

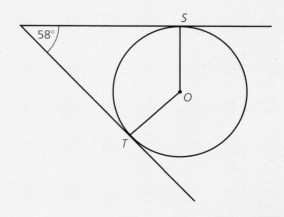

6 *SAT* is a tangent and *BOC* is a diameter of the circle, centre *O*.
Find the following angles, giving reasons for your answers:

   a angle *OAC*   **c** angle *SAB*   **e** angle *AOB*.

   b angle *OAB*   **d** angle *ABO*

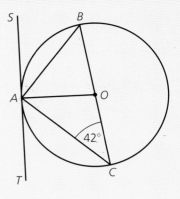

7 *GAF* is a tangent to the circle and *DE* is parallel to *AF*.
Angle *FAD* = 70° and angle *BCA* = 52°.

Find the size of the following angles, giving reasons
for your answers:

   a angle *CAD*   **d** angle *ADE*

   b angle *ACD*   **e** angle *CDE*.

   c angle *CAB*

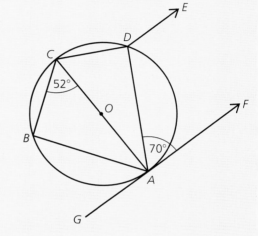

8 *ABCD* are points on a semicircle and *ECF* is a
tangent to the semicircle at *C*.

BC is parallel to the diameter *AD* and
angle *ACB* = 28°.

Find the size of the following angles, giving
reasons for your answers:

   a angle *CAO*   **d** angle *COF*

   b angle *ACO*   **e** angle *CFO*.

   c angle *BCE*

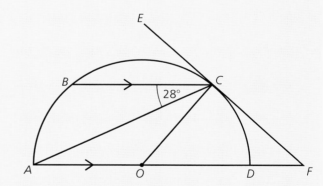

28 Equations and formulae

Learning outcomes:

After this chapter you should be able to:
- transform simple formulae
- solve linear equations with the unknown on both sides
- solve equations with brackets
- solve simultaneous equations.

Formulae are like equations: they contain an equals sign and have terms on both sides of the equals sign.

The difference between formulae and equations is that the variables in a formula stand for definite quantities and the variables in an equation stand for unknown quantities. An equation can usually be solved to find values for the variables.

Learn 28.1 Transforming simple formulae

Transforming formulae is also known as **changing the subject** of a formula.

The subject of a formula is the letter at the start of the formula, on the left of the equals sign. In the formula for the perimeter of a rectangle, $P = 2L + 2B$, the subject is P. You can transform this formula to make L or B the subject. Take the same steps as those you have used to solve equations.

Example

a Make L the subject of the formula $P = 2L + 2B$

b Find the length of a rectangle with breadth 5 cm and perimeter 28 cm.

Solution

a

| $P = 2L + 2B$ | Write the formula down. |

$P - 2B = 2L + 2B - 2B$ — Subtract $2B$ from both sides as you want the term in L on its own.

$P - 2B = 2L$

$\dfrac{P - 2B}{2} = \dfrac{2L}{2}$ — Divide both sides by 2.

$\dfrac{P - 2B}{2} = L$

$L = \dfrac{P - 2B}{2}$ — Rewrite the formula with L as the subject on the left-hand side.

b Substitute $B = 5$ and $P = 28$ in this new formula:

$$L = \frac{28 - 2 \times 5}{2}$$
$$= \frac{18}{2}$$
$$= 9$$

The length is 9 cm.

Study tip

- Start by writing down the formula.
- Look for the term that contains the letter that is going to become the subject.
- You need this term on its own.
- Always finish with the new subject on the left-hand side.

Apply 28.1

1 Rearrange the formula $A = p + q$ to make p the subject.

2 Make k the subject of the formula $M = 3k + 20$

3 Make q the subject of the formula $y = 2p + q + 2t$

4 Rearrange the formula $N = 5(C - 2)$ to make C the subject.

5 Tania uses the formula $v = u + at$ in science.
Make a the subject of the formula.

6 Luiz uses the formula $c = 25 + 9y$ to work out the charge, in \$, for hiring a bicycle for y hours.

   a Make y the subject of the formula.

   b Rafael pays Luiz \$52 to hire a bicycle.
     How many hours is Rafael paying for?

7 The volume of a cuboid is given by the formula $V = lbh$

   a Make b the subject of the formula.

   b A cuboid is 9 cm long and 5 cm high, and has a volume of 270 cm³.
     Calculate the breadth of this cuboid.

8 The formula for the circumference of a circle is $C = 2\pi r$

   a Make r the subject of the formula.

   b The circumference of a circle is 36 cm.
     Calculate the radius of this circle.

9 The formula for calculating simple interest is $I = \dfrac{PRT}{100}$

   a Make T the subject of the formula.

   b Calculate T when $P = 750$, $R = 4$ and $I = 105$

Learn 28.2 Equations with the unknown on both sides

Follow these steps to solve this type of equation:

Step 1: Collect all the terms that contain the
unknown letter on one side.

> Signs belong to the term after them.

Step 2: Collect all the other terms on the other side.

> Take one step at a time.

Example

Solve the equation: $4x + 3 = 10 - x$

Solution

$$4x + 3 = 10 - x$$

$$4x + 3 + x = 10 - x + x \qquad \boxed{\text{Add } x \text{ to both sides.}}$$

$$5x + 3 = 10$$

$$5x + 3 - 3 = 10 - 3 \qquad \boxed{\text{Subtract 3 from both sides.}}$$

$$5x = 7$$

$$\frac{5x}{5} = \frac{7}{5} \qquad \boxed{\text{Divide both sides by 5.}}$$

$$x = 1.4$$

Example

Solve the equation: $3y + 8 = 5y - 7$

Solution

$$3y + 8 = 5y - 7$$

$$3y + 8 - 3y = 5y - 7 - 3y \qquad \boxed{\text{Take } 3y \text{ from both sides.}}$$

$$8 = 2y - 7$$

$$8 + 7 = 2y - 7 + 7 \qquad \boxed{\text{Add 7 to both sides.}}$$

$$15 = 2y$$

$$\frac{15}{2} = \frac{2y}{2} \qquad \boxed{\text{Divide both sides by 2.}}$$

$$7.5 = y$$

Study tip

Collect the terms in y on the side that has the larger number of them already.

Apply 28.2

1 Solve these equations:

a $2x - 4 = x + 3$

b $4y + 3 = 2y + 11$

c $6z + 2 = 7 + 4z$

d $5p - 2 = 8 + 3p$

e $q + 5 = 9 - 3q$

f $3 + t = 17 - 6t$

g $9 + 2a = 4 - 3a$

h $4b - 15 = 10b - 3$

i $4 - c = 7c$

j $15 + d = 4d - 6$

k $5 - 7m = 2 - 6m$

l $14 - 3n = 8 - 6n$

2 Ella solves the equation $7x + 2 = 5 - 2x$

Her first step is $5x + 2 = 5$

What mistake has Ella made?

3 Tomas solves the equation $4y + 2 = 3 - y$

He writes down $3y = 5$

Tomas has made two mistakes.

What are these mistakes?

4 $5a - 1 = \blacksquare - 2a$

The answer to this equation is $a = 2$

What is the number under the block?

5 $3b + \blacksquare = 2 - 2b$

The answer to this equation is $b = -1$

What is the number under the block?

Learn 28.3 Equations with brackets

For equations with brackets such as $2(3x - 1) = 22$, your first step is to remove the bracket.

This usually means multiplying out the bracket.

Once you have removed the bracket, follow the rules for solving equations.

[Hint: In some equations you can start with division instead, as shown in the alternative solution in the first example.]

Example

Solve the equation: $2(3x - 1) = 22$

Solution

$$2(3x - 1) = 22$$

$$6x - 2 = 22 \qquad \boxed{\text{Remember to multiply both terms in the bracket by 2.}}$$

$$6x - 2 + 2 = 22 + 2 \qquad \boxed{\text{Add 2 to both sides.}}$$

$$6x = 24$$

$$\frac{6x}{6} = \frac{24}{6} \qquad \boxed{\text{Divide both sides by 6.}}$$

$$x = 4$$

Alternative solution

You could start by dividing both sides of the equation by 2.

$$2(3x - 1) = 22$$

$$3x - 1 = 11 \qquad \boxed{\text{This method works well here because 22 is divisible by 2.}}$$

$$3x - 1 + 1 = 11 + 1 \qquad \boxed{\text{Add 1 to both sides.}}$$

$$3x = 12$$

$$\frac{3x}{3} = \frac{12}{3} \qquad \boxed{\text{Divide both sides by 3.}}$$

$$x = 4$$

Example

Solve the equation: $11 - 3(y + 2) = 9 - 5y$

Solution

$11 - 3(y + 2) = 9 - 5y$

$11 - 3y - 6 = 9 - 5y$ When you multiply out this bracket, remember $-3 \times +2 = -6$.

$5 - 3y = 9 - 5y$ Simplify the left-hand side by collecting like terms.

$5 - 3y - 5 = 9 - 5y - 5$ Subtract 5 from both sides.

$-3y = 4 - 5y$

$-3y + 5y = 4 - 5y + 5y$ Add $5y$ to both sides.

$2y = 4$

$\dfrac{2y}{2} = \dfrac{4}{2}$ Divide both sides by 2.

$y = 2$

Study tip

Take care with negative terms when you are deciding which side you want to collect y on. For example: $-3y$ is greater than $-5y$.

Apply 28.3

1 Solve these equations:

   a $5(x + 4) = 55$

   b $3(y - 8) = 9$

   c $20 = 4(z - 3)$

   d $2(3 - a) = 14$

   e $4(b + 3) = 18$

   f $13 = 2(5c - 1)$

   g $4(d + 3) = 15$

   h $11 = 4(e + 3)$

2 Solve these equations:

   a $4(k + 2) = 2k + 9$

   b $6(m - 3) = 10 - m$

   c $5n + 3 = 4(n - 2)$

   d $3(2p - 3) = 1 + 7p$

   e $2(5 - 2q) = 8 - 3q$

   f $6 + t = 5(t - 2)$

   g $19 = 6 - 4(x - 3)$

   h $5(y - 7) - 3(2y - 5) + 22 = 0$

3 Geoff thinks of a number, adds 5 and then doubles the result. His answer is 42.

Write this as an equation in x.

Solve the equation to find Geoff's number.

4 Yazmin thinks of a number, subtracts 7 and then multiplies the result by 3. Her answer is 51.

Write this as an equation in y.

Solve the equation to find Yazmin's number.

Learn 28.4 Simultaneous equations

We have seen how to solve an equation containing one unknown. When there are two unknowns we need *two* equations in order to find a solution. The two equations are called **simultaneous equations**.

Solving by elimination

To solve simultaneous equations by elimination, make sure the **coefficients** of one of the unknowns in both equations match.

> The coefficient of a quantity such as x is the number in front of it.

For example: in the equation $4x - 3y = 13$, the coefficient of x is 4 and the coefficient of y is -3.

Then add or subtract the equations so that one unknown disappears.

For example: $3x + 2y = 9$
$5x - 2y = 7$

> These equations are ready to be added.
> The y coefficients match as $+2y$ added to $-2y$ equals zero.

Adding these equations gives $8x = 16$, which can be solved to give x. You then substitute the value of x into one of the original equations to get y.

You always aim to produce an equation in one unknown only, so that you can find that unknown first.

For this pair of equations:

$4x + 3y = 11$

$2x + 3y = 13$

> These equations are ready to be subtracted.
> The y coefficients match as $+3y$ subtracted from $+3y$ equals zero.

Subtracting the second equation from the first gives $2x = -2$, which can be solved to give x.

Example

Solve the simultaneous equations:

$$4x - 3y = 13$$
$$2x + 3y = 11$$

Solution

The coefficients of y are $+3$ and -3, so add the equations to eliminate y.

$$4x - 3y = 13 \quad +$$
$$2x + 3y = 11$$
$$6x \quad\quad = 24$$
$$x = 4$$

Now substitute $x = 4$ in the first equation:

$$4 \times 4 - 3y = 13$$
$$16 - 3y = 13$$
$$y = 1$$

Use the second equation to check your answers by substitution:

$$2x + 3y = 11$$
$$2 \times 4 + 3 \times 1 = 8 + 3 = 11 \checkmark$$

Example

Solve the simultaneous equations:

$$2x + 3y = 5$$
$$2x - 5y = 13$$

Solution

The coefficients of x are $+2$ and $+2$ so subtract the equations to eliminate x.

$$2x + 3y = 5 \quad -$$
$$\underline{2x - 5y = 13}$$
$$8y = -8$$
$$y = -1$$

> **Study tip**
>
> Be very careful when you subtract equations.
>
> Write the equations one under the other and make sure you do the same to both sides.

Now substitute $y = -1$ in the first equation:

$$2x + 3 \times -1 = 5$$
$$2x = 8$$
$$x = 4$$

Use the second equation to check your answers by substitution:

$$2 \times 4 - 5 \times -1 = 8 + 5 = 13 \ ✓$$

If there is no matching coefficient in the pair of simultaneous equations, you have to multiply one or both of them in order to get matching coefficients.

Example

Solve the simultaneous equations:

$$4x + 3y = 6$$
$$3x - 2y = 13$$

Solution

You can make the coefficients of y match by multiplying the first equation by 2 and the second equation by 3, so that $6y$ appears in both equations:

$$4x + 3y = 6 \qquad \boxed{\text{Multiply by 2.}}$$

$$3x - 2y = 13 \qquad \boxed{\text{Multiply by 3.}}$$

Then we have:

$$8x + 6y = 12$$
$$9x - 6y = 39$$

Add these new equations to eliminate y:

$$8x + 6y = 12 \quad +$$
$$\underline{9x - 6y = 39}$$
$$17x \quad\quad = 51$$
$$x = 3$$

Substitute $x = 3$ in the first of your *original* equations, which was $4x + 3y = 6$:

$$3 \times 3 + 3y = 6$$
$$3y = -6$$
$$y = -2$$

Use the second *original* equation, $3x - 2y = 13$, to check your answers by substitution:

$$3 \times 3 - 2 \times -2 = 9 + 4 = 13 \checkmark$$

> **Study tip**
>
> - You must have a pair of terms with matching coefficients.
> - If their signs are the same, subtract the equations (remember this by s s s).
> - If their signs are different, add the equations.

Solving by substitution

In this method, one of the variables in a pair of simultaneous equations can be removed by substitution from one equation into the other. One of the equations has to be rearranged to make x or y the subject.

Example

Solve the simultaneous equations:

$$3x - 2y = 19$$
$$2x + y = 29$$

> **Study tip**
>
> - You can choose whether to solve simultaneous equations by elimination or by substitution.
> - Use the substitution method only when one of the equations can be rearranged easily to give you '$y = \dots$' or '$x = \dots$'

Solution

Rearrange the second equation to make y the subject:

$$y = 29 - 2x$$

Substitute this expression for y into the first equation:

$$3x - 2(29 - 2x) = 19$$
$$3x - 58 + 4x = 19$$
$$7x = 77$$
$$x = 11$$

Substitute this value for x into the expression $y = 29 - 2x$:

$$y = 29 - (2 \times 11) = 7$$

> Check your answer by substitution into the original equation.

Apply 28.4

1 Solve these simultaneous equations. Equations **a** to **d** can be solved by either method. Equations **e** to **i** can be solved more easily by elimination.

a $3a - b = 10$
$a + b = 6$

b $2c + 3d = 11$
$c + 3d = 10$

c $5e - f = 14$
$3e - f = 10$

d $7g + 2h = 9$
$g - 2h = 7$

e $4m - 3n = 0$
$2m + 3n = 9$

f $2p - q = 16$
$2p + 3q = 8$

g $3t + 4u = 3$
$3t + 2u = 9$

h $5v + 4w = 6$
$5v - 3w + 22 = 0$

i $7x + 4y = 25$
$4y = x + 33$

2 The sum of the ages of Adam and Claude is 65 years. Adam is 7 years older than Claude.
Use a pair of simultaneous equations to work out their ages.

3 Beatrice and Clara have $70 between them. Clara has $12 more than Beatrice.
Use a pair of simultaneous equations to find how much money each one has.

4 Solve these simultaneous equations:

a $5a + 3b = 27$
$2a + b = 10$

e $2m - 3n = 15$
$m - 6n = 3$

i $3x + 4y = 37$
$2x - 5y = -6$

b $c + 3d = 22$
$2c - d = 9$

f $2p + 3q = 8$
$3p - 2q = 12$

j $2p - 3q = 4$
$3p + 5q = 25$

c $3d + 2e = 5$
$5d - 6e = 27$

g $4t + 3u = 1$
$12t - 2u = 14$

d $2j + k = 9$
$5j + 3k = 22$

h $7v - 12w = 39$
$5v - 4w = 5$

5 Jake's store sells storage boxes in two sizes.
Large boxes cost $$x$ each and small boxes cost $$y$ each.
Julia buys five large boxes and three small boxes. She pays $48.
Pedro buys two large boxes and three small boxes. He pays $25.50.
Use this information to write down a pair of simultaneous equations and solve them to find the cost of each size of box.

6 Kim buys two adult ferry tickets and three children's ferry tickets. This costs her $35.50
Nicola buys three adult ferry tickets and five children's ferry tickets. This costs her $56.
Use this information to write down a pair of simultaneous equations and solve them to find the cost of each type of ferry ticket.

Assess 28.1–28.4

1 Rearrange the formula $x = 2y + c$ to make y the subject.

2 Make d the subject of the formula $C = \pi d$

3 Make m the subject of the formula $k = 2(m + 5)$

4 The time, T minutes, needed to bake a fish of weight W kg is given by the formula $T = 2W + 7$

a Make W the subject of the formula.

b Find the weight of a fish that takes 16 minutes to bake.

5 The formula for the curved surface area of a cylinder is $A = 2\pi rh$, where r is the radius and h is the height.

    a Make h the subject of the formula.

    b The curved surface area of a cylinder is 350 cm^2.
       The radius of this cylinder is 6.4 cm.
       Calculate the height of the cylinder.

6 Solve these equations:

    a $3x - 1 = 7 + 2x$ **c** $31 - 6t = 3 - 2t$ **e** $5m - 1 = m - 25$

    b $y + 11 = 5 - 2y$ **d** $4k + 3 = 4 + 6k$

7 Solve these equations:

    a $3(p - 11) = 15$ **d** $2(3n - 4) = 1$ **g** $2(c + 8) = 3(c + 7)$

    b $18 = 2(4 - q)$ **e** $4(a - 1) = 3a + 1$ **h** $5k - 3 = 6(3k - 7)$

    c $5(m + 2) = 16$ **f** $7b + 11 = 4(b + 2)$

8 Daniel thinks of a number, adds 9 and then multiplies the result by 5. His answer is 95.
Write this as an equation in n.
Solve the equation to find Daniel's number.

9 Solve these simultaneous equations:

    a $x + y = 11$ **d** $5k + 2t = 16$ **g** $2x - 3y = 8$
         $3x - y = 5$ $3k - 4t = 7$ $3x - 5y = 11$

    b $4p + q = 18$ **e** $3a + 4b = 23$
         $2p - q = 12$ $2a + 3b = 16$

    c $5m - 2n = 3$ **f** $8c + 3d = 2$
         $3m - 2n = 5$ $3c - 2d = 7$

10 The sum of the ages of Maria and Olivia is 59 years.

    Olivia is 11 years younger than Maria.

    Write down a pair of simultaneous equations and use them to work out their ages.

11 Anna buys five rose bushes and three lilies for $81.

    Josef buys two rose bushes and three lilies for $45.

    Use this information to write down a pair of simultaneous equations.

    Solve the equations to find the price of two lilies.

Learning outcomes:

After this chapter you should be able to:

- draw and interpret the graph of a quadratic function
- draw and interpret the graph of a reciprocal function
- solve linear and quadratic equations by graphical methods.

You have drawn straight line graphs in Chapter 26 and in this chapter you will learn how to draw two types of graphs that are curves. You do not use a ruler to join the plots on these graphs, so you have to practise joining them with a smooth curve.

Learn 29.1 Graphs of quadratics

These are examples of **quadratic expressions**: $x^2 + 5$, $3x^2$, $5 + 3x - x^2$.

They all contain a term in x^2. They do not have any terms in higher powers of x, such as x^3 or x^4.

To draw the graph of a quadratic, start with a table of values, as you did for straight line graphs.

The graph of a quadratic expression is a curve, so you have to plot more than three points.

You will be told the range of values of x that is required.

You have to work out the value of y for at least each integer value of x.

Example

a Draw the graph of $y = x^2 - 3$ for values of x from -4 to 4.

b Use your graph to find the values of x when $y = 5$.

Solution

a Start with a table of values.

x	-4	-3	-2	-1	0	1	2	3	4
x^2	16	9	4	1	0	1	4	9	16
$x^2 - 3$	13	6	1	-2	-3	-2	1	6	13

The bottom row gives you the value of y.
The middle row helps you to work this out.

The x-axis goes from -4 to 4 and the y-axis from -3 to 13.

Draw the axes and plot the nine points.

Join the points with a smooth curve.

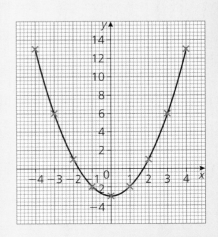

b Draw the line $y = 5$ and find where it crosses the curve.

Answers: $x = 2.8$ and $x = -2.8$

This graph is symmetrical about the y-axis.

> Notice the symmetry of the curve. Graphs of quadratics are always symmetrical.

Example

a Draw the graph of $y = 2x - x^2$ for values of x from -3 to 4.

b Write down the equation of the line of symmetry of this graph.

Solution

Here is the table of values.

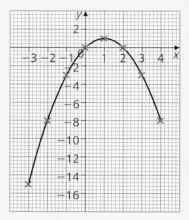

x	-3	-2	-1	0	1	2	3	4
$2x$	-6	-4	-2	0	2	4	6	8
$-x^2$	-9	-4	-1	0	-1	-4	-9	-16
$2x - x^2$	-15	-8	-3	0	1	0	-3	-8

Draw the axes and plot the eight points.

Join the points with a smooth curve.

> Notice the symmetry. The graph does not go far enough to show the next point, $(5, -15)$, which would 'complete' the symmetry.

This graph is symmetrical about the line $x = 1$.

Valley or hill?

If the expression contains $(+)x^2$, the graph will be in the shape of a valley, or part of a valley.

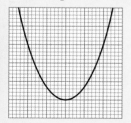 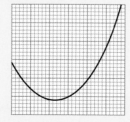 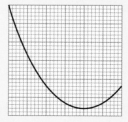

If the expression contains $-x^2$, the graph will be in the shape of a hill, or part of a hill.

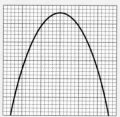 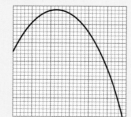 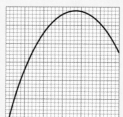

Using a graph to solve a quadratic equation

A quadratic equation usually has two solutions.

Here is the graph from the first example above.

The graph is $y = x^2 - 3$.

You can use this graph to solve the quadratic equation $x^2 - 3 = 0$.

In the equation, y has been replaced by 0.

The solutions will be found on the line $y = 0$ (the x-axis).

They are $x = 1.7$ and $x = -1.7$

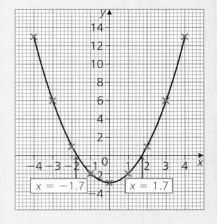

Apply 29.1

1 a Copy and complete the table of values for $y = x^2 + 1$.

x	−3	−2	−1	0	2	3	
x^2	9		1	0		4	
$x^2 + 1$	10		2	1	5		

   b Draw the graph of $y = x^2 + 1$ for values of x from −3 to 3.

   c Use your graph to find the values of x when $y = 4$.

2 a Copy and complete the table of values for $y = x^2 - 5x$.

x	−1	0	1	2	3	4	5
x^2	1			4	9	16	
$-5x$	+5			−10	−15	−20	
$x^2 - 5x$	6			−6	−6		

   b Draw the graph of $y = x^2 - 5x$ for values of x from −1 to 5.

   c Use your graph to find the values of x when $y = -2$.

3 a Copy and complete the table of values for $y = 4 - x^2$.

x	−4	−3	−2	−1	0	1	2	3	4
x^2	16			1	0			9	
$4 - x^2$	−12				4			−5	

   b Draw the graph of $y = 4 - x^2$ for values of x from −4 to 4.

   c Write down the equation of the line of symmetry of this graph.

   d Write down the coordinates of the highest point of the curve.

Study tip

Never draw a quadratic graph with a flat bottom (or top). There will always be a lowest point (or a highest point). Draw your graph with a curve at the bottom (or top).

4 a Copy and complete the table of values for $y = x^2 + 2x - 5$.

[Hint: To find the values of y, add the two middle lines and subtract 5.]

x	−4	−3	−2	−1	0	1	2	3
x^2	16			1				9
$+ 2x$	−8			−2				+6
$x^2 + 2x - 5$	3			−6				10

b Draw the graph of $y = x^2 + 2x - 5$ for values of x from −4 to 3.

c Write down the equation of the line of symmetry of this graph.

d Use your graph to find the solutions to the equation $x^2 + 2x - 5 = 0$.

5 a Copy and complete the table of values for $y = 4 + x - x^2$.

x	−3	−2	−1	0	1	2	3	4
$4 + x$	1	2			5			
$-x^2$	−9				−1			
$4 + x - x^2$	−8				4			

b Draw the graph of $y = 4 + x - x^2$ for values of x from −3 to 4.

c Write down the equation of the line of symmetry of this graph.

d Write down the coordinates of the highest point of the curve.

e Use your graph to find the solutions to the equation $4 + x - x^2 = 0$.

6 a Copy and complete the table of values for $y = x^2 - 3x + 2$.

x	−2	−1	0	1	2	3	4
x^2	4				4		16
$- 3x$	+6				−6		
$x^2 - 3x + 2$	12				0		

b Draw the graph of $y = x^2 - 3x + 2$ for values of x from −2 to 4.

c Write down the coordinates of the lowest point of the curve.

7 The graphs of three quadratic functions are shown in the sketch.

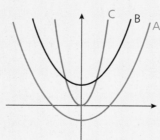

The functions are $\quad y = 3x^2 \qquad y = x^2 + 4 \qquad y = x^2 - 2$

Match the functions to the curves.

Learn 29.2 Graphs of reciprocal functions

The **reciprocal** of x is $\frac{1}{x}$.

$y = \frac{1}{x}$ is the simplest reciprocal function.

For this function, when $x = 0$ the value of y cannot be found.

There is a break in the graph at this value of x, and the function is said to be **discontinuous**.

When x is very small, y is very large, e.g. if $x = 0.001$ then $y = \frac{1}{0.001} = 1000$.

When you plot points for this graph, you have no value of y at $x = 0$.

The diagram shows the graph of $y = \frac{1}{x}$.

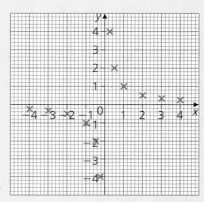

Study tip

- Plot some points where x lies between 0 and 1 to help you to draw the right-hand part of the curve.
- Plot some points where x lies between -1 and 0 to help you to draw the left-hand part of the curve.

Apply 29.2

1 a Copy and complete the table of values for $y = \frac{8}{x}$.

x	-4	-3	-2	-1	-0.8	0.8	1	2	3	4
$\frac{8}{x}$	-2	-2.7			-10					

b Draw the graph of $y = \frac{8}{x}$ for values of x from -4 to 4.

c Use your graph to solve the equation $\frac{8}{x} = 7$.

2 a Draw the graph of $y = \frac{12}{x}$ for values of x from 1 to 8.

b On the same axes, draw the line $y = x$.

c Write down the coordinates of the point where the line crosses the curve.

3 a Draw the graph of $y = \frac{30}{x}$ for values of x from -6 to 6 ($x \neq 0$).

b Use your graph to solve the equations.

i $\frac{30}{x} = 11$ **ii** $\frac{30}{x} = -8$

4 a Draw the graph of $y = -\dfrac{1}{x}$ for values of x from -4 to 4 ($x \neq 0$).

Call this graph A.

b On the same axes draw the graph of $y = \dfrac{1}{x}$ for the same range of values.

Call this graph B.

Which of the following statements are true?

1. Graph A is a reflection of graph B in the x-axis.
2. Graph A is a reflection of graph B in the y-axis.
3. Graph A is a rotation of graph B through 90° clockwise.
4. Graph A is a translation of graph B by the vector $\begin{pmatrix} 1 \\ -1 \end{pmatrix}$.
5. Graph A is an enlargement of graph B with scale factor -1, centre the origin.

Learn 29.3 Solving equations by graphical methods

In Learn 29.1, you were shown how to solve a quadratic equation by finding the values of x where the curve crossed the x-axis. Equations can also be solved by combining quadratic or reciprocal graphs with straight line graphs.

Example

a Draw the graph of $y = 7x - x^2$ for values of x from -1 to 8.

b On the same grid, draw the line $y = 8$.

Use this line to find solutions of the equation $7x - x^2 = 8$.

c On the same grid, draw the line $y = x - 2$.

Use this line to find solutions of the equation $7x - x^2 = x - 2$.

Solution

a First make a table of values.

x	-1	0	1	2	3	4	5	6	7	8
$7x$	-7	0	7	14	21	28	35	42	49	56
$-x^2$	-1	0	-1	-4	-9	-16	-25	-36	-49	-64
$7x - x^2$	-8	0	6	10	12	12	10	6	0	-8

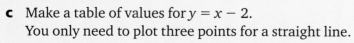

Plot the ten points and join them with a smooth curve.

b Draw the line $y = 8$ right across the grid, to meet your curve in two places.

The solutions of the equation $7x - x^2 = 8$
are $x = 1.5$ and $x = 5.5$

c Make a table of values for $y = x - 2$.
You only need to plot three points for a straight line.

x	0	2	4
y	-2	0	2

Plot the three points and use a ruler to draw a straight line through them.

The line $y = x - 2$ also meets the curve in two places.

The solutions of the equation $7x - x^2 = x - 2$ are $x = -0.3$ and $x = 6.3$

Apply 29.3

1 **a** Copy and complete the table for $y = x^2 + 2$.

x	-3	-2	-1	0	1	2	3
x^2	9		1			4	
y	11		3			6	

  b Draw the graph of $y = x^2 + 2$ for values of x from -3 to 3.

  c On the same grid, draw the line $y = 3 - 2x$.
  Use this line to find solutions of the equation $x^2 + 2 = 3 - 2x$.

2 **a** Copy and complete the table for $y = x^2 - 3x$.

x	-2	-1	0	1	2	3	4	5
x^2	4				4	9		
$-3x$	$+6$				-6	-9		
y	10				-2	0		

  b Draw the graph of $y = x^2 - 3x$ for values of x from -2 to 5.

  c On the same grid, draw the line $y = 5$.
  Use this line to find solutions of the equation $x^2 - 3x = 5$.

  d On the same grid, draw the line $y = 6 - x$.
  Use this line to find solutions of the equation $x^2 - 3x = 6 - x$.

3 **a** Copy and complete the table of values for $y = 3x - 2$.

x	0	1	3
y			7

  b Draw the graph of $y = 3x - 2$ for values of x from 0 to 3.

  c On the same grid, draw the line $y + 2x = 6$.

  d Write down the coordinates of the point of intersection of these two lines.
  [Hint: You could check the answer to part **d** by solving the simultaneous equations.]

4 **a** Copy and complete the table for the equation $y = \dfrac{36}{x}$.

x	1	2	3	4	5	6	7	8
y	36						5.1	

  b Draw the curve $y = \dfrac{36}{x}$ for values of x from 1 to 8.

  c Use your graph to find x when $y = 14$.

  d Copy and complete the table for the equation $9x + 2y = 72$.

x	0	4	8
y		18	

  e On the same axes, draw the graph of $9x + 2y = 72$ for values of x from 0 to 8.

  f The two graphs intersect at two points.
  Write down the coordinates of these two points.

5 a Copy and complete the table for the equation $y = \dfrac{4}{x}$.

x	0.5	1	2	3	4	5
y				1.3		

b Draw the graph of $y = \dfrac{4}{x}$ for values of x from 0.5 to 5.

c Copy and complete the table for the equation $y = 5x - x^2$.

x	0	1	2	3	4	5
$5x$			10		20	
$-x^2$			-4		-16	
y			6		4	

d On the same axes, draw the graph of $y = 5x - x^2$ for values of x from 0 to 5.

e The two graphs intersect at two points.

Write down the coordinates of these two points.

Assess 29.1–29.3

1 a Copy and complete the table of values for $y = x^2 - 8$.

x	-4	-3	-2	-1	0	1	2	3	4
y	8			-7			-4		

b Draw the graph of $y = x^2 - 8$ for values of x from -4 to 4.

c Write down the coordinates of the lowest point on the graph.

d Use your graph to find the solutions to the equation $x^2 - 8 = 0$.

2 a Copy and complete the table of values for $y = 5 - 2x - x^2$.

x	-4	-3	-2	-1	0	1	2
$5 - 2x$	13		9				
$-x^2$	-16		-4				
y	-3		5				

b Draw the graph of $y = 5 - 2x - x^2$ for values of x from -4 to 2.

c Write down the equation of the line of symmetry of the graph.

d Write down the coordinates of the highest point on the graph.

e Use your graph to find the solutions to the equation $5 - 2x - x^2 = 0$.

3 a Draw a set of axes with values of x from 0 to 6 and values of y from -1 to 7.

b On your axes, draw the lines $y = 2x - 1$ and $y = \frac{1}{2}x + 3$.

c Write down the coordinates of the point of intersection of these two lines.

4 a Copy and complete the table of values for $y = \dfrac{3}{x}$.

x	−4	−3	−2	−1	−0.5		0.5	1	2	3	4
y	−0.75			−3	−6						

b Draw the graph of $y = \dfrac{3}{x}$ for values of x from -4 to 4 ($x \neq 0$).

c Use your graph to solve the equations:

i $\dfrac{3}{x} = 2.5$ **ii** $\dfrac{3}{x} = -4.5$

5 a Draw the graph of $y = \dfrac{10}{x}$ for values of x from 1 to 10.

b On the same axes, draw the graph of $y = \frac{1}{2}x$.

c Write down the coordinates of the point where the line crosses the curve.

6 a Copy and complete the table of values for $y = x^2 + 3x - 1$.

x	−5	−4	−3	−2	−1	0	1	2
x^2	25			4				
+ 3x	−15			−6				
y	9			−3				

b Draw the graph of $y = x^2 + 3x - 1$ for values of x from -5 to 2.

c Use your graph to solve the equation $x^2 + 3x - 1 = 0$.

d Copy and complete the table of values for $y = \frac{1}{2}(3x + 5)$.

x	−1	0	1
y	1		

e On the same axes, draw the graph of $y = \frac{1}{2}(3x + 5)$.

f The line crosses the curve at two points.

Write down the coordinates of these two points.

30 Trigonometry

Learning outcomes:

After this chapter you should be able to:

- apply Pythagoras' theorem
- apply the sine, cosine and tangent ratios for acute angles to the calculation of a side or of an angle of a right-angled triangle
- interpret and use three-figure bearings measured clockwise from the North (i.e. 000°–360°).

Right-angled triangles

This chapter will show you how to calculate the length of sides and the size of angles in right-angled triangles.

Learn 30.1 Pythagoras' theorem

Pythagoras was a Greek who was alive around 500 BCE. He was a mathematician and philosopher, and is best remembered for his theorem about right-angled triangles.

Pythagoras' theorem states that if a square is drawn on each side of a right-angled triangle, then the sum of the areas of the two smaller squares is equal to the area of the larger square.

The red triangle is a right-angled triangle.

The sum of the areas of the green squares is equal to the area of the yellow square.

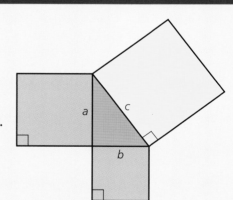

The longest side of the triangle is always opposite the right angle. It is called the **hypotenuse**.

If the shorter sides of a right-angled triangle are a and b, and the hypotenuse is c, then Pythagoras' theorem can be written as:

$$a^2 + b^2 = c^2$$

Using Pythagoras' theorem

Pythagoras' theorem has many uses.

You can split rectangles and isosceles triangles into two right-angled triangles.

These two examples show this.

Solving problems using Pythagoras' theorem

Always draw a diagram.

Isosceles triangles can be split into two congruent right-angled triangles.

Example

Lewis makes a rectangular wooden frame for a door.

To make it rigid, he wants to put in a diagonal piece shown in blue.

Calculate the length of the diagonal.

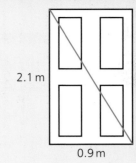

2.1 m

0.9 m

Solution

Shade the diagram to show the right-angled triangle.

$2.1^2 + 0.9^2 = d^2$ | There is no need to draw the squares on the sides of the triangle. The area of the bottom square would be $0.9 \times 0.9 = 0.81\,m^2$.

$4.41 + 0.81 = d^2$ | The square on the left would be $2.1 \times 2.1 = 4.41\,m^2$.

$d^2 = 5.22$ | So the large square would have an area of $0.81 + 4.41 = 5.22\,m^2$.

$d = \sqrt{5.22}$ | (Diagonal)$^2 = 5.22$, so diagonal $= \sqrt{5.22}$.

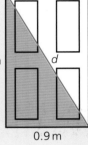

2.1 m

0.9 m

Diagonal, $d = 2.28\,m$ (to the nearest m)

Example

Carla is hanging a large painting on the wall.

She puts two screws in the picture frame and attaches a wire to them.

The screws are 1.5 m apart and the wire is 1.6 m long.

The diagram shows the arrangement.

Calculate how far above the screws the wire will reach.

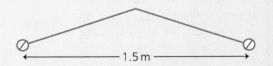

1.5 m

Solution

Draw a sketch and label it.

The triangle is isosceles, so divide it into two congruent right-angled triangles.

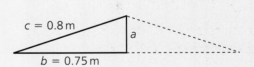

$c = 0.8\,m$

a

$b = 0.75\,m$

Using Pythagoras' theorem:

$$a^2 + b^2 = c^2$$

$$a^2 + 0.75^2 = 0.8^2$$

$$a^2 + 0.5625 = 0.64$$

$$a^2 = 0.64 - 0.5625 = 0.0775$$

$$a = \sqrt{0.0775} = 0.278\,m$$

The wire will reach 27.8 cm above the screws.

Study tip

Pythagoras' theorem only works for right-angled triangles.

Apply 30.1

1 A right-angled triangle has shorter sides of 6 cm and 8 cm.
Find the length of the hypotenuse.

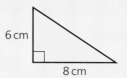

2 Find the length of x in the following diagrams, giving your answers to 1 decimal place.

a

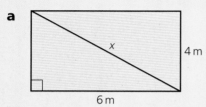

c

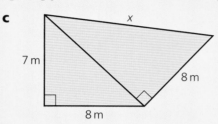

b

3 A right-angled triangle has a hypotenuse of 11 cm and a shorter side of 7 cm.
Calculate the length of the third side.

4 A square has a diagonal of 12 cm. Find the length of side of the square.

5 A builder is constructing scaffolding.
The scaffolding is 6 m wide and 8 m high.
What length of tube do they need for the diagonal?

6 An equilateral triangle has sides of 8 cm.

Calculate:

a the perpendicular height of the triangle

b the area of the triangle.

7 A right-angled triangle ABC has $AB = 4$ cm, $BC = 3$ cm
and $ABC = 90°$.

Attached to the triangle is a rectangle $ACED$, with $CE = 12$ cm.
Calculate the length of:

a AC **b** AE.

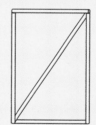

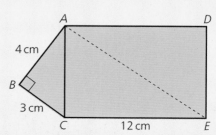

Learn 30.2 Trigonometry

Similar right-angled triangles

If two right-angled triangles have angles of 90° and $x°$, then the third angle of each must be equal to $90° - x°$.

So if two right-angled triangles have a common angle, then they are similar.

For example, all right-angled triangles with an angle of 30° are similar.

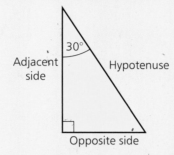

The side **opposite** the 30° angle is half of the **hypotenuse** in all 30° right-angled triangles.

For an angle of 30°, $\dfrac{\text{opposite side}}{\text{hypotenuse}} = 0.5$

This is called the **sine** of 30°.

The third side is called the **adjacent side**, because it is adjacent, or next to, the angle of 30°.

The ratio $\dfrac{\text{adjacent side}}{\text{hypotenuse}}$ is called the **cosine** of 30°.

The ratio $\dfrac{\text{opposite side}}{\text{adjacent side}}$ is called the **tangent** of 30°.

These are usually abbreviated to the first three letters, so, for an angle $a°$, we write:

$$\sin a° = \frac{\text{opp}}{\text{hyp}} \qquad \cos a° = \frac{\text{adj}}{\text{hyp}} \qquad \tan a° = \frac{\text{opp}}{\text{adj}}$$

You can remember these by learning the word SOHCAHTOA.

This is made up of the first letter of each word.

Study tip

You must learn these three formulae.

Or a mnemonic such as 'Some Old Hairy Camels Are Hairier Than Others Are' can help you to remember the rules.

This study of right-angled triangles is called **trigonometry**.

It can be used to find the size of angles or sides in right-angled triangles.

The values of sine, cosine and tangent for any angle can be obtained from your calculator.

Study tip

Make sure your calculator is in 'degree' mode. If it is, a small 'd' or 'deg' will be showing on the display.

Finding the length of a side

Suppose you are 20 m from the foot of a tree. You look up at the top of the tree, and measure the angle from the top of the tree to the horizontal. You find this is 35°.

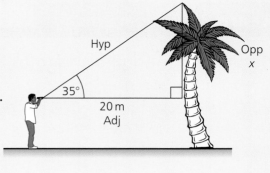

You can use this information to find the height of the tree.

Begin by drawing a sketch and labelling it.

Call the side you want to calculate x.

You already know the length of the adjacent side (20 m). You need to calculate the length of the opposite side.

The formula that has *adjacent* and *opposite* sides in it is the tangent formula.

So $\tan 35° = \dfrac{\text{opp}}{\text{adj}}$.

Your calculator tells you that $\tan 35° = 0.700207538$, so substitute this in the formula:

$$0.700207538 = \frac{x}{20}$$

Solve the equation by multiplying both sides by 20:

$$0.700207538 \times 20 = x$$
$$x = 14.0 \text{ m (to 3 s.f.)}$$

The height from your eyes to the top of the tree is 14.0 m.

(Remember to add the height of your eyes from the ground to this value to get the height of the tree.)

Example

An isosceles triangle has two angles of 70° and a base of 8 cm.

Calculate the length of the other sides.

Solution

First, draw a diagram.

The dotted perpendicular line creates two congruent right-angled triangles with an adjacent side of 4 cm.

Use the left-hand shaded triangle.

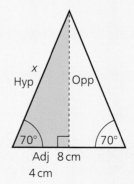

You know the adjacent side (4 cm) and want the hypotenuse, so use the cosine formula:

$$\cos 70° = \frac{\text{adj}}{\text{hyp}}$$
$$0.34202014 = \frac{4}{x}$$

$0.34202014 \times x = 4$ | Multiply both sides by x. |

$$x = \frac{4}{0.34202014}$$

| Divide both sides by 0.34202014 |

$$x = 11.7 \text{ cm (to 1 dp)}$$

Finding an angle

Given two sides of a right-angled triangle, you can use trigonometry to calculate an angle.

In this triangle, you want to calculate the angle $x°$.

The known sides are the *hypotenuse* and the *opposite* side.

These are in the sine formula, so use:

$$\sin x° = \frac{\text{opp}}{\text{hyp}}$$

$$\sin x° = \frac{10.6}{11.2} = 0.94642857$$

To turn a sine back into an angle, you must use the inverse of sine.

The inverse of sine is written as '$\sin^{-1}$'.
You can usually obtain it by pressing the inverse key on your calculator followed by '$\sin$'.

$$x° = \sin^{-1} 0.94642857 = 71.2° \text{ (to 1 d.p.)}$$

[Hint: Answers are usually given to 1 decimal place.]

Example

A shed is 2.4 m wide.

The roof is 2.8 m long.

Calculate $x°$, the angle of the roof with the horizontal.

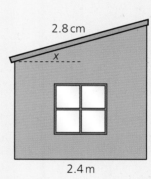

2.8 cm

x

2.4 m

Solution

Label the diagram to show the right-angled triangle.

You know the adjacent side and the hypotenuse, so use the cosine formula:

$$\cos x° = \frac{\text{adj}}{\text{hyp}}$$

$$\cos x° = \frac{2.4}{2.8} = 0.85714286$$

$$x° = \cos^{-1} 0.85714286 = 31.0° \text{ (to 1 dp)}$$

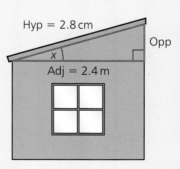

Hyp = 2.8 cm

Opp

x

Adj = 2.4 m

Study tip

- Always draw and label a diagram.
- Always write down the formula you need to use: sin, cos or tan.
- Make sure you can use your calculator to find an angle from the sin, cos or tan.

Apply 30.2

1 Use your calculator to find:

    a sin 46°   **b** cos 76°   **c** tan 45°   **d** cos⁻¹ 0.65   **e** tan⁻¹ 1.34

    Give your answers to 4 decimal places.

2 Calculate the sides and angles marked with letters in the triangles.

3 What angle has a cosine equal to sin 72°?

a
65°
a cm   12.2 cm

c
5.5 cm
$c°$
11.2 cm

e
9 cm   9 cm
$e°$
6 cm

b
55°
7.4 cm
b cm

d
9 cm
$d°$
13.4 cm

f
4 cm
5 cm
$f°$

4 A ladder is 6 m long.
    It rests against a wall at an angle of 75° with the ground.
    How far up the wall does the ladder reach?

5 $AB = 12$ cm, angle $BAC = 67°$. Calculate BC.

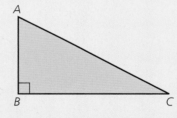

6 $DE = 4$ cm, $DF = 9$ cm. Calculate angle EDF.

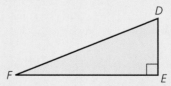

7 $GH = 7$ cm, angle $GIH = 38°$. Calculate GI.

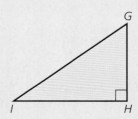

Learn 30.3 Bearings

You can use compass bearings to describe a direction, such as north, or south-east.

A more precise method is to use **angle bearings**.

Angle bearings are measured clockwise, from North.

This is shown in the diagram by the red arrow.

Bearings are always written as three-figure bearings.
If the angle is less than 100°, write a 0 before it.
So a bearing of 47° is written as 047°.

Lucknow is 510 km due East of Jaipur.

Jaipur is 192 km due North of Kota.

To find the bearing of Kota from Lucknow,
you first draw a sketch and label it.

You want to calculate the angle $x°$.

You know the opposite and adjacent sides,
so you use the tan formula:

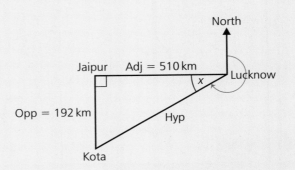

$$\tan x = \frac{\text{opp}}{\text{adj}} = \frac{192}{510} = 0.37647059$$
$$x° = \tan^{-1} 0.37647059 = 20.6° \text{ (to 1 dp)}$$

The bearing of Kota from Lucknow (marked in red) is $270° - 20.6° = 249.4°$

Example

The bearing of Pungol from Kranji is 103°.
Queenstown is on a bearing of 219° from Pungol.
Kranji from Queenstown is on a bearing of 335°.
Pungol and Queenstown are both 19 km from Kranji.
Calculate the distance from Pungol to Queenstown.

Solution

First, draw a sketch and add the bearings and distances.

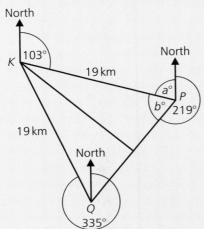

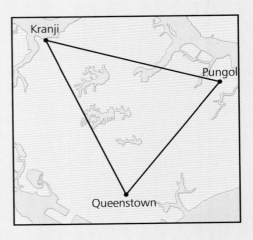

Angle a and angle $103°$ are co-interior angles between parallel lines, and so are supplementary.
So angle $a° = 180° - 103° = 77°$.

Angles $219°$, $a°$ and $b°$ are angles at a point, and so sum to $360°$:

$$b° = 360° - 219° - 77° = 64°$$

$KP = KQ = 19$ km, so the triangle KPQ is isosceles.

Draw a perpendicular from K to PQ, meeting PQ at X.

To find the distance PX, use the cosine formula:

$$\cos 64° = \frac{\text{adj}}{\text{hyp}}$$

$$0.43837115 = \frac{PX}{19}$$

$$PX = 8.329 \text{ km}$$

So the distance from Pungol to Queenstown
$= 2 \times 8.329$ km $= 16.6$ km (to 1 dp)

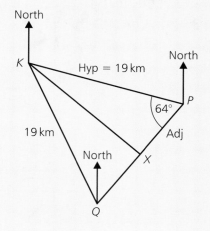

Apply 30.3

1 A ship sails 120 km from port on a bearing of 035°, and then sails due South until it is due East of the port.
How far South did it sail?

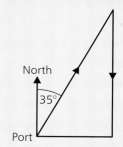

2 A boat is 3 km from a port, on a bearing of 056° from the port.
How far to the East of the port is the boat?

3 B is 5 km from A on a bearing of 050°.
C is 11 km from B on a bearing of 140°.

  a Show this on a diagram.

  b Explain how you know that angle ABC is a right angle.

  c Find the bearing and distance of C from A.

4 X is 50 km due North of Y and 35 km due East of Z.
Calculate the bearing of Z from Y.

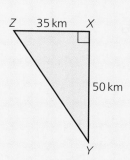

5 *B* is 8 km from *A* on a bearing of 065°.

C is on a bearing of 105° from *A* and 155° from *B*.

Calculate:

 a angle *ABC*

 b the distance from *A* to *C*

 c the distance from *B* to *C*

 d the bearing of *A* from *C*.

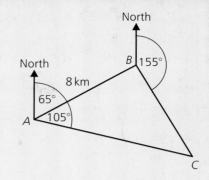

Assess 30.1–30.3

1 *ABC* is a right-angled triangle.

AB = 3 cm and *AC* = 7.2 cm.

Calculate the length of *BC*.

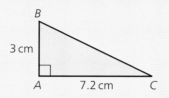

2 *XYZ* is an isosceles triangle.

XY = *YZ* = 10 cm.

XZ = 8 cm.

Calculate:

 a the perpendicular height, *YP*

 b the area of the triangle *XYZ*.

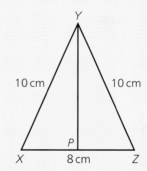

3 A rectangular field is 70 m wide and has a diagonal of length 130 m.

Calculate the length of the field.

4 A right-angled triangle *DEF* has *DE* = 11.4 cm and *DF* = 4.2 cm.

Calculate:

 a the length of *EF*

 b angle *DEF*.

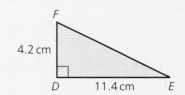

5 A kite *ABCD* has sides of length 8 cm and 12 cm as shown.

The short diagonal *BD* is 12 cm long.

Calculate:

 a the length of the long diagonal, *AC*

 b angle *ABD*.

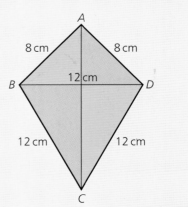

6 ABC is a triangle with $AC = 10.6$ cm and angle $ACB = 38°$.
AX is perpendicular to BC, and $BX = 4.2$ cm.
Calculate:

a the length of AX

b angle ABC.

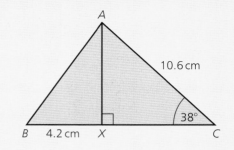

7 A wooden plank rests with one end on the ground
and the other end on a wall of height 1.2 m.
The angle between the plank and the ground is 32°.
Calculate the length of the plank.

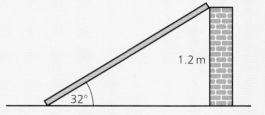

8 A ship leaves a port (P) sailing due East for 30 km and
then due North for 20 km.
On what bearing should it sail to go directly back to the port?

9 A village contains a store, a shop and a church.
The store is 1.2 km from the church, on a bearing of 064°.
The school is due East of the church and due South of the store.

a Draw a sketch of the positions of the store, the shop and the church in the village.

b Calculate the distance of:

i the store from the school

ii the church from the school.

31 Vectors

You used vectors in chapter 16 as a way of describing a translation.

A vector has a magnitude (or size) and a direction.

So a translation moves every point on a shape a fixed distance in a particular direction.

Learn 31.1 Vector notation

There are three common ways of representing a **vector**.

In Learn 16.1, you used column vectors to describe movement from B to C.

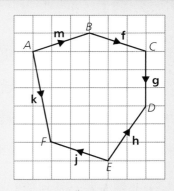

The movement from B to C can be written as $\begin{pmatrix} 3 \\ -1 \end{pmatrix}$.

The first number represents a horizontal movement and the second number represents a vertical movement.

$\begin{pmatrix} 3 \\ -1 \end{pmatrix}$ means 3 to the right (a negative number would indicate left), and 1 down (because the number is negative, it signifies downward movement).

The vector can also be written as $\overrightarrow{BC}$. The arrow indicates the direction from B to C.

It can also be written as **f**. Because you cannot easily write in bold type, when answering questions you indicate a vector by writing $\underset{\sim}{f}$.

Similarly, the vector $\overrightarrow{ED} = \mathbf{h} = \begin{pmatrix} 2 \\ 3 \end{pmatrix}$.

The vector going in the opposite direction is $DE = -\mathbf{h} = \begin{pmatrix} -2 \\ -3 \end{pmatrix}$

Example

Use the diagram above to answer these questions.

a Write $\overrightarrow{AB}$ as a column vector.

b Which vector, written as a column vector, is $\begin{pmatrix} 2 \\ 3 \end{pmatrix}$?

c Which vector has the same column vector as $\overrightarrow{CB}$?

d Write down the column vector AD.

Solution

a $\overrightarrow{AB}$ is 3 units to the right and 1 unit upwards, so is $\binom{3}{1}$.

b $\binom{2}{3}$ looks like the diagram on the right and so is $\overrightarrow{ED}$, or **h**.

c $\overrightarrow{CB} = \binom{-3}{1} = \overrightarrow{EF}$ or **j**

d $\binom{6}{-3}$

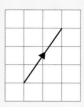

Apply 31.1

1 a Use the diagram to write down the column vector of:

    i $\overrightarrow{AB}$ **iii** $\overrightarrow{EF}$

    ii $\overrightarrow{BC}$ **iv** $\overrightarrow{IJ}$

  b Which vector is equal to:

    i $\binom{2}{2}$ **iii** $\binom{2}{-3}$

    ii $\binom{2}{3}$ **iv** $\binom{-3}{-2}$?

2 *ABCD* is a rectangle.

$$\overrightarrow{AB} = \binom{6}{3} \text{ and } \overrightarrow{BC} = \binom{1}{-2}$$

  a On a square grid, draw the rectangle *ABCD*.

  b If $\overrightarrow{AB}$ = **a** and $\overrightarrow{BC}$ = **b**, write:

    i $\overrightarrow{DC}$ **ii** $\overrightarrow{DA}$ in terms of **a** and **b**.

3 a = $\binom{3}{-3}$, **b** = $\binom{2}{3}$

  a If **a** = $\overrightarrow{AB}$ and **b** = $\overrightarrow{BC}$, copy the diagram and label the quadrilateral *ABCD*.

  b Write:

    i $\overrightarrow{AC}$ and **ii** $\overrightarrow{BD}$ as column vectors.

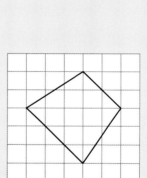

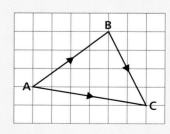

Learn 31.2 Addition, subtraction and multiplication of vectors

Adding and subtracting vectors

The movement from *A* to *B* is represented by the vector $\binom{4}{3}$, and the movement from *B* to *C* by $\binom{2}{-4}$.

You can add vectors by adding the horizontal components and the vertical components separately:

$$\overrightarrow{AB} + \overrightarrow{BC} = \binom{4}{3} + \binom{2}{-4} = \binom{6}{-1}, \text{ or } \overrightarrow{AC}.$$

In vector terms, moving from A to B and then from B to C is identical to moving directly from A to C.

So $\overrightarrow{AC} + \overrightarrow{CB} = \overrightarrow{AB}$

Adding $\overrightarrow{CB}$ is the same as subtracting $\overrightarrow{BC}$.

So $\overrightarrow{AC} - \overrightarrow{BC} = \begin{pmatrix} 6 \\ -1 \end{pmatrix} - \begin{pmatrix} 2 \\ -4 \end{pmatrix} = \begin{pmatrix} 4 \\ 3 \end{pmatrix} = \overrightarrow{AB}$.

Example

a If $\mathbf{a} = \begin{pmatrix} 3 \\ -1 \end{pmatrix}$, $\mathbf{b} = \begin{pmatrix} 1 \\ 5 \end{pmatrix}$ and $\mathbf{c} = \begin{pmatrix} -4 \\ 2 \end{pmatrix}$, find:

    i $\mathbf{a} + \mathbf{b}$ **ii** $\mathbf{c} - \mathbf{a}$

b If $\overrightarrow{AB} = \mathbf{a}$, $\overrightarrow{BC} = \mathbf{b}$ and $\overrightarrow{CD} = \mathbf{c}$, write, in terms of $\mathbf{a}$, $\mathbf{b}$ and $\mathbf{c}$:

    i $\overrightarrow{AC}$ **ii** $\overrightarrow{AD}$ **iii** $\overrightarrow{DB}$.

Solution

a   **i** $\mathbf{a} + \mathbf{b} = \begin{pmatrix} 3 \\ -1 \end{pmatrix} + \begin{pmatrix} 1 \\ 5 \end{pmatrix} = \begin{pmatrix} 4 \\ 4 \end{pmatrix}$

       ii $\mathbf{c} - \mathbf{a} = \begin{pmatrix} -4 \\ 2 \end{pmatrix} - \begin{pmatrix} 3 \\ -1 \end{pmatrix} = \begin{pmatrix} -7 \\ 3 \end{pmatrix}$

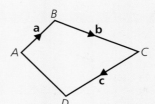

b   **i** $\overrightarrow{AC} = \overrightarrow{AB} + \overrightarrow{BC} = \mathbf{a} + \mathbf{b}$

       ii $\overrightarrow{AD} = \overrightarrow{AC} + \overrightarrow{CD} = \mathbf{a} + \mathbf{b} + \mathbf{c}$

      iii $\overrightarrow{DB} = \overrightarrow{DC} + \overrightarrow{CB} = -\overrightarrow{CD} - \overrightarrow{BC} = -\mathbf{c} - \mathbf{b}$

Multiplying a vector by a scalar

As well as adding and subtracting vectors, you can multiply a vector by a **scalar** (a single number).

The vector $2\mathbf{a} = \mathbf{a} + \mathbf{a}$

If a point is moved through the vector $\begin{pmatrix} 3 \\ -1 \end{pmatrix}$ three times, the overall movement is $3\begin{pmatrix} 3 \\ -1 \end{pmatrix} = \begin{pmatrix} 9 \\ -3 \end{pmatrix}$.

The diagram shows $3\begin{pmatrix} 3 \\ -1 \end{pmatrix}$ as $\begin{pmatrix} 3 \\ -1 \end{pmatrix} + \begin{pmatrix} 3 \\ -1 \end{pmatrix} + \begin{pmatrix} 3 \\ -1 \end{pmatrix} = \begin{pmatrix} 9 \\ -3 \end{pmatrix}$.

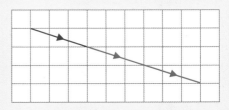

The resultant vector has 3 times the **magnitude** of the original vector and goes in the same **direction**, so is parallel to the original vector.

To multiply a vector by a scalar, multiply each component of the vector by the scalar.

This can be written algebraically:

$$n\begin{pmatrix} x \\ y \end{pmatrix} = \begin{pmatrix} nx \\ ny \end{pmatrix}.$$

If a vector is a multiple of another vector, then the two vectors are parallel.

Example

$\overrightarrow{AB} = \begin{pmatrix} 3 \\ -1 \end{pmatrix}$, $\overrightarrow{AD} = \begin{pmatrix} -1 \\ -4 \end{pmatrix}$ and $\overrightarrow{BC} = \begin{pmatrix} 2 \\ -5 \end{pmatrix}$

a Write $\overrightarrow{DC}$ as a column vector.

b Show that DC is parallel to and twice the length of AB.

Solution

a $\overrightarrow{DC} = \overrightarrow{DA} + \overrightarrow{AB} + \overrightarrow{BC}$

$= -\overrightarrow{AD} + \overrightarrow{AB} + \overrightarrow{BC}$

$= -\begin{pmatrix} -1 \\ -4 \end{pmatrix} + \begin{pmatrix} 3 \\ -1 \end{pmatrix} + \begin{pmatrix} 2 \\ -5 \end{pmatrix}$

$= \begin{pmatrix} 6 \\ -2 \end{pmatrix}$

b $DC = \begin{pmatrix} 6 \\ -2 \end{pmatrix} = 2\begin{pmatrix} 3 \\ -1 \end{pmatrix} = 2\overrightarrow{AB}$

So DC is parallel to and twice the length of AB.

Apply 31.2

1 Calculate:

a $\begin{pmatrix} 4 \\ -2 \end{pmatrix} + \begin{pmatrix} 3 \\ 1 \end{pmatrix}$
         d $2\begin{pmatrix} 4 \\ -1 \end{pmatrix}$

b $\begin{pmatrix} -3 \\ -2 \end{pmatrix} + \begin{pmatrix} 2 \\ -1 \end{pmatrix}$
        e $3\begin{pmatrix} -2 \\ 4 \end{pmatrix} + 2\begin{pmatrix} 3 \\ -6 \end{pmatrix}$

c $\begin{pmatrix} -3 \\ -2 \end{pmatrix} - \begin{pmatrix} -2 \\ 3 \end{pmatrix}$

2 a Write down the column vectors:

    i $\overrightarrow{AB}$
        ii $\overrightarrow{BC}$
        iii $\overrightarrow{CD}$

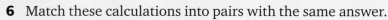

b Calculate $\overrightarrow{AB} + \overrightarrow{BC} + \overrightarrow{CD}$ as a column vector.

c Show that AE is twice the length of CD and parallel to it.

3 $\begin{pmatrix} 4 \\ -1 \end{pmatrix} + \begin{pmatrix} 2 \\ a \end{pmatrix} = \begin{pmatrix} b \\ 3 \end{pmatrix}$

Calculate the values of a and b.

4 $\begin{pmatrix} a \\ 2 \end{pmatrix} - \begin{pmatrix} 2 \\ b \end{pmatrix} = \begin{pmatrix} 1 \\ 4 \end{pmatrix}$

Calculate the values of a and b.

5 $2\begin{pmatrix} 2 \\ a \end{pmatrix} + 3\begin{pmatrix} -1 \\ 1 \end{pmatrix} = \begin{pmatrix} b \\ -1 \end{pmatrix}$

Calculate the values of a and b.

6 Match these calculations into pairs with the same answer.

a $\begin{pmatrix} 4 \\ -1 \end{pmatrix} + \begin{pmatrix} -3 \\ 1 \end{pmatrix}$
        d $\begin{pmatrix} -1 \\ -2 \end{pmatrix} - \begin{pmatrix} -2 \\ -3 \end{pmatrix}$

b $3\begin{pmatrix} -2 \\ 0 \end{pmatrix} - \begin{pmatrix} -5 \\ 1 \end{pmatrix}$
        e $2\begin{pmatrix} 2 \\ -1 \end{pmatrix} + 3\begin{pmatrix} -1 \\ 1 \end{pmatrix}$

c $\begin{pmatrix} -3 \\ -2 \end{pmatrix} + \begin{pmatrix} 2 \\ 1 \end{pmatrix}$
        f $\begin{pmatrix} 3 \\ -2 \end{pmatrix} + \begin{pmatrix} 1 \\ -1 \end{pmatrix} - \begin{pmatrix} 3 \\ -3 \end{pmatrix}$

Assess 31.1–31.2

1 a Write $\overrightarrow{AB}$ as a column vector.

  b Which vector is equal to $\begin{pmatrix} 0 \\ 2 \end{pmatrix}$?

  c Which vector is equal to $\begin{pmatrix} -2 \\ 2 \end{pmatrix}$?

  d $\mathbf{a} = \overrightarrow{AE}$.
  Write **a** as a column vector.

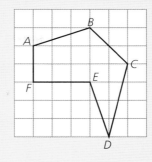

2 $\overrightarrow{PQ}$ is parallel to $\overrightarrow{RS}$ and three times the length.
  If $\overrightarrow{RS} = \begin{pmatrix} 3 \\ -2 \end{pmatrix}$, write down PQ as a column vector.

3 $\overrightarrow{MN} = \begin{pmatrix} 3 \\ -1 \end{pmatrix}$, $\overrightarrow{NP} = \begin{pmatrix} -2 \\ 4 \end{pmatrix}$ and $\overrightarrow{PR} = \begin{pmatrix} 1 \\ 3 \end{pmatrix}$.

  a Show this on a diagram.

  b Calculate the column vectors:

  i $\overrightarrow{MN} + \overrightarrow{PR}$ **ii** $\overrightarrow{MN} + 2\overrightarrow{NP}$ **iii** $\overrightarrow{MN} + \overrightarrow{NP} - \overrightarrow{PR}$

  c Write down the column vector for:

  i $\overrightarrow{MP}$ **ii** $\overrightarrow{NR}$ **iii** $\overrightarrow{MR}$

4 If $\mathbf{a} + \mathbf{b} = \mathbf{c}$ and $\mathbf{a} = \begin{pmatrix} 3 \\ -2 \end{pmatrix}$ and $\mathbf{c} = \begin{pmatrix} 1 \\ 1 \end{pmatrix}$, calculate **b**.

5 $ABCD$ is a parallelogram.
  $\overrightarrow{AB} = \overrightarrow{DC} = \begin{pmatrix} 4 \\ 1 \end{pmatrix}$, and $\overrightarrow{BC} = \overrightarrow{AD} = \begin{pmatrix} 1 \\ -3 \end{pmatrix}$

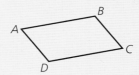

  Calculate:

  a $\overrightarrow{AC}$ **b** $\overrightarrow{BD}$.

6 $BC = \begin{pmatrix} 1 \\ -2 \end{pmatrix}$.

  $\overrightarrow{AB} = 2\overrightarrow{CD}$ and $\overrightarrow{AC} = \begin{pmatrix} 7 \\ -6 \end{pmatrix}$

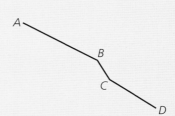

  Calculate:

  a $\overrightarrow{AB}$ **b** $\overrightarrow{CD}$

7 $\mathbf{a} = \begin{pmatrix} 3 \\ -1 \end{pmatrix}$, $\mathbf{b} = \begin{pmatrix} 1 \\ y \end{pmatrix}$ and $\mathbf{c} = \begin{pmatrix} x \\ 2 \end{pmatrix}$.

  a is parallel to **c**, and **a** + **c** is parallel to **b**.
  Calculate the values of x and y.

Practice exam questions

1   Find the size of the five interior angles of a regular pentagon.   *(3 marks)*

2   The diagram shows part of a regular polygon.

Each interior angle of the polygon is 168°.

Calculate the number of sides of the polygon.   *(3 marks)*

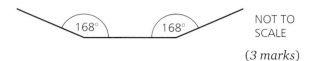

NOT TO SCALE

3   The diagram shows a regular octagon and a square.

Calculate the values of *x* and *y*.   *(3 marks)*

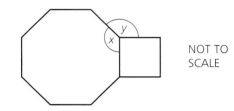

NOT TO SCALE

4   In the diagram, *DE* is a diameter of the circle, centre *O*.

AEB is the tangent at the point *E*. The line *BCD* cuts the circle at *C*.

Angle *CED* = 27°.

   a   Write down the size of angle *DCE*.   *(1 mark)*

   b   Calculate the size of angle *CDE*.   *(1 mark)*

   c   Calculate the size of angle *DBE*.   *(1 mark)*

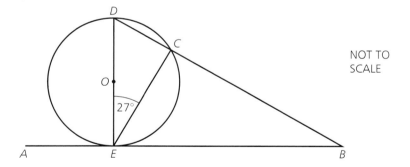

NOT TO SCALE

5   The total cost, *C*, of *n* oranges is given by $C = nk$.

   a   Write *k* in terms of *C* and *n*   *(1 mark)*

   b   What does *k* represent?   *(1 mark)*

6   Make *b* the subject of the formula: $m = ab - c$ *(2 marks)*

7   Solve the simultaneous equations: $8x - y = 17$
$$3x + y = 16$$
    (2 marks)

8   Solve the simultaneous equations: $5x + 4y = 11$

$$3x + 2y = 4$$ (*3 marks*)

9   **a**   Complete the table of values for $y = x^2 - x - 7$.

x	-3	-2	-1	0	1	2	3	4
y	5		-5		-7	-5	-1	

(*2 marks*)

   b   Draw the graph of $y = x^2 - x - 7$, for values of x from -3 to 4.   (*4 marks*)

   c   Use your graph to find solutions to the equation: $x^2 - x - 7 = 0$.   (*2 marks*)

   d   **i**   Draw the line of symmetry of the graph.   (*1 mark*)

   ii   Write down the equation of this line of symmetry.   (*1 mark*)

10   **a**   Complete the table of values for $y = \dfrac{5}{x}, x \neq 0$.

x	-4	-3	-2	-1	-0.5	0.5	1	2	3	4
y	-1.25	-1.7			-10			2.5		

(*2 marks*)

   b   On the grid, draw the graph of $y = \dfrac{5}{x}$ for $-4 \leqslant x \leqslant -0.5$ and $0.5 \leqslant x \leqslant 4$.   (*4 marks*)

   c   Complete the following statement:

   The point $(-1.5, \ldots)$ lies on the graph of $y = \dfrac{5}{x}$.   (*1 mark*)

   d   On the grid, draw the straight line joining the points $(-0.5, -10)$ and $(2, 2.5)$.

   i   Find the gradient of this straight line.   (*2 marks*)

   ii   Write down the equation of this line in the form $y = mx + c$.   (*1 mark*)

11   **a**   The width of a rectangle is x centimetres.

   The length of the rectangle is 2 centimetres more than the width.

   Write down an expression, in terms of x, for:

   i   the length of the rectangle   (*1 mark*)

   ii   the area of the rectangle.   (*1 mark*)

   b   The area of the rectangle is 12 square centimetres. Show that:

   $$x^2 + 2x - 12 = 0$$ (*1 mark*)

   c   **i**   Complete the table of values for the equation $y = x^2 + 2x - 12$.

x	-5	-4	-3	-2	-1	0	1	2	3
y	3	-4		-12			-9		3

(*3 marks*)

   ii   Draw the graph of $y = x^2 + 2x - 12$, for $-5 \leqslant x \leqslant 2$.   (*4 marks*)

   d   **i**   Use your graph to find the solutions to the equation $x^2 + 2x - 12 = 0$.   (*2 marks*)

   ii   Find the length of the rectangle in part **a**.   (*1 mark*)

12 A train can go up a slope if the gain in height is no more than 4% of the length of track.

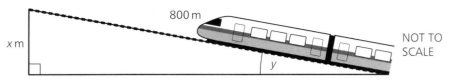

800 m

x m

y

NOT TO
SCALE

a If the length of track is 800 m, calculate the greatest possible gain in height, x m. *(2 marks)*

b The greatest possible angle the train can climb is y°. Calculate the value of y. Show your working. *(2 marks)*

13 A, B, C and D are four towns.

The bearing of B from A is 062°.
Angles BAD and BDC are right angles.
B is due North of D.
A is 11 km from D and B is 14 km from C.

a Write down the bearing of D from A. *(1 mark)*

b Calculate the length BD. *(4 marks)*

c Calculate the length DC. *(3 marks)*

d Calculate the bearing of C from B. *(4 marks)*

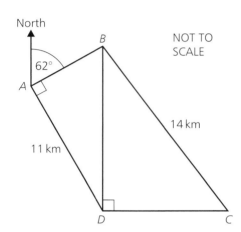

North

B

NOT TO
SCALE

62°

A

14 km

11 km

D

C

14 a Use the diagram to write down the column vector of $\overrightarrow{AG}$. *(1 mark)*

b Which vector is equal to $\begin{pmatrix} -3 \\ 1 \end{pmatrix}$? *(1 mark)*

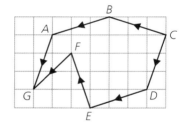

15 $\mathbf{a} = \begin{pmatrix} 2 \\ 1 \end{pmatrix}$ and $\mathbf{b} = \begin{pmatrix} -3 \\ 2 \end{pmatrix}$.

Work out:

a $\mathbf{a} + \mathbf{b}$ *(2 marks)*

b $\mathbf{b} - \mathbf{a}$ *(2 marks)*

c $2\mathbf{a} - \mathbf{b}$ *(2 marks)*

16 $\mathbf{a} = \begin{pmatrix} 2 \\ 1 \end{pmatrix}$, $\mathbf{b} = \begin{pmatrix} m \\ 3 \end{pmatrix}$ and $\mathbf{c} = \begin{pmatrix} 1 \\ n \end{pmatrix}$.

If $2\mathbf{a} - \mathbf{b} = \mathbf{c}$, find the values of m and n. *(2 marks)*

nswers

Assess 1.1–1.2

1
  a natural, integer, square
  b irrational
  c natural, integer, square
  d natural, prime, integer
  e prime, integer
  f none of these

2 1, 2, 4, 5, 8, 10, 20, 40

3 7, 14, 21, 28, 35

4 2, 5

5 **a** 12   **b** 7   **c** 6

6 **a** 60   **b** 60   **c** 90

7
  a 3.999, 4.08, 4.19, 4.2
  b $-5, -4, -2, 7, 8$

8

A factor of 100	20
A square number	36
A prime number	13
Not a natural number	0
A multiple of 8	32
The HCF of 18 and 24	6

9 **a** true   **b** true   **c** false
   d true   **e** false   **f** true

10 4 and 9

11
  a **i** green   **ii** green and blue
     iii green and red   **iv** blue and red
  b 60 minutes

12
  a 7 (1, 4, 9, 16, 25, 36, 49)
  b 3 (64, 81, 100)
  c 2 (121, 144)
  d 2 (169, 196)

Assess 2.1–2.4

1 **a** $8a$ **b** $5b$ **c** c
   d $3d$ **e** $2e - 2c$ **f** $f + 9g$
   g $5h$ **h** $-2m + 6n$ **i** $-2p - q + 5r$
   j $4x + 2y - 7z$ **k** $5t + 1 - 2w$

2 Many possible answers, e.g. $a + 2a + 3b + 5b$.

3 Many possible answers, e.g. $5p - 4p - q - 3q$.

4 $2x + z$; $2x + y + z$; $2x + y + z$, so first expression is
   odd one out.

5 She should have written $5p - 3p$ and $+ 2q + q$.
   Answer is $2p + 3q$.

6 $3x^2$ and $+x^2$, -3 and -2, $+xy$ and $-2yx$

7 **a** $x^2 + x$ **b** $y + 9 + 6y^2$
   c $3mn - 2m^2$ **d** $3pq + 5p + 5q$
   e $8 - 4k + 3k^2$

8 $c^2 + 3c - 2$, $c^2 + 3c + 2$, $c^2 + 3c - 2$,
   so middle expression is odd one out.

9 **a** 17   **b** 11   **c** 7   **d** 28   **e** 48

10 **a** 4   **b** 16   **c** -60 **d** 109   **e** -5

11
  a $(2 \times 8) + (3 \times -5) = 16 + -15 = 1$
  b $x^2 - y^2 = 64 - 25 = 39$,
     $3x - 3y = 24 - -15 = 24 + 15 = 39$

12 $10 \times 9 \div 2 = 45$ Answer 45 l

13 $2 \times 12 = 24$, $2 \times 4 = 8$, $24 + 8 = 32$ Answer 32 cm

14 $75 \div 3 = 25$ Answer 25 km per hour

15 $C = (16 \times 11) + 20 = 196$ Answer \$196

16 $K = 8 \times 35 \div 5 = 56$ Answer 56 km

Assess 3.1–3.3

1 **a** 14 cm²   **b** 8 cm²   **c** 3 cm²

2
  a **i** 34 cm   **ii** 60 cm²
  b **i** 14.4 m   **ii** 9.6 m²
  c **i** 180 mm   **ii** 1350 mm²
  d **i** 82 m   **ii** 360 m²
  e **i** 224 cm   **ii** 3136 cm²
  f **i** 112 m   **ii** 592 m²
  g **i** 250 cm   **ii** 3130 cm²
  h **i** 212 mm   **ii** 1072 mm²
  i **i** 111 cm   **ii** 670 cm²

3 **a** 570 mm²   **b** 25.76 cm²   **c** 1656 cm²

4 **a** 57 m   **b** 254 m²

5 **a** 17.2 cm   **b** 232 cm²

6 1920 mm²

7 **a** 66.4 cm   **b** 337 cm²

8 18.9 m²

Assess 4.1–4.4

1 **a** 4140 mm³   **b** 113 cm³   **c** 675 cm³
   d 7854 cm³   **e** 14 m³

2 **a** 750 cm²   **b** 37 500 cm³

3 **a** 1120 cm³   **b** 684 cm²

4 **a** 78 cm   **b** 158 cm²
   c cuboid   **d** 120 cm³

5 **a** 16 200 mm³   **b** 1440 cm³

6 **a**   **b** 3921 cm²

7 **a** 180 000 cm³
   b **i** 54 cm²   **ii** 1620 cm³   **iii** 111 prisms

8 **a** 11.8 m²   **b** 2120 litres

Assess 5.1–5.2

1 a 18, 21   **b** 14, 12   **c** 64, 125
   d 2, −9   **e** 54, 162

2 a −3   **b** ÷ 2   **c** + 9
   d Square   **e** × 2

3 a 2, 9, 16, 23, 30   **b** 18, 13, 8, 3, −2
   c 1, 2, 5, 14, 41

4 a 11, 12, 13, 14, 15   **b** 4, 7, 10, 13, 16
   c 2, 7, 12, 17, 22   **d** 2, 5, 10, 17, 26

5 a He is not correct.
Using the nth term you get the sequence 3, 5, 7, 9, …
The terms are all odd numbers so 20 cannot be in
the sequence.
OR, if you double an odd or an even number, it is
always even, so adding 1 on to an even number will
always be odd.
   b She is correct.
5th term $= 5 \times 5 - 1 = 24$
1st term $= 5 \times 1 - 1 = 4$
5th term $= 6 \times$ 1st term

6 a $9n$ **b** $2n + 11$ **c** $5 - n$
   d $n \times (n + 3)$ **e** $\dfrac{10}{n}$

7 a 1, 3, 6, 10, 15
   b   **i** $2 \times \frac{1}{2}n(n+1) = n(n+1)$ **ii** $\frac{1}{2}n(n+1) + 2$

8 a

Pattern	1	2	3	4	5
Black dots	1	4	7	10	13

   b $3n - 2$ **c** $3n + 1$ **d** 61   **e** 27

9 a

   b

Diagram (n)	1	2	3	4
Shaded squares	1	2	3	4
Unshaded squares	3	4	5	6

   c   **i** n **ii** $n + 2$
   d $n + n + 2 = 2n + 2$
   e 202   **f** 30

10 a

Pattern	1	2	3	4
Enclosed triangles	6	12	18	24
Lines	12	23	34	45

   b   **i** $6n$ **ii** $11n + 1$
   c $6n + 11n + 1 = 17n + 1$
   d Pattern number 5.
   e Number of triangles = 42.   Number of lines = 78.

Assess 6.1–6.3

1 a −2   **b** +3   **c** +11   **d** −11
   e −15   **f** +24   **g** −3   **h** $\frac{1}{2}$

2 a −8   **b** 10 times
   c Multiplication must be done first.
So $-3 \times 6 - 2 = -18 - 2 = -20$

3 $-2\,°\text{C}$

4 259 metres

5 a +25   **b** +3   **c** −3   **d** +5

6 4 degrees

7 $324

8 a Many possible answers, e.g. $-3 + 8 - 13$
   b $-2 \times +2 \times +2$ There are several possible answers

Assess 7.1–7.2

1 99 minutes

2 a 42739   **b** $157.50

3 $4.60

4 121 minutes

5 Carry out service:
1.2 hours labour @ $70 per hour = $ 84.00
3.5 litres oil @ $8.20 per litre = $ 28.70
4 tyres @ $65 each = $260.00
1 bottle screenwash @ $2.80 = $ 2.80
Total = $375.50

6 133 miles

7 a 117.35 Dinar   **b** 6391.00 Bolivar

8 a 1120   **b** 1505

9 2532.91 Dirham

Assess 8.1–8.6

1 $\frac{7}{15}$

2 a   **i** 0.365   **ii** 0.36   **iii** 0.375
   b 36% $\frac{365}{1000}$ $\frac{3}{8}$

3 a $\frac{3}{4} + \frac{2}{3} = \frac{9}{12} + \frac{8}{12} = \frac{17}{12} = 1\frac{5}{12}$
   b $3\frac{1}{6} - 1\frac{4}{5} = 2\frac{5}{30} - \frac{24}{30} = 1\frac{30}{30} + \frac{5}{30} - \frac{24}{30} = 1\frac{11}{30}$

4 $\frac{1}{4}$

5 a $4\frac{1}{8}$ **b** $12\frac{1}{2}$

6 $45

7 a 140.4   **b** 2.82   **c** 1.176   **d** 35

8 No he is not correct. The multiplication must be done
before the addition and subtraction giving:
$6 + 12 - 1 = 18 - 1 = 17$

Assess 9.1–9.4

1 a $9x + 18$ **b** $14y + 7$
   c $-6 + 4p$ **d** $2 - q$

2 a $3k + k^2$ **b** $4m^2 - m$
   c $2n^2 - 10n$ **d** $6t^2 + 9t$

3 **a** $7f - 6$ **b** $g + 6$
   c $3x + 11$ **d** $4y - 3$

4 **a** **i** $7n - 4$ **ii** $2n - 7$
   b $3n + 6 + 2n - 3 - 5n + 1 = 4$

5 **a** $7(p - 2)$ **b** $5(q + 1)$
   c $2(4 - t)$ **d** $11(v + 5)$
   e $a(a + 3)$ **f** $2b(b - 5)$

6 **a** $n + 9$ **b** $2n$

7 $(8x + 5y)$ cents

8 **a** $x = 6$ **b** $y = -8$
   c $z = 12$ **d** $w = 8\frac{1}{2}$
   e $a = 18$ **f** $c = -5$
   g $d = 0.8$ **h** $e = -1$
   i $m = 12$ **j** $n = 7.2$
   k $p = -50$ **l** $q = 8$

9 **a** $k = 5$ **b** $y = -2$
   c $x = 3$ **d** $z = -4$
   e $w = 1\frac{1}{2}$

10 $3x - 7 = 38; x = 15$

Assess 10.1–10.2

1 **a** and **b**

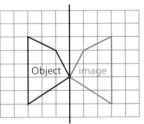

2 **a** and **b**

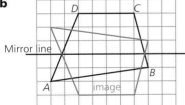

3 **a** and **b**

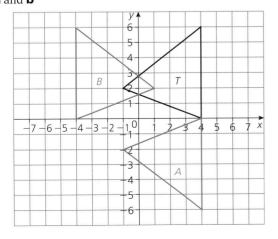

4 **a**, **b** and **c**

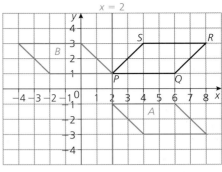

5 **a**, **b** and **c**

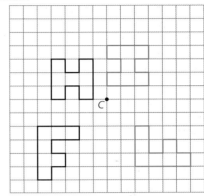

6 **a**, **b** and **c**

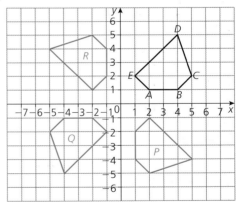

7 **a**, **b** and **c**

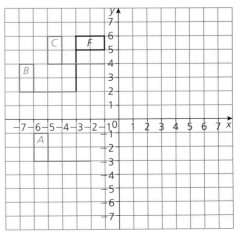

8 **a**, **b** and **c**

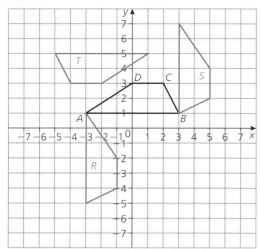

9 **a** Reflection in the *y*-axis

b Rotation of 180° clockwise (or anticlockwise) about (−4, 4)

c Reflection in the *x*-axis

d Rotation of 90° clockwise (or 270° anticlockwise) about (0, 0)

e Reflection in *y* = 2

f Rotation of 180° clockwise (or anticlockwise) about (0, 0)

g Rotation of 90° anticlockwise (or 270° clockwise) about (−1, 4)

h Rotation of 180° clockwise (or anticlockwise) about (−2.5, 5)

10 **a** and **b**

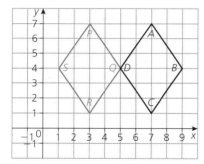

c **i** Reflection in *x* = 5

ii Rotation of 180° clockwise (or anticlockwise) about (5, 4)

Assess 11.1–11.3

1 **a** 49 **b** 64

2 1, 4, 9, 16 and 36

3 **a** 55 **b** 2.25

c 6 **d** 5.6

4 **a** $\frac{1}{16}$ **b** 1 **c** 2.25

d 3 **e** 25

5 **a** 729 **b** 16 **c** 125

d 1 **e** 1

6 **a** −10 **b** −2 **c** −2

d 4 **e** 4

7 **a** **i** 7.5×10^1 **ii** 7.5×10^5 **iii** 7.5×10^{-7}

b **i** 91 200 **ii** 9.12 **iii** 0.00912

8 **a** 6.39×10^4 **b** 1.769×10^8

9 13 km/min

10 23 800 000 km

Assess 12.1–12.3

1 **a** Key: 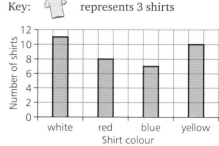 represents 3 shirts

b

2 **a**

Result	Tally	Frequency
Win	⊮⊮ ⊮⊮ ⊮⊮	15
Draw	⊮⊮ |||	8
Lose	⊮⊮ ||	7

b

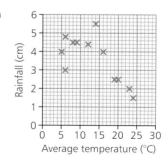

- win
- draw
- lose

3 **a** 2 **b** 29 **c** 4

4 **a**

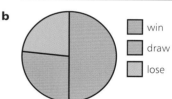

b (Weak) negative correlation

5 **a**

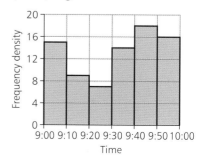

b, d

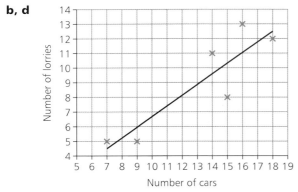

c Positive correlation **e** Eight lorries

6 Votes received

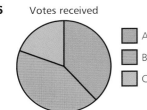

- A
- B
- C

Assess 13.1–13.3

1 **i** Shape A 1, Shape B 3, Shape C 5, Shape D 8
ii Shape A 1 (no rotational symmetry), Shape B 3, Shape C 5, Shape D 8

2

3 **a** **i**

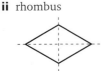

line of symmetry

ii 1 (no rotational symmetry)

b **i** rectangle **ii** rhombus

4 **a** **i** 3 **ii** 3 **b** **i** 2 **ii** 2
c **i** 4 **ii** 0 **d** **i** 6 **ii** 0

5

Name of shape	Number of lines of symmetry	Order of rotational symmetry
Isosceles triangle	1	1 (no rotational symmetry)
Equilateral triangle	3	3
Square	4	4
Rectangle	2	2
Rhombus	2	2
Parallelogram	0	2
Trapezium	0	1 (no rotational symmetry)
Isosceles trapezium	0	1 (no rotational symmetry)
Kite	1	1 (no rotational symmetry)

6 **a**, **b** and **c** Student's own answers.

7 **a** **b** **c**

8 **a** **i** 4 **ii** 4
b **i** 2 triangles shaded and 2 lines of symmetry
ii 2
e.g.

b **i** 2 triangles shaded and 1 line of symmetry
ii 1 (no rotational symmetry)
e.g.

Assess 14.1–14.3

1 $p = 63$ (angles at a point add up to 360°); $q = 64$ (vertically opposite angles are equal); $r = 60$ (angles on a straight line add up to 180°); $s = 81$ (alternate angles are equal); $t = 99$ (angles on a straight line add up to 180°); $u = 99$ (corresponding angles are equal); $v = 99$ (vertically opposite angles)
Note: Alternative reasons are possible.

2 $a = 63$ (angle sum of triangle); $b = 115$ (angles on a straight line add up to 180°); $c = 109$ (angle sum of quadrilateral); $d = 18$ (angle sum of triangle)

3 $a = 55$ (angles on a straight line add up to 180°); $b = 87$ (angle sum of triangle); $c = 87$ (vertically opposite angles are equal); $d = 52$ (alternate angles are equal); $e = 76$ (equal angles of isosceles triangle and angle sum of triangle); $f = 52$ (equal angles of isosceles triangle and alternate angles are equal); $g = 120$ (angle sum of quadrilateral)

4 **a** $x + y = 195$ **b** $x = 65$
c $x°$ is acute, $y°$ is obtuse

5 **a** **i** Isosceles **ii** Trapezium
b $x = 36$ (alternate angles are equal); $y = 72$ (equal angles of an isosceles triangle and angle sum of triangle); $z = 94$ (alternate angles are equal)
Note: Alternative reasons are possible.

6 **a** Kite
b **i** Angle $ADB = 39°$ (equal to angle ADB)
ii Angle $DAB = 102$ (angle sum of triangle ADB)
iii Angle $BDC = 70°$ (symmetry and angle sum of triangle BDC)

7 **a**

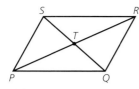

   b Side QR

   c Angle RTS

   d Triangle RTQ

8 **a** **i** Angle $BAC = 53°$ **ii** Angle $DCE = 37°$

      iii Angle $DEC = 53°$

   b Triangle ABC is *similar* to triangle EDC.

   c **i** $AC = 20$ cm   **ii** $DE = 18$ cm

Assess 15.1–15.3

1 $19.60

2 25.5%

3 36.6%

4 14 280

5 15%

6 1617

7 $11.04

8 $283.50

9 $23 320

10 **a** 6.8%   **b** 7.3%

Assess 16.1–16.3

1 **a**, **b**, **c** and **d**

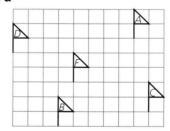

2 **a** and **b**

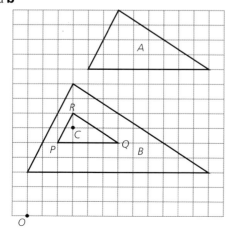

3 **a**, **b** and **c**

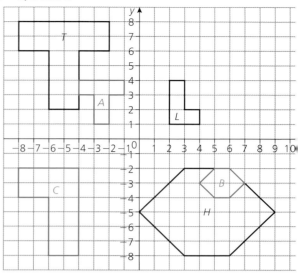

4 **a** Rotation of 90° clockwise about (4, 3)

   b Reflection in $y = -5$

   c Enlargement, centre (2, 0), scale factor 2

   d Translation $\begin{pmatrix} 4 \\ -2 \end{pmatrix}$

5 **a** Translation $\begin{pmatrix} 5 \\ -9 \end{pmatrix}$

   b Reflection in the x−axis

   c Rotation of 90° clockwise about (0, 0)

   d Reflection in $x = -2$

   e Rotation of 180° clockwise or anticlockwise about (0, 1)

   f Rotation of 90° anticlockwise about (0, 0)

   g Enlargement, centre (0, 4), scale factor 3

   h Translation $\begin{pmatrix} -7 \\ -6 \end{pmatrix}$

   i Rotation of 180° clockwise or anticlockwise about (0, 4)

6 Translation $\begin{pmatrix} -4 \\ 2 \end{pmatrix}$, rotation of 180° clockwise or anticlockwise about (4, 3)

   (Also accept enlargement, centre (4, 3) scale factor −1)

Assess 17.1–17.3

1

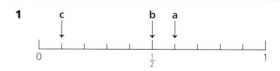

2 **a** $\frac{1}{6}$ **b** $\frac{1}{2}$ **c** $\frac{2}{3}$

3 **a** $\frac{1}{10}$ **b** $\frac{9}{10}$ **c** $\frac{2}{5}$

4 **a** $\frac{1}{2}$ **b** $\frac{1}{3}$ **c** $\frac{2}{3}$

   d $\frac{2}{3}$ **e** $\frac{5}{6}$

5 a $\frac{1}{6}$ **b** $\frac{15}{100} = \frac{3}{20}$

   c $\frac{1}{3}$ **d** $\frac{36}{100} = \frac{9}{25}$

6 a i $\frac{43}{50}$ **ii** $\frac{34}{40} = \frac{17}{20}$

   b Type A is just better

   c 4250

Assess 18.1–18.2

1 a 300 g   **b** 1.7 km

   c 46.72 litres   **d** 1.783 g

   e 56 210 mm   **f** 310 ml

2 a 35 m²   **b** 0.00075 cm³

   c 400 m²   **d** 7.85 m³

3 a 5960 m   **b** 14 900

4 200

5 10

6 a 22 500 mm²   **b** 80

7 a 216 899 484 mm³   **b** 216 899 cm³

   c 217 litres

8 2 cm

Assess 19.1–19.4

1 a 5 : 9   **b** 4 : 3

   c 125 : 16   **d** 1 : 100

   e 14 : 4 : 1

2 a 2 : 7 = **6** : 21   **b** 3.6 : 5.6 = 9 : **14**

   c 3 = 13 : **11**   **d** 0.2 : 12 = 1 : **60**

   e 4 : 0.004 = **1000** : 1

3 a 34 metres   **b** 9 cm

4 a $272   **b** $1768

5 55 metres

6 $136

7 $34.50

8 6 hours

9 The two kg box at 32.5 Rand per kg.

10 3.3 m/s

Assess 20.1–20.3

1 $A(5, 4)$ $B(0, 2)$ $C(-3, 3)$ $D(-1, -4)$ $E(2, -1)$ $F(6, 0)$

2 Kite

3 Yes – all sides same length

4 Valentina is correct

5 a 6.5 l **b** 17 l

   c 3.5 pints

6 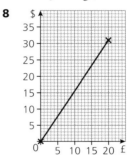   **a** $20

   b $74

   c £11

7 a $20   **b i** $40   **ii** $12

   c B, saving $16

8   **a i** $9

      ii $54

      iii £9.50

      iv £48

   b Multiply both charges by 10 to compare $15 with £16.50

     In **a iii** we found $15 = £9.50 so it is cheaper to send from Australia to the UK

9 a 100 km/h   **b** $\frac{1}{2}$ hour   **c** 40 km/h

10 a 9 min   **b** 60 km/h   **c** 1118

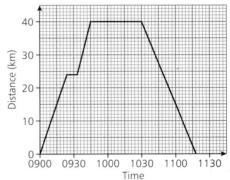

11 a

b 60 km/h

c Between A and B because that is the steepest slope.

12

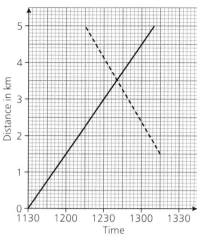

They meet at 1240, $3\frac{1}{2}$ km from Ana's house.

Assess 21.1–21.3

1 $352.80

2 35 hours

3 a $21 775   **b** $4560.42

4 $89 310

5 $22.40

6 a $9.10   **b** $4.55

   c $95.55   **d** 13.75% profit

7 $51.75

8 a $284   **b** 18.3%

9 $120

10 16%

11 $67.50

12 $6489.60

13 Account C (Account A pays $1032; Account B pays $998.91; Account C pays $1084.60)

Assess 22.1–22.4

1 a 6000   **b** 733   **c** 20

   d 44 000   **e** 43 600   **f** 900 000

   g 896 000   **h** 1 302 100

2 a 0.7   **b** 0.035   **c** 0.04

   d 0.0000577   **e** 0.004   **f** 0.0721

   g 0.046   **h** 0.01

3 a 2 000 000 or 2 million   **b** 1 799 600

   c 1 800 000   **d** 1 800 000

4 a 90   **b** 87.2

   c 87.2046   **d** 87.2

5 a 61.1   **b** 60

6 a $\dfrac{10 + 30}{9 - (60 \div 30)}$ **b** 6

   c 5.953

7 a 31 500 ⩽ number of people < 32 500

   b 31 750 ⩽ number of people < 32 250

8 2.325 g/m³ ⩽ density of silicon < 2.335 g/m³

9

Name of moon	Radius in km (lower bound)	Radius in km (upper bound)
Io	1815	1825
Europa	1555	1565
Ganymede	2625	2635
Callisto	2405	2415

10 148.5 cm ⩽ Nijah's height < 149.5 cm

156.5 cm ⩽ Talal's height < 157.5 cm

Minimum difference = 156.5 − 149.5 = 7 cm

Assess 23.1–23.4

1 a

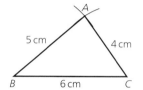

ABC = 41°

b

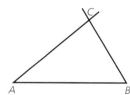

AC = 6.2 cm

c

BC is the diagram with B top right

AB = 8.2 cm

d

ABC = 48°

e

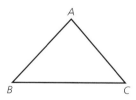

The ambiguous case! BCA₁ = 79°; BCA₂ = 11°

2 a–d

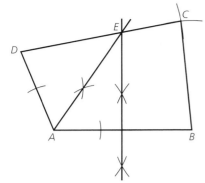

e AE = 9.8 cm

3 **a** 50 cm **b** 10 cm

c

	Scale drawing	Real caravan
Overall length from tow bar to back	9.7 cm	4.85 m
Height from ground to roof	4.5 cm	2.25 m
Caravan body length	7.8 cm	3.9 m
Height of door	3.3 cm	1.65 m
Diameter of wheel	1.3 cm	0.65 m

4 **a** **b i** x = 9.5 m **ii** a = 73°

5 a–e

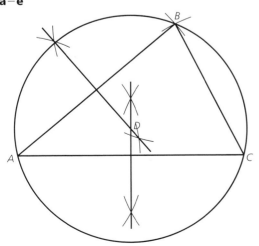

f Circle passes through all three vertices of triangle ABC

Assess 24.1–24.3

1

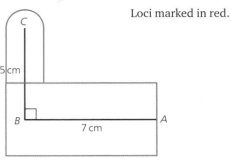

2 Diagram **b** shows the correct locus of points.

3 **a** Loci marked in red.

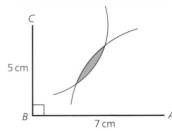

b

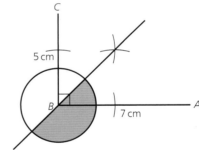

c

4

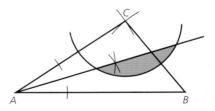

Assess 25.1–25.3

1 5

2 **a** 31.375 **b** 32.5 **c** 33 **d** 17

3 **a** 3.63 (to 3 s.f.) **b** 3 **c** 4

4 **a** 3 **b** 5

5 2, 6, 8, 8

6 The times can be summarised as:

	Mean	Median	Mode	Range
Irma	12.6	12.5	12.3	0.7
Corrine	12.6	12.45	12.4	0.5

The means are the same, Irma has a better mode but Corrine has a better median.

Corrine is slightly more consistent as she has a smaller range, so perhaps she should be chosen.

Or Irma has two times of 12.3, which is better than anything Corrine has done, so maybe Irma should be chosen.

7 a He is using the mean, as the mean will be slightly less than 2, whereas the median and mode will both be 2.

   b No, either of the median or the mode make more sense, as the vast majority of people have two legs.

Assess 26.1–26.3

1 e.g. $(0, -5)$ $(2, -5)$ $(-3, -5)$

2 $x = 3$

3 $(-7, 2)$

4 a b

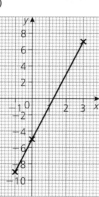

     c $(2.25, 4)$

5 a

x	−2	0	5
y	2.8	2	0

   b

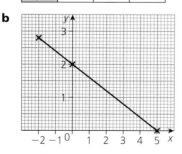

   c No, because $(2 \times 10) + (5 \times -3) = 5$, not 10.

6 a $\frac{1}{4}$ **b** 5   **c** $-1\frac{1}{2}$

7 $5x + y = 15$ can be written as $y = 15 - 5x$, so both have gradient -5.

8 $y = 7 - x$ and $x + y = 2$; $2y + 5x = 3$ and $5x = 7 - 2y$; $x - y = 3$ and $3y + 5 = 3x$

9

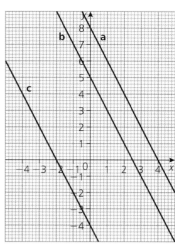

The lines are all parallel but pass through different points on the axes.

10 a $y = 3x - 4$

     b $y = -2x + 6$ or $2x + y = 6$

11 $y = 3x - 5$

12 $y = -\frac{1}{3}x + 3$ or $x + 3y = 9$

13 $y = 13 - 2x$

14 $x + 4y = -1$

15 Gradient AD = gradient $BC = 2$, so these sides are parallel.

Gradient $AB = -\frac{1}{5}$. Gradient $DC = -\frac{3}{4}$, so these sides are not parallel.

A quadrilateral with only one pair of parallel sides is a trapezium.

Assess 27.1–27.2

1 a 24°   **b** 156°

2 36 sides

3 a 10 sides   **b** Decagon

4 $a = 90$ (angle in a semicircle), $b = 56$ (angle sum of triangle), $c = 30$ (equal angles of isosceles triangle), $d = 60$ (angle in a semicircle), $e = 60$ (equal angles and angle sum of isosceles triangle), $f = 90$ (angle between tangent and radius), $g = 28$ (angle sum of triangle), $g = 28$ (angle sum of triangle), $h = 40$ (angle between tangent and radius and angle sum of triangle), $i = 50$ (angle in semicircle and angle sum of triangle), $j = 40$ (angle between tangent and radius), $k = 58$ (equal angles and angle sum of isosceles triangle), $l = 58$ (vertically opposite angles), $m = 61$ (equal angles and angle sum of isosceles triangle), $n = 29$ (angle between tangent and radius), $p = 65$ (angle sum of triangle), $q = 115$ (angle sum of straight line), $r = 32.5$ (equal angles and angle sum of isosceles triangle), $s = 57.5$ (angle in a semicircle), $t = 57.5$ (angle between tangent and radius).

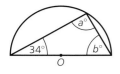

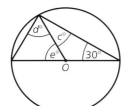

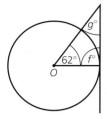

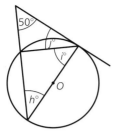

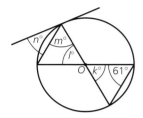

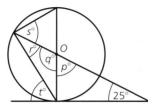

122°

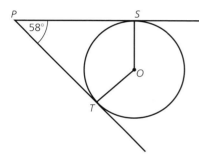

a 42° (equal angles of isosceles triangle *OAC*)
b 48° (angle *CAB* is angle in a semicircle)
c 42° (angle *SAO* is 90° as it is angle between tangent and radius)
d 48° (equal angles of isosceles triangle *OAB*)
e 84° (angle sum of triangle *OAB*)

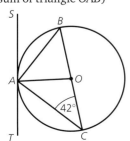

a 20° (angle *CAF* is 90° as it is angle between tangent and radius)
b 70° (angle sum of triangle *ACD*)
c 38° (angle in semicircle and angle sum of triangle *ABC*)
d 110° (interior angles with *DE* parallel to *AF*)

e 160° (angles at point *D*)

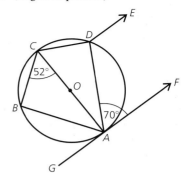

8 **a** 28° (alternate angles, since *BC* is parallel to *AO*)
b 28° (equal angles of isosceles triangle *AOC*)
c 34° (angle *OCE* is 90° as it is angle between tangent and radius)
d 56° (alternate angles, since *BC* is parallel to *AO*)
e 34° (angle between tangent and radius and angle sum of triangle *CFO*)

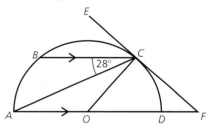

Assess 28.1–28.4

1 $y = \dfrac{x - c}{2}$

2 $d = \dfrac{C}{\pi}$

3 $m = \dfrac{k - 10}{2}$

4 **a** $W = \dfrac{T - 7}{2}$ **b** 4.5 kg

5 **a** $h = \dfrac{A}{2\pi r}$ **b** 8.7 cm

6 **a** $x = 8$ **b** $y = -2$
c $t = 7$ **d** $k = -\frac{1}{2}$
e $m = -6$

7 **a** $p = 16$ **b** $q = -5$
c $m = 1.2$ **d** $n = 1.5$
e $a = 5$ **f** $b = -1$
g $c = -5$ **h** $k = 3$

8 $5(n + 9) = 95; n = 10$

9 **a** $x = 4, y = 7$
b $p = 5, q = -2$
c $m = -1, n = -4$
d $k = 3, t = \frac{1}{2}$
e $a = 5, b = 2$
f $c = 1, d = -2$
g $x = 7, y = 2$

10 $M + O = 59$
$O = M - 11$
Maria is 35
Olivia is 24

11 $5r + 3l = 81$
$2r + 3l = 45$
2 lilies cost $14

Assess 29.1–29.3

1 a

x	−4	−3	−2	−1	0	1	2	3	4
y	8	1	−4	−7	−8	−7	−4	1	8

b

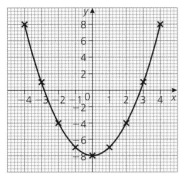

c $(0, -8)$
d $x = -2.8$ and $x = 2.8$

2 a

x	−4	−3	−2	−1	0	1	2
5 − 2x	13	11	9	7	5	3	1
−x²	−16	−9	−4	−1	0	−1	−1
y	−3	2	5	6	5	2	−3

b

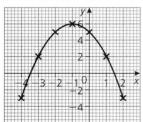

c $x = -1$
d $x = -3.5$ and $x = 1.5$

3 a b

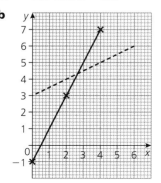

c $(2.7, 4.3)$

4 a

x	−4	−3	−2	−1	−0.5
y	−0.75	−1	−1.5	−3	−6

	0.5	1	2	3	4
	6	3	1.5	1	0.75

b

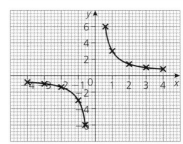

c i $x = 1.2$ **ii** $x = -0.7$

5 a b

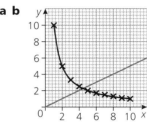

c $(4.5, 2.2)$

6 a

x	−5	−4	−3	−2	−1	0	1	2
x²	25	16	9	4	1	0	1	4
+3x	−15	−12	−9	−6	−3	0	+3	+6
y	9	3	−1	−3	−3	−1	3	9

d

x	−1	0	1
y	1	2.5	4

b e

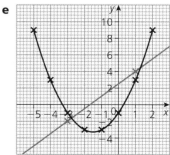

c $x = -3.3$ and $x = 0.3$
f $(-2.8, -1.7)$ and $(1.5, 4.5)$

Assess 30.1–30.3

1 7.8 cm

2 a 9.2 cm   **b** 36.7 cm

3 109.5 m

4 a 12.1 cm   **b** 20.2°

5 a 15.7 cm   **b** 41.4°

6 a 6.5 cm   **b** 57.1°

7 2.3 m

8 236.3°

9 a

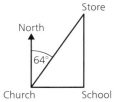

b i 0.52 km   **ii** 1.08 km

Assess 31.1–31.2

1 a $\begin{pmatrix} 3 \\ 1 \end{pmatrix}$ **b** $\overrightarrow{FA}$ **c** $\overrightarrow{CB}$ **d** $\begin{pmatrix} 3 \\ -2 \end{pmatrix}$

$\begin{pmatrix} 9 \\ -6 \end{pmatrix}$

3 a

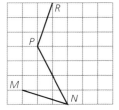

b i $\begin{pmatrix} 4 \\ 2 \end{pmatrix}$ **ii** $\begin{pmatrix} -1 \\ 7 \end{pmatrix}$ **iii** $\begin{pmatrix} 0 \\ 0 \end{pmatrix}$

c i $\begin{pmatrix} 1 \\ 3 \end{pmatrix}$ **ii** $\begin{pmatrix} -1 \\ 7 \end{pmatrix}$ **iii** $\begin{pmatrix} 2 \\ 6 \end{pmatrix}$

4 $b = \begin{pmatrix} -2 \\ 3 \end{pmatrix}$

5 a $\begin{pmatrix} 5 \\ -2 \end{pmatrix}$ **b** $\begin{pmatrix} -3 \\ -4 \end{pmatrix}$

6 a $\begin{pmatrix} 6 \\ -4 \end{pmatrix}$ **b** $\begin{pmatrix} 3 \\ -2 \end{pmatrix}$

7 $x = -6, y = -\frac{1}{3}$

Glossary

2-way table a table used to show two different pieces of information.

A

acute less than 90°.

acute-angled triangle a triangle with all of the angles less than 90°.

adjacent side the side adjacent to the known or required angle in a right-angled triangle.

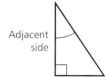

Adjacent side

alternate angles angles formed on opposite sides of a transversal between parallel lines.

ambiguous case something that can have two different possible answers.

analogue showing a reading with a moving hand on a dial (opposite of **digital**).

angle a turn or change in direction.

angle bearings angles measured clockwise from North to describe a direction.

angle bisector a line that cuts an angle in half.

angle of rotation

annual salary amount of money a person is paid per year.

appreciate increase in value.

appreciation the increase in value of an item.

arc part of the circumference of the circle.

area the amount of space inside a 2-D shape.

average a single value that is used to represent a set of data.

average speed the ratio of distance ÷ time.

axes (singular: **axis**) fixed reference lines for the measurement of coordinates.

B

bar chart in a bar chart, the frequency is shown by the height (or length) of the bars. Bar charts can be vertical or horizontal.

base number the number which is being raised to a power.

biased of an outcome that is distorted and not as expected .

BIDMAS order in which operations are performed: **B**rackets, **I**ndices (powers: squares, cubes, …), **D**ivision, **M**ultiplication, **A**ddition, **S**ubtraction.

bisect cut in half.

bonus an extra payment.

C

capacity the amount a container holds when it is full.

Cartesian coordinates two axes at right angles.

centre of enlargement the lines joining corresponding points on an object and its image all meet at the centre of enlargement.

centre of rotation fixed point at the centre of a rotation.

certain having a probability of 1.

changing the subject changing which letter is on the left-hand side of a formula.

circle the locus of a point moving at a given distance from a fixed point.

circumference the distance around the outside (perimeter) of a circle.

coefficient the number in front of a quantity such as x.

common factor a factor that is common to two or more numbers or terms.

common multiple a multiple that is common to two or more numbers.

composite shape a shape made from simple shapes.

compound interest interest which is added to the principal.

congruent having exactly the same size and shape.

consecutive next to each other.

continuous data data that can have any value within a range.

conversion graph a graph used to convert from one unit of measurement to another.

convert change one unit of measurement to another.

correlation a connection between two sets of data.

corresponding angles angles formed on the same sides of a transversal between parallel lines.

cosine the ratio of the adjacent side to the hypotenuse.

cost price the original price of an item you are selling.

cross-section a face formed by cutting through an object at right angles.

cube a 3-D solid consisting of six square faces.

cube number the number you get when you multiply three lots of the number together.

cube root opposite of cubing a number

cuboid a 3-D solid consisting of six rectangular faces.

currency the unit of money that is used in a country. Different countries use different currencies.

cylinder a 3-D solid with a circle as its cross-section.

D

decrease go down in value.

degree unit of measurement for angles

nominator the number on the
:tom of a fraction.

posit money paid to start with.

preciate decrease in value.

preciation the decrease in value of
item.

meter the distance from one point
the circumference to another point
sing through the centre.

Diameter

ference the difference between
cessive terms of a linear sequence.

jital showing a reading as numbers
a display (opposite of **analogue**).

ect proportion two quantities that
rease by the same ratio.

ected number a positive or negative
nber or zero.

ection the direction of a vector.

continuous having a break .

count an amount taken off the
ing price of an item.

crete data data that can have only
tain values within a range.

uble time rate of pay that is twice the
mal hourly rate.

ge the line where two faces of a solid
et.

argement a transformation in which
shape of an object stays the same,
: its size usually changes.

ually likely outcomes outcomes that
e the same probability.

uidistant at the same distance.

uivalent fractions fractions that are
ual in value.

ent a set of outcomes in probability.

pand multiply all the terms inside
ckets by the term outside the brackets
posite of **factorise**).

experimental probability the ratio of
the number of times the event occurs to
the total number of trials.

expression a series of terms connected
by addition and subtraction signs.

exterior angle the angle you turn
through at each vertex when going round
the perimeter of a polygon.

F

face the surface of a solid which is
enclosed by edges.

factor a whole number which divides
exactly into another whole number .

factorise take a common factors outside
a set of brackets (opposite of **expand**).

fair unbiased.

formula rule expressed in words or letters.

frequency (plural frequencies) the
number of times a data item occurs.

frequency table a table showing total
number (frequency) against data values;
like a tally chart but with a number
instead of tallies.

G

gradient a measure of how steep a line
is.

GST (General Sales Tax) tax added to the
selling price of something.

H

highest common factor (HCF) the
largest factor which is common to two or
more numbers.

hire purchase way of buying items
and paying for them over a number of
months.

horizontal at right angles to the vertical.

hourly rate of pay rate of pay for each
hour worked.

hypotenuse the longest side of a right-
angled triangle. It is always opposite the
right angle.

I

image the new shape after a
transformation.

impossible having a probability of 0.

included angle the angle between two
given sides.

income tax tax paid on the money you
earn.

increase go up in value.

index power of a number.

index form (**index notation**) a way of
writing a number using powers.

inequality a statement about the
relative size or order of two objects using
$<$, $\leqslant$, $>$ and $\geqslant$.

infinite continuing for ever.

instalments equal regular payments.

integers ... $-5, -4, -3, -2, -1, 0, 1,$
$2, 3, 4, 5, ...$

intercept where a line crosses the y-axis.

interest the charge for borrowing or
lending money.

interior angle the angle inside a
polygon.

inverse something that is reversed in
order or effect.

inverse proportion a relation between
two variables, in which one variable
increases as the other decreases.

irrational number a number that
cannot be written as a fraction.

L

least common multiple (LCM) the
lowest multiple that is common to two or
more numbers.

like terms terms containing the same
variables raised to the same power, which
can be combined by adding or subtracting.

line a one-dimensional figure extending
infinitely in both directions.

line of best fit a straight line that goes
between points on a graph, passing as
close as possible to all of them.

line of symmetry the fold line when a
2-D shape can be folded so that one half
fits exactly over the other.

line segment a one-dimensional figure
that does not extending infinitely in both
directions.

line symmetry symmetry in which a 2-D
shape divides a shape into two congruent
halves which are mirror images of each
other.

linear equation an equation that does not contain any powers or roots of x or y such as x^2 or XXX.

linear sequence a sequence in which the difference between consecutive terms is the same for all terms.

locus (plural: **loci)** the path followed by a moving point.

loss if you sell something for less than you paid for it, you make a loss.

lower bound the smallest possible value of a rounded quantity.

lowest common denominator the lowest common multiple of the denominators of two or more fractions.

magnitude the size of a vector.

mapping the process which changes one number into another number.

mean a way of calculating how much each value would be if all the values were shared equally.

median the middle value, when data are put in order.

mirror line a **line of symmetry**.

mixed number a fractions that consists of a whole number part and a fractional part.

modal of the score or class with the highest frequency.

mode the score with the highest frequency.

multiple the product of an integer with another integer.

mutually exclusive having no outcomes in common.

natural number the counting numbers, 1, 2, 3, 4, 5, …

negative correlation as one set of data increase, the other set of data decreases.

negative integer any negative whole number.

net a 2-D pattern that can be cut out and folded to form a 3-D shape.

no correlation the points on a graph do not appear to follow a trend.

nth term this phrase is often used to describe a 'general' term in a sequence; if you are given the nth term, you can use this to find the terms of a sequence.

numerator the number on top of a fraction.

object the original shape before a transformation.

obtuse greater than 90° but less than 180°.

obtuse-angled triangle a triangle with one of the angles more than 90°.

odometer an instrument that measures the distance a car has travelled.

operations $+, -, \times, \div$.

opposite side the side opposite to the known or required angle in a right-angled triangle.

Opposite side

order of rotational symmetry the number of different positions in which a shape looks the same during a complete turn.

origin the point where graph axes cross, where both coordinates are zero (0, 0).

outcome result.

overtime extra hours worked.

parallel parallel lines are the same distance apart everywhere along their length.

per annum every year.

perimeter the total distance around the edges of a shape.

perpendicular at right angles (90°).

perpendicular bisector a line that cuts a line in half at right angles.

pictogram in a pictogram, the frequency is shown by a number of identical pictures.

pie chart in a pie chart, frequency is shown by the angles (or areas) of the sectors of a circle.

point the intersection of two lines.

polygon a two-dimensional shape with straight sides.

position-to-term rule a rule for a sequence linking the term number to the value of that term.

positive correlation as one quantity increases, the other increases.

positive integer any positive whole number.

power the number of times a base number is multiplied.

prime number a number that has exactly two factors.

principal the amount of money invested

prism a 3-D solid whose cross-section the same throughout its length.

probability a value between 0 and 1 (which can be expressed as a fraction, decimal or percentage) that gives the likelihood of an event.

probability scale a scale on which probabilities are shown.

profit if you sell something for more than you paid for it, you make a profit.

proportion comparing one part to the total amount.

quadrant the axes divide the page into four quadrants.

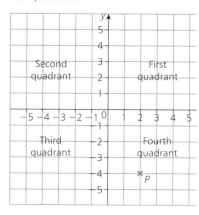

quadratic function a function in which x^2 is the highest power of x.

...litative descriptive but not ...merical.

...antitative numerical.

...ius (plural: radii) the distance from ...e point on the circumference to the ...tre.

...nge the difference between the largest ...m and the smallest item in a set of ...ta.

...te the rate of interest per year for ...rrowing or lending money.

...te of change the ratio of a change ...one variable to a change in another ...iable.

...tio comparing two or more quantities ...th each other.

...tional number any number that can ... written in the form $\frac{p}{q}$, where p and q ... integers.

...al number any rational or irrational ...mbers.

...ciprocal a fraction turned upside ...wn.

...ciprocal function a graph involving a ...ciprocal such as $y = \frac{1}{x}$.

...curring decimal a decimal with an ...finite number of decimal places, in ...hich the last digit or group of digits are ...peated.

...flection a transformation that gives an ...mage which looks like the reflection of ...e object in a mirror.

...flex greater than 180° but less than ...50°.

...gular having all sides equal and all ...ngles equal.

...elative frequency
$$\frac{\text{the number of successful outcomes}}{\text{the total number of trials}}.$$

...ght angle an angle of 90°.

...ght-angled triangle a triangle with ...ne of the angles 90°.

rotation turning an object through a given angle about a fixed point.

rotational symmetry looking exactly the same after a rotation of less than 360°.

rounding replacing a number with one that is approximately equal .

rule a general statement .

scalar a single number.

scale drawing accurate drawing that shows the exact shape but does not use the actual size.

scale factor a number that tells you how many times bigger the object is than the image.

scatter diagrams are made by plotting points on a graph, they are used to see if there is a correlation between sets of data.

sector an area of a circle cut off by two radii and an arc.

selling price the price you sell something for.

semicircle half a circle.

sequence a set of numbers or patterns with a given rule or pattern.

significant figures the digits of a number.

similar having the same shape, but being different in size.

simple interest the charge for borrowing or lending money.
$$I = \frac{PRT}{100}.$$

simplest form the form with the smallest possible whole numbers in the numerator and the denominator of a fraction, or the smallest possible whole numbers in a ratio.

simplifying collecting the like terms.

simultaneous equations two equations with two unknowns.

sine the ratio of the opposite side to the hypotenuse.

solid a three-dimensional shape.

solve work out.

square number the result of multiplying an integer by itself.

square root opposite of squaring a number.

standard form a way of writing very large and very small numbers using a number between 1 and 10 multiplied by a power of 10.

strong correlation a correlation in which the points on a graph are very close to a line of best fit.

substitution replacing the letters in an expression with numbers to find its value.

surface area the total area of the faces of a solid.

tally chart a method of showing a set of data.

tangent
1. A straight line that touches a curve at only one point.
2. The ratio of the opposite side to the adjacent side in a right-angled triangle.

term an expression forming part of a sequence, or an equation.

terminating decimal a decimal with a finite number of decimal places.

term-to-term rule a rule for a sequence linking one term to the value of the next term.

time-and-a-half an hourly rate of one-and-a-half times the normal hourly rate.

transformation a change of the position or the size of a shape.

transforming changing the subject of a formula.

translation a transformation in which the object moves across the page, but is not rotated or reflected.

transversal a line that cuts two or more parallel lines.

trial an experiment that is repeated a large number of times.

triangular numbers - 1, 3, 6, 10, 15, ...

trigonometry the study of right-angled triangles.

unitary method finding the value of one unit of a quantity.

unknown a value you are trying to find.

unlike terms terms containing different variables which can be combined by adding or subtracting.

upper bound the largest possible value of a rounded quantity.

variable a quantity that can take different values.

VAT (Value Added Tax) tax added to the selling price of something.

vector way of writing a change of position in two directions.

Venn diagram a way of showing the elements of sets in a diagram.

vertex (plural: **vertices)** a point where three or more edges of a solid meet.

vertical a line at right angles to the horizontal.

volume the amount of space inside a 3-D shape.

weak correlation a correlation in which the points on a graph are not close to a line of best fit.

weekly wage the amount of money a person is paid per week.

x-**coordinate** the first number in a pair of coordinates to identify the position of a point on a graph.

y-**coordinate** the second number in a pair of coordinates to identify the position of a point on a graph.

Index